THE KILLING GROUND

THE
KILLING GROUND

The British Army, the Western Front
and the Emergence of Modern Warfare
1900–1918

TIM TRAVERS

Professor of History
University of Calgary

PEN & SWORD MILITARY CLASSICS

First published in 1987 by Allen & Unwin
Published in this format in 2003 by
PEN & SWORD MILITARY CLASSICS
an imprint of
Pen & Sword Books Ltd
47 Church Street
Barnsley
South Yorkshire
S70 2AS

© Tim Travers, 1987, 2003

ISBN 0 85052 964 6

A CIP record for this book is
available from the British Library

Printed in England by
CPI UK

For Heather, Jessica and Nicholas,
and for
Bee and Hugh

Contents

PART IV
Remembrance and Recrimination

Plates

Maps

Acknowledgements

I would like to thank all those who gave advice and encouragement at various stages during the lengthy preparation of this book. Without such support manuscripts may not be attempted, much less completed. First, I would particularly like to acknowledge the long-standing support and encouragement of Brian Bond, who did much to maintain morale. At a critical stage Paul Kennedy kindly offered to read the manuscript, and provided valuable advice. In the very early stages of research, Toby Graham made useful suggestions, although he would probably disagree with some of the results. Others who offered friendly advice and support were Holger Herwig; Michael Geyer, who kindly sent me his as yet unpublished manuscript on the German army; and in my own department, Chris Archer and David Bercuson. Naturally none of the above bears any responsibility for the contents of the book, and all errors of fact and interpretation are my own.

I am grateful to the trustees of the Killam Fellowship for providing free time to write and largely conclude the manuscript. I am also grateful to the University of Calgary for providing a publications subvention to assist with maps and photographs. I wish, further, to express my appreciation to the following for their kind permission to cite and quote from private papers and copyright sources: the Trustees of the Liddell Hart Centre for Military Archives for the Liddell Hart, Montgomery-Massingberd, G. S. Clive, Edmonds, Macleod, Kiggell and Maurice papers, and the representatives of the Robertson and Spears families for their respective papers; Earl Haig for the Haig papers; the Trustees of the General Sir Aylmer Haldane papers; Mrs Maxse and the County Archivist of the West Sussex Record Office for the Maxse papers; the Rawlinson family for the Rawlinson papers in the National Army Museum, London, and Churchill College, Cambridge; the Imperial War Museum for the Archibald, Boraston, Butler, von Donop, Fitzgerald, Haldane, Horne, Jeudwine, MacDougall, Maxse, Smith-Dorrien, Stephens and Wilson papers; the Royal Artillery Institution for the Anstey, Rawlins and Tudor papers; the British Library for the Hutton and Smith-Dorrien papers; the National Army Museum for the Milward, Rawlinson and Roberts papers; the Trustees of the National Library of Scotland for the Haig and Aylmer Haldane papers; the editors of the *Journal of Contemporary History* for permission to publish extracts from two articles that originally appeared in that journal; A. P. Watt Ltd on behalf of the Literary Executors of the Estate of Robert Graves; and William Heinemann Ltd for permission to quote from Cecil Lewis, *Sagittarius Rising*. Every effort has been made to trace and secure permission from copyright holders for all material under copyright that is quoted in this book. If I have inadvertently infringed upon such rights, I offer sincere apologies.

Bill Mills did yeoman service in researching the biographies of many senior British officers, and then carefully prepared the maps with great attention to detail, accuracy and function. Shannon Mercer also assisted with the biographies. Joyce Woods cheerfully typed the entire first draft of the manuscript and made subsequent changes (luckily the word processor had arrived). Liz von Wolzogen efficiently supervised the allocation of tasks, provided long-term support and encouragement, and willingly worked herself on various drafts. At a late stage Jodi Steeves launched enthusiastically into retyping changes and last minute work with the word processor. Marjory McLean also kindly helped prepare some chapters, and in the background Olga Leskiw provided support to the others in the office.

Librarians and archivists in all the libraries, museums and archives mentioned were extremely helpful, while the visual experts at the Imperial War Museum willingly guided me through their extensive collection of First World War photographs and films.

Finally, but first in other senses, I acknowledge the help and encouragement of family: my parents, who were always supportive; my parents-in-law, who helped in many ways; and my wife Heather and children Jessica and Nicholas, whose love and humour kept the ship afloat.

Abbreviations

AAG	Assistant Adjutant General
ADC	Aide-de-camp
ADMT	Assistant Director of Military Training
ADSD	Assistant Director of Staff Duties
AG	Adjutant General
APM	Assistant Provost Marshal
AQMG	Assistant Quartermaster General
BEF	British Expeditionary Force
BGGS	Brigadier General, General Staff
BL	British Library
Cab	Cabinet Office paper at PRO
CCC	Churchill College, Cambridge
CGS	Chief of the General Staff
CIGS	Chief of the Imperial General Staff
C-in-C	Commander-in-Chief
CO	Commanding Officer
CRA	Commander Royal Artillery (usually a Brigadier commanding Divisional artillery)
CSO	Chief Staff Officer
DA	Director of Armaments
DDSD	Deputy Director Staff Duties
DMI	Director Military Intelligence
DMO	Director Military Operations
DMT	Director Military Training
DSD	Director Staff Duties
FSR	Field Service Regulations
GHQ	General Headquarters
GOC	General Officer Commanding
GOCRA	General Officer Commanding Royal Artillery (at Corps HQ)
GQG	French Army High Command (*Grand Quartier Général*)
GSO 1	General Staff Officer, First Grade
GSO 2	General Staff Officer, Second Grade
GSO 3	General Staff Officer, Third Grade
HE	High Explosive
I	Intelligence
IWM	Imperial War Museum

JRUSI	*Journal of the Royal United Services Institute*
KCL	King's College, London University
MGGS	Major General, General Staff
MGO	Master General of the Ordnance
MGRA	Major General Royal Artillery
NAM	National Army Museum
NLS	National Library of Scotland
OHL	German Army High Command (*die oberste Heeresleitung*)
PRO	Public Record Office
PSC	Passed Staff College
QMG	Quartermaster General
RA	Royal Artillery
RAI	Royal Artillery Institution
RFA	Royal Field Artillery
RFC	Royal Flying Corps
RGA	Royal Garrison Artillery
RHA	Royal Horse Artillery
USM	*United Service Magazine*
WO	War Office
WSRO	West Sussex Record Office

Introduction

The Killing Ground, first published by Allen and Unwin in 1987, was an attempt to understand the ideas underlying the British approach to warfare on the Western Front during the First World War, as well as a consideration of Sir Douglas Haig's comprehension of modern warfare. It seemed that one way to do this was to look at the British Army before World War I, and to look at the education of Sir Douglas Haig [Commander in Chief of the British Expeditionary Force (BEF) from late 1915 to 1919], especially his time at the Staff College from 1896 to 1897. Then the concept was to follow the British high command through to 1918, with particular attention to the battle of the Somme in 1916, followed by a discussion of the way the British Official History dealt with, and provided an inner knowledge of, the Passchendaele offensive of 1917, and the BEF defence against the German March 1918 offensive. It was not possible to cover the whole war on the Western Front in detail, and there were some considerable gaps in the book, notably 1914, much of 1915, the first half of 1917, and most of 1918 after the end of the German Spring offensives. Some of these gaps were covered by the publication of *How the War Was Won: Command and Technology in the British Army on the Western Front, 1917-1918* (1992), which looked at the period from Passchendaele to the end of the war, and more recently *Gallipoli 1915* (2001), which went back to 1915, albeit from the perspective of a different theatre than the Western Front.

When research began on *The Killing Ground* in the early 1980's, there was very little being published at the time on the operational and technical side of the British Expeditionary Force on the Western Front. One notable exception was Shelford Bidwell and Dominick Graham's fine book, *Fire-Power: British Army Weapons and Theories of War, 1904-1945*, published in

1982. Graham provided the chapters on pre-World War I and Western Front material, and showed the way toward understanding the technical and theoretical context of the war from the British point of view. A number of other talented specialists such as Ian Beckett, Brian Bond, David French, John Gooch, Martin Middlebrook, Keith Simpson and David Woodward investigated important aspects of the war, yet there did not seem to be an overview of the war from the British point of view, apart from the technical approach of Dominick Graham. However, on the subject of Sir Douglas Haig, the analysis of specific British offensives, and the year 1918, there did exist the earlier work of John Terraine, who shouldered the rather lonely task of defending the reputation of Haig in a number of books. Perhaps partly because Terraine operated outside the academic establishment, his views at the time did not convert the general public or the academic world. Yet Terraine's ideas sometimes acted as a foil for parts of *The Killing Ground*.

Since *The Killing Ground* was published, the historiography of the First World War has exploded, with literally hundreds of books published. Among many others, some can be noticed, for example a generally critical biography of Haig by Gerard de Groot, published in 1988, and two well balanced volumes on Sir Henry Rawlinson, and the battle of Passchendaele, published by joint authors Robin Prior and Trevor Wilson in 1992 and 1997 respectively. Then, starting with Paddy Griffith's *Battle Tactics of the Western Front* (1994) there emerged an important revisionist school of historians, who aimed to rehabilitate the reputation of Sir Douglas Haig, and to reveal the tactical efficiency of the British Expeditionary Force and its commanders. Among the recent publications of this informal school are Gary Sheffield's moderate and nicely reflective *Forgotten Victory: The First World War: Myths and Realities* (2001), and selected chapters in Peter Liddle ed., *Passchendaele in Perspective: The Third Battle of Ypres* (1997), and in Brian Bond and Nigel Cave eds., *Haig: A Reappraisal 70 Years On* (1999).

Very generally, it can be said that this informal revisionist school praises Haig for his administrative and logistic efforts at GHQ [General Head Quarters], while the strategy of attrition is seen as the correct approach to winning the war. Haig is also viewed as a more intelligent and open minded commander than the rather isolated and difficult individual that normally depicts his character and leadership. The revisionists also assert that if Haig is to be criticised for his leadership in 1916 and 1917, then he should equally be congratulated for his role in the victory of 1918, though this argument seems to be something of a non sequiter. Similarly, the revisionists claim that GHQ was much more in touch with the army and conditions at the front than hitherto was thought to be the case for the 1915 to 1917 period. In regard to the growing efficiency of the BEF, the revisionists argue that the BEF made considerable tactical progress during the Somme in 1916, and continued a strong learning curve through 1917 and 1918. This conclusion seems quite reasonable, indeed it would be strange if a learning curve did not take place. Undoubtedly, the all arms approach of the last stages of 1917 and through 1918 was successful and commanders at all levels became more efficient due to their experience of warfare and the expected learning curve. The revisionists therefore suggest that victory in 1918 came about due to the greater tactical ability and capable leadership of the BEF at all levels. Among the more insistent of the revisionist claims is that Haig and GHQ generally were not as opposed to technology as is sometimes claimed.

It is not possible in this Introduction to debate all these topics. However, one or two issues can be raised as they relate to *The Killing Ground*. Firstly, *The Killing Ground* does not generally discuss the tactical competence or not of the BEF, apart from comments on the battle of the Somme, both the first day, and subsequent fighting. Although revisionists will argue that the Somme was a British success, this still seems difficult to accept, especially if the unhappy method of comparing the casualties of the British, French and German forces involved is applied. In this context, *The Killing Ground* does advance the argument that there was an underlying pre-war paradigm among senior British officers which tended to see the human battlefield as the normal method of waging war, and so pre-war thinking tended to stress moral qualities as the means of crossing the costly fire swept zone. Despite the obvious heavy reliance of the BEF on artillery and other weapons at the Somme, this still seems a useful idea, and can be supported by the continuing emphasis during most of the war on the infantry as the decisive element of warfare, to be assisted by all other arms, rather than as a partner of these arms. In the end, the concept of an all arms partnership did emerge by 1917 and was fully employed in winning the war in 1918.

The Killing Ground spends much time considering the abilities of Sir Douglas Haig, and here one or two points can be made. One argument advanced in the book that seems to have irritated some historians is that Haig learnt at Staff College the concept of the three or four act structured offensive: preparation, including wearing down the enemy and drawing in the enemy reserves; then the decisive attack; and finally, the exploitation. In fact, a better way of expressing the structured offensive would have been to describe it as an approach to an entire campaign rather than as being specific to a single offensive, and also to remove the offending word "structured", which does not alter the meaning of the concept. Yet there is no doubt that Haig did learn this basic idea, and it does underly his approach, for example, to planning the Somme in 1916. The problem was that conditions of the time prevented the wearing out fight and the drawing in of enemy reserves in 1916, and in fact a decisive offensive never did take place, rather a series of offensives made the difference in 1918. Another point raised by the revisionists relates to Haig's understanding of technology, which *The Killing Ground* does not discuss very much. In general it can be said that Haig was keen to use all technology, but that he sometimes asked technology to adapt to his plans rather than setting plans that made the best use of the available technology. The obvious example here is Haig's choice of Passchendaele as a battlefield, which definitely hindered both his artillery and other kinds of technology such as the tanks.

A further point that is an issue with the revisionists is the assertion in *The Killing Ground* that Haig's style of command produced a rather isolated leadership. This was partly produced by Haig's own forbidding character, and partly produced by British army principles of command. Despite efforts to see Haig as a more amenable character, and the evidence that Haig did visit units and commanders, it appears that Haig and his GHQ were often rather detached from front line conditions. One reason to believe this is the fact that some key members of GHQ, such as Kiggell [Chief of Staff] and Charteris [Director of Intelligence], were replaced in early 1918, while newcomers to GHQ found there was indeed much to remedy. For example, Brigadier General Charles Bonham-Carter, appointed to GHQ on 12 October 1917 to take charge of the Training Branch, wrote "When I arrived I was horrified by the lack of knowledge at GHQ of the conditions under which fighting in the Ypres Salient was being carried out. During the last month of the fighting they were very bad indeed and I do not believe for a moment that they were realized." He continued: "The Operations Staff did not make proper use of the means at their disposal for keeping in close touch with the formations and units in front. General Kiggell was a tired man. Butler [Deputy Chief of Staff] was occupied with organisations and training. J.H. Davidson [Director of Military Operations] was over-driven; though he visited frequently the higher commanders, it was not possible for him to keep personal touch with forward formations. This lack of contact and knowledge was harmful."[1]

There is a classic story told that when Kiggell visited the battlefield after the end of the Passchendaele campaign, he is alleged to have become upset and said: "Good God, did we send men to fight in that?" In fact it appears that the officer concerned was not Kiggell but Davidson, and that he was not weeping, but "holding his hands to his face to show that he was dumb to enquiries and not to hide tears."[2] Whatever the truth of the incident, the story symbolises the continuing debate over the effectiveness of Haig and GHQ during the war. In spite of the valuable work of the revisionists, it seems likely that Haig and his headquarters will always be primarily associated with the Somme and Passchendaele battles. However, it is useful that such controversies exist, and predictably in the future the pendulum will swing again, and other viewpoints will emerge. In the meantime, this re-issue of *The Killing Ground* can hopefully still contribute to the ongoing debate over the nature of the pre-war British army, and the role of Haig, GHQ and the BEF on the Western Front during the First World War.

Notes

1 Major General Charles Bonham-Carter, "Autobiography", chapter IX, Section 2, pp. 5-6, Bonham-Carter papers, 9/2, Churchill College, Cambridge.
2 The Kiggell story seems to have originated with Brigadier General J.E. Edmonds, the British Official Historian, and was publicised by the military historian Liddell Hart: Liddell Hart, 'Note on conversation with Edmonds', 7 October 1927, Liddell Hart papers, 11/1927/17, Liddell Hart Centre for Military Archives, King's College, London University. The Davidson story comes from the interview of Sir John Davidson by G.C. Wynne [an official historian working on the Passchendaele campaign], 21 April 1945, Cabinet 45/144, Public Record Office, Kew Gardens, London.

PART I

Understanding the Edwardian Army

[1]

The System at Work

Promotions, Dismissals and the Personalized Army

In 1937 Brigadier General Sir James Edmonds, the official historian, met with Captain Basil Liddell Hart, the historian of the First World War, and outlined some promotion procedures he perceived to exist in the British army before the First World War. These procedures Edmonds considered to be an unofficial system, and in his opinion this 'system' had damaged the British army to a considerable extent. With some degree of exaggeration, Edmonds argued that before the Boer War, 'no one in the Army ever took the profession seriously'. But, said Edmonds,

> Things greatly improved after the Boer War, yet it was astonishing in how few years the elementary lessons of that war were forgotten in training. The army suffered above all, and always had done, from the system. The careers of promising officers were too much at the mercy of one man. [General] Sir Charles Douglas, for example, when AG [Adjutant General] and CIGS in turn, had done a lot of harm – he chose all the wrong men and penalised any who had ideas and originality.

Edmonds then listed the names of four CIGS, and declared that General the Hon. Sir Neville Lyttelton had favoured Riflemen (Rifle Brigade officers) for promotion; General Sir William Nicholson gave preference to India service officers; General the Earl of Cavan* preferred any who had crossed the Piave river (Cavan had been in charge of operations for the Tenth Italian army on the Piave front in 1918); and Field Marshal Lord Milne promoted those who had been in Salonika (Milne had commanded the British Salonika force from 1916–20). Again, there was exaggeration in Edmonds's remarks, yet also a basis of fact.

Next Edmonds turned his attention to General Sir Henry Wilson,* whom he disliked, and recounted how Wilson had engineered his own appointment to command the Staff College in 1906. According to Edmonds, who learnt the details from his old chief, Lyttelton, Wilson first disposed of two rivals, Lieutenant General Sir Henry Lawson and Major General Sir Thomas Capper, by offering the former command of the Dublin Infantry Brigade and the latter command of the Indian Staff College at Quetta. Wilson could do this because he held the post of Deputy Director of Staff Duties at the War Office; he was also able to produce his own list of candidates made up, he said, by Major General Hutchinson, who was actually on sick leave at the time. Wilson placed this list in front of Lyttelton, the CIGS, with an unsuitable name at the top of the list – that of General May, who was reportedly dull and pompous but well-read – and then told Lyttelton: 'The next name on the list, Sir, is mine'. Lyttelton apparently said to Wilson, '"you will do", as he told me [Edmonds] with a smile, he wanted to be off to Lords to see a Royal [i.e. real] tennis match'. Wilson did in fact command the Staff College at Camberley from 1906–10.[1]

Even if exaggerated, Edmonds's assertions merit further consideration, since they do seem to indicate some deeper structural problems in the British army. This chapter will in fact argue the awkward transitional nature of the Edwardian army, and then examine the personalized system which existed in the army, particularly in regard to promotions, and will stress the importance of the 'protector-*protegé*' relationship. Then the question of removals or dismissals will be addressed, especially in regard to GHQ leverage and personal rivalries. The latter aspect will involve a detailed analysis of the problem of the reserves at the battle of Loos (September 1915) and the subsequent removal of Sir John French. Specific types of removals will be suggested, including that of the scapegoat. The chapter will then turn to a discussion of cover-ups, and alterations in the military record and in the *Official History*. Finally, certain conclusions will be reached regarding the transitional nature of the army, caught between traditional and professional ideals.

The army in the period 1900–14 was going through a particularly anxious transitional phase. It was developing from a small volunteer force, geared to the defence of empire and the waging of small colonial wars – essentially a small, traditional army – toward a much larger-scale force (later conscripted), capable of waging continental war, competent in staff work and the handling of modern weapons. It was becoming essentially a professional army. This transition from traditional to professional proved lengthy and difficult, and it has been argued that the struggle between the technical, professional approach and the traditional 'gentlemanly' ideal produced tensions within the officer corps,[2] as one ideal replaced the other, or as both uneasily co-existed. This situation seems to have been particularly evident in the decade before the First World War, as growing pressures to professionalize the British officer came up against an officer corps whose members often favoured reform, but whose attitudes and ethos remained essentially traditional.

On the one hand, reforming pressures were brought into the open by reports, committees and commissions, such as the Royal Commission on the Boer War (1904), the Education of Officers Committee Report (1902), the Esher Committee (1904), and the Haldane reorganization of the army (1906–07). All these were attempts to professionalize the army in line with the 'efficiency' movement of the period. Also, the lessons of the Boer War and the Russo-Japanese war, plus some technical innovations such as the short Lee Enfield rifle, heavier quick-firing artillery and the Vickers machine-gun, forced a discussion of new tactics, ideas and weapons. On the other hand, traditional attitudes in the officer corps remained strong if not overwhelming, and these attitudes either led to a misunderstanding of change, or most frequently tended to divert changes into acceptable channels.[3]

Traditional attitudes in the Edwardian officer corps also reflected the public school experience, whence most officers originated. Public school education stressed such values as group loyalty, deference and obedience to the accepted hierarchy, an opposition to politics and intellectual matters, and an emphasis on self-assurance and character. Values such as these were not conducive to criticism of the prevailing army system, nor to the ready acceptance of a purely professional officer corps.[4] Furthermore, there was a strong tendency to perpetuate the way in which senior army officers, the aristocracy and the royal family seemed to 'own' the late Victorian army. Patronage and social connections, the seniority promotion system, the lack of a general staff and of socially acceptable staff college training, leadership of the Volunteer and Militia system, colonial 'small war' heroes and personalities – all tended to personalize the late Victorian and Edwardian army, and to produce an army that acted as an instrument in preserving traditional attitudes.[5]

The convergence and frequent conflict of these two concepts of war in the Edwardian period – the traditional gentlemanly ideal and the technical, functionally competent, professional ideal – produced an awkward transition period for the officer corps. Some officers attempted to merge the two ideals. Douglas Haig, for example, certainly did his best to professionalize Aldershot Command just before the war and create a common doctrine for the army, while at the same time clinging to traditional nineteenth-century ideas about morale and cavalry. Other officers kept the two ideals separate, and adhered to one or the other, such as the new fire power/technical theorists, Major McMahon and Captain J. F. C. Fuller.* But other officers found it impossible to make the transition from traditional to professional, as in the case of the unfortunate Major Geohegan.[6]

The outbreak of war in 1914 accelerated the process of conflict and adjustment between the two ideals, and the result was a painful pro-fessionalization during the war, which apparently generated anxiety among senior officers and staff. This anxiety, and the attempt of a still largely traditional officer corps to fight a modern (technological/fire-power) war as though it were a fully prepared and professional group of senior officers and staff, led to a strong tendency to cover up errors during the war, and to achieve alterations in the subsequent military record and then in the *Official History*. At the same time, the continuing strength of the traditional ideal permitted considerable leeway for personal rivalries in the field, and for undue personal influence and distortions in the matter of promotions and removals. Before turning to the question of cover-ups and alterations, therefore, it will be useful to look first at the personalized system of the Edwardian army, and its role in the area of promotions and dismissals.

Long after the war, Edmonds claimed that 'in 1914 the army was still very feudal in its status, and great personages, even great ladies, exercised the higher patronage'. General Noel Birch,* Major General Royal Artil-lery (MGRA), at GHQ in 1916, thought that the British army in the First World War was an amateur army, while he saw the German army as professional.[7] This does not mean that at the lower levels the army was not well trained and well led in 1914, or that serious efforts were not being made to modernize and re-equip the army in the Edwardian period, despite financial restrictions, but simply that the ethos and attitudes of the officer corps at the higher levels of command were often traditional, leading to the existence of an unofficial personalized system, through which the army operated. Despite a widespread conviction that in 1914 the British army was a professional army, in fact the British officer corps on the eve of the war was still largely Victorian in many of its attitudes, with an overwhelming emphasis on the influence of individual personali-ties, and on social and regimental hierarchies.[8] The system operated through the influence of dominant personalities, of social traditions, and of personal friendships and rivalries.

Of prime and natural importance to senior (and junior) officers was the question of promotion. At the time of the Boer War, senior appointments were in various hands – the Secretary of State for War, the Military Secretary, the War Office, the Commander-in-Chief, etc. – but much of what transpired in the way of promotion was heavily influenced by the feud between the Field Marshal Lord Roberts (Indian) Ring and the Field Marshal Lord Wolseley (African) Ring. This feud had severe repercus-sions in South Africa, and did much to stifle initiative in the War Office.[9] But although belonging to one ring or another could have beneficial or negative results for the careers of individual officers, there was another significant variable. It would seem that in the 1890s and early 1900s it was essential to have senior protectors who would push the career of a *protegé.* This was natural in many ways, being the result of friendship or belief in the capacity of a junior officer, yet the overall impression is of an Edwardian army given over to struggles for promotion through personal influence rather than any disinterested or neutral evaluation. Even after a Selection Board of eight members was set up in 1885, personal rivalries continued to block or promote individuals. For example, the future General Sir Aylmer Haldane* asked the CIGS Nicholson to help him become Brigadier General, General Staff (BGGS) of Eastern Command under Major General Sir Arthur Paget, because General Sir Ian Hamilton*, Haldane's enemy, was on the Selection Board, and always opposed him. Due to Nicholson, Haldane did become BGGS to Paget, but in 1911 General Sir Charles Douglas became CIGS and would not have Haldane on his staff because he said Haldane had not got on well with him as a regimental brother officer.[10]

In fact Aylmer Haldane is a good example of the system of protector and *protegé* in operation. Aylmer Haldane was the *protegé* of the future CIGS Nicholson, and in 1900 wrote to the latter hoping for brevet promotion and appointment to his staff. Nicholson said that he would promote his interests, and in 1901 he told Haldane that he would obtain a key staff job for him in the new War Office (under Nicholson). Haldane did join the new General Staff, although in 1905 he was writing again to Nicholson hoping to be made a full Colonel. Then by a stroke of fortune his cousin, R. B. Haldane, became War Minister in 1906, and Aylmer Haldane was able to reciprocate by urging R. B. Haldane to appoint Nicholson as CIGS. Whether Aylmer Haldane actually achieved this by his own efforts is not clear, however he thought he had, and Nicholson did become CIGS in 1908. Aylmer Haldane seemed set for promotion, and indeed, as previously mentioned, became BGGS to Paget. Then came the disfavour of Douglas's rule as CIGS and again difficulties for Haldane. But Haldane was 'rescued' by the First World War, and the command of 3 Division. As a result, however, of reverses at the St Eloi craters in April 1916, he ran foul of Douglas Haig, who tried to remove him, having concluded that Haldane was only a good defensive general. Nevertheless, General Sir William Robertson,* the CIGS in 1916, was a friend of Haldane's, and in August 1916 Haldane was appointed to command VI Corps. Subsequently, he did well at Arras in 1917 and his career prospered.[11]

Despite the problems in April 1916 at St Eloi and again in July 1916, when he was forced to make a hurried attack,[12] Haldane was an intelligent commander and deserved the promotion which admittedly he eagerly sought. But his career shows that it was important to have a protector, and the same thing occurred with Douglas Haig. Like Haldane, Haig was an efficient officer, with a similar desire for promotion, and again like Haldane, was well-connected socially. Haig was the better read of the two, partly due to his Staff College training, but like Haldane, he too needed to be the *protegé* of someone. Initially Haig found two cavalry protectors, Major General Evelyn Wood* and Colonel John French.[13] Already in 1895 the latter wanted Haig to be his staff officer, a position which he actually filled during the South African war. Meanwhile Haig wrote and narrowly failed the Staff College examination in 1893, but was accepted in 1896 by special nomination.[14]

Haig passed successfully out of Staff College and then joined the Sudan campaign. According to Haig's letters in 1898 it was Major General Evelyn Wood who obtained Haig his position in the Sudan, and who then offered to get him a job at the Horse Guards by speaking to Wolseley. It was in the Sudan campaign also that Haig started his practice of writing private letters to the Prince of Wales (nicknamed 'Tum'), and confidential letters to Major General Evelyn Wood (a preview of Haig's confidential letters to the king and Kitchener in 1915).[15] At this point an event occurred which was indirectly to assist Haig in his promotion prospects, although there is no evidence that he acted with this mind. It would appear that Colonel John French got into financial difficulties in 1899, and Haig offered to bail him out with a loan guarantee of £800 (or £1200 if necessary): 'I have wired that I'll produce the £800. It would be a terrible thing if French was made a Bankrupt – such a loss to the Army as well as to me personally. For of course we can do a lot here together towards improving things.'[16] After this incident, French pushed Haig's interests at every opportunity, although it should be noted again that there is no evidence Haig intended this action to help his own career, and indeed French had shown interest in Haig's career as early as 1895. Nevertheless, whether because of Haig's own talents as a staff officer in South Africa, or because French felt obligated or wanted to promote the career of a fellow cavalryman, there is no doubt that French worked hard to advance Haig's interests as his *protegé*.

This was not always an easy matter because it was in South Africa that Haig ran into the rivalry between the Roberts Indian Ring and the Wolseley African Ring. Haig seems to have been an 'African', and the result of this alignment could be seen when French told General Sir Redvers Buller in November 1899 that he wanted to make Haig his Assistant Adjutant General (AAG). Haig confidently told his sister, Henrietta, that he would be made AAG, yet Roberts picked his own man, the Earl of Errol, instead. So Haig settled for the rank of Lieutenant Colonel and command of the 3rd Cavalry Brigade. After a short time (and some letters home castigating Roberts as a 'foolish old man' and scarcely fit to be Commander-in-Chief) Haig then became Chief Staff Officer (CSO) to French's Cavalry Division. Next, French wired the War Office in November 1900 requesting a particular cavalry regiment for Haig, but apparently another officer was appointed to command instead. However,

Haig was not disheartened, partly because the new Military Secretary was Sir Ian Hamilton, and although a prominent Roberts Indian, he was 'a friend of mine, and will I know do his best for me when he gets home – He promised French that I would be offered the first Regt. which was in need of a Comy officer from outside; and he asked me to let him know my wishes'.[17] Also in 1900 French suggested that Haig become an Aide-de-Camp (ADC) to the queen 'because that at once gives one the rank of full colonel', while Evelyn Wood wanted Haig to command a cavalry regiment because the Cavalry had not done so well in South Africa up to that time (August 1900).[18]

In the event Haig stayed on as CSO to French's Cavalry Division, a fact which apparently angered Haig's sister, Henrietta, who wrote in December 1900 upbraiding French for not helping Haig enough. Haig loyally replied 'don't think for a moment that French has not done his best for me. – He is only too anxious to help me on, but I think in remaining on as his Chief Staff Officer I did the best for the Cav-Div^n, for him and myself.' There may have been some basis for Henrietta's suspicions, since Kitchener apparently wondered at this time whether French was promoting Haig as far as he could – but only as a staff officer. Kitchener asked himself: 'Is French really trying to help Haig, or is he tired of Haig and does he want to shunt him to make room for some young *protegé* of his own?' The doubt was probably unjustified, and although Henrietta returned to the attack in November 1901, Haig once more told her, 'Now as I have told you often the General [French] wrote to Evelyn [Wood] several times about me and the others recommending me for all sorts of things'.[19] In fact Haig was appointed to command the 17th Lancers in 1901, but it was also in 1901 that Roberts and the Indians claimed the Horse Guards from Wolseley, causing Haig's influence (and Henrietta's) to decline in that direction. However, before that happened, Haig had written to Henrietta in July 1901 seeking some way of appointing his relation Oliver Haig as ADC, despite his inexperience: 'So you will have to arrange with the "Lady Killer of Pall Mall" [i.e. Wolseley] as French calls him.'[20]

The presence of Roberts at the Horse Guards apparently did prevent Haig from getting the job that he wanted. In June of 1902 Haig had told Henrietta that General French 'has kindly said that he is going to insist on my being appointed to command the Aldershot Cavalry Brigade. But of course he may fail in getting his way.' (French was now General Officer Commanding (GOC) at Aldershot.) In due course Roberts did turn down Haig for that appointment and instead Haig was told to remain with the 17th Lancers. This elicited two uncharacteristically bitter letters from Haig, one in August 1902 declaring that Roberts would give command of the Cavalry at Aldershot to someone else because the nursery and rooms at the Aldershot Cavalry GOC's official house will suit 'Dear Mrs. So and

So', and the other in September 1902 arguing 'So no doubt some of Roberts' pals (or ? Lady R's pals) have been chosen' for the post.[21]

In the end Haig was appointed by Kitchener as Inspector General of Cavalry in India, while later on the combination of his own talents, the continuing efforts of French,[22] and the interest of others such as Lord Esher, R. B. Haldane and the king,[23] enabled Haig to get the crucial post of Director of Military Training (DMT) at the War Office in 1906. Thereafter Haig's career continued to prosper, until finally Sir John French was removed as Commander-in-Chief of the BEF in late 1915, and Haig replaced him. Edmonds claimed that until that moment, French continued to clear the path for Haig, doing so because he wished to secure promotion for the cavalry. Hence French sent General Sir Horace Smith-Dorrien* home, and got General Sir Charles Monro sent to India, thus getting rid of two of Haig's rivals.[24] If so, it is ironic that Haig should have been partly responsible later for French's own removal. It is likely that French wanted to promote cavalry men, but in this case he was particularly pushing Haig's career, as he had done since 1895, and so it is not clear that the cavalry connection was the main reason for removing Smith-Dorrien and Monro. In any case, the careers of Haldane and Haig illustrate the role of *protegé* and protector – roles which were necessary because that was the way the system worked.

Edmonds was not being critical when he reported such matters but simply recording the facts. Indeed, Edmonds himself had the Director of Military Intelligence, Colonel Sir John Ardagh, and then Haig, as protectors. Edmonds and Haig became friends at Staff College, to the extent that Edmonds allowed Haig to use his notes for three days during a field exercise, and later on in 1914 Haig protected Edmonds at a critical point when Edmonds collapsed through strain. Later still, after the war, Edmonds loyally repaid Haig by generally preserving Haig's reputation during the writing of the *Official History*, particularly the volume on Passchendaele.[25] Neither Haig, Edmonds, French or Haldane are to be particularly criticized, for what was happening was the slow transition under twentieth-century pressures of a small, colonial-oriented, traditional, above all personalized army, into a much larger, professional, and technically oriented army; and this transition caused the personalized senior level promotion system to become antiquated, as it were, in mid-stream.

Nor was the system simply one of protectors and *protegés*. There were many countervailing currents, such as the 'Cavalry' thesis of Edmonds, who maintained that after Haig obtained the post of Commander-in-Chief, he continued French's policy of promoting cavalrymen – Gough, Allenby,* Byng* and Birdwood,* for example – who all commanded armies.[26] It seems that in some cases there was the natural element of friendship involved here, but Haig also liked 'thrusters', and cavalrymen were usually 'thrusters'. On the other hand Haig also tried to promote men such as General Sir Richard Haking,* who was a 'thruster' but also an infantryman. To complicate matters further, Haig apparently singled out General Sir Hubert Gough, not only as a Cavalry 'thruster', but also as his *protege*. According to Edmonds, Haig was much taken with Gough, and later offered to resign to save him (Gough) in 1918. In more concrete terms, Aylmer Haldane observed the removal of various Corps commanders in June 1916, such as Lieutenant General Sir Edward Fanshawe* and Lieutenant General Sir Charles Ferguson, and remarked, 'It seems pretty clear that Haig is getting rid of all Corps Crs., who are senior to Gough, who is to command the 2nd Army operation'.[27]

Hence all that can be concluded here is that French and Haig did favour cavalrymen, but there were other reasons for promotion too. In fact a study of some other examples of promotion shows how personalized and idiosyncratic the system could be. Aylmer Haldane, who was admittedly no great friend of Sir Ian Hamilton's, recorded how Hamilton got himself made senior to Nicholson by having his promotion to Major General antedated to the date of his arrival in South Africa, although he was still only a Colonel when at Ladysmith. (Hamilton had his own problems in South Africa, however. When he was appointed chief of staff to Kitchener in November 1901, Kitchener saw him as a rival; he feared that he himself would be sent home, and replaced perhaps by Hamilton. So, reportedly, he would not let Hamilton do anything, and if Hamilton wrote a minute, Kitchener would allegedly blue-pencil it out of recognition.)[28] In another case, Edmonds recalled that Robertson, the future CIGS, was once senior staff officer, grade two (G2), in the Intelligence Department at the War Office. It happened that a certain high level servant wanted his brother-in-law, who had not passed Staff College, to be G2 in the Intelligence Department. Nicholson, the DMI at that time, objected, but the civil servant achieved his end by increasing the staff to include another staff officer, grade one (G1), and two more G2s, to allow his relative in, and to please others. So Robertson became a Colonel and G1, and was promoted over others, including Edmonds, in order to make space in the G2 ranks for the civil servant relative. Edmonds did add, however, that Robertson's elevation was deserved. This took place between 1904 and 1906. In regard to Edmonds himself, Aylmer Haldane mentioned that in 1911 it was 'thanks to me mainly' that Edmonds was promoted to be G1 of 4 Division – Edmonds and Haldane had gone to Russia together in 1908 and had become friends.[29]

Reviewing the question of senior promotions before the war, one is struck by the presence of a highly personalized system in which the influence of friends and enemies made an enormous difference to a man's career. It is also noticeable that a confusing variety of influences made themselves felt. These ranged from personal, regimental and arm rivalries, to the question of whom one was or was not with at Staff College,[30] and to the influence or otherwise of powerful individuals as protectors, besides the traditional army reliance on simple seniority. And there was not only the question of who got promoted and how, but also of who was passed over and why. Space forbids a detailed view of this aspect, but it is evident that personal rivalries played a large role. Edmonds claimed, for example, that Arthur Paget was the best choice to command III Corps in 1914, but was passed over because he had had a row with Sir John French on manoeuvres in 1913.[31] Allowing for the biases (and sometimes bitterness) of well-placed observers such as Edmonds, Haldane, Haig, Liddell Hart, Wilson, and so on, it is still clear that the promotion system left much to be desired in the Edwardian army, and reflected an amateur army caught in a changing world. It would only be fair to add that other prewar European armies, particularly the French, suffered many of the same defects in regard to their promotion systems (see Epilogue). In the British case, the Edwardian army simply continued the arbitrary procedures of the South African War,[32] but with the advent of the First World War certain changes did take place.

After 1914 there were two main changes in the BEF regarding promotion prospects: a large number of incompetent officers were sent home, and GHQ began to exercise very considerable leverage over the attitudes of senior commanders through GHQ's ability to promote or send home officers. At the same time the Commanders-in-Chief, French and Haig, continued the South African and traditional precedent of making personal appointments. For example, in April 1916 Aylmer Haldane stated that Haig's military secretary, Teck, came to him and asked Haldane if he knew of any good officers for promotion to staff work, 'as his chief [Haig] had come to an end of those whom he knew personally!' On 21 June 1916 Haldane made a similar critical comment, upon hearing of Haig's appointment of the melancholy Hamilton-Gordon to command IX Corps.[33] The nature of Haig's appointments caused so much concern that the king himself tried to stop the practice, telling Haig on 8 August 1916 that senior promotions should come from London and not GHQ.[34] Haig demurred, and the practice went on, although with increasing limitations and, finally, according to Henry Wilson, Haig was prevented from personally appointing Army or Corps commanders after September 1916.[35]

The limitation on Haig's powers after September 1916 and the king's actions stemmed, it would appear, from Haig's attempt in August 1916 to appoint Haking to command First Army. Haking's earlier Corps attack at Fromelles on 19 July 1916 had been an abject failure,[36] although not all the blame rested with Haking,[37] since GHQ had actually ordered the attack. Haig, making the best of the failure, commented that the attack was of value through the experience of shelling and fighting for new troops.[38] But, in any case, Haking's appointment to an army command after this costly failure was strange. Wilson wrote on 5 August 1916, 'If this is so [Haking's appointment] it only shows how hopelessly out of touch GHQ is with what we all think of Haking'. Robertson agreed, and apparently prevented the appointment, for it was given to Major General Horne.*[39] Haig's rebuff over Haking, and the limitation subsequently placed on GHQ's ability to appoint Army and Corps commanders, did not prevent GHQ from continuing to exercise very considerable leverage over Army and Corps commanders, and indeed over all senior officers. This occurred through reports on how offensive-minded senior officers were, and through the general knowledge that the way to get promoted was always to be enthusiastic about attacking, regardless of the drawbacks.[40] Earlier examples include the case of Major General the Hon. Sir Julian Byng in Gallipoli, who advised evacuation unless further support was forthcoming. Byng held firm against Kitchener's opposition, and by January 1916, when the evacuation was complete, Byng found that eight Major Generals had been promoted over his head.[41] However, Byng's career was not blighted, and he went on to command an Army. Not so happy was the career of Major General R. G. Broadwood, who apparently declined to launch attacks that could not succeed. Broadwood was reported by his Corps commanders Major General A. G. Godley and then Haking for lack of fighting spirit. Colonel Allanson was G1 to Broadwood's Division, and he recalled that as a result of these reports Broadwood got himself killed, leaving instructions that he wished to be buried between a subaltern and a soldier. Allanson concluded by saying that moral courage of this sort was rare, because to speak one's mind caused one's career to suffer.[42]

However, the leverage that GHQ operated was not only through promotions for offensive-minded commanders, but also more powerfully, through dismissals. Edmonds remarked in 1916 in a letter to Spenser Wilkinson that there was 'only one form of order and that is to attack. Generals who protest and point out the folly of attempting to rush fortifications are *degommés*'.[43] *Degommer* means to unstick, and the practice of removing senior officers and sending them home became known as 'degumming', a worthy successor to the South African war practice of removing unwanted officers to the town of Stellenbosch, hence being 'Stellenbosched'. Edmonds also commented that Haig had once told him he had sent home (degummed) more than 100 Brigadiers, but was forced to keep some Corps and Division commanders because there weren't any better officers around. Perhaps for this reason, or because removing Corps commanders was obviously awkward for GHQ, Edmonds also claimed that Haig did not sack Corps commanders for inefficiency, such as Horne, General Sir Walter Congreve* and Lieutenant General Sir Aylmer Hunter-Weston,* although he did remove divisional generals.[44] Such a scale of senior officer dismissals gives pause for thought, and a study of the material shows that there were four main causes of removal: (1) poor health and/or incompetence, (2) personal rivalry and animosity, (3) failure in action and as a lever to encourage the offensive spirit and (4) as scapegoats.

Unquestionably, many officers (senior and junior) were unfit and/or incompetent when the war started. Aylmer Haldane, who trained and commanded 10th Infantry Brigade of 4 Division before and during the war, was strongly critical of his GOC, Major General T. D'O. Snow,* and of a great many other officers in his command prior to the war. Haldane relates how one officer in his Brigade went mad in 1913, and one night killed several chickens belonging to his commanding officer. Strangely, this officer (and another) were cashiered for bankruptcy rather than (mental) illness. Haldane had tried in vain to get rid of a certain Colonel Churcher before the war. Subsequently Churcher's conduct at Mons was such that he was then sent home. The commanding officer of the 2nd Royal Dublin Fusiliers had colitis, but the doctors would not agree to his dismissal, so it was not until Le Cateau that he too was removed. Overall, Haldane recalled that three out of four Battalion commanding officers were not fit for command, and all had been sent home by the end of September 1914.[45] General Snow survived as GOC, but was probably lucky to do so.[46] Haldane may have been over-critical, but the ratio of incompetent officers in 10th Infantry Brigade was probably not unique. At the higher levels of command, many officers were physically unfit, even if mentally alert. Lieutenant General Sir Archibald Murray, chief of staff to Sir John French, collapsed from strain on 26 August 1914, the critical day of Le Cateau, while General Sir James Grierson, selected to command II Corps, collapsed on his way to the front in 1914. Grierson was a competent and widely-read officer, perhaps the most qualified to be chief of staff, but in the Edwardian fashion was overweight and unfit. Edmonds recalled that Grierson used to go red in the face when bending over, due to high blood pressure, and his medical officer issued Grierson's staff with penknives so that he could be bled when his blood pressure rose too high. Sadly, Grierson's collapse resulted in his death in 1914.[47]

Secondly, most personal rivalries and animosities pre-dated the war, and this was the case between Henry Wilson and Douglas Haig's circle. Wilson was extremely critical of Haig's generalship from the beginning, and Haig found Wilson too clever, too fond of the French, and an intriguer. Although the record is not crystal clear, it seems that in May 1916 Haig thought he had found an opportunity for removing Wilson, who in early 1916 had been given command of IV Corps. Major Armytage, a staff officer from Haig's GHQ, had visited Wilson's front on 25 May 1916, and reported back to Haig that the commanding officer of a

Brigade in IV Corps was ignorant of the situation. Haig remarked that IV Corps should not have kept so incompetent a Brigadier, and that IV Corps had been the most efficient in the army before Wilson took over, but that he had failed as commander. Two days after this incident, Haig sent GHQ Generals Butler* (Deputy Chief of Staff) and Charteris (Brigadier General, Intelligence) over to the IV Corps HQ Mess, and they reported back to Haig that IV Corps staff were despondent and pessimistic. In fact Wilson claimed that his staff were playing a joke on Charteris and pulling his leg (which seems likely from the conversations Charteris reported), but Haig evidently felt he had enough reason to degum Wilson. Fortunately for Wilson, Monro (GOC First Army, containing IV Corps) supported his Corps commander, and told Haig that he had seen Wilson, that the Corps' situation was difficult, and that things would improve.[48] Wilson was saved – an example it seems of an unsuccessful attempt at degumming.[49]

Another example of rivalry that stemmed from prewar days concerns the relationship between Sir John French and General Smith-Dorrien. The origins of the rivalry are obscure, but may well lie in Edmonds's assertion that Sir John French wished to hinder rivals to the promotion prospects of Haig. Edmonds later remarked in a private letter that '"Smith D" ... went home for special reasons which one cannot publish in the history ... [Smith-Dorrien] was got rid of by French because he stood in Haig's way of the Commander in Chiefship'. There may also have been simple incompatibility between French and Smith-Dorrien, and between Haig and Smith-Dorrien. In any case, Aylmer Haldane first encountered the problem at the annual 1909 manoeuvres, when Sir John French summed up in favour of General Paget and against General Smith-Dorrien, 'to the extent of being unfair to him [Smith-Dorrien]'. Later, when Smith-Dorrien replaced Grierson as commander of II Corps against French's wishes, the problem emerged again and Smith-Dorrien told Edmonds that at the battle of Mons on 23 August 1914 Sir John French gave the order: 'The BEF will give battle on the line of the Conde (Mons) canal'. But when Smith-Dorrien asked 'Do you mean to take the offensive or stand on the defensive?', Sir John French went off and whispered with his Chief of Staff, Sir Archibald Murray, and then retorted, 'You do as you are ordered and don't ask questions'. According to the historian John Terraine, Sir John French's control over this battle was tenuous, and when Smith-Dorrien saved the situation a few days later at Le Cateau, against Sir John French's orders, it might be predicted that Smith-Dorrien would be removed. This became fact at Ypres in 1915.[50] Smith-Dorrien himself claimed that, starting in February 1915, Sir John French began to inflict 'pin pricks' on him, for example the removal of Lieutenant General Forestier-Walker as his II Corps Chief of Staff because Sir John French said Forestier-Walker could not be spared as he was wanted immediately to command a division training in England. But two months later Forestier-Walker was still waiting to command the division. It was personal feeling only, remarked Smith-Dorrien.[51] At this point in time, it is now impossible to untangle the primary reasons for this rivalry, but it did exist and it did have consequences in terms of operations and efficiency.

Personal rivalries have always existed in large organizations and it is natural that they should, but these rivalries in South Africa and the First World War were allowed to have unfortunate results, due to the personalized style of the British senior command. A controversial example concerns Haig, Sir John French again, and the question of the Reserves (21 and 24 Divisions of XI Corps) at the Battle of Loos, 25 September 1915. This question is significant because this failure gave the Cabinet and Kitchener, Haig and Robertson the opportunity to replace Sir John French.[52] Generally, Sir John French has been blamed, particularly by Haig, for keeping the Reserves too far back so that they could not move up in time to support Haig's First Army attack at Loos, and for keeping the Reserves in Sir John French's own hands, and only reluctantly handing them over to Haig when it was too late to exploit the breakthrough.

It would appear that by now Sir John French was jealous of Haig (and Kitchener), and that he did keep back the Reserves, but whether this was because he did not really believe in the success of the battle,[53] or because he wanted to be able to claim the victory for himself,[54] or because he wanted to compel Haig to conform to his plan for the battle,[55] or because he thought in traditional terms of a Napoleonic general reserve, to be used at the discretion of the Commander-in-Chief,[56] is not clear. Nevertheless, Sir John French *did* accede to Haig's own request of 19 September 1915 that the Reserves be placed on the line Noeux-les-Mines–Beuvry by daylight on 25 September 1915, which would have put them approximately six and a half miles from the Loos start line.[57]

Subsequently Haig argued that he had wanted the Reserves closer than Noeux-les-Mines–Beuvry, and had made this point at the GHQ conference at St Omer on 18 September 1915.[58] In fact, from both First Army files and his diary, Haig seems to have been more concerned on 18 September with the possibility of postponing the attack if the wind was not favourable for the use of gas.[59] No doubt Haig *did* want the Reserves closer, but from his letter of 19 September to GHQ he seemed content with his own request that the 'heads of the two leading Divisions of XI Corps should be on the line Noeux-les-Mines–Beuvry by daylight on 25 September'. Moreover, Haig's own diary entry for 23 September 1915 also suggests that he was satisfied with the arrangements 'the three divisions [21, 24 and Guards] will, I hope, be close up in the places where I have arranged to put them, and will go forward as soon as any opportunity offers'. This entry implies that Haig considered the line Noeux-les-

Mines–Beuvry to be 'close up', and that the Reserves would be ready to go forward, not immediately the assault began, as the *Official History* states, but when 'opportunity offers', i.e. at some later time.[60] The situation is further complicated by the fact that General Haking, commanding the Reserves (XI Corps), was of the opinion that Haig originally intended XI Corps to fill the gap between IV and I Corps in the attack, and not act as a reserve at all.[61]

Therefore, the Reserves *did* arrive at the time and place requested by Haig, and the question then turns on whether Sir John French refused to hand over the Reserves early enough on 25 September to exploit the success of the assault. The timetable shows that Haig requested XI Corps to move forward at 8.45 a.m. on 25 September, and in fact Sir John responded by ordering XI Corps to move at 9.30 a.m. Haking thereupon issued orders to his XI Corps Divisions to move, but since he did not have telephone communication with his divisions, the orders went via liaison officers. Consequently it was 10.30 a.m. before XI Corps received the orders, and approximately 11.15 a.m. before the first units actually moved forward. Thereafter the heavy congestion of roads and railway crossings delayed the march of the two reserve divisions, whose leading units did not begin to arrive at the front for at least another three hours, i.e. approximately 2.30 p.m., by which time it was too late.[62]

Douglas Haig was quick to blame Sir John French and GHQ for the fiasco, but the issue is not clear cut in deciding who was really responsible for the slow arrival of the Reserves. Originally, Haig's *protegé*, General Haking, had said that the slow movement of the Reserves to the front was due to the presence of First Army troops in the area. But then, perhaps under pressure, Haking contradicted himself and noted that First Army had made the 'most careful arrangments ... to ensure that the two roads were kept clear', and blamed the troops instead for their poor march discipline. Haig concurred.[63] Further investigation revealed, however, that the troops had not been delayed by poor march discipline, but by the faulty arrangements of both GHQ and First Army in not keeping the roads (and especially the railway crossings) clear for the troops. Brigadier General F. B. Maurice (BGGS, GHQ) later admitted 'GHQ should have made arrangements for assisting the march of newly formed Divisions. I think now this was a bad oversight on my part'.[64]

Haig also argued that Sir John French had not actually handed over the Reserves officially to First Army until they reached the British trenches in the afternoon of 25 September, thus delaying their deployment. In fact, a scrutiny of the telephone logs of Sir Henry Rawlinson (GOC IV Corps) in the southern sector of the Loos attack casts some doubt on this statement. According to this document, First Army (Haig) telephoned Rawlinson (IV Corps) at 9.41 a.m. on 25 September to say that XI Corps (Haking) had been put under First Army command. And during the morning and early afternoon Rawlinson telephoned First Army and XI Corps several times to say that 21 Division (of XI Corps) was slow in starting and marching, etc., all participants apparently acting as though First Army was already in command of the Reserves. Further corroboration comes from Henry Wilson's diary and Robertson's correspondence at the time, which both seem to suggest that the effective handing over of the Reserves to Haig took place around 9.30 a.m., while the IV Corps War Diary states that it took place at 9.40 a.m.[65]

In private correspondence immediatly after Loos, Haig did not initially criticize either the location of the Reserves or their handling by Sir John French, but only the newness and inexperience of the two Divisions. On 5 October 1915 Haig wrote to his brother, 'Two new Divisions were placed behind my attacking troops as a Reserve – They had just landed in the country and poor d—ls had never seen a shot fired in earnest. Consequently they were not much good. Otherwise I think we would have been right through the enemy's second line as well as his First.' Haig may have been referring to the next day, 26 September, when the two Divisions did not perform well. But it is significant that on 5 October 1915, Haig did not see Sir John French as the culprit. However, by 2 November 1915, Haig now told his brother that Sir John French had kept the 'Reserves under his own hand so long that they did not arrive in time to be of use'. Here the blame lies with Sir John French in regard to the time of hand-over, although there is no criticism of the original location of the Reserves.[66] On the other hand, Haig's diary entry for 27 September 1915 criticizes Sir John French for not moving the divisions up closer to the attack line before the battle, while a letter to Kitchener on the 29 September 1915 switches to the criticism that French had handed the Reserves over too late.[67] What may have happened was that Haig had seen that his critique of GHQ for not having the Reserves closer than Noeux-les-Mines–Beuvry was not a solid argument because of his own First Army letter to GHQ on 19 September 1915 requesting that very location, and because the advance of the two divisions across the congested First Army area could not easily be blamed on bad march discipline, despite Haking's assertions.[68] Hence it was convenient to switch to arguing that Sir John French was at fault for not handing the Reserves over earlier. The snag here, besides the contrary information listed above, was that regardless of whose command they were under, the divisions could not have arrived in time anyway, and it was clear that they *had* been ordered to move within forty-five minutes of Haig's request.

The whole question of the Reserves at Loos revealed the problems of a personalized army, to say nothing of indifferent staff work, and painfully slow communications at all levels.[69] Sir John French must also assume much of the blame, and his evolving rivalry with Haig was certainly destructive. The results of Loos dramatically escalated the animosity between Haig and French, and Haig's letter to Kitchener, criticizing French's handling of the Reserves, was instrumental in the removal of French, and his replacement by Haig, with all that resulted in the next three years of war. Haig considered himself to be in the right, although his later defence to Edmonds makes interesting reading, both regarding First Army area traffic control[70] and the general situation at Loos: 'It is so easy to say this or that was to blame; but when the facts are gone thoroughly into, it is found that the very best and seasoned troops, under the very best Staff arrangments, could not have overcome an impossible situation.' Yet 'the sad part', he concluded, 'is to realise, that all this could and ought to have been avoided – It was due to the obstinacy and conceit of one man [Sir John French]'.[71] A sad end to the original relationship of protector and *protegé* between French and Haig.

Sir John French's removal[72] was a case of dismissal at the very summit of the BEF. It would appear that the same thing was tried against Haig by Robertson and a small group who apparently wanted Haig's removal in early July 1916, with Robertson replacing Haig as Commander-in-Chief. Henry Wilson believed that Robertson wanted Haig's job, and got further details from General Foch (commander of the northern group of French armies at the Somme), who said that Robertson had suggested to Haig and then to Joffre (French Commander-in-Chief) that the Somme offensive be called off. If Haig had then himself suggested the offensive be called off, he would have been *degommé*. In the event, Haig decided to continue the Somme, and the success on 14 July 1916 relieved the pressure. But two weeks later, another serious situation arose for Haig, relating to the high casualties and heavy criticism of those at home. Alan Fletcher, a member of Haig's staff, wrote to Lady Haig, wanting to enlist Lord Northcliffe on Haig's side and to use Lord Derby and Lord Esher as well, although Lady Haig thought of Esher as a fair-weather friend, and considered Asquith, too, to be an enemy of Haig's. Haig, initially reluctant, agreed to use the Northcliffe card: 'the chief [Haig] at last quite realised that Northcliffe could do a service to the country to appease any feelings that our losses had been well earned and to explain what we had done ... Even the chief said, "I think the man will do good and he means to help the whole show I can see".' So Northcliffe was invited to visit GHQ at the end of July 1916, and apparently succeeded in deflecting criticism of GHQ at home.[73] At the same time, Robertson (nicknamed privately by Haig as 'The Iron Ration') was obviously still at odds with Haig, and his letter of 29 July 1916 referring to the casualty list and his own ignorance of the situation at the Somme aroused Haig, who scribbled on the letter that Robertson had spent eight to ten days with the Army since 4 July 1916, and added 'Not exactly the letter of a CIGS! – He ought to take responsibility also!' Haig seemed to imply that there was something to take responsibility for, and his refusal to go to London to see the War Committee probably had something to do with concern over the criticisms he would face and his possible removal, apart from the need to stay at GHQ on a daily basis while the battle continued.[74] In any case, Haig was not removed, as Sir John French had been, despite another attempt at the end of the Somme, and a more serious attempt led by Henry Wilson, Lloyd George, the Cabinet, and Sir John French, as a result of the German March 1918 offensive.

Removals/degummings at the highest levels could and did take place through personal rivalry, although on a necessarily limited scale. Much more frequent, however, were removals due to failure in action at lower levels, and degummings to encourage the offensive spirit. Some of these lower level degummings may also have involved personal feelings, for example when Major General the Hon. Stuart-Wortley* was removed as GOC of the North Midland Division after 1 July 1916 (perhaps also for corresponding privately with the king, although most agreed he was a poor commander), and Brigadier Oxley,* who was sent home after his Brigade failed to hang on to Contalmaison on 7 July 1916 (but perhaps also because of earlier rivalry at the Staff College).[75] Whether these removals were fully justified is now hard to evaluate, but what is clear is that the fear of degumming and the fear of not being seen to have the right offensive attitude gave GHQ very considerable leverage. Nor was it only GHQ – all levels of senior command could and did initiate dismissals. Edmonds once mentioned a strange 1918 experience with General Sir Hubert Gough:[76]

> I heard him [Gough] complain that his troops had 'no blood lust', the officers 'no spirit of the offensive'. Whilst I was having tea in the 'B' Mess of his headquarters he came in and said, 'I want to shoot two officers'. There was an astonished pause, and the A.P.M. [Assistant Provost Marshal] said, 'Beg your pardon, Sir, there are no officers under sentence'. Gough looked at him as if to say, 'you fool', and explained, 'Yes, I know that, but I want to shoot two officers as an example to the others'. And he got them.

Faced with obviously hopeless attacks, commanders were reluctant to complain, suggest alternatives, or even refuse to attack, for fear of GHQ reprisals, although some brave souls did so. Orders had to be obeyed of course, but as Aylmer Haldane pointed out, one could not suggest difficulties.[77] Along the same lines, an officer of 20 Division Artillery wrote 'It was common talk that no Divisional Commander dared say his Infantry were unfit to attack for fear of being sent home'. George Lindsay, a Brigade commander, declared in regard to the 14 November 1916 attack at the Ancre that the ground was impassable, but 'to tell unpalatable truths of this kind was unpopular with those above, and led to one being considered not to have the right amount of "the fighting spirit".

This undoubtedly led people to hesitate to tell the whole truth.' The commander of 43rd Infantry Brigade was ordered to renew the attack on Ginchy at 6.55 p.m. on 15 September 1916, and wrote that he only did this to save his reputation – half-jokingly he remarked that he was more afraid of his superiors than of the enemy.[78]

Some commanders did refuse to attack, but it was obviously a step that took 'great moral courage' as an officer of 95th Brigade said of his commanding officer, who at Morval on the eve of the 25 September 1916 attack, refused to go ahead with it because 200 men of his regiment were sick. This officer regretted that he did not do the same, for his own attack on 25 September 1916 cost his regiment 12 officers and 200 men, a 50 per cent casualty list due to poor staff work, enemy shelling, and impossible conditions of mud and rain.[79] History does not record what happened to the commanding officer who refused to attack at Morval. More often and more naturally commanding officers felt compelled to attack, regardless of circumstances, as was the case with the GOC of 38 Division in early July 1916. But this commanding officer, Major General Sir Ivor Philipps,* apparently concerned for his men, sent his Brigades to attack Mametz Wood on 7 and 8 July 1916, with instructions not to press the attack if machine-gun fire was met. General Horne, GOC XV Corps, told GHQ that the attacks were not even launched, and on 9 July Philipps was degummed. Major General Kiggell,* Chief of Staff at GHQ, wrote ominously on 9 July that 38 Division had failed at Mametz with 'quite insignificant losses'. He added that the future performance of 38 Division could erase doubts about the Division. On 10 July under a new GOC, Major General Watts,*38 Division took the greater part of the wood. Horne had in fact been wrong for the attacks of 7 and 8 July had taken place, despite problems with time and communications, and Kiggell was wrong, for 38 Division did suffer considerable casualties. Philipps had shown moral courage in cancelling one attack by 115th Brigade of his Division due to lack of time for preparation, although he did not cancel another by 113th Brigade on 8 July when there was equally no time. No doubt Philipps was not an experienced commander, but the impression is that Horne and GHQ got rid of Philipps (and also Major General Pilcher,* GOC of 17 Division, in XV Corps, who did not succeed in taking Contalmaison) because they simply failed and declined to press the attack when success was likely to be very costly.[80]

An ominous feature of GHQ (and Army) leverage, expressed by Kiggell's reference to casualties, was the simplistic notion that attacks that failed with considerable casualties were given a sympathetic hearing at Army and GHQ, whereas attacks that failed with light casualties were inevitably condemned. Major General Furse,* GOC 9 (Scottish) Division, put the matter bluntly to General A. A. Montgomery, Chief of Staff, Fourth Army, when referring to the costly wood fighting of July 1916: 'At the present time, most Brigadiers and Battalion Commanders believe that if they held a wood as lightly as I suggest, and then lost it, they would be degummed, not so much for losing the wood as for not losing enough men in trying to hold it. This may be quite a false idea, but I believe it to be prevalent.' Certainly this *was* GHQ's thinking, for example Haig's castigation of 49 Division for not holding on to positions around the Ancre in early September 1916, was due he thought to troops not really attacking because 'total losses of this division are under a thousand'![81]

This was difficult enough, but commanding officers also faced another dilemma. On the one hand, failures were sent home, but on the other hand, commanding officers, who knew that failure was coming and complained beforehand, were equally likely to be degummed or at least disgraced. The 'before and after' problem is well illustrated by the story told by Colonel (later Brigadier General) Kentish,* with 14th Brigade at the Ancre (November 1916). He reported on the very poor conditions prior to the assault, but in reply the 'Brigadier several times said to me "Kentish I can't send your reports on, I should lose my job!"' The Brigadier lost it anyway, together with the Divisional commander, the GSOs 1 and 2, two Brigadiers and two Brigade Majors.[82] The Divisional commander who lost his job on this occasion was Major General Rycroft,* GOC 32 Division. It would appear that Rycroft was apprehensive of Gough, because of an earlier failure on 3 July 1916 at Thiepval under Gough's command. According to the GSO 1 of 32 Division, Gough failed to fix the blame for the 3 July 1916 failure on the Division, but when in October the Division was once more returned to the Somme, under Gough's command, Rycroft, knowing that Gough 'had got it in for us', turned to the GSO 1 'and said wryly this would be his undoing unless we went to Rawlinson's Army. So he just hadn't the kick in him to stand up to Gough ...' In the event the difficulties of November 1916 were largely caused by the impossible conditions, so much so that when 32 Division went into the line to relieve 2 Division, and prepare for the attack, the GSO 1 of 2 Division, 'confessed they didn't really know where the then front line was'.[83] Hence Rycroft and the others were degummed for failure, although the reason for the failure really rested with Gough.[84]

Removal for failure blends easily into degumming or disgrace as a scapegoat and this seems to have been the case with Rycroft and the other staff officers. In fact removals for failure as scapegoat had a ritualistic quality. One of the better documented situations concerns Major General Fanshawe's removal after the problems of the Canadians at the St Eloi craters in the spring of 1916. Involved were General Plumer,* then GOC of Second Army; Fanshawe, the V Corps commander; Aylmer Haldane, GOC 3 Division; Major General Turner,* GOC 2 (Canadian) Division; Lieutenant General Alderson, GOC Canadian Corps; and Haig. Initially Haig came to Plumer's Second Army HQ after the debacle, and wished to dismiss Haldane for the poor defence of the craters. Meanwhile Haldane felt that the real culprit was Turner who did not know whether his Division was actually holding the craters. Haig wrote to Fanshawe via Plumer, wishing to dismiss Haldane, and Plumer simply passed the letter on to Fanshawe who stood up for Haldane. Plumer was at the time in danger of being removed himself as GOC Second Army because of various other errors, and so he refused to defend Haldane. Plumer remained, partly because Haig apparently felt he was a true gentleman, and wanted to keep him on. Turner was safe, according to Haldane, because 'Haig determined to remove me [Haldane] as he could not sacrifice the Canadians and wanted a scapegoat'. Haldane in turn was saved because Fanshawe acted as a gentleman and stood by his Divisional commander, and so it was Fanshawe who was eventually sacrificed and removed from his Corps command. A short time later, Alderson was also removed as the Canadian commander, and replaced by General Sir Julian Byng. The St Eloi craters had proved rather damaging to senior commanders![85]

Various other scapegoats can be identified. For example, Brigadier General Sandilands,* of 35 Division, Fifth Army, recalled that on 26 March 1918, at the time of the major German spring offensive, when Fifth Army was in full retreat, he went into Fifth Army HQ at Amiens to try to find the location of his Division. The room was full of junior officers, to whom Sandilands said 'What on earth are you doing running away for like this?' There was dull silence, but in the corner there was an officer sitting on a chair with his mouth wide open and a doctor prodding at his teeth. The officer sprang up and said 'What the Hell are you doing here?' It was Gough, GOC Fifth Army. Sandilands left hastily, and continued to search for his 35 Division. It transpired that Lieutenant General Sir Walter Congreve (GOC VII Corps, Fifth Army) had given orders for Major General Franks's 35 Division to advance to the line of the Ancre. Franks refused, as his Division had just retired eight miles from there and could not easily turn around. Franks was removed from his command by Gough, a scapegoat for the Fifth Army confusion, asserted Sandilands.[86] Gough himself was soon forced to resign as a result of March 1918, although he too was an obvious scapegoat.

Promotions and removals, personal rivalries and interventions were all part of a system that displayed a traditional rather than a professional approach to modern war. This was not the fault of middle and junior levels of the British army, which was working hard to catch up with reality. If anything the army was simply a reflection of Edwardian society and of an outdated view of warfare. Yet another result of the conflict between the traditional ideal of the army and the pressure of a modern war, was the attempt, first, to cover up errors during the war, secondly, to alter the military record, and thirdly, to achieve alterations in the subsequent *Official History*. To an extent this was natural, obviously few

23

like to be seen in a negative light, yet the net result was to create a distorted image, while the extent of the reworking of the image is also surprising.

The official historian, Edmonds, believed that his task was simply to write the story, but not to pass judgement. His method of dealing with sensitive events was to either tone down offending passages, or to place awkward evidence in footnotes or appendices, or more usually simply to confine the text to facts, without drawing critical conclusions. In addition, Edmonds tended increasingly to defend the GHQ point of view, and sometimes altered the text to support Haig and GHQ, especially in regard to the 1917 Passchendaele volume. However, Edmonds also had his biases, which grew with time and resulted in criticism of some senior commanders, for example Gough in 1917, and General the Hon. Sir Julian Byng in 1918. The *Official History* treatment of 1916, 1917 and 1918 is analysed in Chapters 8 and 9, but the general conclusion must be that Edmonds often altered passages to suit the criticism of senior commanders, and certainly sought to diminish the worst errors. An example of this concerns Lieutenant General Allenby's desire to order 'relentless pursuit' of the enemy after the first stage of the battle of Arras, over the protests of three Divisional commanders. This event was described in the *Official History*, but not Allenby's orders. However, Edmonds went on to note that Allenby was shortly 'Stellenbosched' to Palestine, 'where all failures were consigned' for his handling of the Arras offensive.[87] Yet this attitude was reasonable when compared to the treatment accorded other sources of evidence by some senior officers.

There were first the expected efforts of some to alter the evidence or cover up blunders at the front. To take the first of three examples, the Brigade Major of 36th Infantry Brigade (12 Division, Fourth Army) claimed that 'the whitewashing habit was well established' on the Western Front, although this usually took the form of Commanding Officers altering stories to bring credit on their own troops. This Brigade Major himself altered a draft narrative at his Commanding Officer's orders, so as to present a better picture.[88] Edmonds recalled that Lieutenant General Sir Archibald Murray was a big offender, when Chief of Staff to Sir John French in 1914, since he apparently altered the time that orders were received or sent out, although he was given away by the stamp of the duty clerk which contained the correct time. Then the Commanding Officer of the 19th London Battalion was dismayed at the falsification of the record at Divisional HQ in 1917 by his Divisional GOC.[89] Not all such stories can be taken at face value, but there appeared to be an effort by some, as might be anticipated, to alter the record. More frequent, no doubt, was the simple omission of facts, as Major General Jeudwine* pointed out in regard to prior warnings of the German counter-attack of 30 November 1917 (Cambrai), which were not subsequently recorded in the War Diary of Byng's Third Army.[90]

Falsification of the record becomes more serious (at least for historians!) when evidence is specifically removed. According to General Pope-Hennessy, assistant to Edmonds for Volume 1 of the *Official History*, GHQ orders four to nine, relating to 1914, were found to be missing. It was alleged that Henry Wilson had ordered them removed since they reflected badly on the shaken state of mind of GHQ in August and September 1914. However, the orders were later found at a lower level, in Corps files.[91] In his unpublished 'Memoirs' Edmonds claimed that on 26 August 1914, GHQ departed rapidly from St Quentin to Noyon, without leaving cable communications with Corps, and that on 3 September 1914, GHQ again left rapidly from Dammartin, with Henry Wilson instructing the staff to 'Drive like hell for Paris'. According to a witness, it was Wilson who had ordered GHQ orders four to nine destroyed.[92] Most spectacular, perhaps, was the attempt, according to Edmonds, of the Fourth Army staff at the Somme to cover up their and Rawlinson's difficulties on 1 July 1916 by removing the Fourth Army War Diary and substituting a later narrative. Edmonds was careful in his unpublished memoirs not to name names, but simply related the anonymous story of the removal of the War Diary. Then later when Edmonds 'wrote to the Chief of Staff [of Fourth Army in 1916] to enquire what had become of the diaries he [Montgomery-Massingberd] replied that the "narrative took the place of the diaries". I have pasted this letter into the lid of the box where the diaries should be, and the narrative lies.'[93] Edmonds actually identified the staff officers concerned when he told Liddell Hart about the cover-up in 1931, and also his suspicions as to why the substitution was made.[94] Liddell Hart also claimed that the Fourth Army Staff tried to recall and destroy their May 1916 'Tactical Notes' after the failure of 1 July 1916.[95]

Another form of personal intervention in the way that events were recorded concerns the published personal diaries of senior officers (to say nothing of memoirs and autobiographies). There seemed to be general caution concerning the diary of General J. Charteris (Brigadier General, Intelligence at GHQ in 1916 and 1917). Edmonds declared, 'It is whispered among the initiated that it [Charteris's diary] is a fake. *Before* the event he was invariably wrong.'[96] Probably the most important GHQ diary is that of Field Marshal Haig. This diary was accepted by the *Official History*, and since then has been frequently used as evidence, while large sections have been published by Lord Blake as *The Private Papers of Douglas Haig 1914–1919* (London, 1952). However, the diary is a rather 'cool' and careful document, and Liddell Hart was not always satisfied with the veracity of the entries. He wrote to Lieutenant Colonel A. H. Burne in 1935 that Haig's diary was fallacious regarding the advance to the Aisne in that it said he was active in speeding up the advance, whereas the Divisional War Diary showed the opposite.[97]

Edmonds, who was in charge of the transcripts of Haig's Diary, and was familiar with the process of typing it up, declared that it was not all written up at the time, and that some things were inserted later.[98] Edmonds's comments are easy enough to substantiate, and Haig made no effort to claim otherwise; for example, an entry for 23 October 1916 quotes a German Regimental order dated 29 October 1916, and a letter from Lloyd George to Haig inserted in the middle of the entry for September 1916 has a note written by Haig referring forward to a letter from Robertson written on 14 October 1916.[99] Corroborative evidence comes from letters written by Lady Haig to Edmonds, soon after Haig's death, in which she states that Haig did not have time 'to correct the words of the last volumes', implying that earlier transcript volumes had been corrected. Lady Haig also asked Edmonds to 'put right any little passages hurriedly written at the Front which may not read well', and in a subsequent letter Lady Haig stated that she herself had omitted various passages 'as Douglas would have done ... and he proposed altering some words in the diary which I have done – where he pointed [to] them at the time we were putting them together'.[100] All this is understandable, but at the least future historians should recognize some potential areas of conflict.

In conclusion, the existence of the personalized system shows that the weakness in the training and quality of officers before the First World War (the Esher Committee in 1904 found it almost impossible to find competent officers for senior posts)[101] resulted in an idiosyncratic promotions and removals system based on arms rivalry and personal favouritism as much as merit.[102] In other words, a largely non-existent system was necessarily replaced by an ad hoc, personalized system. Apart from personal influence and distortions, the removal of unfit and/or incompetent senior officers can also be seen as a crude selection system that the Staff College and military academies had failed to apply earlier when training these same officers.[103] But, fundamentally, the matter of a personalized and distorted promotions and removals system, and of personal rivalry in the field, can be traced back to the continuing strength of the amateur, traditional ideal of war, as that ideal proved incapable of meeting the grim reality of a technological, barely understood, war. In short the British army was caught in a transitional stage of development when the First World War broke out as indeed was the case with other European armies, particularly the French army.

The same general argument can be applied to the problem of cover-ups, and of distortion and alteration of evidence, namely that the British senior officer corps before the First World War was still very much a traditional group, although often striving to become a fully professional corps. One indication that this was a difficult process, or an uncongenial one, concerned General Paget, GOC Eastern Command before the war, who very rarely visited his office in 1909, but preferred other activities. In fact Paget was so lax that when in 1911 he commanded one of the forces at the annual army manoeuvres, he did not actually attend the manoeuvres, but spent his time in London. Consequently, Aylmer Haldane, his BGGS, had to give details of the manoeuvres to Paget while on the train from London to Salisbury, and a summary of what had happened, so that Paget could put forward a narrative of his forces' activities and answer questions at the post-manoeuvre discussion. Another example of traditional attitudes within the army occurred in Ireland in 1912, when at the post-manoeuvre discussions regarding the use of aeroplanes for reconnaissance, it was generally agreed that aeroplanes were useful for strategic but not tactical reconnaissance, because of the length of time required to deliver messages. Major General Groves, then a junior officer, disagreed, and suggested signals or dropping messages. There was a frozen silence, reported Groves, and afterwards his regimental commander called him in, tore a strip off him, calling him a 'young puppy' for raising his voice in the Divisional GOC's presence, and said he had let down the regiment.[104]

In summary, the system, operating in a transitional army, was at fault, and in this matter the army was really a faithful reflection of Edwardian society. This conclusion leads to another point, namely, that historians should perhaps pay more attention to the concept of the army and its activities as a 'system' rather than focusing on individuals. This should serve to divert attention away from the faults and merits of individual Commanders-in-Chief, which has hitherto largely characterized First World War historiography. The same approach could be used in examining the South African war, where much the same problems were encountered in 1899–1902, namely poor staff work leading to cover-ups, damaging rivalries, a personalized system of promotions, and a dismissals system as frequent as in the First World War.[105]

For a number of reasons the British senior officer corps had learnt slowly during the period 1900–14, as was also the case in the French army. Perhaps there was no easy means by which this could rapidly be done. But behind this reluctance to insist on basic structural changes there seems to have lurked, among many British officers, a simple desire to perpetuate the privileges and attractions of the late Victorian and Edwardian army, with its pleasant life, social networks and traditional ideals.[106] Change was attempted, and modernization did occur. Yet, fundamentally, the urgency to make basic alterations was lacking in the British officer corps before 1914, and the lessons of the South African war and the Russo-Japanese war were often altered to fit the traditional ideal. But when the Edwardian army was compelled to change through the *force majeure* of the First World War, senior officers found there was much to be hidden and many reputations to be saved.

Notes

1 Liddell Hart, Talk with Edmonds, 23 April 1937, 11/1937/30, Liddell Hart Papers, KCL; Edmonds, 'Memoirs', chs XX and XXVIII, Edmonds Papers, 3, KCL.

2 Corelli Barnett, 'The education of military elites', in Rupert Wilkinson (ed.), *Governing Elites* (New York, 1969), p. 206. A useful comparison of amateur and professional pressures on the Edwardian officer is in Brian Bond, *The Victorian Army and the Staff College 1895–1914* (London, 1972), ch. 6. Of value here is Edward M. Spiers, *The Army and Society, 1815–1914* (London and New York, 1980), ch. 8 and pp. 229, 246, 281–2. Spiers suggests a useful list of ideas that would encompass the late Victorian, traditional, 'gentlemanly' ideal of war: that the human factor in war was predominant; that, all things being equal, the attacker would always win; that warfare did not essentially change; that war was moral and practical and did not require theory or doctrine; and that technology was a tool to be used, rather than a new major factor in warfare. Spiers also argues that few lessons were learnt from the South African war, and he seems to suggest little fundamental change in the attitudes of the three arms before 1914. On the other hand, the professional, technical ideal would emphasize doctrine and theory; the increasing importance of technology and resulting tactical and strategic changes; the necessity for high quality staff training and staff work; and the willingness to learn lessons from experience, to accept criticism, and to innovate.

3 See T. H. E. Travers, 'Technology, tactics and morale: Jean de Bloch, the Boer War, and British military theory, 1900–1914', *Journal of Modern History*, vol. 51, no. 2 (1979), *passim*.

4 Corelli Barnett, op. cit., pp. 195–6; G. F. Best, 'Militarism and the Victorian public school' in Simon and Bradley (eds), *The Victorian Public School* (Dublin, 1975), pp. 139–43; Rupert Wilkinson, *Gentlemanly Power* (Oxford, 1964), *passim*.

5 Gregory Phillips, *The Diehards: Aristocratic Society and Politics in Edwardian England* (Cambridge, Mass. and London, 1979), p. 100 and ch. 5; Giles St Aubyn, *Edward VII* (London, 1979), ch. 10; Sir Charles Petrie, *Scenes of Edwardian Life* (London, 1965), ch. 8; Gwyn Harries-Jenkins, *The Army in Victorian Society* (London, 1977), pp. 100, 158, 165, 169, 199–200, 270–8; W. S. Hamer, *The British Army, Civil–Military Relations, 1885–1905* (Oxford, 1970), pp. 18, 25, 245; Spiers, *Army and Society*, pp. 229, 249.

6 For Haig at Aldershot, 'Aldershot Command. General Staff and Administrative Staff Tours. June 1913', 69/53/4, Maxse Papers, Imperial War Museum (hereafter IWM). On the new 'professionalism' of McMahon and Fuller, see T. H. E. Travers, 'The offensive and the problem of innovation in British military thought 1870–1915', *Journal of Contemporary History*, vol. 13, no. 3 (1978), pp. 531–53. Just before the war Major Geohegan, 6th Battery, Royal Field Artillery, made great efforts to learn how to shoot a modern battery, and was even coached in the evenings by his junior officer, Archibald, but simply could not learn, and was 'forced to resign', Major General S. C. M. Archibald, unpublished memoirs, pp. 67–8, PP/MCR/11, Archibald Papers, IWM.

7 Edmonds to Barclay, 7 April 1950, 1/2, Edmonds Papers, KCL; Noel Birch to Edmonds, 29 June 1938, Cab 45/132, Public Record Office (hereafter PRO).

8 A good example is the reception accorded Robert Graves, when he joined the 2nd Battalion of the Royal Welch Fusiliers in 1916, Robert Graves, *Goodbye to All That*, Penguin edn (Harmondsworth, 1960), ch. 14.

9 Thomas Pakenham, *The Boer War* (London, 1979), p. 250. Spiers describes the Edwardian promotion system in his *Army and Society*, p. 249.

10 Haldane, Diary, 28 October 1908, 20 July 1911, Haldane Papers, National Library of Scotland (hereafter NLS).

11 Haldane, Diary, 20 August 1900, 7 April 1901, 11 April 1901, 23 April 1905, 6 December 1905 (including an insert dated 1925 declaring that Nicholson became CIGS due to Aylmer Haldane's pressure on R. B. Haldane), 28 October 1908, 28 July 1916 (including an insert dated 24 December 1947 which recalled Edmonds's comment to Aylmer Haldane concerning Haig's view of Aylmer Haldane as only a good defensive general), 6 May 1916 (for Robertson's friendship), Haldane Papers, NLS.

12 Brigadier Potter to Edmonds, no date, complaining of Haldane's over-confidence in this hurried attack, 'you'll do it on your head, Potter!', Cab 45/136, PRO.

13 Haig to Henrietta (his sister), 12 June 1895, 4 July 1895, 6b, Haig Papers, NLS.

14 H. J. Creedy to Duff Cooper, in Creedy to Edmonds, 21 March 1935, Edmonds Papers, 1/2, KCL; according to an unsubstantiated claim by Edmonds, there was a certain amount of royal influence which enabled Haig to enter Staff College and overcome both a medical problem (colour blindness) and his poor marks in mathematics, Liddell Hart, Talk with Edmonds, 16 December 1935, 11/1935/117, Liddell Hart Papers, KCL.

15 Haig to Sir Evelyn Wood, 15 March 1898, Sir Evelyn Wood to Haig, 25 May 1898, Haig to Sir Evelyn Wood, 7 September 1898, 6g; and Haig to Henrietta, 21 April 1898 and 15 September 1898, 6b, Haig Papers, NLS.

16 Haig to Henrietta, 16 May 1899, 6b, Haig Papers, NLS. Sir John French apparently ran into other problems besides financial – he once ran away to Pondicherry with a Eurasian girl, according to Edmonds, and went absent without leave. He was saved by Lieutenant Colonel R. G. Kekewich, Liddell Hart, Talk with Edmonds, 1933, 11/1933/32, Liddell Hart Papers, KCL.

17 Haig to Henrietta, 15 November 1899, 26 November 1899, 22 February 1900, 14 May 1900, 30 November 1900, 6c, Haig Papers, NLS.

18 ibid., Haig to Henrietta, 9 July 1900 and 7 August 1900.

19 ibid., Haig to Henrietta, 14 December 1900 and 26 November 1901. For Kitchener's doubts, see Victor Sampson and Ian Hamilton, *Anti-Commando* (London, 1931), p. 155.

20 Haig to Henrietta, 28 July 1901, 6c, Haig Papers, NLS; Pakenham, *The Boer War*, p. 457.

21 Haig to Henrietta, 25 August 1902 and 17 September 1902, 6c, Haig Papers, NLS. Roberts was reportedly anti-Cavalry, Spiers, *Army and Society*, p. 245.

22 Sir John French had written in 1906, 'I think there is every chance of the billet about which we talked being vacant within the next six or eight months', Haig to Henrietta, 8 February 1906. See also Haig to Henrietta, 13 December 1905, 'I heard from French two weeks ago that he hoped matters wd. soon be settled for me to come home', 6d, Haig Papers, NLS.

23 Haig and Henrietta's relationship with the king was apparently close, and the king did make his wishes known regarding military appointments. Whether Haig would anyway have obtained the post of Director of Military Training is probable, although perhaps not certain, Haig to Henrietta, 4 October 1903 (from Balmoral) and 28 March 1906, 6d, Haig Papers, NLS.

24 Edmonds to Swinton, 21 March 1950, 2/5/18, Edmonds to Barclay, 7 April 1950, 1/2, Edmonds, 'Memoirs', ch. XXVI, p. 13, Edmonds Papers, KCL. Cf. also Edmonds's comment to Liddell Hart that Sir John French never thought

Haig would supplant him, and so pushed him on, Liddell Hart, Diary, 7 June 1927, 11/1927/—, Liddell Hart Papers, KCL. On the other hand Henry Wilson thought Smith-Dorrien was incapable and should have been sent home, Wilson, Diary, 15 March 1915, 27 April 1915, DS/MISC/V, Wilson Papers, IWM.

25 Edmonds, 'Memoirs', ch. XX, p. 27, and ch. XXVII, p. 2, Edmonds Papers, KCL. Edmonds also argued that Major General A. A. Montgomery, CGS to Fourth Army, and later CIGS, got on by Rawlinson's protection, Liddell Hart, Talk with Edmonds, 23 September 1929, 11/1929/15, Liddell Hart Papers, KCL. Liddell Hart, Talk with Edmonds, 27 October 1933, 11/1933/24, Liddell Hart Papers, KCL; Edmonds, 'Memoirs', ch. XXIV, Edmonds Papers, KCL. See below Chapter 8.

26 Edmonds to Barclay, 7 April 1950, 1/2, Edmonds Papers, KCL.

27 Edmonds, 'Memoirs', ch. XXVIII, Edmonds Papers, KCL; Haldane, Diary, 30 June 1916, Haldane Papers, NLS. See below Chapter 8.

28 Haldane, Diary, 26 April 1901, Haldane Papers, NLS; cf. Pakenham, *The Boer War*, pp. 535–6.

29 Edmonds, 'Memoirs', ch. XIX, p. 8, Edmonds Papers, KCL; Haldane, Diary, 1 February 1911, Haldane Papers, NLS.

30 Edmonds thought this important, and felt that Major General Sir Ernest Swinton did not get command of the Tank Corps because he was not 'passed Staff College', and therefore not a member of the 'Union', Edmonds, 'Memoirs', ch. XIV, p. 282, ch. XXVII, p. 21, Edmonds Papers, KCL.

31 Liddell Hart, Talk with Edmonds, 5 February 1937, 11/1937/4, Liddell Hart Papers, KCL. Edmonds may have overlooked here the negative influence of Paget's involvement with the Curragh incident.

32 For example, Roberts's 'petticoat government' in South Africa, Pakenham, *The Boer War*, pp. 448–9, and cf. Haig's complaints to Henrietta about Lady Roberts, see above note 21.

33 Haldane, 'Autobiography', vol. 2, p. 385, Haldane Papers, NLS. In regard to Hamilton-Gordon, Haldane wrote that the former had never commanded a battery before, and because of his melancholy manner, was nicknamed 'Sorry Jim'. 'He is, however, a friend of Haig's, and, as Teck remarked, Haig prefers to provide for his friends first.' On the other hand, there is no doubt Haldane was disappointed at not getting a Corps himself, Haldane, Diary, 21 June 1916, Haldane Papers, NLS; but Henry Wilson also reported that Major General E. S. Bulfin saw Hamilton-Gordon's appointment as 'Haig's idea of a joke', Wilson, Diary, 6 August 1916, Wilson Papers, IWM.

34 Haig, Diary, 8 August 1916, WO 256/11, PRO.

35 Wilson, Diary, 7 September 1916, Wilson Papers, IWM.

36 Wilfred Greene (61 Division HQ) to Edmonds, 13 May 1937, Cab 45/134; Lieutenant Colonel Parry Jones to Edmonds, 13 October 1937, Cab 45/136; Hereward Wake (61 Division HQ) to Edmonds, 12 March 1937, Cab 45/138, PRO.

37 Although all those present did blame Haking, for example Captain Landon and Brigadier General A. Gordon of 182nd Infantry Brigade, who thought of the 19 July attack as hopeless. 'Haking was always "Butcher Haking" after this battle', Captain Landon to Edmonds, 2 April 1937, Cab 45/125, PRO.

38 Haig, Diary, 20 July 1916, WO 256/11, PRO.

39 Wilson, Diary, 5 August 1916, 20 August 1916, 21 August 1916, Wilson Papers, IWM.

40 Haldane, Diary, 5 February 1916 (Allenby's offensive ideas got him command of an army and rank of Lieutenant General), 6 May 1916, Haldane Papers,

NLS. Captain Landon (182nd Infantry Brigade) to Edmonds, 2 April 1937, Cab 45/135; George Lindsay (2 Division) to Edmonds, 28 June 1937, Cab 45/135; F. Wilson (20 Division) to Edmonds, 26 [?] 1936, Cab 45/138, PRO.

41 Major General G. S. Clive, Diary, 16 May 1916, Cab 45/201/2, PRO.

42 Liddell Hart, Talk with Colonel Allanson, 19 August 1937, 11/1937/69, Liddell Hart Papers, KCL. Rawlinson tells the story of how in June 1915 GHQ forced First Army to make an attack by threatening to offer the attack to Second Army if First Army refused. The original reluctance came about because of lack of ammunition, Rawlinson, Diary, 7 June 1915, Rawlinson Papers, Churchill College, Cambridge (hereafter CCC).

43 Edmonds to Spenser Wilkinson, 15 March 1916, 2/1, Edmonds Papers, KCL.

44 Edmonds to Barclay, 7 April 1950, 1/2, Edmonds Papers, KCL; Liddell Hart, Talk with Edmonds, 31 October 1929, 11/1929/17, Liddell Hart Papers, KCL. Elsewhere, Liddell Hart surmised that Horne was not the best of army commanders, but was safe because he was a Scot and the only gunner to command an army, Liddell Hart, Diary, 10 February 1928, 11/1928/—, Liddell Hart Papers, KCL.

45 General Sir Aylmer Haldane, Shorncliffe Diary, entries for 19 February 1913, [?] March 1913, 3 May 1913, 24 July 1913, 20 September 1913, 31 October 1913, 18 June 1914, 'Postscript', 69/36/1, Haldane Papers, IWM.

46 See Edmonds's comment to Liddell Hart that Snow was often more worried by GHQ than by the enemy, as at Gommecourt, 1916; and Snow's defence, that Gommecourt was stronger than he realized, Talk with Edmonds, 22 April 1937, 11/1937/30, Liddell Hart Papers, KCL; Snow to Edmonds, 9 January 1931, Cab 45/137, PRO.

47 Liddell Hart, Talk with Edmonds, 5 February 1937, 11/1937/4, Liddell Hart Papers, KCL; Liddell Hart, *History of the First World War*, pp. 33–4.

48 The story can be pieced together from Wilson's Diary, entries for 27–30 May 1916, Wilson Papers, IWM, and Haig, Diary, entries for 27 May–2 June 1916, WO 256/10, PRO. One of Haig's complaints against Wilson was the latter's 'infatuation for the French', ibid., 28 May 1916. In fairness, it should be noted that R. N. Harvey, who was apparently present at St Eloi in 1916, had a low opinion of the officer concerned and of Wilson, saying that Wilson's orders read like 'field day at Aldershot where nothing matters', R. N. Harvey to Edmonds, 22 February 1929, Cab 45/130/St Eloi, PRO.

49 Haig notes on 23 June 1916 that Henry Wilson 'seems to acquire a more evil look each time I see him', and cannot understand how Wilson's CGS, du Pree, admires Wilson, Haig, Diary, WO 256/10, PRO.

50 Haldane, Diary, 23 September 1909, Haldane Papers, NLS. The information comes from Edmonds in three ways, Edmonds, 'Memoirs', ch. XXIII, p. 14, Edmonds Papers, KCL; Liddell Hart, Talk with Edmonds, 7 December 1933, 11/1933/26, Liddell Hart Papers, KCL; Edmonds to Acheson, 30 July 1950, Cab 103/113, PRO; John Terraine, *Mons*, Pan edn (London, 1972), pp. 68–70. Edmonds also asserted that Haig and Smith-Dorrien were not friendly, and that their two chiefs of staff, J. Gough and Forestier-Walker, were even more antagonistic, and that this had unfortunate results in regard to the co-operation of I and II Corps at Le Cateau, Liddell Hart, Talk with Edmonds, 5 February 1937, 11/1937/4, Liddell Hart Papers, KCL. See also Terraine, *Mons*, pp. 123–4, 131, 134–5. Another official historian, Acheson, also stated that Haig did not like Smith-Dorrien, Acheson to Edmonds, 27 July 1950, Cab 103/113, PRO.

51 Smith-Dorrien to Edmonds, 16 May 1923, 2/1, Edmonds Papers, KCL. The rivalry of Smith-Dorrien and Sir John French continued after the war in

various antagonistic volumes, and in some revealing letters between Smith-Dorrien and the official historian Major Becke. These letters do not reflect well on Sir John French, and include some allegations against Haig, for example, Haig's 'fabrication' of what Smith-Dorrien told Sir John French on 24 August 1916, and Haig's *sauve qui peut* order on 26 August 1914, Smith-Dorrien to Major Becke, 1 December 1919, 29 December 1919, 16 April 1920, p. 365, Smith-Dorrien Papers, IWM.

52 Wilson, Diary, 12 August 1915, 24 September 1915, 29 September 1915, 2 October 1915, Wilson Papers, IWM; Haig, Diary, Haig to Kitchener, 29 September 1915, WO 256/5, PRO. Lieutenant Colonel B. Fitzgerald, Diary, 5 October 1915, PP/MCR/118, Fitzgerald Papers, IWM.

53 Lieutenant General Sir R. D. Whigham to Edmonds, 9 July 1926, and Robertson to Edmonds, 10 August 1926, Cab 45/121, PRO.

54 Rawlinson believes Sir John French wanted to throw in the Reserves at the last minute, and so 'win the victory himself', Rawlinson to his wife, 29 September 1915, 5201–33–66, Rawlinson Papers, NAM.

55 A. A. Montgomery-Massingberd to Liddell Hart, 29 September 1927, I/520/—, Liddell Hart Papers, KCL. (Montgomery added Massingberd to his name in 1926, but for convenience Montgomery will be used.)

56 Haig, Diary, Robertson to Haig, 1 October 1915, WO 256/5, PRO; Haig's comments on Loos *Official History* draft ch. XV, p. 1, dated by Haig 20 February 1927, Cab 44/28, PRO.

57 Haig, Diary, 19 September 1915, WO 256/5, PRO; J. E. Edmonds, *Military Operations, France and Belgium, 1915, Battles of Aubers Ridge, Festubert and Loos* (London, 1928), p. 276.

58 Haig's comments on Loos *Official History* draft ch. XV, p. 1, dated by Haig 20 February 1927, Cab 44/28; and comments dated 7 January 1928, p. 6, Cab 44/27, PRO.

59 Haig, Diary, 18 September 1915, WO 256/5, PRO; Haig to GHQ, 18 September 1915, WO 158/184, PRO.

60 First Army (Haig) to GHQ (French), 19 September 1915, WO 106/390 (Loos File), PRO; Haig, Diary, 23 September 1915, WO 256/5, PRO; Edmonds, *Military Operations, France and Belgium, 1915* (1928), p. 276.

61 Haking's comments on Loos *Official History* draft, no date, p. 9, Cab 44/28, PRO.

62 Telephone conversation of Lieutenant General Sir Henry Rawlinson, 25 September 1915, 5201–33–67, Rawlinson Papers, NAM. Haig comments on Loos *Official History* draft ch. XV, pp. 11, 13, 20–21, dated by Haig 7 January 1928, Cab 44/27; and Haking comments on Loos chapter, p. 10, Cab 44/28, PRO. Even here there are discrepancies: Haig, loc. cit., p. 20, states that 64th Infantry Brigade of 21 Division left at 12.00 p.m. and arrived at 4 p.m., while the Provost Marshal of First Army (who should know) states that 64th Infantry Brigade left between 2 and 2.30 p.m., and then bivouacked for four hours on the way! Similarly the Somerset Light Infantry of 63rd Brigade did not leave until 2.30 p.m., E. R. Fitzpatrick (Provost Marshal of First Army) to General Staff, 12 November 1915, WO 106/390, PRO. The inference is that even if the order to move had gone out promptly as Haig requested at 8.45 a.m., the Reserves would very probably still have arrived too late.

63 Haking to First Army (Haig), 3 November 1915, and Haig to GHQ, 4 November 1915, WO 106/390, PRO.

64 Major General Sir Frederick Maurice to Edmonds, 10 January 1926, Cab 45/120, PRO.

65 Telephone conversation of Lieutenant General Sir Henry Rawlinson, from the commencement of the attack, 25 September 1915, 5201-33-67, Rawlinson Papers, NAM; Wilson, Diary, 29 September 1915, Wilson Papers, IWM; Haig, Diary, Robertson to Haig, First Army GHQ, 29 September 1915, WO 256/5, PRO; War Diary of General Staff of IV Corps, 25 September 1915, 41, Montgomery-Massingberd Papers, KCL. It is confusing but fair to add that Sir John French wrote that he felt he handed over the two Divisions at 11 a.m. [!], Haig, Diary, Sir John French to Kitchener, 9 October 1915, WO 256/5, PRO.

66 Haig to Bee (his brother John), 5 October 1915 and 2 November 1915, 214b, Haig Papers, NLS.

67 Haig, Diary, 27 September 1915, and Haig to Kitchener, 29 September 1915, WO 256/5, PRO. Haig's letter to Kitchener was of a secret nature, and stemmed from the request of the king and Kitchener for Haig to write confidential letters to them, evidently regarding Sir John French, Haig, Diary, 14 July 1915, WO 256/4, PRO.

68 Haking's retraction of his earlier statement that First Army's congested area was at fault, is interesting. 'I wrote this letter [regarding First Army problems] when I was very busy preparing for an attack ... and the above mentioned statement was based on my own memory of verbal statements made to me by the GOCs of 21 and 24 Divisions on the night of the 25th [September 1915] at Vermelles, where I was giving final instructions for the attack next day ... I may have been mistaken about this, because I know that the most careful arrangements were made by First Army.' GOC XI Corps (Haking) to Advanced First Army, 3 November 1915, WO 106/390, PRO.

69 Most of the letters in Cab 45/120/Loos show that just about everything that could go wrong did go wrong, for example Lieutenant Colonel H. J. C. Piers (24 Division) to Edmonds, 17 June 1926, on poor staff work; Lieutenant General Sir Robert Whigham to Edmonds, 9 July 1926, on mistakes at GHQ and XI Corps HQ; Major General Sir Archibald Montgomery (Chief of Staff, IV Corps) to Edmonds, 11 January 1926, who blamed the obstinacy of both Haig and Sir John French; and General Sir William Robertson (then Chief of Staff to Sir John French) to Edmonds, 10 August 1926, admitting to 'vacillation' and 'hesitation' on the part of Sir John French, Cab 45/120, PRO.

70 'Ammunition and food supply trains had to run of course, but even if the railway authorities had known what could they have done? ... The fact should be recognized the whole area was terribly over congested!' Haig's notes on 1927 draft of Loos ch. XV, vol. 4, dated 7 January 1928 by Haig, p. 9, Cab 44/27, PRO.

71 Haig to Edmonds, 7 January 1928, 11/4/59, Edmonds Papers, KCL.

72 Aylmer Haldane felt Haig had been mainly instrumental in Sir John French's removal, Haldane, 'Autobiography', vol. 2, p. 405, Haldane Papers, NLS. See also a very interesting letter from Haig to Oliver Haig (nephew), 31 October 1915, 334d, Haig Papers, NLS.

73 Alan Fletcher, GHQ, to Lady Haig, 22 July 1916 and 25 July 1916 (with Lady Haig's annotations), E. G. Thompson, GHQ, to Lady Haig, 28 July 1916, 144, Haig Papers, NLS.

74 Haig, Diary, Robertson to Haig, 29 July 1916, WO 256/11, PRO.

75 Liddell Hart, Talk with Edmonds, 31 October 1929, 11/1929/17, Liddell Hart Papers, KCL; see also J. F. C. Fuller to Edmonds, 5 June 1929, Cab 45/133; Frank Lyon to Edmonds, 10 June 1929, Cab 45/135; and Charles Page to Edmonds, 1 June 1929, Cab 45/136, PRO, who all three thought Stuart-Wortley poor. On Oxley, Liddell Hart, Diary Notes, 15 May 1930, reporting a talk with Edmonds, 11/1930/15, Liddell Hart Papers, KCL.

76 Edmonds to G. C. Wynne, 17 February 1944, Cab 45/33, inside Cab 45/140, PRO.
77 Haldane, 'Autobiography', vol. 2, p. 332, Haldane Papers, NLS.
78 F. Wilson (20 Division Royal Artillery) to Edmonds, 26 [?] 1936, Cab 45/138; George Lindsay (Brigade Commander 2 Division) to Edmonds, 28 June 1937, Cab 45/135; Morant (43rd Brigade Commander) to Edmonds, 2 April [?], Cab 45/136, PRO.
79 E. W. Flanagan (CO 1st East Surrey Regiment), to Edmonds, 27 November 1935, Cab 45/133, PRO.
80 Kiggell to Rawlinson, 9 July 1916, and Horne to Fourth Army, 13 July 1916, WO 158/233, PRO; Major Drake Brockman to Edmonds, [?] February 1930, Cab 45/132, and Colonel L. Price Davies (113th Infantry Brigade), to Edmonds, 6 March 1930, Cab 45/133, PRO. Edmonds, *Military Operation, France and Belgium, 1916, 2nd July 1916 to the End of the Battles of the Somme* (London, 1938), pp. 28–54.
81 Major General W. T. Furse to Major General Sir A. A. Montgomery, 26 July 1916, 47, Montgomery-Massingberd Papers, KCL; Haig, Diary, 4 September 1916, WO 256/13, PRO.
82 Brigadier General L. Kentish to Edmonds, 19 November 1936, Cab 45/135, PRO.
83 E. G. Wace (G1 32 Division) to Edmonds, 30 October 1936, Cab 45/138; Lieutenant Colonel H. J. N. Davis (CO 15th Highland Light Infantry) to Edmonds, 10 November 1936, Cab 45/133; see also Austin C. Girdwood (G2 32 Division) to Edmonds, 30 June 1930, Cab 45/134, PRO.
84 Gough apparently knew little of conditions at the front, according to George Jeffreys of 58 Brigade, 19 Division, for Gough 'had no notion of the physical strain on the troops of even a few hours in the line under such conditions', George Jeffreys to Edmonds (referring to 14–19 November 1916) 23 October 1936, Cab 45/135, PRO. This was one of those occasions that the GOC (Bridges, 19 Division) did protest (to Gough) but to no avail.
85 Haldane, Diary, 18 April 1916, 20 April 1916, 22 April 1916 (including Edmonds to Haldane, 17 March 1931, and Haldane's note of 17 March 1931), 6 May 1916, 24 June 1916 (including the story of Haig's letter), 25 June 1916, 30 June 1916 (including the occasion for Fanshawe's demotion to Divisional commander); and Haldane, 'Autobiography', vol. 2, p. 382, Haldane Papers, NLS; Haldane to Edmonds, 28 January 1929, Cab 45/130/St Eloi, PRO; Haig to Lady Haig, 18 February 1916, 143, Haig Papers, NLS; Haig, Diary, 22 June 1916, 23 June 1916, WO 256/10, PRO. For Alderson and the Canadian side, D. J. Goodspeed, *The Road Past Vimy: The Canadian Corps 1914–1918* (Toronto, 1969), pp. 57–8.
86 Brigadier General Sandilands (GOC 104th Infantry Brigade, 35 Division, Fifth Army) to Edmonds, 14 August 1923, Cab 45/192, PRO. Sandilands had serious doubts also about General Sir Walter Congreve (GOC VII Corps) at this time, and Congreve's BGGS, Hore-Ruthven. See Sandilands's account in Appendix I.
87 Edmonds to Acheson, 19 July 1950, Cab 103/113, PRO. No doubt Edmonds was slightly exaggerating when he said that all failures went to Palestine! Ironically, this demotion of Allenby turned out to be a lucky break for him, since he made his name in the Middle East campaign. Edmonds's claim that he altered the text in order to agree with the version of Cyril Falls, the official historian writing the account, by inserting a 'NOT' in the text, is not easy to follow in the published version, Edmonds, *Military Operations, France and Belgium 1917, The German Retreat to the Hindenburg Line and the Battle of Arras* (London, 1940), p. 378.

88 D. F. Anderson to Edmonds, 6 April 1936, Cab 45/132, PRO; Sandilands also altered his account of the Loos battle to help the GOC of 44 Brigade, Colonel Sandilands (then CO of 7 Cameroons, 44 Brigade) to Edmonds, 9 February 1926, Cab 45/121, PRO.

89 Liddell Hart, Talk with M. Cuthbertson, 23 November 1933, 11/1933/25, Liddell Hart Papers, KCL. The Divisional GOC was Major General Bruce-Williams.

90 Notes and suggestions by General Jeudwine, Cab 45/182/Part 2, PRO.

91 Liddell Hart, Talk with General Pope-Hennessy, 27 May 1937, 11/1937/43, Liddell Hart Papers, KCL.

92 Edmonds, 'Memoirs', ch. XXIV, pp. 5B, 14–15, 18, Edmonds Papers, KCL; Liddell Hart, Talk with General Pope-Hennessy, 27 May 1937, 11/1937/43, Liddell Hart Papers, KCL.

93 Edmonds, 'Memoirs', ch. XXXII, p. 12, Edmonds Papers, KCL. The Chief of Staff of Fourth Army in 1916 was Major General A. A. Montgomery.

94 Talk with Edmonds, 22 January 1931, 11/1931/3, Liddell Hart Papers, KCL. Edmonds thought that Rawlinson and his staff (Montgomery and Luckock) removed the War Diaries because on 1 July 1916 Rawlinson did not exploit the success on his right against Montauban, but wanted to move against the unbroken Thiepval sector in the centre. However Gough, put in charge of the two relevant Corps, X and VIII, refused to attack. Liddell Hart later repeated the story, and included the information that when the General Staff protested the criticisms of Fourth Army in the *Official History* (Montgomery was now Adjutant General), the missing War Diary made the General Staff give way, 'Some Odd Notes for History', 1933, 11/1933/35, Liddell Hart Papers, KCL.

95 Liddell Hart, Note on the CIGS, Montgomery-Massingberd, 1934, 11/1934/64, Liddell Hart Papers, KCL. Edmonds thought that generally there was a lot of suppression of documents, Liddell Hart, Talk with Edmonds, 11 November 1937, 11/1937/88, Liddell Hart Papers, KCL.

96 Edmonds to Liddell Hart, 14 May 1934, 1/259/76, Liddell Hart Papers, KCL. The archive librarian at the Imperial War Museum argued that Charteris's Diary was actually a reworking of his letters home to his wife (private interview, September 1979).

97 Liddell Hart to Lieutenant Colonel A. H. Burne, 3 October 1935, 1/131/91, Liddell Hart Papers, KCL. Liddell Hart makes the same statement in his book, *History of the First World War*, p. 93, footnote.

98 Liddell Hart, Talk with Edmonds, 27 March 1935, 11/1935/68, Liddell Hart Papers, KCL.

99 Haig Diary, entries for 23 October 1916 and 21 September 1916, WO 256/13, PRO.

100 Lady Haig to Edmonds, 10 February [1928] and 3 November [1928], 11/4/61 and 11/4/67, Edmonds Papers, KCL. It is of interest to note what Lord Blake has to say, namely, Haig 'did not, when revising his diary, make any important changes in what he had originally written. He does not appear to have deleted anything, but he did sometimes add a sentence or a paragraph'. Robert Blake, 'Introduction', *The Private Papers of Douglas Haig, 1914–1919* (London, 1952), p. 13. On the other hand, some passages that Haig originally wanted omitted were included in the final Edmonds typewritten edition of the diary. Generally speaking, the diary does appear unusually 'cool' and devoid of strong personal feelings or statements, which can be found instead in letters between Haig and Lady Haig.

101 Harries-Jenkins, *The Army in Victorian Society*, p. 100; Liddell Hart, *History of the First World War*, p. 33.

102 A good example was the case of Arthur Paget, a guardsman, who failed to get command of III Corps partly because of his involvement in the Curragh incident, and partly because of a row with Sir John French on manoeuvres in 1913, but was still able to secure the III Corps command for another guardsman, Lieutenant General Sir William Pulteney; Liddell Hart, Talk with Edmonds, 5 February 1937, 11/1937/4, Liddell Hart Papers, KCL.

103 Haig himself anticipated that in the event of war many peace-time officers would have to go, Haig to Edmonds, 31 August 1911, 11/4/3, Edmonds Papers, KCL.

104 Haldane, Diary, October 1909 generally, 10 May 1911 and 11 May 1911, Haldane Papers, NLS; Liddell Hart, Diary, 29 March 1927, 11/1927/—, Liddell Hart Papers, KCL.

105 Pakenham, *The Boer War*, pp. 179, 318, 368, 448. The similarities between the South African war and the First World War from the point of view of the British army, suggest an historical periodization that links these two wars together, and sees the change-over from the traditional to the professional ideal around the time of the Second World War.

106 Much the same attitude seems to have prevailed between the two world wars, cf. Brian Bond, *British Military Policy Between the Two World Wars* (Oxford, 1980), ch. 2.

[2]

The Cult of the Offensive and the Psychological Battlefield

Following the South African war, the Edwardian army entered a period of transition. There were numerous commissions, reports, committees and reorganizations which did much to modernize what was essentially a Victorian, colonial-oriented army. Many officers were concerned to professionalize their own roles in the decade between the South African War and the First World War, and there was therefore a considerable ferment of ideas, with some junior and senior officers reading widely; with some testing of new weapons and rearmament; with expanded training in areas such as musketry; the issue of new Field Service Regulations and other manuals; and considerable discussions of weapons, strategy and tactics in various forums.[1]

However, there were several stumbling blocks which detracted from much of this reforming effort and left the army still in a transitional phase when the anticipated war actually arrived in August 1914. These stumbling blocks included the short and inevitably unknown time period between 1902 and 1914, and the financial stringency of military budgets in the Edwardian era. There was also the normal, traditional regimental and 'arm' prejudices of the Victorian army. These will be discussed more fully in Chapter 3.

Of particular interest here were the ideas and mental horizons of the prewar British officer corps, which ultimately led to the acceptance of an unrealistic cult of the offensive. This cult of the offensive emerged as the result of three central ideas: (1) recognition of the influence of fire-power; (2) a pessimistic and anti-modern attitude, which included suspicion of the reliability of working-class recruits; and (3) an understanding of warfare as structured, ordered, and therefore potentially decisive.

The British army recognized and accepted the emergence of fire-power as a major factor in modern warfare, but reacted by overemphasizing the offensive just because of the very difficulty of troops crossing the deadly and terrifying fire-swept zone and still continuing the assault. (This problem will be addressed more fully in Chapter 3.) The desire to stress the offensive spirit was exacerbated however by a pessimistic or anti-modern strain of thought that revolved around a deep suspicion of the likely behaviour of the new urban recruits when under fire, and this was further reinforced by a rather simple Social Darwinism. There was also an anti-intellectual ethos which rejected theory and doctrine, thereby under-cutting alternative concepts to the cult of the offensive. Finally, there existed an underlying assumption that warfare was understood, and that future battles were likely to take place within a structured and 'reliable' framework. In fact, prewar thinking considered the battle of the future to be a three or four-stage affair, with each stage following a recognized and predictable pattern. If this was so, then the army with the strongest offensive spirit would clearly win the decisive victory. This concept will be explored more fully in Chapter 4, but it too helped to create the British cult of the offensive.

Of course the prewar British army was not the only one to promote this cult. Indeed traditional interpretations have stressed the prewar influence of French thought via army officers such as Foch, Langlois and de Grandmaison. But recent studies have shown that all major European armies shared this prewar fascination with the offensive.[2] Why was this? Various reasons have been advanced to explain the existence of this European-wide prewar phenomenon. They include the need of large organizations like armies to operate in a predictable, structured environment which an offensive strategy can potentially produce; and the fact that a decisive, offensive strategy appears inherently attractive in promoting the idea of a competent army organization, and in offering the benefits of a short, decisive war.[3] The above reasons were probably present in British military thinking before 1914, and there is no doubt that an unofficial cult or doctrine of the offensive *did* develop in the prewar British army. The British army did re-emphasize, in the face of rapidly developing fire-power, and the emergence of the town-bred masses, the centrality of human qualities in war, and the image or paradigm of the psychological battlefield. These two concepts – the cult of the offensive and the psychological battlefield – were to remain as strong underlying assumptions among many senior officers, including GHQ, during the war itself.

The staff and officers of the Edwardian army really reflected Edwardian society, with its good and bad points, its class structure and its underlying social and national trends. The officer corps was traditionally conserva-tive and often anti-intellectual, in line with Edwardian upper middle-class prejudices, and this is reflected in a typical, although not total, rejection of doctrine. This anti-intellectualism had something to do with class attitudes, something to do with Social Darwinism, something to do with Victorian empiricism, and something to do with nineteenth-century colonial warfare. For example, asked to write an introduction to the Wolseley series of military classics, Field Marshal Lord Wolseley declared in 1897, 'I hope the officers of Her Majesty's Army may never degenerate into bookworms. There is happily at present no tendency in that direction, for I am glad to say that this generation is as fond of danger, adventure, and all manly out-of-door sports as its forefathers were.'[4] Wolseley's Social Darwinism was as explicit as his anti-intellectualism in his autobiography, published in 1903: 'any virile race can become paramount . . . if it possesses the courage, the constancy of purpose and the self-sacrifice to resolve that it will live under a stern system of Spartan military discipline, ruthlessly enforced by one lord and master, the King'. Wolseley was much concerned by 'unmanly vices' and overcivilized nations, and felt that only war could restore 'manliness' and 'virility'.[5]

The acceptance of Social Darwinism was very widespread among army officers in the late Victorian and Edwardian period,[6] and it fitted in only too well with the anti-intellectual tendency of the army, and with the growing mistrust of the urban-bred working classes. Lieutenant General Baden-Powell fitted all these strands together in his *Scouting for Boys*, which counselled sports, manliness, self-discipline, and duty to the state, as the keys to national success. He criticized loafing, hooliganism, cigarette smoking, watching football (soccer), self-abuse, listening to agitators, and vices such as drinking and gambling – all these signified loss of self-control, and hence loss of manliness and lack of patriotism. The solution was to take part in sports, and of course scouting, whose whole object was 'to form character in the boys – to make them good citizens'. For Baden-Powell the real enemy was the loss of individual self-control, which necessarily meant the loss of national discipline and patriotism, and hence the loss of military instincts. Watching football was almost criminal:

> thousands of boys and young men, pale, narrow-chested, hunched-up, miserable specimens, smoking endless cigarettes, numbers of them betting, all of them learning to be hysterical as they groan or cheer in panic unison with their neighbours – the worst sound of all being the hysterical scream of laughter that greets any little trip or fall of a player.

Instead, what Baden-Powell wanted was 'manhood, unmoved by panic or excitement, and reliable in the tightest of places. Get the lads away from this – teach them to be manly, to play the game . . . and not be merely onlookers and loafers'. The opposite to manliness was loss of self-control, but also signs of female characteristics as perceived by Baden-Powell:

'manliness can only be taught by men, and not by those who are half men, half old women'. (Baden-Powell's strictures on manliness are perhaps ironic in that Edmonds was sceptical of Baden-Powell's abilities in defending Mafeking when in command of the besieged forces in that town during the South African war. Then, when Mafeking was relieved, Baden-Powell was given a column, but this was shortly contained in West Luxembourg by a few Boers. Subsequently, Lord Roberts sent Baden-Powell home by placing him in charge of raising the South African Constabulary.)[7]

Mistrust of the working classes in their urban centres was high, and many officers feared that under the pressures of invasion or war, popular sentiment would lead to surrender or to suing for peace. In 1913 Major Stewart Murray expected urban panic and riots in the event of war, while the future CIGS, Major General Robertson, thought in 1912 that there was a mischievous spirit of disloyalty to the Crown abroad, and counselled a return to 'reverence for authority'. A large majority of officers in the 1910–14 period seemed to feel the same, and the General Staff conference of 1910 felt the need to discuss the question of patriotism. One solution was offered at the conference by Brigadier General Kiggell, who believed that it was a sexual question, in the sense that ladies ought not to have anything to do with men who refused to serve their country in the event of war. This general fear of the new urban working-classes fitted in well with Social Darwinism, and officers like Major General Sir Walter Knox argued that the 'physically deteriorated race of town-bred humanity' was getting dangerously low in the 'scale of virility'.[8]

Parallel to these currents went the anti-intellectualism noted above, and evident in late Victorian soldiers such as Wolseley and Knox. Obviously there were a great number of officers who did read, and who were well-educated, among them Staff College graduates like Haig and Edmonds. But equally there was an undoubtedly strong current of opinion that deprecated doctrine, theory and critical reading. The future Commander-in-Chief of the BEF, Sir John French, reportedly applied to the War Office librarian for Hamley's *Operations of War*, but could not digest it, and never asked for another book. However, General Sir Francis Davis thought that Sir John French *had* read some military books, although without understanding, and had followed army practice by quoting tag ends and clichés. An unkind story also had it that Sir John French claimed to know some of the French language, but when speaking to a group of French officers early in the war in French, after a certain period of time voices from the back ranks shouted '*traduisez*'. The unfortunate Sir John had to explain that he was already speaking in French.[9]

Anti-intellectualism was also partly anti-modernism. For example, a report on the education and training of officers in 1902 included evidence from the Assistant Commandant at Woolwich, Lieutenant Colonel Murray, who argued that science subjects were detrimental to character and leadership, although classics might be acceptable:[10]

> We would rather have a classically educated boy than one who has given his mind very much up to Electricity and Physics and those kinds of subjects. We want them to be leaders in the field first ... I think the man who has a strong turn for science does not at the same time develop the soldierly side of his nature. Power of command and habits of leadership are not learned in the laboratory ... Our great point is character; we care more about that than subjects.

This sort of tendency led also towards a rejection of doctrine and theory. Numerous officers, particularly in the 1912–13 period, wrote articles decrying doctrine, and in its place suggesting experience, surprise, initiative, imagination, genius, intelligence, common sense, and so on.[11]

Along with anti-intellectual and anti-modern trends went a certain lack of professionalism among some Edwardian officers. Edmonds, for example, gave an unflattering portrait of the prewar War Office in his unpublished Memoirs. He was a Sapper, who knew that he was not in a fashionable branch of the army, but instead relied on his brains for advancement. He was seemingly jealous of his contemporaries in the Cavalry and other socially acceptable arms, and was rather contemptuous of those who achieved promotion through social networks rather than ability. He considered that he and several other capable officers were emerging as a kind of ginger group, bringing a new sense of professionalism to the army, but he felt they were facing an uphill battle and this lent his comments an occasionally bitter tone. However his critical stance did cause him to reveal aspects of the army that might not otherwise have seen the light of day.

Edmonds attended Staff College in 1896 and 1897, and he made rather pungent remarks about some of his fellow candidates. Generally he noted that the Royal Engineers called the Staff College a 'two year loaf', and he objected to the nomination system whereby eight out of thirty-two candidates were admitted as 'favourites of fortune' by nomination rather than by examination. He also felt it a great mistake for reports on candidates to be made by the Commanding Officer and Staff rather than by their fellow students. Appointed to the Intelligence branch of the War Office, Edmonds noticed the perpetual rivalries for precedence that went on in the labyrinths of the old War Office. He also recalled that the hour for arrival was 11 a.m. (10 a.m. for clerks), and that Field Marshal Lord Wolseley expected everyone to ride in the Park every morning. When any officer at the War Office wanted to go on leave, he wrote a message, such as 'away until the 12th' and fixed it to his table with his office pen knife, and then departed, leaving his door open. In contrast, in the Intelligence

Department at Queens Gate, leave was hard to obtain.[12] At the War Office, the distribution of work was strange. When Haig went there in 1908 he found an infantryman writing *Cavalry Training*, and Edmonds's relative, Birkbeck, was faced with writing three manuals simultaneously, *Infantry Training*, *Songbook of the British Army* and *Handbook of the 4.5 inch Howitzer*.[13]

Edmonds was also critical of prewar staff work both at divisional level and above, particularly during army manoeuvres. In his own 4 Division, there were only two staff officers, whereas in wartime the establishment was six. The only practice his divisional GOC, Snow, got at commanding the division was the three or four days at the annual army manoeuvres, and these were neither terribly successful nor practical. For example, practising retirements were forbidden by General Sir Charles Douglas (an officer whom Edmonds considered unintelligent). Sir John French had problems at the 1913 manoeuvres, when his two Corps diverged, and his opponent, Gough, refused to stay still; while the winter 1913–14 General Staff war game, designed to test the workings of the BEF's GHQ, resulted in total confusion. Later, in 1915, all of the BEF's GHQ staff were changed, except for one captain, who kept the letter register. These problems with the staff-command structure came back to haunt the BEF in August and September 1914, when Sir John French and his GHQ did not make a particularly good showing. For example, there seemed to be poor co-operation between the I and II Corps in their retreat, while both Corps staff forgot to check whether the forest of Mormal was occupied by the enemy.[14]

Edmonds's view was a little jaundiced perhaps, but the general atmosphere and his factual comments are probably accurate enough. Other prewar diaries reveal the same sort of staff-command problems as Edmonds depicted,[15] but at lower levels one is conscious of an army training hard, yet finding difficulty in coming to grips with 'modern' warfare. Major General Archibald recalled his prewar days as a Lieutenant in the Royal Field Artillery, when training emphasized speed as the thing that counted. During the 1913 manoeuvres, the Commanding Officer, later Major General Uniacke, had formed the whole Brigade of three six-gun batteries into a line on Salisbury Plain, with a round up the spout, just to see how quickly the first round could be got off. Archibald pointed out that targets were only engaged by observation, not by map, and there was no night shooting. Calibration and adjustment for atmosphere were unknown, and field use of the 6 inch batteries was not contemplated. Liaison between artillery and infantry was virtually nil, no effort was made to find out from the infantry what was wanted, and in fact infantry and artillery fought separate battles. Finally, training was difficult because officers were frequently away on courses, or on leave. And the courses themselves sounded fairly leisurely – Archibald's veterinary course in 1910–11 did no work after lunch.[16]

The trends in the Edwardian officer corps so far discussed have given a rather pessimistic view of the early twentieth-century army. Social Darwinism, class-conscious fears, anti-intellectualism, a preference for traditional Victorian social and military practices – these were all backward-looking or negative attitudes. Change and reform did take place, but within this rather apprehensive and anti-modern set of attitudes. Ironically, however, while the British army in general rejected any fixed doctrine of war (partly because of a preference for flexibility, and partly because of anti-intellectual trends), nevertheless a doctrine *did* emerge, although it was necessarily 'unofficial'. This was the doctrine of the offensive at all costs. As noted previously, this doctrine initially developed as an antidote to the arrival of modern fire-power – just because fire-power now made the offensive very difficult, *therefore* the offensive must be heavily over-emphasized. With this went anti-intellectual and anti-modern trends; the officer corps' pessimistic evaluation of the patriotism of town-bred army recruits; and the underlying concept of the structured and predictable battle. The difficulty was that because an offensive strategy was likely to be very costly in manpower in the face of modern weapons, the doctrine of the offensive must take account of this and still remain offensive. The solution was to prepare the nation, the army and the individual soldier for heavy losses, and to over-emphasize the required discipline or moral qualities of the nation, army and soldier. This would hopefully enable the potentially unreliable individual soldier to overcome fire-power on the battlefield. The future losses of the Western Front can, in a sense, be said to have been 'prepared' by this and other European countries' reaction to the emergence of modern fire-power.

This unofficial cult of the offensive was argued via several sequential theses in the 1902–14 period, namely (1) that new weapons (fire-power) had definitely arrived and now influenced the battlefield to a high degree; nevertheless (2) the fire-power lessons of the South African war (1899–1902) were abnormal and not typical and so could not be seen as undermining the future of offensive strategy; furthermore (3) despite high losses the Japanese had defeated the Russians in Manchuria (1904–5) through offensive spirit, cold steel and high morale rather than fire-power; hence (4) the nation, the army and the individual must be taught to suffer losses because the essential but reliable offensive strategy of the next war would be very costly; moreover (5) offensive tactics must actually aim at heavy losses because this was the reliable and sure way of getting through enemy defences and fire-power; and therefore (6) because of these factors and the very stress of modern war, the individual soldier must either be more highly disciplined, or develop a much loftier sense of individual enthusiasm and initiative, or feel himself an organic fighting unit of a virile nation. It was agreed that the end result was to be the higher morale of the individual and the army; and (7) that, in summary, the offensive must be maintained at all costs, the more so because of the doubts concerning the patriotism of the town-bred recruits and the very difficulty of the offensive. (Nevertheless a few officers did begin to question the cult of the offensive, particularly in the 1912–14 period.)[17] Taken together, this 'unofficial' doctrine or cult of the offensive, and solutions to the problems of the offensive, amounted to an image of war that might be termed the 'psychological battlefield'.

Looking at the seven theses, sometimes argued in combination and sometimes singly, it can be seen that there was undoubtedly general agreement about the first thesis, namely, the significance of fire-power, and the difficulty of crossing the fire-swept zone.[18] In regard to the second, there was a surprisingly widespread belief in the abnormality of South Africa. In the 1902 Committee appointed to consider the education and training of officers, the army crammer T. Miller Maguire was questioned by the headmaster of Eton, Dr Warre:[19]

> 'Has it not been studiously inculcated in various quarters that the Boer War must not be taken as an example in Tactics, and so on, as everything would be different in a European war?' T. Miller Maguire, 'Yes, but its effect has not been to cause more reading about any wars ... The younger officers are worse than for a generation.' Dr. Warre, 'But they have studiously said that ... giving it as a reason why they should not read more ... "This Boer War is altogether on a different plan from what a war in Europe would be, and therefore you will not learn much by it!" 'T. Miller Maguire, 'That has been said over and over again.'

A long line of officers repeated the same argument about South Africa,[20] and even the military theorist and Staff College lecturer, Colonel G. F. R. Henderson, declared that South Africa was abnormal and displayed 'peculiar conditions'. It was typical of the general army reaction that at the same time Henderson should admit the revolution in war created by 'modern fire', i.e. the flat trajectory of the small bore rifle and smokeless powder.[21]

Concerning the third thesis, there was an initial reaction after the Russo-Japanese war to stress the use of machine-guns and fire-power, but by 1909–10 the tide had turned, and fire-power was officially devalued.[22] The most remarkable rejection came from Lieutenant General Ian Hamilton, who wrote in 1910:

> Blindness to moral forces and worship of material forces inevitably lead in war to destruction. All that exaggerated reliance placed upon chassepots and mitrailleuses by France before '70; all that trash written by M. Bloch [the Polish theorist of war] before 1904 about zones of fire across which no living being could pass, heralded

nothing but disaster. War is essentially the triumph, not of a chassepot over a needle-gun, not of a line of men entrenched behind wire entanglements and fireswept zones over men exposing themselves in the open, but of one will over another weaker will.

What was needed was an army 'formed, trained, inspired by the idea of the attack'.[23] Despite some opposition from a minority fire-power school of thought, there was general agreement that the lessons of the Russo-Japanese war lay in the area of offensive tactics and morale.[24] As Major General Altham* remarked in 1914, the 'Manchurian campaign has wiped out the mistaken inference from South African experiences that bayonet fighting belonged to the past'.[25]

The fourth thesis, the concept of accepting heavy losses due to the use of new weapons/magazines/fire, etc., was once more a reluctant conclusion of most officers. As with the other theses, this led to an emphasis on the offensive, but in this case an over-emphasis because senior officers feared that their juniors and the men would be reluctant to close with the enemy in the face of heavy losses. Major General Altham spelled out the problem and offered a solution – to over-emphasize the offensive just because of the likely losses of the attack. 'The ideal of the final decisive charge must be ever in the mind of the attacking infantry, to sustain them in enduring the punishing losses of the passage of the fireswept zone, to draw them on to victory.' Hubert Gough anticipated 25 per cent losses in the assault, and Major General Knox in 1914 anticipated a loss list of some 20,000 in the first engagement of the BEF and commented, 'We surely have some work before us to steel and discipline the heart of the nation to face this possibility'. Colonel Maude, Major Pollock (editor of the *United Service Magazine*), the observers in Manchuria, and the official manuals – all stressed the necessity to suffer loss in order to drive the assault home.[26] Unfortunately, these predictions or self-fulfilling prophecies became reality a few years later, and so the General Staff found it necessary in 1915 (and later) to continue stressing the 'suffer losses' thesis in regard to the offensive:

> The attitude of the British mind at home appears to be that any loss in defence may be joyfully accepted as a sign of true bulldog tenacity against odds, but that losses incurred in attack are lamentable and unjustifiable unless the attack ends in the complete and decisive defeat of the enemy. This feeling is beginning to be reflected in the Army and the consequences may be serious. No war was ever won by troops in which this spirit prevailed.

Similarly, in 1917, before the battle of Passchendaele commenced, Robertson did not want the French to get away from the 'idea of heavy fighting and heavy losses'.[27]

The fifth thesis was a corollary of the previous one, and simply argued that a sufficiently large mass of troops would always succeed. This thesis was also related to the underlying idea that warfare was structured and predictable. Thus the future General Sir Ivor Maxse* argued in 1910–11 that 'masses of men in sufficient lines one behind the other will go through anything'. This was to urge the concept of human 'weight' behind the attack – and the same message occurred in Major General Butler's November 1915 offensive plan that called for twenty-five 'waves' of men to ensure success. Kiggell's pre-Somme offensive instructions to Divisions also stressed human weight and impetus, so that to make sure of the capture of a trench line 'four or more lines [of men] have usually succeeded'. GHQ therefore actually prepared for heavy losses: 'All must be prepared for heavy casualties.'[28]

The sixth thesis proposed various solutions to modern war, which all emphasized the creation or re-creation of a new type of human being. Nearly all officers favoured meeting the new fire-power conditions with either more discipline, more individualism, or a more virile nation which would produce a more virile soldier. Some wanted a combination of all three, and some, caught up in the prewar argument over voluntarism or conscription, opted for individualism/enthusiasm if they were voluntar- ists, and discipline if they were conscriptionists. Some were not quite clear, as for example Colonel Henderson, who was a voluntarist, and wanted individual initiative, but also wanted higher discipline of the individual and moral training. However, he opposed mechanical disci- pline, in the same way as Lieutenant Colonel James, who stated flatly: 'Battle fighting is less mechanical, and a much higher development of the individual intelligence is needed to carry it to a successful conclusion.'[29] One thing that nearly all officers were agreed on was that the new conditions of warfare, experienced firsthand in South Africa and second- hand in Manchuria, placed far greater stress on the individual and therefore required a different kind of training of the soldier. In 1904 Haig declared 'the main lesson of the [South African] war is that modern conditions of warfare entail higher training of the individual'. Lieutenant General Sir Ian Hamilton argued that the South African war marked a very important epoch in the evolution of military tactics, which was that 'we are entering upon a period when the efficiency of an army will depend far more upon the morale and the high training of individuals who compose it than upon the mere numbers of those who may be available'. Lieutenant General Sir William Gatacre thought that the individual should be trained into a 'sharp fighting machine'. In contrast Lord Roberts thought the solution was 'training the men to act as individuals and not as machines', while Wolseley seemed to be torn between discipline and *esprit de corps*, but essentially came down on the side of discipline as against individual initiative.[30]

What was happening was that officers were really dividing into two rather vague camps. There were those who feared the response of soldiers under the greater stress of modern war and therefore opted for higher discipline (these were often conscriptionists, who also feared invasion, and therefore wanted a disciplined nation-in-arms); and there were those who wanted to liberate the enthusiasm and willingness to fight of the individual (these were normally the voluntarists, who were less concerned about invasion, and who opted for smaller, more intelligent and efficient armies. They were often Social Darwinists, wanting to make use of the fighting instincts of the British race).[31] An example of the conscriptionist 'discipline' school was Field Marshal Lord Roberts, who had changed his mind since 1904 and in 1911 now declared that modern war required 'above all, discipline in the highest sense of the word, the active, conscientious, unwavering resolve to carry out instructions'. Roberts thought that success in war might depend on the extent to which the 'fighting front is constantly and normally in organic unity with the whole body politic'. On the other hand, officers like Major General Smith-Dorrien wanted 'individual initiative and intelligence', while Sir Ian Hamilton wanted to release the fighting spirit in the 'souls of our race', and contended that 'war searches the innermost part and the uttermost corner. It is on [individual] moral forces we must stand or fall in battle.'[32]

The two schools of thought often converged, however, and individuals often changed sides, so that in the end many believed that the soldier of the future must actually have both individuality and mass discipline. Major General Baden-Powell told Roberts that 'though the development of individuality may tend to loosen hard-and-fast discipline, this should be replaced by substitution of a higher moral tie, by setting up an ideal of loyalty and patriotism to influence the men'.[33] Lieutenant Colonel F. B. Maurice wanted both initiative ánd self-subordination, leading to a happy medium of 'the spirit of playing the game for the side'. L. S. Amery of *The Times* sought discipline, but discipline on a higher plane, i.e. moral quality, or conscious discipline of the mind and will. Captain Charles Vivian wanted obedience and understanding because of the new 'scientific warfare', and even Hamilton came around to a mixture of enthusiastic individualism and the momentum and coherence of what he called 'communism'.[34] Similarly, Major Lawson desired both discipline and moral qualities, while Colonel Maude opted for a strange mixture of discipline and *élan* moulded together by the will power of the commander.[35] It would seem that a dialectic between individual initiative and mass discipline existed, which resulted in a consensus that officers generally termed a 'higher' combination or synthesis. Often the higher synthesis was phrased in Social Darwinian images that saw the individual soldier as part of an organic unity within a patriotic nation.

Finally, the seventh thesis, that of the offensive at all costs, or rather the offensive spirit at all costs, was an encapsulation of the previous theses and was judged to be really self-explanatory.[36] The offensive was diligently pressed by almost all senior officers, who were afraid of the converse, that troops would normally be fearful or unreliable in crossing the fire-swept zone. This very danger together with the previous theses, all combined to produce an 'unofficial' doctrine or cult of the offensive. Among many others, Brigadier General Haking disparaged the defensive and exalted the attack – even if the stronger force was on the defensive and the weaker on the offensive, still the offensive 'will win as sure as there is a sun in the heavens'. For Haking, the modern battlefield was simply a question of morale and human nature, indeed once one had mastered one's own human nature (which was 'always for defence and never for attack') then the problem of the attack was solved. The real battle was for control over the morale of one's own troops, so that company training 'is one constant struggle against human nature'. Haking was not unusual in fearing for the offensive spirit of the modern, democratic soldier, and the result with Haking and others was a violent swing to the spirit of the offensive as a sure antidote to fire-power. 'One often hears it stated that with modern weapons the defence has gained over the attack ... If, however, it was possible to visit the front line of attack and talk to the officers, N.C.O.s and men, and then go over to the defenders' trenches and talk to them, one would discover several reasons why the attack is better than the defence.' These reasons were all essentially moral, and so for Haking and others the image of war just prior to 1914 was that of a stressed but self-disciplined human battlefield.[37] Because of the overwhelming emphasis on human solutions to modern fire-power[38] – in the unequivocal words of the War Office in 1909, 'Moral force in modern war predominates over physical force as greatly as formerly'[39] – an image or paradigm of future war evolved that can be summarized as the 'psychological battlefield'.

The 'psychological battlefield' was an image that appealed most to the Social Darwinists like Colonel Maude, but was accepted by almost all officers, who argued that moral qualities were the bedrock of the attack, other things being equal. A few officers of the minority fire-power school like Colonel C. E. Calwell and Major B. F. S. Baden-Powell (brother to the founder of the Boy Scouts) considered that the attack across open ground should only be attempted under certain specific circumstances, but most argued for the offensive spirit under all circumstances, and training manuals stressed the psychological conditions of the decisive bayonet charge of the infantry.[40] Similarly, a questioner at the General Staff conference in 1913 asked whether fire should precede forward movement, or if this was 'opposed to the psychological conditions of the battlefield'.[41] It was simply accepted by the senior staff and officer corps that the crucial moment of the battle, the final assault, was always going to be psychological (i.e. the right moment for the charge, and the success or failure of the charge), and that the strain of modern war required a psychologically-conditioned soldier. Officers often quoted Napoleon's maxim that in war the moral predominated over the physical in a ratio of three to one, and there also continued to be a considerable interest in the determination and character of the commander or leader.[42]

Because of the psychological conditions of the battlefield, some officers even advocated closed formations in the attack, so that the troops could gain comfort from close proximity to each other, under intense fire.[43] Even the minority fire-power school of thought contained curious anomalies. Captain J. F. C. Fuller's 1914 article, 'The procedure of the infantry attack: a synthesis from a psychological standpoint', argued for an instinctual battlefield. 'It is the strength of the unconsciously or subconsciously acquired habit, rather than the conscious acts due to direct education, which, when death surrounds the soldier, urge him forward.' Fuller concluded, 'we must not forget that we have soldiers behind us and not heroes, and that the fight is a complex moral action and not a mechanical and soulless exploit'. Another fire-power article by Major Rooke in 1914 advocated the use of rifle-thrown hand grenades, dynamite, machine-guns etc., in crossing the fireswept zone, plus portable shields-spades to protect the attacker, but he too reverted to group psychology in describing the moment for the charge, when the line 'divining by a collective intuition, a sort of *sentiment du fer*, the favourable instant, hurls itself forward'.[44] Advocating the combination of both fire-power technology and the psychological battlefield occurred partly because both Fuller and Rooke recognized that the modern battlefield was likely to be very stressful, partly because official manuals called for both fire and movement, and partly because the prevailing sentiment for the offensive via the psychological battlefield was so strong in the army. No doubt, too, the prevailing European intellectual trends of anti-positivism had some effect, particularly on Fuller.[45]

The overwhelming response of the General Staff and both senior and junior officers was to argue that modern fire-power weapons could be overcome by psychological/human qualities, rather than by corresponding fire-power/technological tactics. This is reflected in the strategic concept of the decisive battle to which the whole army subscribed in Field Service Regulations (FSR) where the words used have a moral quality, derived from Clausewitz. When Haig, who was responsible for writing the FSR, describes the decisive battle in his 1907 volume on the Cavalry, the struggle becomes personalized: the sudden decisive blow on the enemy's centre of gravity, then the breakdown of the enemy, whose will-power starts to fail and who must be pressed until overthrown and demoralized. The connotations are of a small-scale individualized conflict, and the constant references to morale ('Success in battle depends mainly on moral [*sic*], and a determination to conquor', wrote Haig), give a sense of a personal, almost schoolboy-like conflict.[46]

This sense of an individual conflict on a psychological battlefield is confirmed by the language used as the First World War evolved. Initially, warfare was consciously seen as straightforward, because of the known human qualities required, and because senior officers could not accept that war had changed from the earlier, understood, structured and reliable pattern. Hence the demands from GHQ and other HQs during the Somme to take such and such a position 'at all costs', and hence the language used which betrays an adherence, at one level, to a psychological image of war. Sometimes the enemy was simply individualized, as in a GS memo in December 1915 – 'When *he* is "all out" on the defensive ... and *his* sting has been drawn and success against *him* at any one point is likely'; or when Robertson wrote to Rawlinson in June 1916, advising the latter to give him [the Bosche] plenty of artillery and machine-gun fire 'until *he* is dug out of *his* holes. As you know *he* is hard up for reserves ... and once you can stir *him* up we should be able to accomplish much.' In turn Rawlinson wrote to Colonel Wigram* on the eve of the 14 July 1916 assault, 'I think I can promise to give *him* a real good beating ... [and] to hunt *him* if anything like real demoralization sets in in *his* ranks'. Rawlinson's letter is full of references to a personalized enemy.[47]

More common, however, was a sense of 'beating', 'thumping', 'shaking' the enemy as in a schoolboy fight.[48] Major General G. S. Clive* reported in March 1915 that the enemy had been given a 'good shaking up'; Lieutenant Colonel Fitzgerald, however, was concerned in September 1915 that the Guards had been 'biffed out' of the Chalk Pits; while Major General F. B. Maurice was happy that in October 1915 'We have given the Germans a really bad shake and I hope will give them another soon'. By 1916 a certain frustration was beginning to show, and the language became a little more colourful. In June 1916 General Maxse wanted to give the Germans a 'good thump', but by August 1916 he felt it was necessary 'to beat him continuously on the head from now till winter; and begin again in the early Spring'. Meanwhile Major General A. A. Montgomery told Maxse in August 1916 that he hoped soon to give the Bosche 'another good smash'. For his part Kiggell believed in July 1916 that the Bosche was 'badly rattled', while the artillery fire 'shook their nerves to pieces', and again that the Bosche was 'a good deal rattled'. Charteris was equally optimistic – in August 1916 he argued, 'We are jostling them pretty hard and they must know they are going to be jostled harder in the future'. By October 1916 Charteris was still very sanguine: '*His* [the Germans'] tail is down, he surrenders freely, and on several occasions he has thrown down his rifle and ran away'.[49]

By 1917 the grim reality of 'modern' war had sunk in, and fewer remarks of this kind were being made, although in April 1917 Henry

Wilson confidently predicted that 'We shall knock the Bosches about to such an extent that everyone who runs can read what our proper course is'.[50] There is a serious danger in over-interpreting such language, but at a deep level in 1915 and 1916 staff and senior officers did seem to think of warfare as more predictable and simpler than it actually was, and were puzzled when offensives didn't conform to the prewar paradigm of the structured battle, and decisive results through high morale. Instead of rethinking basic ideas about modern warfare there was a strong tendency to reinforce the paradigm of the structured, psychological battlefield and indulge in the 'more and more' syndrome. To take a few examples, in May 1915 F. B. Maurice claimed that 'We must keep hammering away and to do that must have more and more men and more and more ammunition'. When battles went wrong, there was an even stronger tendency to call for 'more and more' thus in July 1916 General Maxse wanted 'more and more fresh Divisions'; in August 1916, Fourth Army HQ called for a future offensive on a huge front with two or three armies attacking instead of one; and in October 1916 Henry Wilson wanted a future battle involving one and a half million men and equivalent to two Somme offensives.[51]

Another aspect of the organized, psychological battlefield was the continuation into the First World War of theses 4, 5 and 6 in regard to a basic mistrust of the offensive spirit of the troops. Haldane reported that on the outbreak of war in August 1914 he issued orders to his Infantry Brigade of 4 Division regarding the carrying of white handkerchiefs by the men, and ordered officers to exercise strict discipline because of many new men. Subsequently Haldane reported that on 14 July 1916 he put the New Army Battalions in front of 3 Division's attack because he felt they were less reliable. In fact the white handkerchiefs were not used in 1914 and the New Army Battalions on 14 July were keen.[52] Rawlinson in particular seemed to be initially suspicious of the morale of his men, starting in November 1914 when he told the Master General of the Ordnance (MGO), Lieutenant General Sir Stanley von Donop, that German trench mortars were affecting morale and added, 'It is hard enough to keep them in their trenches as it is owing to the heavy casualties we have had in officers'. But by March 1915 Rawlinson could write to Kitchener, about his men, 'it has astonished me how and why their moral has increased rather than deteriorated during their life in the trenches'. Next year, in April 1916, Rawlinson still worried about the soldierly instincts of his men, and considered that the lack of military instinct of the men could be overcome by discipline and leadership, for 'There is no one more easily influenced for good or bad than the British soldier by the example of his superiors'. And finally, in October 1916, Rawlinson was still vaguely puzzled to find that the New Armies and Dominion troops 'have fought with a bravery and determination which one had never dared to hope for'.[53]

Rawlinson's attitude seemed to be that of upper-class distrust of the military instincts of the 'men', together with a corresponding emphasis on discipline. Others thought the same. For example Major General Bridges,* GOC 19 Division, felt in September 1916 that while the spirit of the men was splendid, they laboured 'under the disadvantage of being of unsporting habits and lacking those soldier instincts which generations of military service alone can supply'. General Sir Reginald Stephens,* GOC 5 Division and then X Corps, believed in September 1916 that 'slightly wounded men and people with shell shock have not the strongest of hearts: many of them ought never to leave the ranks'. Stephens wanted officers to be 'hard-hearted with these sort of people' and came to the conclusion that 'lack of discipline' was the reason for their problems, 'We are much too easy going an army'.[54] Dominion troops were particularly suspect when it came to discipline, especially Australian troops. Curiously enough Australians were recognized to have fighting instincts, but not soldierly instincts, i.e. self-discipline and automatic obedience to officers. Hence the cure was discipline, and the reaction of Lieutenant General Sir Archibald Murray to this problem reflects his attitude that modern war could not be fought with troops that showed individualistic enthusiasm, but only by disciplined troops in a controlled situation.[55]

Another indication of the army's unease over the psychological battle-field and thus the attitude of the troops, came from the way in which troops were 'controlled' in their periods 'at rest' by continuous digging and fatigues. The nature of the war compelled this, but arrangments could have been made, as in the French army, to relieve the men from much of the work. Moreover, the multitude of complaints by officers that units were actually too tired to fight reveals that continuous work was assigned for other reasons than efficiency.[56] It is apparent from the many complaints that overworking of soldiers was done as a matter of routine and that it had something to do with ignorance on the part of Divisional staff, and something to do with exerting control over the soldiers.[57] Austin Girdwood, GSO 2 of 32 Division, on 1 July 1916, wrote that his Divisional GOC and GSO 1 knew nothing about the infantry or how to handle them, and that the

> real cause of the failure of the 32nd Division is that the wretched Infantry were literally exhausted long before the day of the attack. Units were kept in the trenches for too long at one time without a relief and there was far too much digging and most of it was quite useless and haphazard. The GSO 1 considered that if the strength of a Battalion on paper was 500 men at least 450 should turn out for working parties.

Hence the men were exhausted physically and morally, wrote Gird-wood.[58]

The clearest indication of the desire to regulate and control the troops, arising from a fear of their individuality, comes in General Sir Charles Monro's conference on 4 August 1915. Monro told his divisional commanders that 'Order and regularity in trenches must be of the nature we are accustomed to in barracks. Elaborate orders must be drawn up to provide for everything and "go as you please" methods must be suppressed.' This apparently was particularly the case in preparing food: 'Everlasting cooking in the trenches not to be allowed and the "individual" soldier must be merged in his units and controlled by his section commander day and night.' And just in case the men were puzzled as to why they were in France, 'it must be properly explained to them why we are fighting and the great part they are playing in the welfare of the Empire'. Monro believed self-respect was crucial, and this he translated into smartness, 'The strictest attention must be paid to turn out, guards, saluting etc. in order to keep off slackness which is common to trench warfare'.[59]

It is apparent that the comments of Monro and other senior commanders were based on a prewar image of war that focused on the psychological battlefield, controlled by discipline and/or soldierly instincts. After the Somme, Major General A. A. Montgomery, Chief of Staff, Fourth Army, declared that the most important of the general principles were still 'drill and discipline'. Drill in the formation required for the attack, and discipline to 'obey by instinct, without thinking, so that in times of stress they will act as they are accustomed to do and there shall be no hesitation in obeying an order'.[60] No doubt Montgomery feared for the training and ability of the new officers and men, yet what he and Monro and others espoused was essentially a prewar style of fighting that saw the conflict of moral qualities as the central focus of success or failure in battle.

Complementary to these aspects of the psychological battlefield were underlying assumptions about what the offensive was supposed to achieve. Robertson was reported as saying in a prewar address to the Staff College: 'Go for your man as soon as you can; only by the offensive can you win'.[61] There was a general consensus that the idea of the decisive offensive meant attacking men, i.e. closing with and destroying the main enemy army in a structured, four-stage, decisive battle. The way to do this in 1900–14 was for the preparatory fight to pin and exhaust the enemy along the front, draw in the enemy reserves, and then artillery preparation for the final decisive infantry assault with the bayonet. The assault was meant to achieve 'annihilation' by dislodging the enemy from their defensive position, causing demoralization and, above all, a retreat. Then the cavalry was to confirm the victory by a vigorous pursuit. But it was never very clear whether the assault was to be against the position the enemy was holding, so that victory was represented by the *retreat* itself, or whether victory was represented by the capture of the *ground* the enemy had been holding, or by the physical surrender, wounding or killing of the main enemy army, i.e. by the numbers captured or made casualties; or indeed a combination of all these possibilities. In any case the final assault was going to be decisive and quick, and tactics were really subordinated to strategy. This was just the reverse of what Haig and his colleagues had learned at the Staff College in regard to the French army in 1870: 'In 1870 the French payed [*sic*] more attention to tactics than to strategy, and believed that success was to be won by materiel alone!'[62]

The problem in 1914 was that the British army pendulum had swung too far the other way, and now the army trained for strategic results via the decisive offensive, relying ultimately on morale and discipline. It did not pay sufficient attention to tactics. More important perhaps was the absence, even strategically, of clear goals. There was no official doctrine, resulting in the confusion that developed from 1914 following, over whether to gain ground; whether to kill the enemy as the primary goal; whether to attempt a breakthrough; or whether the 'bite and hold' principle should be applied (i.e. to bite off a piece of ground and invite the enemy to counter-attack). In the end two main schools of thought developed. First, the breakthrough concept (rush through the various enemy lines of defence, aim at deep objectives, gain ground, stress high morale, force the enemy out of the trenches, restore mobility, and use the General Reserve 'and the cavalry to reap victory); and secondly, the deliberate advance concept ('bite and hold', kill Germans, use artillery as a massive preparation so the infantry could walk in, ignore cavalry, aim at limited objectives, use artillery power rather than morale, use ground to invite and repel counter-attacks).

The first set of ideas were human-centred, and were espoused by, among others, Haig, Gough, and GHQ in 1916 and 1917; the second set of ideas were weapon-centred, and were espoused by Kitchener, Robertson, Rawlinson, Birch and most of Fourth Army staff in 1915, 1916 and 1917. The first concept was predominant in 1916 and part of 1917, because of the seniority of the proponents, and 'ground' became a symbol of victory and defeat, a question of territoriality.[63] The front line of trenches had 'to be held at all costs', and if lost, 'must be regained at once'.[64] In August 1916, General Sir Neill Malcolm,* Chief of Staff to Gough, GOC Fifth Army, wrote that 'energetic measures and offensive action' were needed, and ground should be gained: 'Every yard of ground gained has great consequences, both material and moral.'[65] The overall sense of ground as an end in itself may also be gauged in a postwar comment by General Perceval, GOC 49 Division, about his Corps commander, Lieutenant General Morland: 'I think that Morland like many others did not like to report to his superiors that he had given up a yard of ground to the enemy.'[66] On the other hand, Robertson in July 1916 told Kiggell, 'Before the war our theory was that anybody who could make ground should make it. This is a dangerous theory until we get through the enemy's trenches.'[67]

However by August 1917, with the evolution of elastic lines of defence, Kiggell and GHQ had changed their minds, although Gough apparently had not. In August 1917 Kiggell wrote a blunt letter to Gough in the midst of Passchendaele telling him that limited objectives were the key: 'Boche beating, not gain of territory. Beat him first and then *en avant*.'[68] The argument here is that the gain-ground supporters were really human-centred and optimistic, the heirs of the cult of the offensive and the psychological battlefield. Victory was achievable and could be won by following the three- or four-stage offensive, and then relying on discipline, morale and sheer courage. On the other hand, the weapon-centred school was pessimistic about decisive results and about what offensives, morale and discipline could achieve, and had earlier and reluctantly come to the conclusion that artillery and not manpower was the key. They were the heirs of the prewar minority fire-power school of thought, but even they expected a return to 'normal psychological' conditions when mobility was restored to war, and the enemy could be demoralized and beaten.

In summary, the prewar Edwardian army came to terms with modern (fire-power) warfare and urban society by developing two powerful sets of ideas: an unofficial doctrine or cult of the offensive, and the associated concept of the psychological battlefield. Both these sets of ideas stemmed from a pessimistic understanding of modern society, coupled with an apprehensive appreciation of modern fire-power, and from institutional preferences for a decisive, predictable, structured, discipline-oriented battlefield. But when the army was confronted by the severe reality of the first years of the war, the officer corps then divided into two schools of thought, human-centred and 'optimistic'; and weapon-centred and 'pessimistic', as Chapter 6 will show. Both these basic concepts were to persist into 1918 and beyond.

Notes

1 For example the Edwardian library of Captain John Bowen-Colthurst, Royal Irish Rifles, contained several military volumes, which had all been read and underlined, including L. S. Amery, *The Problem of the Army* (London, 1903); Lord Roberts, *A Nation in Arms* (London, 1907); Colonel C. E. Calwell, *Small Wars*, 3rd edn (London, 1906); Spenser Wilkinson, *Britain at Bay* (London, 1909); the military correspondent of *The Times*, *Essays and Criticism* (London, 1911); the military correspondent of *The Times*, *The Foundations of Reform* (London, 1908); and Lieutenant Colonel W. H. James, *Modern Strategy*, 2nd edn (London, 1904) (private collection). Regarding specific reforms, see Bidwell and Graham, *Fire-Power*, Book 1; John Gooch, *The Plans of War: the General Staff and British Military*

Strategy c.1900–1916 (London, 1974); Hew Strachan, *European Armies and the Conduct of War* (London, 1983), chs 6–8.

2 These concepts are discussed in articles by S. Van Evera, 'The cult of the offensive and the origins of the First World War', and Jack Snyder, 'Civil-military relations and the cult of the offensive, 1914 and 1984', *International Security*, Vol. 9, no. 1 (1984), pp. 58–146. There is also a very useful article in the same issue by Michael Howard, 'Men against fire: expectations of war in 1914', and a stimulating introduction by Paul Kennedy, 'The First World War and the international power system'. See also Jack Snyder, *The Ideology of the Offensive: Military Decision Making and the Disasters of 1914* (Ithaca, NY, 1984).

3 ibid., S. Van Evera, 'The cult of the offensive', and Jack Snyder, 'Civil-military relations'.

4 Wolseley to W. H. James [the army crammer], 1897, in 'Introduction', in Major W. H. James (ed.), Count Yorck von Wartenburg, *Napoleon as a General*, 2 vols (London, 1902), Vol. 1, p. v.

5 Field Marshal Viscount Wolseley, *The Story of a Soldier's Life*, 2 vols (London, 1903), Vol. 2, p. 368, and Vol. 1, p. 20.

6 Among many examples were Lord Roberts and the National Service League/ conscription group generally. But the voluntary enlistment group such as Ian Hamilton and Colonel Maude were also Social Darwinists. A study of articles in the *United Service Magazine* in the 1910–14 period reveals a strong emphasis on Social Darwinism. A good example is an article by 'Ubique' in 1913. 'Ubique' ûsed a Social Darwinian, anti-intellectual argument to advance the thesis that 'the more virile of modern nations' always had the offensive spirit, for example the Japanese. British youths watching football matches lacked 'discipline and reverence', as did 'the listless flabby loafer ... [of the] towns'. Hence 'Ubique' consciously linked patriotic, virile people with offensive strategy and tactics, while declining or degenerate people opted for a defensive strategy or tactics, 'Ubique', 'The offensive spirit in war', *USM*, Vol. 67 (September 1913), pp. 637–43.

7 Lieutenant General R. S. S. Baden-Powell, *Scouting for Boys: a Handbook for Instruction in Good Citizenship*, revised edn (London, 1908), pp. 280, 263, 266, and *passim*. Liddell Hart, Talk with Edmonds, 16 May 1930, 11/1930/3, Liddell Hart Papers, KCL. In the same conversation Edmonds also claimed that Baden-Powell spent much of his time in Mafeking, and while in charge of the Constabulary, designing fancy uniforms. The uniforms of the Constabulary were the origin of the Boy Scout uniforms. On the other hand Pakenham, *The Boer War*, pp. 396 ff., sees Baden-Powell in a positive light, even if Kitchener and Roberts did not favour him, ibid., p. 496.

8 Major Stewart Murray, 'The internal condition of Great Britain during a great war', *Journal of the Royal United Services Institute* (hereafter *JRUSI*) (December 1913), pp. 1587–8; Major General Robertson, 'Final address to the officers of the senior division, Staff College', 30 November 1912, *Army Review*, Vol. 4 (April 1913), p. 341; Brigadier General Kiggell, speaking in *Report of a Conference of General Staff Officers at the Staff College, 17–20 January 1910*, Staff College Library, Camberley, p. 76. Major General Sir Walter Knox, *The Flaw in our Armour* (London, 1914), p. 138. See also 'Ubique', 'The offensive spirit in war', *USM*, Vol. 67 (September 1913), pp. 642–3, and several other *USM* articles of the same period; and Captain Holmes Wilson, *Offence, Not Defence, or Armies and Fleets* (London, 1907), pp. 89–90, 156–7, claiming that invasion would produce anarchy and the white flag in London and elsewhere.

9 Edmonds, 'Memoirs', ch. XXIII, Edmonds Papers, KCL; General Sir Francis Davis to Edmonds, 21 February 1936, 2/1, Edmonds Papers, KCL.

10 Lieutenant Colonel A. M. Murray, evidence, *Report of the Committee Appointed to Consider the Education and Training of Officers of the Army*, Cmnd Paper 983 (1902), Parliamentary Papers, Vol. 10, p. 188. Another report in 1903 recommended hunting as indispensable and polo as educational for cavalry officers, *Report of the Committee ... to Enquire into the Nature of the Expenses Incurred by Officers of the Army*, Cmnd Paper 1421 (1903), Parliamentary Papers, Vol. 10, pp. 15, 21.

11 'Veto', 'Is "Doctrine" a delusion?', *USM*, Vol. 66 (November 1912); 'Mousquetaire', 'Heretical doctrines of war', *USM*, Vol. 66 (January 1913); A. W. A. Pollock (ed.), 'Strategy in theory and practice', *USM*, Vol. 67 (July 1913); Major General Robertson, 'Final address to the officers', *Army Review*, Vol. 4 (April 1913). Captain Musgrave deprecated the lack of doctrine, 'Various aspects of preparation for war', *Army Review*, Vol. 5 (July 1913).

12 Edmonds, 'Memoirs', chs XIV ff., Edmonds Papers, KCL.

13 Liddell Hart, Talk with Edmonds, 28 December 1933, 11/1933/31, Liddell Hart Papers, KCL. John Gooch gives a more rounded picture of the prewar War Office in his *Plans of War*.

14 Edmonds, 'Memoirs', chs XXII, XXIII, XXIV, Edmonds Papers, KCL. See also Terraine, *Mons*, pt 2, for similar criticism, although implicit rather than explicit.

15 For example, Aylmer Haldane's Diaries.

16 Major General S. C. M. Archibald, Royal Field Artillery, PP/MCR/11, IWM. In contrast, in the Boer War, the Boer artillery did utilize indirect fire, W. A. Griesbach, *I Remember* (Toronto, 1946), p. 274.

17 'Osman', 'Attack and defence', *USM*, Vol. 66 (December 1912), p. 308; 'Pax', 'Offensive or defensive?', *USM*, Vol. 68 (February 1914), p. 537; Major General E. S. May, 'Freedom of manoeuvre', *Army Review*, Vol. 4 (April 1913).

18 T. H. E. Travers, 'Technology, tactics and morale: Jean de Bloch, the Boer War, and British military theory, 1900–1914', *Journal of Modern History*, Vol. 51 (June 1979), pp. 264–86. See also, at random, Major B. F. S. Baden-Powell, *War in Practice* (London 1903); Lieutenant Colonel W. H. James, *Modern Strategy* (London 1903), pp. 166–7; and a host of articles, e.g. Major Budworth, 'Horse Artillery in cooperation with Cavalry', *Cavalry Journal*, Vol. 9 (January 1914), pp. 13–14. Most articles and books after the South African and Russo-Japanese wars emphasized the importance of fire-power, e.g. Colonel C. E. Calwell, *Tactics of To-Day*, 2nd edn (Edinburgh and London, 1909), pp. 2–33 and *passim*; and most important, Colonel G. F. R. Henderson, *The Science of War* [articles dated 1892–1903] (London, 1905), pp. 24 ff. and *passim*. See also Major Lawson (The Greys), 'How can moral qualities best be developed during the preparation of the officer and the man for the duties each will carry out in war?' (Prize Essay), *JRUSI*, Vol. 58 (April 1914), pp. 432, 458–9.

19 *Report of the Committee Appointed to Consider the Education and Training of Officers of the Army*, Cmnd Paper 983 (1902), Parliamentary Papers, Vol. 10, p. 101.

20 Major B. F. S. Baden-Powell remarked, 'It has often been urged' that because the South African war was 'so peculiar' and unlikely to recur, the lessons learned there 'are hardly worth study'; *War in Practice*, p. 7, and cf. his brother Major General R. S. S. Baden-Powell, writing to that effect, ibid., p. 13; James, *Modern Strategy*, pp. 156–7.

21 Henderson, *Science of War*, pp. 369, 371–2, 376, 381.

22 See Chapter 3 and, for example, Kiggell in *Report of a Conference of General Staff Officers at the Staff College, 17–20 January 1910*, Staff College Library, Camberley, p. 27.

23 General Sir Ian Hamilton, *Compulsory Service* (London, 1910), pp. 121–2, 148.

24 Again, as a random example among many, the editor's footnote to Henderson, *Science of War*, p. 153, reads 'The assurance with which frontal attacks were pronounced impossible ... after the South African war, and the complete refutation of those critics by the successes of the Japanese, are well worthy of note'. See also Bidwell and Graham, *Fire-Power*, pp. 31–2.

25 Major General E. A. Altham, *The Principles of War Historically Illustrated* (London, 1914), p. 205. See also Major G. Gilbert, *The Evolution of Tactics* (London, 1907), pp. 178–81.

26 Altham, *Principles of War*, p. 204; Hubert Gough to Roberts, 10 March 1910, Roberts Papers, 7101–23–223, NAM; Knox, *The Flaw in our Armour*, p. 66; Major General Brooke, 'Some reflections', *USM*, Vol. 26 (January 1903), p. 377; [Major Pollock] (ed.), 'Arms and methods in war', *USM*, Vol. 26 (March 1903), p. 627; Lieutenant Colonel Maude, *The Evolution of Modern Strategy* (London, 1905), p. 146; Lieutenant Colonel Maude, *Notes on the Evolution of Infantry Tactics* (London, 1905), p. x. See, for example, the reports of Lieutenant Colonel Aylmer Haldane, Colonel Waters, and Major Home from Manchuria on the need for determined assaults, despite heavy losses, in *The Russo-Japanese War: Reports from British Officers Attached to the Japanese Forces in the Field*, 3 vols (London, 1908), Vol. 1, p. 73, Vol. 2, p. 519, Vol. 3, pp. 205–15; *Field Service Regulations*, Part I, *Operations* (London, 1909), pp. 107, 111, and 114; *Infantry Training* (London, 1914), pp. 127, 134, 146–7 and 163; Colonel Lonsdale Hale (ed.), Major General Haig, *Cavalry Studies Strategical and Tactical* (London, 1907), pp. 7, 142, 173, 180.

27 The General Staff, 'The Offensive under present conditions', 15 June 1915, no. 27, pp. 102–3, WO 158/17, PRO. Robertson, 'Memorandum', 30 April 1917, WO 106/311, PRO. No doubt Robertson was suspicious of French intentions at this time.

28 Maxse, 'Notes on Company Training: 3rd Lecture', no date, but *c*.1910–11, 69/53/1, Maxse Papers, IWM; Major General Butler, Advanced First Army to GOC First Army, November 1915, 69/10/1, Butler Papers, IWM, Kiggell, GHQ, 'Training of Divisions for Offensive Action', 8 May 1916, p. 2, 5201–33–70, Rawlinson Papers, NAM.

29 Henderson, *Science of War*, pp. 412, 374. To his credit Henderson did accept that a revolution in war had occurred, and that his earlier writings might be out of date; James, *Modern Strategy*, p. 165.

30 Evidence at the *Royal Commission on the War in South Africa*, Parliamentary Papers, Vol. 60 (1904), p. 386; Vol. 61 (1904), pp. 404, 107, 273.

31 Major Roper-Caldbeck, *The Nation and the Army* (London, 1910), pp. 21, 215; and Denis Hayes, *The Conscription Conflict* (London, 1949), pp. 42, 63. The debate over conscription has recently been reviewed in R. J. Q. Adams, 'The National Service League and mandatory service in Edwardian Britain', *Armed Forces and Society*, Vol. 12, no. 1 (1985), pp. 53–74.

32 General Smith-Dorrien, 'Introduction', in Altham, *Principles of War*; Field Marshal Earl Roberts, *Fallacies and Facts: an Answer to Compulsory Service* (London, 1911), pp. 94, 247, and see also pp. 239–40, where Roberts claims that Hamilton stands for enthusiasm over discipline; Sir Ian Hamilton, *A Staff*

Officer's Scrap-Book during the Russo-Japanese War (London, 1905), Vol. 1, p. 12; General Sir Ian Hamilton, *Compulsory Service* (London, 1910), p. 131.

33 Major General Baden-Powell to Roberts, 12 January 1904, 7101–23–6, Roberts Papers, NAM.

34 Lieutenant Colonel F. B. Maurice, 'The use and abuse of the initiative', *Army Review*, Vol. 7 (July 1914), pp. 8, 12; L. S. Amery, *The Problem of the Army* (London, 1903), pp. 181–2; Captain Charles Vivian, *The British Army from Within* (New York and Toronto, 1914), p. 12; General Sir Ian Hamilton, *National Life and National Training* (London, 1913), p. 17.

35 Major Lawson, 'How can moral qualities' op. cit., pp. 435–6; Maude, *Evolution of Modern Strategy*, pp. 11–12.

36 For example, a series of articles by Captain Green, Royal Artillery, 'The shadow of the sword', *USM*, Vol. 68 (May, August and September 1914), especially August 1914, p. 486 and September 1914, p. 611. Most officers agreed with Green, although there were some doubters in the 1912–14 period.

37 Brigadier General R. C. B. Haking, *Company Training* (London, 1913), pp. 103, 264, 462, 223 and *passim*. Among senior officers concurring were Roberts, Wolseley, Hamilton, Maude, Haig, R. S. S. Baden-Powell and many others, often using Social Darwinian imagery.

38 The clearest exposition of this concept comes from Colonel Maude, who strongly attacked the concept that 'the slaughter in battle is determined by the nature of the weapon and not by the man', Colonel Maude, *War and the World's Life* (London, 1907), p. 69. For a general summary, see Travers, 'Jean de Bloch; the Boer War, and British military theory', op. cit., pp. 264–86.

39 *Training and Manoeuvre Regulations 1909* (War Office: London), p. 4.

40 *Infantry Training* (War Office: London, 1914), pp. 2–3, 134, 146, 149, 160, 163.

41 *Report of a Conference of General Staff Officers at the Staff College, 13–16 January 1913*, Staff College Library, Camberley, p. 65.

42 Haking, *Company Training, passim*; Altham, *Principles of War*, pp. 296, 303 ff.; Haig, *Cavalry Studies*, pp. 174–5; *Training and Manoeuvre Regulations 1909*, pp. 1–2, 4–5; Major Lawson, 'How can moral qualities', op. cit., pp. 433, 443, 456; 'Xenophon', 'Character training', *Cavalry Journal*, Vol. 8 (January 1913), *passim*; Major Redway, 'A study in defensive war', *USM*, Vol. 68 (June 1914), p. 293.

43 Major Lawson, 'How can moral qualities', op. cit., p. 459; Maude, *War and the World's Life*, p. 46.

44 Captain J. F. C. Fuller, 'The procedure of the infantry attack: a synthesis from a psychological standpoint', *JRUSI*, Vol. 58 (January 1914), pp. 65–6, 84; Major G. H. J. Rooke, 'Shielded infantry and the decisive frontal attack', *JRUSI*, Vol. 58 (June 1914), pp. 774, 782, 783.

45 Travers, 'Jean de Bloch, the Boer War, and British military theory, op. cit., p. 284.

46 Haig, *Cavalry Studies*, pp. 142, 174–5.

47 Haig, Diary, 'A Paper by the General Staff on the Future Conduct of the War', 16 December 1915, p. 13 (my italics), WO 256/7, PRO; Robertson to Rawlinson, 15 June 1916 (my italics), 1/35/99, Robertson Papers, KCL; Rawlinson to Colonel Wigram, 13 July 1916 (my italics), 5201–33–18, Rawlinson Papers, NAM.

48 The schoolboy image is common in prewar Social Darwinian language, emphasizing the duty of playing the game for the side, i.e. as a unit in an

organic whole, Lieutenant Colonel F. B. Maurice, 'The use and abuse of the initiative', *Army Review*, Vol. 7 (July 1914), p. 12; and of course, Baden-Powell, *Scouting for Boys*. But also in many other articles, for example Colonel Simpson, 'An open letter', *USM*, Vol. 68 (January 1914), pp. 402, 414; and Captain Green, 'The shadow of the sword', *USM*, vol. 68 (September 1914), p. 609.

49 G. S. Clive, Diary, 11 March 1915, 2/1, Clive Papers, KCL; Fitzgerald, Diary, 28 September 1915, PP/MCR/118, Fitzgerald Papers, IWM; F. B. Maurice, Diary, 2 October 1915, 3/1/4, Maurice Papers, KCL; General Maxse to Tiny [Maxse], 29 June 1916, 10 August 1916, Maxse Papers, West Sussex Record Office (hereafter WSRO); Kiggell to Robertson, 14 July 1916, 1/22/56, Robertson Papers, KCL; Charteris to Macdonogh, 13 August 1916 and 1 October 1916 (my italics), WO 158/897, PRO.

50 Henry Wilson to Robertson, 22 April 1917, 73/1/6, Wilson Papers, IWM.

51 F. B. Maurice, Diary, 23 May 1915, 3/1/4, Maurice Papers, KCL; Maxse to Tiny [Maxse], 16 July 1916, Maxse Papers, WSRO; 'Appreciation', HQ Fourth Army, 5 August 1916, pp. 7–8, 5201–33–18, Rawlinson Papers, NAM; Wilson, Diary, 28 October 1916, Wilson Papers, IWM.

52 Haldane, Diary, 7 August 1914, 69/36/1, Haldane Papers, IWM; Aylmer Haldane to Edmonds, 11 December 1929, Cab 45/134, PRO.

53 Rawlinson to von Donop, HQ IV Corps, 7 November 1914, and Rawlinson to Kitchener, HQ IV Corps, 6 March 1915, 5201–33–17, Rawlinson Papers; Rawlinson, 'Fourth Army Tactical Notes', 11 April 1916, pp. 1–3, 5201–33–70, Rawlinson Papers; Rawlinson, 'Notes on Operations between 14 September and 3rd October, 1916', p. 13, 5201–33–69, Rawlinson Papers, NAM.

54 T. Bridges, 'Some Further Notes on the Recent Operations', 9 September 1916, p. 1, 47, Montgomery-Massingberd Papers, KCL; General Sir Reginald Stephens, 'Lessons from the Recent Offensive Operations', *c.* September 1916, pp. 9–10, 69/70/1, Stephens Papers, IWM.

55 Lieutenant General Sir A. J. Murray (GHQ Mediterranean Expeditionary Force), to Robertson, March 1916, pp. 55–7, Murray–Robertson Correspondence, vol. 3, Egypt 1916–17, 52463, British Library (hereafter BL).

56 Denis Winter, *Death's Men: Soldiers of the Great War* (London, 1978), pp. 158–9; Lyn Macdonald, *Somme* (London, 1983), pp. 242–3.

57 Edwardes (Fourth Division) to Edmonds, 8 April 1936, Cab 45/133; N. Luxmore (Highland Light Infantry) to Edmonds, 15 May 1930, and Ian Lindsay (168 Brigade) to Edmonds, 16 May 1936, Cab 45/135, PRO; Major General Milward, Diary, 8 May 1916, 6510–143–5, Milward Papers, NAM.

58 Brigadier General Austin Girdwood (GSO 1, 32 Division) to Edmonds, 30 June 1930, Cab 45/134, PRO.

59 General Sir Charles Monro, 'Secret, Notes of Conference, 4 August 1915, by Sir Charles Monro', 69/53/6, Maxse Papers, IWM.

60 Major General A. A. Montgomery, 'Notes on the Lessons of the Operation on the Somme', *c.* November 1916, 48, Montgomery-Massingberd Papers, KCL.

61 Robertson, 'Address to Staff College', no date, but *c.*1913, cited in Major Lawson, 'How can moral qualities', op. cit., p. 443.

62 Haig, '1870 Campaign' (notes from 1896–7), Tactics, 17, Haig Papers, NLS.

63 Eric Leed, *No Man's Land: Combat and Identity in World War I* (Cambridge, 1979), *passim*.

64 'Tactical Training and the Organisation of Works of Defence', Third Army, 1915, p. 1, 37, Montgomery-Massingberd Papers, KCL.

65 N. Malcolm (MGGS, Fifth Reserve Army), Memo, 3 August 1916, WO 158/344, PRO.

66 Major General Sir Edward Perceval (GOC 49 Division), referring to the period 1 July to 14 July 1916, to Edmonds, 29 May 1930, Cab 45/190, PRO.
67 Robertson to Kiggell, 5 July 1916, 4/3, Kiggell Papers, KCL.
68 Kiggell to Gough, 7 August 1917, 5/114, Kiggell Papers, KCL.

[3]

Morale, Fire-power and Technology, *c.*1900–1918

Through the image of the psychological battlefield and the unofficial cult of the offensive, the Edwardian army attempted to come to terms with the hard reality of the new fire-power technology. Because of the continuing development of this technology (and contrary to popular opinion) most officers and staff before 1914 were aware that the next war would be extremely unpleasant and involve very heavy losses. For example, Colonel Meinertzhagen noted in his diary in 1913, 'work at the Staff College also makes me realise what a ghastly business the next war is going to be'.[1] These losses would be inflicted by the new fire-power available in the shape of improved rifles, artillery, and machine-guns.[2] Although none could know the exact date of the outbreak of the First World War, most knew from about 1910 onwards that a major war with Germany was likely.[3] As a result the army was obliged to confront with some urgency the problem of integrating the human side of war with new and still developing technology. This was particularly the case in regard to the offensive, since the new fire-power was generally useful for defence and not attack.[4]

The central problem faced by senior officers and staff seems to have been the severe mental difficulty of integrating, or 'linking' together, what were really two different entities or images of war. On the one hand there were morale and human qualities, in fact the cult of the offensive and the psychological battlefield; and on the other hand, fire-power and new weapons, in fact the technological battlefield. On another level this became the problem of relating tactics to fire-power, and many officers such as Haig and Gough found the transition from one image to another difficult. Fire-power and technology in the shape of new weapons was readily accepted, but the problems of integration into the human side of the equation had not been thought through. A good example of this mental difficulty can be seen in the historical evolution of the machine-gun – a piece of technology that was the essence of fire-power and of divergence from the human face of war.

British army reaction to the early French *mitrailleur* of 1870–1 was to see the gun as an artillery piece and consequently, while advocating the introduction of Gatlings, to reassure the artillery arm that 'the Committee [of 1870] wish it to be distinctly understood that they do not for a moment contemplate their [the Gatlings] supplanting or displacing a single field gun'. Notwithstanding this reassurance (which may have had something to do with the fact that five out of the seven members of the committee were artillery officers!), the Director of Artillery in 1872, Sir John Adye, rejected the *mitrailleur* as a weapon of 'limited powers, and of such exceptional use' that it was 'far more likely to prove an encumbrance than an assistance to the Army'. Adye conceded the *mitrailleur* might be useful for defence, but declared it was 'doubtful whether exceptional compli-cated weapons for purposes so rare should be maintained'. Adye was overruled, but certain attributes of the gun became fixed in the army's mind through these early discussions – the machine-gun was complicated and delicate, it was vulnerable because slow and visible, useful in defence but not attack, it seemed like an artillery piece but was rejected by the artillery, and above all, its uses were fleeting and exceptional.[5] Most of these attributes, particularly the last, stayed with the gun into the First World War, over forty years later.

Summarizing the early reaction to the gun, and recalling that the true machine-gun with an automatic gas recoil system was not invented until 1884 by Hiram Maxim and then not introduced into the army until 1894, it is clear that the *mitrailleur* faced two main obstacles in the British army. First, traditional loyalties to other arms shunted the gun to a peripheral status, except in colonial warfare; and second, since the gun did not clearly belong to any particular arm or have any particular constituency, this meant that its role was also fixed as peripheral – as a weapon of unusual or exceptional use. The important point to note is that the British army, represented by senior officers, accepted the new technology readily enough, with few exceptions. But having accepted what was a new source of fire-power, albeit imperfect, the army directed the gun into acceptable and traditional patterns. The problem was not getting the gun accepted as a piece of technology, but what was done with it.

Through the 1880s and 1890s, the machine-gun was found to be valuable in colonial warfare, yet the problems offset the virtues, such as the difficulty of choosing between different patterns of gun, and the hazards of transporting the gun and its ammunition in the field. It remained in artillery eyes as a rival to the field gun, and in other eyes continued as a bulky, awkward subsidiary to other weapons on the defence. Officers understood that it could deliver a high volume of fire, but the emphasis was on obtaining a better quality weapon rather than larger quantities of machine-guns.[6] With the South African war the machine-gun emerged as an important weapon, although still with problems of size and transport (60 pounds plus water), vulnerability to jamming, and mechanical problems (the water-cooled Maxim either froze or steamed), while the War Office Committee of 1901 noted that its tactical role was not well understood.[7] However, the South African war did focus attention on the machine-gun and split those who thought about it into three schools, whose attitudes persisted into and through the first years of the World War. These were first the enthusiasts, such as Major General F. W. Kitchener (brother to the Field Marshal), Major E. H. Allenby (the future Army commander), and Lieutenant Colonel W. P. Campbell; secondly, the cautious or muddled progressives (the great majority of officers), who usually saw the weapon as useful in defence; and thirdly, the opponents (some artillery and cavalry officers, and some uninterested senior officers such as General Sir Neville Lyttelton), who apparently did not want to discuss the gun at all.[8]

A 1901 War Office machine-gun committee did make recommendations for the Infantry Training manual of 1902, but the results of the South African war were not clear-cut from the point of view of the machine-gun,[9] partly because of its mechanical failures, but mainly because of its size, visibility, and problems of transportation. A surviving film from the South African war vividly reveals some of the problems. It shows ten men attending several horses, who are carrying the .303 Maxim, tripod and ammunition. An attempt is made to take the equipment off the horses, and after much milling around, confusion and dust, this is finally achieved. After considerable delay the sizeable gun is eventually mounted on a large tripod, ready for action.[10] In addition to these problems, the officer in command of the machine-gun section in South Africa was usually a junior and uninfluential, and was soon removed to other duties.

With the Russo-Japanese war of 1904–5, the viability of the machine-gun was definitely established, particularly in regard to its status as a fire-power weapon. War Office reports from Manchuria stressed the value of the gun, although discussion now centred on the *organization* of the weapon – should machine-guns be brigaded, should there be a battery organization, was it a cavalry weapon, could it replace artillery, and so on – while its official tactical role remained the same as thirty-five years earlier, 'Machine-guns are essentially weapons of opportunity'. The gun was supposed to assist the infantry and cavalry, although the two guns of the infantry Battalion still needed one officer and fourteen other ranks to handle them.[11]

In fact the problem of the machine-gun was still the same as in 1870–1, it was accepted as a piece of technology, but not as part of the army. Umpires at manoeuvres ignored the gun, while the unwritten army rule was to just 'stick them in somewhere', and hard thinking about machine-gun tactics was generally avoided.[12] But starting around 1909–10, due to the tense international situation, and particularly because of reports of other countries adding larger numbers of machine-guns to their establishments, there was a definite push from the then CIGS, Nicholson, and from Major C. W. Scott, a staff officer under the MGO. In a report on machine-gun equipment, dated 18 April 1911, Major Scott pointed out that a minute from the MGO of 8 March 1910, had said 'No new machine-gun is to be considered at present'. Whether this was because the MGO was waiting for new types of machine-guns, or for a new calibre cartridge, or was inactive because of financial restraints, or whether there was a certain amount of inertia, is not clear. However, the Royal Navy had pushed ahead on its own with trials of a new Vickers light machine-gun, and the CIGS did not intend to let the matter drop. As a result of a letter from the CIGS to the MGO on 25 March 1911, the MGO was persuaded to go ahead with trials of the light Maxim. The correspondence leaves no doubt that the CIGS was pressing for action, while the MGO, waiting for new machine-gun patterns and possibly a new cartridge, was dragging his feet.[13] As a result two Vickers .303 machine-guns were sent for trial in 1911, with a view to 'supplying immediate requirements with this gun', although these were supplied first to the cavalry in 1912 and only later to the infantry.[14]

At the same time, much the same process was occurring with automatic rifles. Here again the tense international situation, the realization that some other countries were experimenting with these weapons, and pressure from the CIGS, Nicholson, caused tests to go ahead. The reports of the Committee on Automatic Rifles show repeated testing failures, while the CIGS kept pressing for more action. However, a final report in January 1914 stated there would be nothing for 'some years to come'.[15] Strangely enough, the Lewis gun, which could be considered tactically as an automatic rifle (as was recognized in 1915),[16] was available in 1912 for testing, but was being fitted into aircraft, for aircraft to aircraft use. This research seems to have been stimulated by the Small Arms Committee, and the first firing of the Lewis gun from a plane occurred on 24 July 1912. The Lewis gun, however, was not available to the infantry until the end of 1914.[17] A final example from this period (1912) concerns machine-guns for anti-aircraft fire. Again the staff of the MGO and Kiggell, then Director of Staff Duties, pressed the matter forward, while this time Colonel Ruggles-Brise, Commandant of the School of Musketry, Hythe, dragged his feet in suggesting reasons why the anti-aircraft machine-gun should not be developed. The matter was complicated by Kiggell who wanted a tripod that enabled the gun to be used both vertically against aircraft and horizontally against troops. The argument over tripods dragged on and the trials were finally halted in November 1914.[18]

The introduction and evolution of the machine-gun as a new piece of technology over a number of years shows that the technology itself was readily accepted, but that the internal logic of the technology, i.e. the role of the machine-gun, was consciously or unconsciously resisted. After the Russo-Japanese war it was harder to escape the fire-power logic of the weapon, but conscious or unconscious tactical confusion still relegated the machine-gun to secondary status. At the highest levels, notably from the CIGS, Nicholson, there was pressure to test and produce a new lighter Vickers gun and an automatic rifle, but this pressure ran into technical difficulties and delays from departments such as the MGO's that had actually to produce the weapons. It is perhaps significant that in the 1909–14 period, an automatic rifle did not actually emerge; the Vickers light machine-gun was first tested by the Royal Navy; the Lewis gun was first tested for use in aeroplanes; the Vickers light machine-gun was issued first to the cavalry in 1912 rather than the infantry (even if there were reasons for this, there were also reasons in the opposite direction); and much time was spent testing an anti-aircraft machine-gun, which likewise did not appear.[19] The likely reason for these factors, apart from technical problems and financial exigency, is that the tactical role for the machine-gun had not yet been worked out. Indeed, at the 1910 General Staff conference, the CIGS admitted there was confusion over instructions and tactics and that a machine-gun manual had been under consideration for some time in the General Staff. There were various opinions, he said, but doctrine would emerge. Probably because of the re-armament with the new Vickers light machine-gun a new doctrine did not emerge, and the first tactical doctrine specifically for machine-guns seems to have come from a memorandum by Robertson on 26 May 1915 advocating the brigading of machine-guns.[20] Until then, discussion of machine-gun tactics was split between *The Handbook for the .303 Maxim* (1907), *Cavalry Training* (1907), *Field Service Regulations 1909* (1910), and *Infantry Training* (1914).

The machine-gun, together with other existing and projected weapons, formed a central focus of the wider fire-power debate that took place in the British army before 1914. Yet, as in the case of the machine-gun, it can be argued that the most basic problem was how to integrate technology and the image of the human-centred battlefield. Again, as with the debate over the machine-gun, there seemed to be three basic prewar schools of thought regarding fire-power: the small group of fire-power enthusiasts led by Major McMahon of Hythe; the large middle ground of cautious or muddled progressives; and a significant opposition group, formed of various factions, some apathetic, some defending traditional loyalties, and some more worried about the morale of the attack. Underlying much of the fire-power debate was a curious reluctance to enunciate doctrine, as outlined in Chapter 2. The argument was always the same – that to lay out doctrine, by which all the pieces of the army were to fit together, was to 'stereotype' methods, tactics, and strategy. The army disliked doctrine because common sense was preferred, because stated doctrine was vaguely un-British since it carried continental overtones, and because doctrine limited initiative and flexibility. There was justification for avoiding a fixed doctrine at an evident time of change, yet there was an intellectual lassitude about senior officers that deprecated a theoretical approach. The official word in early 1914 was that doctrine was not acceptable, particularly in regard to fire and movement methods, and the reason again given was that doctrine introduced 'stereotyped' methods.[21] What was actually meant by this was revealed in discussion at the General Staff conference of January 1914. Colonel du Cane* (then an artillery staff officer) remarked that the French were inclined to the human, psychological and moral factor in war, and so were less stereotyped tactically. Du Cane went on to describe a French article that did emphasize fire-power tactics in the approach over open ground, but admitted that such laid-down tactics would not appeal to a number of British officers. Indeed, Brigadier General Sir Archibald Murray rejected the French ideas as introducing a stereotyped fire and movement doctrine. What was actually being said in this discussion was that doctrine, or stereotyped methods, damaged the morale or human factor in war, and deprived men in the attack of their desire to close with the enemy at all costs.[22] In other words, doctrine and fixed fire-power tactics were rejected, not because they might be wrong, but because they did not fit the Edwardian image of war as the human battlefield. In the last analysis, doctrine, fire-power and technology were viewed with caution, yet their very necessity and presence caused the older image of war as a matter of discipline and courage to be re-emphasized.

A crucial point in the British army's turn away from an emphasis on fire-power occurred at the General Staff conference in 1910. It was at this conference that Major McMahon outlined his minority fire-power views. However, Brigadier General Kiggell responded by saying that although after the South African war the General Staff had said that fire decides combat, and that the sword and the bayonet were out, 'this idea is erroneous and was proved to be so in the late war in Manchuria. Everyone admits that. Victory is won actually by the bayonet, or by the fear of it. This fact was proved beyond doubt in the late war.' Although other officers present such as Brigadier General May said that the machine-gun was extremely important, the CIGS reinforced Kiggell's point by noting that War Office manuals had now changed from 'The decision is obtained by superiority of fire' to 'A superiority of fire makes the decision possible'. The CIGS went on to say that some officers had objected to McMahon's claim that volume of fire was more important than accuracy, but that McMahon had really meant to convey the fact that the accuracy of a volume of fire depended on individual accuracy, 'and with this view we shall, I think, all agree'. The CIGS was actually more interested in obtaining general agreement than in staking new ground, and his devaluation of McMahon's statement together with his reference to accuracy showed that the General Staff really had come down on the side of the Edwardian human paradigm of war.[23]

The issue of the machine-gun at the General Staff conferences showed that the acceptance of technology was not a simple 'yes' or 'no' question. Rather, the prevailing human paradigm of war meant that while the technology of the machine-gun and its fire-power was accepted, it was accepted only under certain limitations of number and role. These limitations meant that the General Staff for various reasons did not increase the prewar number of machine-guns per Battalion beyond two,[24] while the role of the machine-gun was seen as supplementary, namely, that of a weapon of 'opportunity' and of reserve fire. Another sign of the times was the reaction to J. F. C. Fuller's previously mentioned 1914 article on the tactics of penetration. Despite certain misunderstandings by Fuller,[25] his April 1914 lecture, subsequently printed as an article in November 1914, offered an alternative to the British army concepts of the wearing-out battle and decisive assault. Fuller called for mass infantry penetration by means of quick firing artillery and flanking machine-gun fire, with the light infantry of the future armed with machine-guns preceding and flanking the attack. Although Fuller had not thought hard enough about the actual function of the projected fire-power of his plan, it was at least a starting point for further discussion. But F. B. Maurice and Kiggell told Fuller he was 'lacking in military judgement', and that British army doctrine, *Field Service Regulations 1909*, 'was envelopment, more envelopment and always envelopment. I had Yalu, Nan Shan, Liao Yang and Mukden thrust down my throat, but I was not convinced',[26] wrote Fuller.

The problem as some saw it, was to convert the British army from a fundamental belief in the human battlefield, to a belief in combined manpower and fire-power, and the technology and tactics to support this. The problem was obviously not a simple one, as the attitude of Aylmer Haldane makes clear. Haldane had gone to Manchuria in 1904 and 1905 and had seen the effect of machine-guns on attacking troops, and he told the 1909 General Staff conference that in Manchuria it was 'impossible to take a position which is well defended by machine-guns until these guns have been put out of action'. Yet at the same 1909 conference Haldane argued that although the infantry now thought a thick attacking firing line absurd and wanted to advance on a very wide dispersed front, yet the infantry should also realize 'it is by obtaining superiority of fire and not by avoiding loss that infantry alone can win battles'. Haldane therefore opted for a thick attacking line, and Kiggell in the same debate wanted three, four or five men per yard to get the decisive attack home, as could be learnt, he said, from military history. Haldane (and Kiggell) realized the power of the machine-gun, yet saw it as a defensive weapon, and because the attack was the crucial element of infantry tactics, the fire-power of the machine-gun was altered conceptually to fit in with the absolute necessity of the attack, and it was simply assumed that achieving superiority of fire meant putting more men in the firing line. The concept of allowing weapons to achieve the same fire-power with fewer rather than more men did not fully occur to the staff. Ultimately the staff expected the crucial element to be manpower, despite anticipating heavy losses.[27] If the prewar machine-gun had been lighter and had been conceived of as a less visible and vulnerable offensive weapon, as some officers such as Lieutenant Colonel G. M. Lindsay* were saying at the GHQ Small Arms School later on in 1917, then tactics would have been adapted to the weapon rather than the other way round.[28]

At the risk of making generalized assertions, it would appear that senior officers before the war were mostly adherents to a paradigm of war that fixed on the psychological battlefield as the key element of warfare, with the real problem being whether the troops had the courage and the will to cross the fire-swept zone, suffer heavy casualties in the attack, and still keep going. The problem of facing defensive fire-power had become partially a moral problem[29] – would the troops actually face up to modern fire-power? Robertson put the matter clearly in January 1914, when he expressed the general fear of senior officers regarding the determination of the troops – the army must do nothing to 'interfere with the desire of the troops to push into the fight at all costs'. And in a 1906 discussion regarding machine-guns, a Colonel Inglefield simply doubted whether troops would go forward at all against heavy fire.[30]

The manpower and morale orientation of most senior officers continued into the war, so that it was not until 10 May 1918 that the first full official doctrine regarding machine-guns as a separate arm emerged, actually from First Army HQ. In this document, and in earlier lectures from the machine-gun exponent, G. M. Lindsay, the point was stressed that it was fire-power that counted, not numbers, and it was machines that must replace men. 'The strength of a force', wrote Lindsay in April 1916, 'is frequently judged by the number of the individuals of which it is composed. This point is fundamentally wrong.' Lindsay had talked to GHQ in May 1916 about his concept of 'Machine-Gun Forces', with little result apparently, although at lower levels there was some development of the machine-gun organization.[31] In fact in 1916 at GHQ there was some confusion about the provision of machine-guns and Lewis guns, Haig in March 1916 wanting fewer machine-guns, and Kiggell in May 1916 wanting more. Furthermore, there was a considerable argument in late 1915 between the CIGS and the Adjutant General (AG), the former wanting more guns, which would replace men, while the latter evidently thought men the more useful and no doubt worried about where to find sufficient men for machine-gun training.[32]

Underneath all this discussion, however, was a fundamental vision of war which could not easily integrate technology involving fire-power with a human-oriented battlefield. There existed a fatal breach between the two. A glance at *Infantry Training* (1914) shows how the General Staff who wrote the manual devalued fire-power in contrast with the emphasis placed on the human aspect of the battlefield. Partly this was because the infantry must be encouraged at all costs to push across the deadly fire-zone and assault the enemy. But partly it was a difficulty in thinking through the consequences of fire-power. Thus when discussing the machine-gun the 1914 infantry training manual argued that because of its concentrated fire a small error would cause it to miss the target entirely, whereas the target would 'probably be struck by several shots from riflemen making the same error in aim or elevation'. This was to argue that inaccuracy was valuable when done by a rifle but not when done by a fire-power weapon! After listing various other limitations of the machine-gun, including the by now mandatory reference to the expenditure of ammunition being out of proportion to results (without stopping to think what results were actually being considered – one wonders if the General Staff paid any attention to the Hythe School of Musketry results with the machine-gun), the authors of the infantry training manual concluded with the traditional forty-year-old opinion: 'Machine Guns are essentially weapons of opportunity'. Then when the infantry training manual considered the machine-gun in defence, the logic became tortuous. Machine-guns would lose their mobility when permanently allotted to the defensive line (surely a tautology), and machine-guns could rarely be used as a reserve of fire for special purposes because the enemy's intentions would not be known in advance (another self-fulfilling tautology). So, 'For these reasons it should be exceptional to employ more than a limited number of guns with the firing line in a defensive position'.[33]

The authors of *Infantry Training* (1914) had not been able to bridge the gap between fire-power technology and the human-centred battlefield when discussing the machine-gun. They also found difficulty when considering how to link fire-power in the assault and the morale of the defence, when choosing the moment of the attack. Doctrine stated that the climax of the attack was the final assault, made possible by superiority of fire over the defenders. Yet 'Premature attempts to assault an enemy who has not been demoralized by previous exposure to well-directed fire are, however, likely to be repulsed with heavy loss'. Generally, however, the assault must proceed without halting to seek cover because of the 'moral effect on the enemy' of the assault. A determined advance has the greatest effect 'on the nerves and ['military' was deleted here] spirit of the defenders'. Therefore the 'ultimate object of demoralizing the enemy and then assaulting him must always be kept in view'.[34] The problem with this scenario was that the authors of the infantry training manual were trying to tie together two incomparable or incompatible entities, a mechanical superiority of fire and a human loss of morale. At the General Staff conference in 1909 Colonel du Cane had put his finger on this vulnerable linkage when he said that troops reached the final fire position, and then did not know what to do, because 'It is extremely difficult to judge whether you have gained sufficient moral superiority over your enemy to allow of a successful assault being delivered'. The only solution Colonel du Cane (and Kiggell, Haldane and others) could arrive at was simply to accentuate the human side of the equation by putting more men into the firing line until moral superiority was presumably guaranteed. In other words, the success of the assault, which was supposed to be predicated on fire superiority, could only be translated or linked to moral superiority and success by heavily weighting the human side of the equation. Or, more accurately, because there was often no obvious observable linkage between fire-power and moral superiority, staff officers basically gave up the game and ultimately emphasized the human assault 'at all costs'.[35]

Much the same difficulty can be noticed with prewar infantry training as reported by Brigadier General Maxse with the 1st Guards Brigade at Colchester and Aldershot, and as described by Aylmer Haldane with 10th Infantry Brigade at Shorncliffe. Maxse seemed to be trying to bridge the gap between fire-power technology and the human battlefield by stressing on the one hand individual efficiency, and on the other 'masses of men in sufficient lines one behind the other [which] will go through anything'. Aylmer Haldane was influenced by French authors, and he emphasized rapid rushes forward and the use of the bayonet following fire, rather than combined fire and movement. Evidently he was worried enough by memories of the South African habit of infantry not pushing forward to relegate fire-power to a lesser role, despite his Manchurian experience, and to stress the moral value of the bayonet charge. Hence in August 1912 he watched the 1st Royal Irish Fusiliers charge 150 yards across open ground and conceded it was rather far, 'but in actuality the enemy would have probably flown when bayonets were fixed'. On other occasions he wrote in his diary 'bayonets not to be fixed too soon as otherwise the effect on the enemy will be less', or he reprimanded umpires for allowing the defence to hold on too long, or he wanted to practise the men 'in cheering to strengthen their lungs and make them cheer as loud as possible so as to effect, by vibration, the enemy's nerves'.[36] Clearly Haldane had solved the problem of linking fire-power and human nature by largely ignoring the problem and insisting that human nature could do the job more or less by itself. Fire and movement was the official link, but for Haldane, movement and morale were all.

The artillery was also the subject of considerable prewar debate and discussion, and here too the link between fire-power and the human battlefield was a difficult one to forge. Fortunately this subject has been ably covered elsewhere,[37] but it is clear that prewar co-operation between artillery and infantry was largely absent, and that most General Staff officers were not well informed about artillery needs and desires. They thought that the artillery was merely an accessory to infantry, and did not appreciate the enormous fire-power that modern artillery could produce. As a result there was little interest, for example, in counter battery work, and instead an emphasis on the mobile human-centred battlefield,[38] while the tendency of Manchuria towards siege war was termed by the General Staff in 1909 to be 'exceptional'.[39] Haig, for example, thought of moving warfare, to which the artillery should adapt. He could not decide how the fire-power technology of the artillery should *primarily* be used – whether it would be a force that demoralized and neutralized the defenders, or a physically destructive force that destroyed obstacles. Because of his cavalry instincts he basically favoured the former, but he normally confused or integrated the two. Hence in evidence presented after the South African war, Haig declared that the object of the artillery is 'to level at a distance the material, intellectual and moral obstacles that prevent the victorious forward advance of the other arms of the force'. Haig concluded that concentration and rapidity were the keys to the 'moral effect of all firing'. It can be seen that for Haig the battlefield was a predictable place where moral forces played a primary role, and so he felt that the function of artillery was also primarily to demoralize or neutralize the defenders, although he also recognized the physically destructive power of the arm.[40] Ironically, if Haig had had his way in regard to a short bombardment on 1 July 1916 at the Somme, followed by a rapid advance, that day might have turned out better, providing the wire could have been cut and the objectives were not too distant.

Haig's understanding of the artillery, therefore, related to his basic understanding of the modern battlefield as an organized arena for the triumph or defeat of an army through its morale. Thus the link between artillery and man was solved by Haig in the prewar period by simply assimilating the artillery to the human side of the equation, by seeing the fire-power technology of the artillery as only an accessory to the human battlefield. Indeed, in jotting down notes from an 1896 Staff College lecture, Haig at one point wrote, 'It must be recollected that Infantry wins battles, and the artillery is the auxiliary arm!' This attitude seems to have remained with Haig, since he subsequently had difficulty in seeing the infantry and the artillery as equal partners.[41]

One more example of the process of linking technology and the human-centred battlefield is worth considering, namely the tank. Leaving aside the controversial question of the origins of the tank, it would appear that the Army Council, the War Office and GHQ were somewhat naturally reluctant to divert resources from arms they were familiar with to an experiment that was still in its infancy in 1914 and 1915. Thus there was considerable resistance to this technical alternative, and Major General Sir Ernest Swinton* claimed that in February 1915 the War Office turned down the tank idea. In turn the War Office argued, in the person of Major General Sir Geoffrey Scott-Moncrieff, Director of Fortifications and Works at the War Office, that Swinton's 'visit on the 4th January [1915] was however most important because you came from GHQ. The Army Council would not agree to me initiating schemes unless GHQ either asked me to do so or gave approval'. Swinton concluded 'It would appear to have been against etiquette and good taste for the military brains in this country to have put forward anything to defeat the enemy?'[42]

Swinton implied that it was his initiative at GHQ that set the ball rolling, but T. G. Hetherington, a member of the Admiralty Landship committee, declared that it was neither the War Office nor GHQ that supplied the specifications for the tanks, and that Swinton was wrong. In fact it was Lloyd George who supplied the specifications, wrote Hetherington, and it was the War Office who said that wire could not be forced. In 1915 Hetherington visited GHQ at St Omer, as tank designs were under way, and was received by Major Hutchinson, later Lord Hutchinson, who refused permission for Hetherington to check conditions of wire and trenches, and lectured Hetherington's tank group on their waste of public money.[43]

Nevertheless, the tank was developed, and was first used at the battle of the Somme, in September 1916. The reception of the tank by Fourth Army and GHQ was coloured, of course, by its newness, and subsequently by a realization of its lack of durability. Moreover, there was a belief in GHQ that tanks should be used, but not if their production interfered with the output of any other war material.[44] But in August and September 1916, the reaction of senior staff was to bridge the gap between the tank as a new form of technology and the human battlefield by turning the tank into one of the three traditional arms. Thus in August 1916 GHQ argued that tanks should use surprise and rapid movement and get to close quarters with the enemy rather like cavalry; or should be used as 'extra weight' against strong points, i.e. as a replacement for dense infantry ranks; or finally should be used as light mobile artillery.[45] Like the artillery, the tank was seen as auxiliary to the infantry, and like the machine-gun, it proved difficult for senior staff officers to conceive of the tank as a weapon with a logic of its own, and particularly with tactics of its own. Yet it must be said also that GHQ and Fourth Army staff *were* open to the idea of using tanks, in fact Haig was perhaps desperate to use them as a breakthrough weapon, just as he had been eager to use gas on 25 September 1915 at Loos.

It would appear that there were several opinions regarding the tank in 1916. One group, including the Secretary of the War Council, Lieutenant Colonel Maurice Hankey, Swinton, Fuller, Lloyd George and Winston Churchill, strongly supported the use of tanks but wanted to keep them a secret until they could be used in a large-scale mass attack. Another group, headed by Haig, but including some divisional commanders like Aylmer Haldane, wanted to use the tanks as a surprise, breakthrough weapon, relying upon moral effect and boldness. Then Kiggell at GHQ, and Rawlinson and his Fourth Army HQ, were willing to use the tanks, but were cautious about their value, and thought them vulnerable to artillery fire. Finally, there was a detached and sceptical group comprising most officers, who either did not think about the tank at all, or thought that they would not be useful, or did not want to consider them until they had been proven in action. This amorphous group included Kitchener, Robertson, Gough and various divisional commanders, and in their favour it must be said that the tanks of 1916 *were* slow, vulnerable, unreliable and exhausting to their crews.

It is instructive to consider the arguments between Haig and Rawlinson over the use of tanks for the 15 September 1916 offensive. Initially Rawlinson had been very sceptical about their value, although Haig had shown interest from an early date. Then Rawlinson saw a demonstration in August 1916 and wrote in his diary: '"Tanks" at St Riquier 3 p.m. Interesting show. Less visible and less noisy than I expected. They will be most useful at night. Doubtful if possible use by day in line.' Two days later Rawlinson made out his plan for the 15 September offensive, using tanks. Remembering the success of 14 July 1916 and keeping in mind his thoughts about the night use of tanks, Rawlinson suggested that tanks should be kept a mystery as long as possible, but if they were to be used, should not be used in daylight because of vulnerability to artillery fire. Instead they should attack at night with infantry and then be withdrawn. Haig objected to all of this, jotting down notes on Rawlinson's plan such as tanks 'shd. be thrown with *determination* into the fight, regardless of cost!', and that tanks could be used in daylight since 'the country has valleys and covered and concealed approaches'. The night attack idea was not feasible, noted Haig, and the whole plan was far too cautious, 'So use tanks boldly, press success, demoralise enemy and try and capture his guns'.[46] Loyally Rawlinson retired and drew up his plan again with tanks to be used in daylight, but keeping ahead of the infantry. Once again Haig objected, writing a note on Rawlinson's new draft that infantry and tanks should start together, with the infantry attacking trenches and the tanks attacking strong points, while two or three tanks should push forward to the enemy support and reserve trenches. Despite Haig's comments, Rawlinson apparently stuck to his idea of tanks keeping ahead of the infantry, and these ideas were ratified after the offensive by Kiggell at

GHQ, who in early October 1916 argued that tanks should arrive at the enemy trenches ahead of the infantry, but only by fifty yards. However Kiggell was quite clear that tanks were 'entirely accessory to the ordinary methods of attack, i.e. to the advance of infantry in close cooperation with artillery'.[47]

Summarizing GHQ and Fourth Army attitudes toward the tank in 1916, the reaction was one of cautious acceptance of it as a piece of new technology, as in the case of the machine-gun, but with a tendency to slot that piece of technology into understood and 'traditional' roles. This was natural in 1916 due to the novelty of the tank, and not surprisingly Haig saw it as a kind of armoured cavalry shock and surprise weapon, while Rawlinson thought of it primarily as armoured infantry, depending on the night or day plan. Both had difficulty in relating it to the human battlefield, and GHQ had problems in developing tactics that firmly brought together man and machine.

However, there were also innovative ideas held by tank proponents, and also by some Divisional and Corps commanders, for example Aylmer Haldane who in October 1916 conceived of a form of *blitzkrieg* warfare. Haldane wanted to use tanks for flattening wire, with predicted artillery firing at zero hour only, the use of mines and light railways, and aeroplanes to bomb enemy HQs and key points. In early November 1916 Haldane considered using tunnels, mines, short-range trench mortars and Lewis guns to break the first line, long-range guns for the second line, and tanks to break the third line, perhaps on the second day of the offensive. Going faster was a matter of better tactics and administration, thought Haldane, although a lecture on 13 November 1916 by Major General Elles* (commander of the Tank Corps in France) disillusioned him as to the reliability of the tank.[48]

By 1917 its poor mechanical performance had led to something of a rejection syndrome and senior officers expected very little from the tank, especially if it was to be used over the poor ground selected for the Passchendaele offensive. Elles reported that, before Passchendaele, 'GHQ and Fifth Army were perfectly frank upon the point that regarded any success by tanks as a windfall ... and tanks must take their chance. Every resource was to be put in whether it pulled its full weight or not.'[49] In August 1917, during the Passchendaele offensive, GHQ's attitude to the tank was conditioned by its continuing poor durability and by its almost self-fulfilling difficulties, and consequently led to a re-emphasis on the tank's accessory status. A letter from Kiggell to Gough at this time argued that tanks should be used for rounding up pockets of resistance, but this would be *after* the attack had passed on. They could be used in woods also (one wonders how) and for wire-cutting and against machine-guns not destroyed by artillery. If tanks could go faster, they could be used with cavalry – again Kiggell could not visualize tanks replacing cavalry (or infantry) – or by simply assisting other arms. Finally Kiggell summarized, echoing the way in which the machine-gun had been described in 1914: 'In fact their [tanks] uses will always be special and subject to suitable conditions'.[50]

In August 1917 J. F. C. Fuller and Elles tried to persuade GHQ of the need for a separate tank offensive, but were turned down due to an alleged lack of infantry divisions to support the attack.[51] Then after the failure of Passchendaele was officially recognized, the successful Cambrai tank offensive went ahead in November 1917, despite different opinions over the objectives of the tank plan. However in 1918, Haig and GHQ remained sceptical about the tank, and J. F. C. Fuller later claimed that Haig issued an order in April 1918 to disband one tank Brigade in order to supply infantry reinforcements during the spring 1918 German offensive. But Fuller hung up the order, saw Churchill and Henry Wilson privately and saved the Brigade.[52] According to Elles, Haig and GHQ were not alone in 1918 in adopting a detached viewpoint, willing to use the tank as an extra resource, but not giving it a role that reflected its own logic; in other words, accepting the tank, but not really thinking through the capability of a new weapon. Elles maintained that non-tank officers were divided into two camps:[53]

> those who believed, and some passionately, in the possibility of the tank and those who disbelieved entirely. We were well in the middle of 1918 before there was any considerable body of the opinion that the advantages and disadvantages of the new weapon might be weighed against each other. Up to that time there were neither pro's nor anti's and no half way opinion at all.

The reason for this evolution of opinion seems to be that acceptance of a piece of technology in the prewar and First World War period tended to follow a particular pattern. Taking the machine-gun and the tank as examples, the following evolution is seen to take place: (1) the invention and introduction of the new piece of technology, with some resistance at the higher staff levels and some arm resistance; (2) after a certain period of time, ready acceptance of the technology, especially at middle and lower levels of the officer corps; but then an important stage occurs, (3) a corresponding reluctance to think through the logic of the new weapon, and therefore a tendency to relegate the weapon to traditional, peripheral or subordinate roles. At this important stage (4) there emerge small but vigorous groups of supporters and opponents, with a large middle ground of mostly non-thinkers; but (5) from the small support group there emerge further one or two individuals who articulate appropriate tactics for the new weapon, which eventually enable the weapon to assume either a semi-autonomous or separate role according to its own logic, and which firmly integrate the weapon into the tactical system of the army.

There also seem to be two other underlying fundamentals in the more general context of dominant fire-power technology and the major new pieces of technology – the machine-gun, the tank and the aeroplane.[54] First, the difficulty in finding the right connection or linkage between man and technology, between morale and fire-power, and thus secondly the difficulty of making the shift from the image of the psychological battlefield to the image of the technological battlefield. In other words, this is a shift from a qualitative image of war to a quantitative image. In his introduction to Jacques Ellul's book, *The Technological Society*, John Wilkinson remarks that it is the essence of technique (organization, methods, means) '*to compel the qualitative to become quantitative*, and in this way to force every stage of human activity and man himself to submit to its mathematical calculations'.[55] For some time, warfare had been assuming quantitative aspects, but in the period 1900–14 most British senior staff and officers still conceived war to be essentially qualitative, i.e. human centred. Yet the essence of the new fire-power technology *was* quantitative in the sense of requiring war to become ever more mathematical and calculable, and the human-oriented, qualitative battlefield was in fact in the process of eroding into quantitative terms during 1914 and 1915. It seemed that war had become a matter of precision and calculation, while earlier conceptions of morale and discipline were difficult to apply in 1914–18 just because they could not be measured. This did not mean they were no longer important, but simply that the quantitative logic of war altered their importance, despite efforts to continue to make morale a central factor, for example in GHQ's analyses during the Somme.

Some examples of the quantitative impulse can be seen in the emergence of the 'wastage' return in early 1915.[56] Of course the Adjutant General's office had always calculated numbers of men required, but now the language of war revealed the way in which war had become primarily quantitative. For example, in 1916 the AG's office issued a 'Memo on Wastage of the Forces in the Field' which reduced the matter of losses to a new kind of calculation. Wastage was seen as 6.15 per cent of the men in the field, while 510 Battalions × 971 men per Battalion × 29.673 weeks average Battalion time in the field equalled 14,694,366 'regular infantry man weeks'. Then the memorandum moved on to banking language, noting deficits, credits and surplus of 115,000 men by the end of September 1916. However, the memorandum considered that a thirty-division offensive would lead to 195,000 casualties (an underestimation for the Somme of around 250 per cent), so that the surplus would be 'consumed'. And after the offensive there would be 'further expenditure of men'.[57]

Another example of the urge to quantitative precision came with the development of the large-scale artillery timetable. Already in April 1915 the First Army had called for an elaborate artillery timetable and the strict adherence of the infantry to it, so that 'The whole operation can be regulated with the greatest precision'.[58] A similar example of the mathematical impulse occurs in November 1915 when Butler, MGGS First Army, sensing the new logic of the battlefield, conceived of a plan to break through, based on calculations of weight and depth for the attack. There would be five lines of attackers for breaking through three lines of defence, and each line of attack would have five waves of men. Hence the normal attack would require twenty-five waves of men, and Butler worked out a precise distance × frontage × men equation.[59] This sense of the mathematical or structured offensive was carried over into the Somme with its careful artillery plan and attacking waves, so that an officer at VIII Corps HQ recalled how the mass of detail for 1 July 1916 dispensed with all initiative. There was a seventy-six page scheme for the offensive, and a 365-page supplement from Division.[60] This impulse, with its centralizing tendencies, seems to have reached its zenith at the time of the Passchendaele offensive, when a Corps commander insisted to Division that even two platoons in Battalion reserve be given very specific tasks.[61] As General von Bulow (commander of the German Second Army) maintained later, the war had become a war of administration, even tactically, so that there was no leadership or touch with the fighting troops.[62]

Von Bulow recognized that the very nature of war had changed, and it was *not* simply because of the unexpectedly larger numbers of men involved or the centralizing tendency of artillery control. Prewar thinking *was* largely qualitative, and yet an enforced evolution did take place during the war towards a technological paradigm that Jacques Ellul saw as quantitative, i.e. an image or paradigm of war that relied heavily on technique, method and calculation. In other words most senior officers continued to think in terms of the morale-oriented battlefield, yet the inexorable logic of the war compelled a parallel, tacit acceptance of technique and quantification. Thus the problem of the linkage between morale and fire-power, between the human battlefield and the technological battlefield, was eventually 'solved' by the assimilation of the former into the latter, although GHQ and many senior officers such as Field Marshal the Earl of Cavan declined to acknowledge this process throughout the war.[63]

Notes

1 Meinertzhagen, Diary, 19 May 1913, Quetta, cited in Colonel Meinertzhagen, *Army Diary 1899–1926* (London, 1960), p. 53. Books and articles on tactics between about 1910 and 1914 stressed this point, e.g. Haking, *Company Training* (1913) and Altham, *The Principles of War* (1914).

2 Bidwell and Graham, *Fire-Power*, Book 1.

3 Gooch, *The Plans of War*, ch. 9.
4 Strachan, *European Armies*, pp. 114–17, 120.
5 'Report of the Special Committee on Mitrailleurs', November 1870, p. 749/3, WO 33/22; 'Abstract of Proceedings of the Department of the Director of Artillery, for the Quarter ending 31 March 1872', 1 February 1872, p. 929/51, His Royal Highness the Commander-in-Chief, p. 929/51, and 'Second Report of the Special Committee on Mitrailleurs', November 1871, pp. 1317/3, 1318/4, WO 33/24, PRO.
6 'Machine Guns for Land Service, a Brief History', 6 May 1886, WO 32/8901, PRO. Even the smaller Gardner gun required 1 officer, 9 other ranks and 4 mules!
7 'Report of the Special Committees on (1) the 1 pr. Automatic QF Gun (Pom Pom), and (2) Machine Guns, 1901', September 1901, pp. 7–8, WO 32/9029, PRO.
8 'Reports on Equipment from South Africa. Machine Guns: Cavalry, Mounted Infantry and Infantry', no date, WO 108/267, PRO. Major General Kitchener's evidence was unusual in its strong approval of the gun, ibid., pp. 23, 62. Lyttelton's apathy in 1901 can be found in WO 32/9029, PRO.
9 'Report of Special Committee', 1901, Major General C. W. H. Douglas (replacing Major General Lyttelton), WO 13/483, PRO.
10 Boer War, Reels 01 and 02, IWM 1025, Imperial War Museum film archive.
11 'Infantry Training (1908), Amendment (1909)', p. 4, cited in Captain R. V. K. Applin, *Machine Gun Tactics* (London, 1910), pp. 238, 241. War Office Reports from Manchuria can be found in WO 33/350, PRO.
12 Major F. V. Longstaff and A. Hilliard Atteridge, *The Book of the Machine Gun* (London, 1917), p. 4; Lieutenant General Sir Ian Hamilton, 'The training of the troops during 1906', *JRUSI*, Vol. 50 (December 1906), pp. 1521–2; Applin, *Machine Gun Tactics*, p. 106.
13 'Machine Guns. Relative value of various patterns', Machine Gun Equipment (Report), C. W. Scott, Director of Artillery (hereafter DA), under Master General of the Ordnance, 18 April 1911; CIGS to MGO, 25 April 1911; MGO to CIGS, 28 April 1911; CIGS to MGO, 12 May 1911; MGO to DA, 29 May 1911; MGO to CIGS, 9 June 1911, in WO 32/7067, PRO.
14 'Proceedings of the Small Arms Committee', 1911, Minute 1197: 5, 15 July 1911, Supply 6/534, PRO.
15 'Interim and Final Reports by the Committee on Automatic Rifles', and letters from the CIGS, Nicholson, dated 28 October 1910 and 24 November 1911, urging progress. Final Report, 22 January 1914, WO 32/7071 PRO; also WO 33/504 and WO 33/571, PRO.
16 Lieutenant General W. R. Robertson to Field Marshal the Commander-in-Chief, 28 November 1915, 'Machine Guns', 20b, WO 32/11392, PRO.
17 'Question of a Light Machine Gun for Military Aeroplanes' (1912 ff.), WO 32/7069 PRO; MGO, 'New Armies 1914–1915; Arms and Ammunition', indicating 25 Lewis guns in hand on 1 November 1914, and 25 more per month, escalating to 100 per week starting March 1915, WO 161/22, PRO.
18 'Machine Gun Fire versus Aircraft' (1912–1914), WO 32/9089 PRO.
19 Bidwell and Graham, *Fire-Power*, pp. 53–5, offering perhaps a more sympathetic interpretation.
20 CIGS, in *Report of a Conference of General Staff Officers at the Staff College, 17–20 January, 1910*, Staff College Library, Camberley, p. 32; Robertson, CGS, GHQ, Confidential 'Memo', 26 May 1915, no. 23, General Staff Notes on operations, WO 158/17 PRO. See also C. D. Baker-Carr, *From Chauffeur to Brigadier* (London, 1930), p. 79.

21 Despite all this, there was a belated recognition by some senior officers in the 1910–14 period that there should at least be common doctrine in regard to tactics, for example, Haig, 'Memorandum on Army Training in India, 1910–1911', 91g; 'Aldershot Command General Staff and Administrative Staff Tours, 1913', 91a in Haig Papers, NLS; and Altham, *The Principles of War*, p. vi.

22 Brigadier General du Cane and Major General Sir Archibald Murray, in *Report of a Conference of Staff Officers at the Royal Military College, 12–15 January, 1914*, Staff College Library, Camberley, pp. 75 ff. Other references to doctrine or stereotyped methods can be found in various places, e.g. General C. W. H. Douglas, 'Annual Report of the Inspector General of the Home Forces for 1913', p. 333, WO 163/20, PRO; and even in Captain J. F. C. Fuller, 'The tactics of penetration', *JRUSI*, Vol. 59 (November 1914), p. 389.

23 *Report of a Conference of General Staff Officers at the Staff College, Held under the Direction of the CIGS, 18–21 January 1909*, pp. 65–8; *17–20 January 1910*, pp. 26–31; *13–16 January 1913*, pp. 65–7; *12–15 January 1914*, pp. 75–7, Staff College Library, Camberley.

24 See Bidwell and Graham, *Fire-Power*, pp. 48 ff.

25 ibid., pp. 25–6.

26 J. F. C. Fuller to Liddell Hart, 16 August 1926, 1/302/96, Liddell Hart Papers, KCL.

27 *Report of a Conference of General Staff Officers at the Staff College, 18–21 January, 1909, Held under the Direction of the CIGS*, Staff College Library, Camberley, pp. 11, 19, 68.

28 G. M. Lindsay (GHQ Small Arms School) to [?] 14 December 1917, 73/60/1, General Lord Horne Papers, IWM.

29 See for example the ruminations of Altham, *The Principles of War*, pp. 26 ff., although Altham also advocated night attacks, pp. 255 ff., 269 ff.; and Haking, *Company Training*, pp. 223 ff.

30 *Report of a Conference of General Staff Officers at the Staff College, 12–15 January 1914*, p. 77, and *Report of a Conference and Staff Ride as Carried out at the Staff College by Senior Officers of the General Staff, January 1906*, p. 126, Staff College Library, Camberley.

31 G. M. Lindsay to Lord Horne, 30 January 1919; W. H. Anderson, MGGS First Army, 'First Army Policy regarding the Employment of Machine Guns', 10 May 1918; G. M. Lindsay, 'Some Suggestions on the Strategical and Tactical Value of Machine Guns', 9 November 1915, revised 26 April 1916, pp. 1–3; and G. M. Lindsay (GHQ Small Arms School) to [?], 14 December 1917; all in 73/60/1, General Lord Horne Papers, IWM. For lower-level development and problems, see J. Miller to Edmonds, 13 July 1935, Cab 45/136, PRO, regarding II Corps appointment of a machine-gun officer to Corps HQ in September 1916; and two critical letters about mishandling of machine-guns, G. H. Sawyer to Edmonds, 14 May 1930, and Captain Basil Sleigh to Edmonds, 11 December 1929, Cab 45/137, PRO.

32 Haig, Commander-in-Chief, 3 March 1916, 20, and Kiggell, CGS, to Secretary, War Office, 19 May 1916, 37a, in 'Machine Guns', WO 32/11392, PRO; correspondence between the CIGS (Murray) and the AG, from September 1915 to November 1915, including a sharp letter from the CIGS to the AG, 14 November 1915, 20, in 'Formation of the Machine Gun Corps', WO 32/5453, PRO.

33 'Infantry Training', 1914 (draft copy with corrections), General Staff, WO, 1914, pp. 81–5, 69/53/4, Maxse Papers, IWM.

34 ibid., pp. 57–62.
35 *Report of a Conference of General Staff Officers at the Staff College, 18–21 January, 1909*, pp. 10, 19, Staff College Library, Camberley; and ibid., *12–15 January, 1914*, p. 77.
36 Maxse, 'Fire Control', 18 January 1911; 'Notes on Company Training, 3rd Lecture', 1911; 69/53/1, Maxse Papers, IWM. Haldane, Shorncliffe Diary, 14 May 1912, 14 August 1912, 28 August 1912, 19 June 1914, 69/36/1, Haldane Papers, IWM.
37 Bidwell and Graham, *Fire-Power*, chs 1–3.
38 Colonel S. W. H. Rawlins, 'A History of the Development of British Artillery in France 1914–1918', no date, unpublished ms, pp. 88–92, MD/1162, Rawlins Papers, Royal Artillery Institution (hereafter RAI); General Noel Birch to Edmonds, 8 July 1930, Cab 45/132, PRO.
39 Major General Sir Stanley von Donop, 'The Supply of Munitions to the Army', unpublished ms, WO, 1919, p. 31, 69/74/1, von Donop Papers, IWM.
40 Colonel Haig, Evidence at *Royal Commission on the War in South Africa*, Parliamentary Papers, vol. 61, 1904, pp. 403–4. (This view continued into the war, cf. Haig, Diary, 11 May 1915, WO 256/4, PRO.) See also Haig's handwritten notes and underlining in 'Report of General Percin on the Inspection held in 1910', and Major Radcliffe, 'Report on the French Artillery, 1911', in Haig, 'Reports on French Artillery Training, 1910–1911', 90, Haig Papers, NLS.
41 Haig, 'Notes on the Waterloo Campaign', August 1896, 7, Haig Papers, NLS. For Haig's later attitudes see Chapter 4.
42 E. D. Swinton to Liddell Hart, 11 January 1930 (including quotation from a letter to E. D. Swinton by Major General Sir G. K. Scott-Moncrieff, dated 29 September 1919), 1/670/—, Liddell Hart Papers, KCL.
43 T. Gerard Hetherington to Edmonds, 23 October 1934, Cab 45/134, PRO.
44 L. W. Savile (HQ 6 Division) to Edmonds, 5 June 1935, Cab 45/137, PRO; Bidwell and Graham, *Fire-Power*, pp. 135 ff. Haig Report, rough draft, 9 February 1916, 45a, 'Tanks', WO 158/831, PRO.
45 GHQ, 'Preliminary Notes on Tactical Employment of Tanks', August 1916, Cab 45/200, PRO.
46 Rawlinson, Diary, 26 August 1916, 5201–33–26, Rawlinson Papers, NAM; Rawlinson to GHQ, Fourth Army Proposals, 28 August 1916 (with Haig's notes dated 29 August 1916) Fourth Army Papers, 188, WO 158/235, PRO.
47 Rawlinson to GHQ, 31 August 1916 (with notes by Haig dated 1 September 1916), Fourth Army Papers, 198, WO 158/235, PRO; Rawlinson, Diary, 7 September 1916, 5201–33–26, Rawlinson Papers, NAM; Kiggell, GHQ, 5 October 1916, 'Note on use of Tanks', Fourth Army Papers, 241, WO 158/235, PRO.
48 Haldane, Diary, 22 October 1916, 4 November 1916, 13 November 1916, Haldane Papers, NLS.
49 Elles to Edmonds, 24 December 1933, in 'Ypres 1917 and yours of 19 December 1933', Cab 45/200, PRO. See also 'Passchendaele' and '1917', ibid.
50 Kiggell to Gough, 7 August 1917, 5/114, Kiggell Papers, KCL.
51 Edmonds, Note of a conversation with Lieutenant General Sir Hugh Elles, 29 October 1934, in '1917'; and Elles to Edmonds, 24 December 1933, in 'Ypres 1917 and yours of 19 December 1933', Cab 45/200, PRO.
52 E. D. Swinton to Edmonds, 22 January 1946, 2/5/12, Edmonds Papers, KCL; J. F. C. Fuller to Liddell Hart, 16 August 1926, 1/302/96, Liddell Hart Papers, KCL; Bidwell and Graham, *Fire-Power*, p. 137.

53 Elles to Edmonds, 4 September 1934, in 'Arras 1917', Cab 45/200, PRO.

54 Judging by the Royal Flying Corps policy statement of August 1916, which emphasized the moral effect of the aeroplane, senior air staff also had considerable trouble integrating this new piece of technology with the human side of the equation, Denis Winter, *The First of the Few: Fighter Pilots of the First World War* (London, 1982), pp. 15–16.

55 John Wilkinson, 'Translator's Introduction' in Jacques Ellul, *The Technological Society*, Vintage edn (New York, 1964), p. xvi. The original French edition was published as *La Technique* in 1954.

56 The first two 'wastage' returns of early 1915 can be seen in Creedy–Kitchener Papers, WO 159/3, PRO. Of course 'wastage' was not invented in the First World War, see for example the War Office 'wastage' prediction of 1906, WO 8813, PRO. However, from early 1915 on, 'wastage' became the normal British way of thinking about manpower in the First World War.

57 Haig, Diary, 'Memo on the Wastage of the Forces in the Field prepared by the AG's Branch', no date, but *c.* 22 May 1916, 44, WO 256/10, PRO.

58 First Army General Staff (Butler) to Corps, Divisions and Brigades, 'General Principles for the Attack', 13 April 1915, p. 1, 5201–33–67, Rawlinson Papers, NAM.

59 Butler, MGGS, First Army, 'Strength required to pierce front', November 1915, pp. 1–2, 69/10/1, Butler Papers, IWM.

60 H. C. Rees (VIII Corps HQ) to Edmonds, 14 November 1929, Cab 45/137; also W. G. Dobbin to Edmonds, 21 January 1931, Cab 45/133, PRO. Curiously enough, in view of his later criticism, Liddell Hart in 1916 was much impressed by the systematic advance on 1 July 1916, with 100 yards between each wave, four to five yards between each man, etc., Liddell Hart, 'Impressions of the Great British Offensive on the Somme', by a Company commander who saw three and a half weeks of it, 7/1916/22, Liddell Hart Papers, KCL.

61 Henry A. Fletcher [?] (Guards Division) to Edmonds, 15 July 1938, Cab 45/187, PRO. Because artillery tended to dominate offensive tactics, and because Corps controlled the artillery plan, there did exist this strong centralizing tendency focused towards Corps command. However this tendency was itself part of the mathematical spirit engendered by fire-power technology and the internal logic of artillery and other weapons.

62 Liddell Hart, Talk with von Bulow, 8 March 1932, 11/1932/9, Liddell Hart Papers, KCL.

63 At the Staff College Academy Banquet in 1924, Field Marshal the Earl of Cavan, then CIGS, recalled with dismay that Sir Ian Hamilton had criticized (in the 1924 debate on Army estimates) the continuing 'cult of the bayonet', and had suggested doing away with two-thirds of the infantry and putting the remaining one-third in machines. Cavan, who had commanded XIV Corps in the war, commented that this was highly dangerous, 'it is rating the machine higher than the man', and he asserted that it is 'the man that counts', 'Academy Banquet 1924' in Cavan Papers, WO 79/69, PRO. See also Bond, *British Military Policy, passim.*

PART II

Understanding Command: the Evolution of a Commander-in-Chief

[4]

Douglas Haig,
the Staff College,
and the Continuity of Ideas

Perhaps the most severe problem faced by commanders in high positions before and during the First World War was to understand the fundamental nature of modern war. Some commanders did not seem fully to realize that a problem existed. Brigadier General Rees, for example, described as a 'marvellous advance' the destruction of his Brigade on 1 July 1916, when 'hardly a man of ours got to the German Front Line'.[1] Rees was obviously more concerned here with the discipline and gallantry of his men than with the results of their assault, and such thinking shows how difficult it was for officers with a nineteenth-century background to come to grips with modern warfare. A similar kind of statement came from the General Staff of GHQ in November 1915, when contesting a Ministry of Munitions assertion that 200 machine-gunners were equal in effectiveness to 1,000 riflemen: 'In short, the introduction of the Machine Gun has not, in the opinion of the General Staff, altered the universally accepted principle that superior numbers of bayonets closing with the enemy is what finally turns the scale and is the ultimate object of fire.'[2]

A useful way to pin down the components of the late nineteenth-century concept of war and the reaction of those holding that concept to the emergence of a twentieth-century technical image, is to review the evolution of Douglas Haig's ideas through Staff College in the late nineteenth century, the South African war, and his tours of duty in India (1909–11) and as GOC Aldershot Command (1912–14).

Douglas Haig attended Staff College from 1896 to 1897, and it would appear that the central lessons of these two years stayed with him into the First World War and beyond. Understandably, the Staff College curriculum included the study of Napoleonic warfare, especially the 1806 and 1815 campaigns. Other important campaigns included the Franco-Prussian war in its first year (1870) and the American Civil War. Certain

85

themes emerged from these studies, and form what may be called the late nineteenth-century ideal of war as learnt by Haig. Certain truths were expounded to Haig by his teachers at Staff College, and it is noteworthy that Haig's notebooks show very little sense of independent criticism. Indeed he was not an independent thinker, and his Staff College concepts were applied, with few changes, to the battles of the Somme some twenty years later.

What were these ideas, learnt in 1896 and 1897? First, that the principal army of the enemy was the main target and must be attacked, that this army could only be defeated by concentrating superior force at the decisive point, and that the aim was to achieve a decisive victory. This could be done by engaging the enemy on a wide front, wearing out the enemy and drawing in his reserves, and then the decisive blow by one's own general reserve. The infantry was the chief arm for winning battles,[3] and the artillery existed mainly to support the infantry, while only the cavalry could exploit the success of the infantry (whose chief role was to dislodge the enemy), and make the victory decisive. At this point Haig's attention was often drawn to the cavalry exploitation after the battle of Jena in 1806. Success in battle depended to a large extent on morale, and on the quality of the Commander-in-Chief. Morale and discipline were extremely important, both because of the destructive nature of modern war, and because the British were likely to use 'green' or undisciplined troops.

Leadership by the Commander-in-Chief was crucial – he should have determination and singleness of purpose, and it was better to have one guiding idea than that it should be the very best idea. Also it was better to do something rather than nothing. The Commander-in-Chief should only set out the strategic objectives – the details and execution of those objectives should be left to subordinates. On the other hand, his authority was impaired if he permitted subordinates to advance their own ideas. The Commander-in-Chief should also ensure unanimity at GHQ. Before the battle he could only intervene by positioning the various Corps, and during the battle by controlling the reserves. More generally, the Commander-in-Chief should always be prepared to incur risks in order to win, and should mystify and mislead the enemy whenever possible. Tactically, the essence of Napoleonic warfare was the role of the Advanced Guard. This was the entity that reconnoitred, protected the main body of the army, then attacked and pinned the main enemy army, drew in his reserves, deceived him and found weak points so that the decisive blow could be struck.[4]

Underlying these central themes of Haig's Staff College lessons was a fundamental vision of war as mobile but controlled, limited in time (in fact time was of the essence), susceptible to determined leadership, and structured so that battles took place in series of separate but automatically consecutive acts, as in a play. In fact Haig's notes often give the impression that warfare had lost Napoleon's creativity and had become symmetrical and predictable – Act I: the advance; Act II: the engagement and fire fight; Act III: the assault and decision; Act IV: the exploitation. Nor did Haig forget this structured concept, for his comments in June 1913 as Director of the Aldershot Command General Staff and Administrative Staff Tours repeated what he had learnt earlier. The acts of battle were the same now as ever, he told his listeners: (1) the preparation for the decisive attack, (2) the decisive attack, (3) the exploitation. There is no doubt that for Haig in 1913 the modern battle was structured, short, reasonably simple, and predictable. Moreover each act of the battle led necessarily to the next act. Much of Haig's later indecision about the preparation and proper tactics for the Somme and Passchendaele can be traced back to this vision of a structured battle, and his subsequent puzzlement that war had somehow escaped its proper or normal boundaries. In fact this sense of the structured three or four act battle was not confined to Haig, but was implicitly or explicitly understood in the army as the likely future course of battle tactics. So, for example, around 1910 Brigadier General Maxse gave a lecture to his troops on the three act Battle, in which Act I was the fire fight, Act II the decision, and Act III the annihilation of the enemy.[5] It is not too much to say that the prewar Edwardian army had returned in this way to the formalized attitudes of the eighteenth century, and that many officers were later surprised at the way in which the First World War seemed to have escaped the prewar 'guidelines' laid down for it, particularly in regard to the decisive offensive.

Another underlying message in Haig's notes was the Clausewitzian emphasis on human nature and morale – success in war required the highest moral qualities in the Commander-in-Chief and in the army – these were the ultimate determinants of Victory. Courage, stamina, enthusiasm, determination, disciplined obedience, all these were easily understood moral values which fitted in well with Victorian attitudes and with the frequent 'savage war' campaigns of the nineteenth century. Haig's notes also reveal a fundamental preoccupation with the offensive at all costs, for only the decisive offensive could influence war. In this Haig and his fellow officers had to take account of Clausewitz, who had annoyingly argued that the defensive was actually stronger than the offensive. The solution for Haig and others was simply to argue, as did Charteris, Haig's future chief of intelligence, in a 1907 Staff College paper, that nevertheless only the offensive could lead directly to 'decisive results'.[6] The important point about this was that warfare had to be *decisive*, and here one can see the underpinnings of the massive offensives of 1916 and 1917, both of which aimed at *decisive* results.

Finally, there was an imbedded sense in Haig's notes that he and other officers had come to a final understanding of modern warfare – there was

only one 'normal' kind of war[7] – decisive, offensive, mobile but structured, and won by morale and determined personal leadership. This
predictable kind of warfare was not expected to change drastically,
and the continued stress on unchanging principles helped to reinforce
the concept of 'normal' war.[8] During the First World War, Haig often
reiterated 'normal' concepts, thus in 1917 when arguing against diversions, he told the War Cabinet, 'It has always been accepted as the
most effective form of war to attack and destroy the enemy's strongest
forces as soon as possible'. And it is noticeable, even after the First
World War that Haig felt only the battle of the Aisne (September 1914)
had been 'a normal Battle in Europe' because of mobility, influence of
weather, use of ground etc., while evidently the years 1915–18 were not
normal.[9]

It is also the case that in Haig's notes and exercise books at Staff College
there was only a partial sense of the evolution of warfare towards modern
weapons and fire-power; the campaigns of Napoleon were given equal
validity with the lessons of 1870–1, although the Staff College lecturers
were certainly trying to come to grips with modern warfare. It was agreed
that superiority of fire before the final assault was vital, that loose order
was required in the attack in order to avoid losses, and that mass artillery
fire at the decisive moment was crucial. And there was an interesting
lecture from a Major Jackson at Chatham in October 1896, who talked
on the subject of 'Modern Forts' and how to take them. Major Jackson
recommended howitzers firing at 4,000 yards range, which would enable
the infantry attack to get within 300 yards. Then Pioneers would be
needed to cut wire entanglements in front of the fort, since neither
shrapnel nor high explosive could cut wire. Finally the attacking troops
should rush the fort while the artillery bombardment kept the defenders in
their 'casemates'. Major Jackson's ideas were eminently sensible,
although it was not clear how the 'pionniers' might freely cut the wire
while under fire. However, while Major Jackson saw the key to the
successful investing of the fort as the ability to move howitzers to within
their range of the fort, this could only be done in the old style, 'Whichever
side has the pluck and courage to carry his artillery forward will gain a
great moral advantage if not more'.[10]

Major Jackson's references to howitzers, wire and siege warfare were
all progressive in terms of the unknown future, but his lecture remained
isolated in contrast to the overall emphasis on the decisive battle, and the
impression gained from Haig's extensive notes at the Staff College is that
of moving forward while looking backward. Nor can one be surprised, for
later on when General Noel Birch attended an actual course on fortifications at Chatham, there was an illustrated lecture on the Russo-
Japanese war, showing 'dugouts, real trenches and tunnels', yet Birch
remarked that these ideas were not fully appreciated, and there seemed to

be no means by which these lessons could be widely absorbed and transformed into general discussion and then into doctrine.[11]

The Staff College, and Haig, did accept the fact of modern fire-power, but while making adjustments to tactics, they came to the conclusion that, other things being equal, it was ultimately simple solutions such as morale, discipline and leadership that decided battles. So the problem of modern fire-power was to be solved by intensifying morale, discipline and leadership rather than by using that same fire-power to devise appropriate solutions and tactics. This was not always the case, as noted above in Major Jackson's lecture 'Modern Forts', and tactics were modified, but how was the fire fight, for example, to be won? Haig noted at one point that the defence would probably stop firing either because of the attacker's fire, or simply from fatigue. Then the firing line would unleash a stronger fire, and the noise of whistling bullets 'acts sharply upon the morale of the defenders who are already somewhat shaken by long hours of fighting'. In other words, the offence was inherently or morally stronger than the defence. Haig noted that leaders were wanted along the firing line with pluck – an obvious point – for 'we shall always win by reason of pluck: and, if it is not the only cause of victory, it is always the most essential factor and the one without which we cannot hope to succeed'.[12]

The 1896 introductory lecture at the Staff College had commenced by turning attention away from modern weapons and towards human nature: 'War . . . is a contest between two human intelligences rather than between two bodies of armed men'. Ligny and Waterloo were won by 'sheer power of brain' and not so much by the fighting.[13] While there was an element of truth in this, the emphasis tended to distract Haig and others from appreciating fully the changes that were taking place. Nowhere was this more evident than in Haig's notes on the place of cavalry in modern warfare. His notes on the Waterloo campaign, taken in August 1896, stressed that the recent tendency to reduce cavalry in favour of artillery and infantry was 'a fatal error' because only the mounted arm could win the decisive victory – success in battle simply opened the way for the cavalry to achieve the decision.[14] As a cavalry man, Haig would not easily change his mind on this point, and he expected no less of his cavalry in 1916, 1917 and 1918.

Nevertheless, how was the cavalry to face modern weapons? Here was the late nineteenth-century concept and the twentieth-century technical image of war, not in conflict, but talking past each other, as Thomas Kuhn argued would happen when he discussed the problem of an individual transferring allegiance from one mental paradigm to another.[15] This was the crux of Haig's problem: having given allegiance to the late nineteenth-century concept of war, which essentially focused on human nature, he could not, and subsequently never did, transfer his allegiance fully to a twentieth-century technical image of war. Hence he would write down in his Staff College notes:[16]

> Modern arms of precision have no doubt been improved, but the human heart and pluck is just the same so that the hand which holds the arm of death trembles just as much or possibly more than in the old days. More, because in a few minutes very heavy losses can be inflicted and the short service system contributes and provokes panics.

And in 1916 he was to hope that the 1 July Somme offensive would succeed because the enemy second line would be rushed on the basis of panic among the defenders.

Haig (and his teachers) were attempting to come to grips with modern fire-power, but were in fact simply sliding past the problem. At this time Haig was reading French military writers, particularly Colonel du Picq and General Maillard (the professor of infantry tactics at the Ecole de Guerre). Haig copied down Maillard's views on cavalry into his notes:[17]

> To believe that Cavalry can effect nothing against Infantry because the latter is now armed with a long range repeating rifle, is to suppose without proper reason, that surprises are no longer possible, that leaders will never again make mistakes, that troops will always be in good heart, and ready at any moment for fighting, that they will never be affected by fatigue or hunger nor by the results of an unsuccessful fight ... Such conclusions are contrary to human nature because surprises, misunderstandings, mistakes, and failures will constantly recur and Cavalry will be at hand to take advantage of them.

Then Haig quoted Colonel du Picq, who argued that rifled guns and arms of precision had in no sense altered cavalry tactics because these weapons were, in effect, *too* precise. Haig appeared to develop these ideas and wrote down in his notebook three reasons why the role of cavalry would increase in the future. First, the greater extension of the modern battlefield would provide more cover for the cavalry. (Here Haig apparently forgot why the modern battlefield *was* more extended.) Secondly, Haig reverted to the 'human nature' thesis of the late nineteenth-century concept of war: 'The increased range and killing power of modern guns will augment the moral exhaustion, will affect men's nerves more and produce greater demoralisation amongst the troops – These factors contribute to provoke panic and to render troops (short service soldiers nowadays) ripe for attack by Cavalry!'[18] Finally, he argued that the longer the range of modern guns the more important would become the rapidity and mobility of cavalry. This was reasonable, but still did not solve the problem of fire-power versus cavalry, and was an adaptation of a similar argument by the Russian commander in the Balkans (1877–8), General M. D.

Skobelev. Haig also frequently presented the argument in his notes that cavalry could expect to suffer heavy losses, and made comparisons with severe Napoleonic cavalry losses at Eylau and Essling.[19]

Essentially, he was simply reaffirming his belief in the late nineteenth-century concept of war – an ideal which centred on structure, decision, mobility and human nature – in fact the cult of the offensive and the psychological battlefield, and he understandably rejected the future idea that new kinds of technology might become of central importance. Again, the two ideals or paradigms did not confront one another, but simply slid past each other, as when Haig noted the power of machine-guns in a paper on cavalry manoeuvres, written just before the turn of the century. Machine-guns were valuable as an independent arm, he said, but 'It is of paramount importance that the Manoeuvres of the Cavalry should not be hampered – which must often happen if [machine-gun] lines of fire are multiplied and divergent'. Perhaps the very distance between the old and the new prohibited any engaged discourse between the two. For example, Haig's notes from 1896–7 on cavalry tactics really represent a world that had already passed away:

> The [Cavalry] combat should not resolve itself into a melée which can bring about no decisive result. It should, on the contrary, come about with the violence of a released spring, with the force of moral ascendancy, at the threat of which the enemy saves himself by flight. This known philosophical fact should determine the conduct of cavalry: that is that the physical shock hardly ever takes place, it is replaced by the moral shock of two wills! Only combats unscientifically entered into end in a melée.

When it came to the employment of artillery in preparation for the cavalry assault, Haig's notes stressed the strictly auxiliary role of the guns and the lack of time, 'the few precious minutes which are available for the artillery to produce an effect'. Finally, in executing the attack, Haig wrote down that 'when the GOC raises his sword to signify that the moment for deployment has come, each Brigadier leads forth his command'.[20] These notes reveal the deep gulf in the understanding of warfare between the old and the new – within two years Haig was to witness the cavalry in action in the Sudan, yet within only sixteen more years he was to experience an entirely different form of warfare in Europe in 1914. The point is that these two different conceptions or images of war did not, and could not, relate to each other. The individual could not readily transfer aspects from one to the other, nor could lessons or solutions be shifted from one to the other. Instead one ideal would have to be fully abandoned and the other fully accepted. But in 1897 Haig somewhat naturally left the Staff College with the older human-centred image fixed in his mind, although the tenacity with which he clung to these ideas was to be remarkable.

With the help of Major General Sir Evelyn Wood, Haig was appointed to serve in the Sudan campaign (where he actually criticized the charge of the 21st Lancers at Omdurman as poorly conceived),[21] and then when the South African war broke out, he went on to become chief of staff to John French's cavalry division. The South African war confirmed Haig's Staff College understanding that the Commander-in-Chief must run risks in order to win, that cavalry were still valuable in war and, more controversially, that cavalry were effective 'in spite of modern guns!'[22] After the South African war, he was appointed Inspector General for Cavalry in India from 1903–6 and continued to stress the value of offensive-minded cavalry, telling Lieutenant General Sir Edward Hutton in 1903 of manoeuvres where 'the umpires attach too much value to the killing power of the rifle, and constantly give faulty decisions, and force the Cavalry to adopt a passive role. I know of no instance in the South African war where a *vigorous offensive* of either British or Boer was stopped by rifle fire alone from an unprepared position.'[23] No doubt the last two words in the sentence were significant.

In 1906 Haig was appointed to the War Office to be Director of Military Training and then Director of Staff Duties in 1907. Here he was responsible for preparing the Field Service Regulations (FSR) and for attempting to inculcate a sense of uniformity in the army regarding strategy, tactics, and staff organization. The FSR and Haig's letters at this time continued to reinforce the lessons of his Staff College years, with an emphasis on Clausewitz, the spirit of the offensive, and the traditional idea that 'Success in war depends more on moral than on physical qualities'. As he wrote to Kiggell in 1911 regarding the first volume of *Field Service Regulations*, 'I rubbed in the absolute necessity for having the *will to conquer!*'. FSR, Part 1, also summarized the methods of the offensive battle – a hard-fought preparatory action along the whole front by the Advanced Guard, the wearing out of the enemy, drawing in his reserves, and then the decisive assault by the general reserve.[24] All of this could be found in Haig's Staff College notes, with one important exception, the changing role of the Napoleonic Advanced Guard, which was transformed and explained in Haig's Staff Tours in India (where he was appointed in 1909 as Chief of Staff), and at Aldershot (where he became GOC in 1912).

The India Staff Tour of 1910 showed that Haig's original conception of the Napoleonic Advanced Guard, learnt at Staff College, which was primarily to do reconnaissance, and then to protect the main army (including deceiving, pinning and holding the enemy),[25] was now developed into a more active offensive role. Not only was the Advanced Guard to obtain information, so that the Commander-in-Chief could 'see', as in Napoleon's day, and also to engage the enemy in order to deceive and hold them back, but all this was now transformed into the official preparatory or 'wearing out' fight. This vigorous preparation was supposed to take place along the entire battlefront, to wear out the enemy, draw in his reserves, and find or create a weak point for the decisive attack.[26] This concept was further developed at Aldershot, when Haig became GOC. In the 1913 Staff Tour at Aldershot, the Advanced Guard now was to obtain important tactical positions of ground along the whole front, even into the enemy's second line of resistance, as part of the preparatory or 'wearing out' fight. It was a sign of Haig's simple, structured and mobile vision of war that although he saw this as a lengthy preparation, it would only last a few hours, or a day or more at most, while in the next stage, the artillery preparation before the decisive attack was also to be very short, perhaps only a quarter of an hour. The emphasis that Haig placed on mobile warfare and thus on the Advanced Guard concept is illustrated again by the army manoeuvres of 1913, where Brigadier General Maxse, who was with Haig, remarked on the fact that Haig kept the Advanced Guard well in front of the main force for three consecutive days.[27]

The point of this discussion of the Advanced Guard is that Haig felt it to be the crucial root of the Napoleonic method, and in its transformed role he was preparing to use it in 1915 and 1916. In fact he would have fully applied Advanced Guard tactics at the Somme except that he considered the battle of Verdun had already performed the preparatory or 'wearing out' function.[28] But when the decisive blow at the Somme failed in July 1916, GHQ stated on 2 August 1916 that the army was now in 'the "wearing out" battle' and that the decisive blow would actually be in the second half of September, using the 'last reserves' for the decisive assault.[29] Therefore the Advanced Guard idea was applied throughout August and the first half of September 1916, while the transformed Napoleonic conception of battle had been at the basis of Haig's planning of the Somme campaign.

Apart from this transformed concept of the Advanced Guard, Haig was also fundamentally trying to apply the ideal of the three or four Act Napoleonic battle at the Somme, but the new warfare was just not susceptible to the simplicity and logical sequence implied by preparation, the drawing in of reserves, decisive assault and exploitation. Haig was aware that preparation had become very important, utilizing the Advanced Guard concept, and in India and at Aldershot he stressed this stage or act of the battle, but his weak point was artillery. He had learnt at Staff College the normal nineteenth-century concept that infantry was the key arm, and that artillery was there to assist the infantry forward, with the cavalry to exploit. Hence there remained in his thinking (and in the army generally) the idea that the artillery primarily *assisted* the infantry. It is true that Haig most often conceived of the artillery assisting during the preparation and he always emphasized the combination of all arms in the decisive assault, but fundamentally in nineteenth-century fashion he thought of infantry as the arm that would or would not win the battle.[30] In other words, Haig underestimated, like most others, the role of the artillery, and tended to separate the roles of the three arms, despite pronouncements on combination and co-operation. This was to be the case at the Somme, where the preparation was done by the artillery, the assault by the infantry, and the exploitation, theoretically, by the cavalry.

In fairness to Haig, official doctrine at this time (1910) did state that the object of artillery fire was to 'assist the forward movement of the infantry', and there was a general lack of understanding of fire-power, and of the artillery in particular.[31] Haig's own conception of artillery before the First World War was motivated by his stress on mobility. He had learnt in the Sudan and the South African war that field artillery was mobile, and in Staff College his notes revealed that artillery sometimes could and should be moved into the firing line with the infantry; and while in India and at Aldershot, he believed that field artillery should be prepared to advance in support of the infantry to close range of the enemy.[32] Of greater interest was his comments in 1911 on French reports of artillery training in 1910 and 1911. In these reports Haig continually underlined those sections that emphasized the mobility of artillery, and the need for artillery to hit moving targets. At one point, he read that it was a mistake to bring a battery into action in the open at the start of a battle, and wrote, 'Why?', '!' in the margin – this one comment reveals his incomprehension at that time of counterbattery fire.[33] Haig was, of course, not alone in failing to appreciate artillery tactics. A covering letter with the French artillery reports by Colonel Fairholme, British Military Attaché in Paris, remarked that the British school of gunnery did not pretend to do tactics, that in the *Memorandum on the Training of the Royal Horse Artillery and Royal Field Artillery, 1910*, there was only one page on fire tactics, and that because gunnery and tactics were separated, nobody did artillery tactics, which were 'slurred over and taken for granted'.[34] Nor can it be said that the French were much in advance in artillery tactics, for they relied on speed and simple targets, and General Percin's 'Report' denigrated counterbattery work, and laid down that an offensive artillery duel was to be avoided.[35]

The changing importance of artillery was difficult for almost everyone to understand, and part of the problem for Haig and many others was to visualize just how powerful fire-power had and would become. Hence in 1911 Haig simply supposed that the offense would always triumph over the defence. '*Success lies with the offensive*. Entrenchments were a valuable weapon of the defence. But entrenchments, however good, were only a pallative [*sic*] of the loss that would be incurred. No defence of a position, however well entrenched, could hope to gain the victory by passive defence.'[36] Perhaps Haig was thinking about the battle of Tel-el-Kebir (1882) where, according to his pre-Staff College notes, the Battalion which entrenched themselves for a fire fight lost heavily (80 men), while the other three Battalions that went through with the bayonet without checking 'lost less than 80 amongst them'.[37] Or perhaps Haig, who was in India in 1911, had not yet received the War Office *Memorandum* of December 1910 that cautioned against too much optimism in the attack, 'which shows a failure to appreciate the effect of the fire of modern weapons'.[38]

What, therefore, had Haig learnt at the Staff College in 1896 and 1897 – lessons which, reinforced by the Sudan and South African campaigns, he was to carry over into the First World War and specifically into the planning and execution of the Somme and Passchendaele? In short, what was the basic vision or ideal of war that he tenaciously carried with him from the nineteenth century into the twentieth century?[39]

He had learnt, and clung to, an ideal of war that formed a paradigm of what 'normal' war should be. This was that the principal army of the enemy was the main objective (hence his later opposition to diversions, for example, at Salonika); the main enemy army would be defeated in a decisive offensive, which would be divided into three or four consecutive acts (manoeuvre, preparation, attack, exploitation); within these stages, the role of the Advanced Guard was paramount, to reconnoitre, protect, pin down, deceive and, especially, engage and wear down the enemy in the preparatory stage; the engaging and using up of the enemy reserves during preparation was the key. This had to be done before the general reserve could launch their decisive attack; it was necessary to incur risks in order to win, and it was essential to concentrate superior force at the decisive point. Then, victory almost always went to the side with the highest morale, discipline and offensive spirit, and these were qualities that the infantry needed above all, for they were the only arm that could actually force the decision, while the artillery would assist the infantry and the cavalry would exploit what the infantry had gained.

At root, this was a kind of warfare that was structured. The enemy was expected to fight in much the same way with the same weapons, and therefore the difference between the two sides was not really weapons, tactics or strategy (although the Germans preferred envelopment and the French the central offensive with the general reserve), but the determination of the Commander-in-Chief and the offensive-minded morale of the often 'green' troops. Not only was warfare organized, it was also mobile, so that battles would be relatively short and decisive affairs, even if the war itself might last a long time due to the need to wear down the enemy nation. The main difference between this Napoleonic style of warfare and the reality at the turn of the twentieth century was fire-power, but even so it was thought that fire-power would mainly assist and make possible the infantry assault, which was still the centre-piece of warfare.

But the infantry assault could only take place if the enemy was demoralized by fire. Hence in the end warfare still revolved around the individual, and because of the increasing impact of fire-power the individual must be more disciplined and must expect to suffer heavy losses.[40]

This paradigm of war was essentially still Napoleonic, still pre-industrial, although its structured nature carried strong overtones of the eighteenth century rather than the nineteenth century. Haig applied this set of ideas to the Somme, as is apparent from his diary during 1915 and 1916, where many entries deal with the preparation, the wearing out and the decisive assault, with the emphasis on the transformed role of the Advanced Guard in the preparatory or 'wearing out' stage of the battle. In 1916 he followed his Staff College notes in planning to engage along as wide a front as possible, then would follow the drawing in of the enemy reserves, and the decisive assault by the main reserve, by surprise if possible.[41] At various other times, Haig hoped that cavalry would exploit success in 1916 as in 1806; he declared it was necessary to take risks to get superior force at the decisive point in 1916 just as formerly; and he argued that the Commander-in-Chief should deceive and mislead the enemy as in former times. Hence in 1916 he ordered the First, Second and Third Armies to deceive and mislead before the 1 July 1916 assault, although this was more difficult in static warfare than in Napoleon's day.[42]

Of course Haig was not alone in attempting to apply an earlier ideal to twentieth-century warfare. A host of senior officers maintained the same attitude, particularly in regard to morale and discipline, as might be expected, since they were following FSR doctrine. Charteris, Haig's chief of intelligence at the Somme and Passchendaele, wrote later that 'the issue of any war is – as I think it is – decided by morale tipping the balance of a practical equality of numbers and material'. The General Staff in August 1915 stated baldly, 'human nature is the dominant factor in war, and no arguments to the contrary, however specious, can alter this fact'. In December 1915 the General Staff felt that the Germans could give way to panic, as happened to the French in 1870, since 'the "moral" of their men is deteriorating'. Rawlinson and Montgomery's Fourth Army tactical notes of April/May 1916 also stressed discipline and morale in the opening pages of that document, 'this war will be won by superior discipline and morale'.[43] Naturally, morale and discipline were very important and nobody denied this, but the problem arose when senior officers thought of these qualities as war-winning weapons, or as substitutes for technical or tactical change – Haig believed, for instance, in May 1915 that the way to take machine-guns was by grit, determination and the qualities of the stalker.[44]

His experience at the Staff College was of particular significance when applied to the role of the Commander-in-Chief. He learnt that the Commander-in-Chief must be a determined leader, who must display singleness of purpose. In fact it was better to stick to one guiding idea, even if it was not the very best plan or idea, than to change it. (This apparently had its influence on Haig when he pursued the battles of the Somme and Passchendaele longer than seemed desirable.) He had also learnt that the 'authority of the Commander-in-Chief is impaired by permitting subordinates to advance their own ideas', and that 'There must be unanimity at HQ'. These concepts, when added to Haig's rather rigid and aloof character, evidently did much to isolate GHQ during 1916 and 1917, and gave it an unnecessarily authoritarian aspect. Finally, Haig noted down that 'Interference of superiors with details really pertaining to subordinates, paralyses initiative'. The Commander-in-Chief should select strategic objectives but not anticipate details, or attempt to intervene on the battlefield, except in the use of the general reserve or in allocating Corps their places on the battlefront. 'The chief duty of the higher command is to prepare for battle, not to execute on the battlefield. After having clearly indicated to subordinate leaders their respective missions, we must leave the execution to them.' This idea goes far in accounting for the critical vacuum in leadership between Haig and Rawlinson, and then between Haig and Gough, during the preparations respectively for the Somme and Passchendaele, particularly in the matter of tactics.[45]

In conclusion, the most remarkable aspect of Haig's experience at the Staff College (supplemented by the Sudan and South African war campaigns) was the tenacity with which he (and other senior officers) carried the ideas of 1896 and 1897 into the First World War. The concepts he had learnt at Camberley were applied, with changes in detail rather than substance, to the strategic planning and execution of the battles of the Somme and Passchendaele. The basis was laid for the application of the late nineteenth-century concept of war to the twentieth-century technical fire-power reality. However, by far the greatest problem was the way in which the late nineteenth-century paradigm failed to come to grips with the twentieth-century paradigm – one set of ideas simply did not engage the other emerging set of ideas because the act of conversion to a fundamentally different kind of war was essentially an emotional one that was extremely difficult to make. In order to follow this argument, it will be useful to look at Haig's GHQ in 1916, and to see how Haig's own character fitted in with his Staff College training in running his GHQ and the war after 1915.

Notes

1 Notes by Brigadier General Rees (GOC 94th Infantry Brigade, 31 Division), on 1 July 1916, 1/21/27/2, Robertson Papers, KCL. Similar sentiments can be found in Colonel E. Vansittart to Edmonds, 25 January 1926, Cab 45/121, PRO.

2 'The Question of Training Men for Employment with the Machine Guns now under Supply', General Staff, GHQ, 23 November 1915, 1/9/35, Robertson Papers, KCL.

3 Only the infantry could actually *dislodge* the enemy. Fire could frighten and force the enemy to conceal himself, and cavalry could pursue, but the central effort of the attack was to get the enemy moving, preferably backwards, and only the infantry could do this.

4 These general themes are to be found in Haig's Staff College notebooks, 1896–7, particularly those concerning tactics and strategy: 7, 'Notes on Waterloo Campaign'; 10, 'Military History Papers', 1896; 11, 'Staff Duties', 1897'; 16, 'Tactical Training of Officers'; 17, 'Tactics' (1870 campaign); 18, 'Tactical Notes'; 19, 'Strategy I'; 20, 'Strategy II'; 24, 'Military History Exam (concerning the campaigns of 1862 and 1866)'; 31, 'Tactical Notes', in 3155, Haig Papers, NLS. See also Brian Bond, *The Victorian Army and the Staff College 1858–1914* (London, 1972), *passim*.

5 Haig's notes visualize a battle divided into four Acts, or sometimes three, in his unpaginated notebook, 'Tactics (1870 campaign)', 17, Haig Papers, NLS. This structured approach to the battle may help explain why it was difficult for Haig to change strategy (or battle tactics) during the First World War. Director's Comments [Haig], 'Aldershot Command. General Staff and Administrative Staff Tours, June 1913', p. 20, 69/53/4, Maxse Paper, IWM; Maxse, 'Notes on Company Training: 3rd Lecture', no date, but 1910–11, 69/53/1, Maxse Papers, IWM.

6 Captain Charteris, R.E., 'The Relative Advantages of Offensive and Defensive Strategy', 1907, Indian Staff College, WO 79/61, PRO.

7 This sense of 'normality' occurs frequently in later references to the First World War, which was of course not normal, according to senior officers. In May 1915 the Director of Military Intelligence (DMI) saw the trench deadlock as 'an abnormal state of affairs', General Military Review, DMI, 15 May 1915, p. 3, WO 106/1519, PRO; R. H. K. Butler (MGGS First Army) in November 1915 considered the war to be 'peculiar' and 'to a certain extent new', Butler to GOC First Army, November 1915, p. 1, 69/10/1, Butler Papers, IWM; Robertson thought the 1916 conditions were 'not at present normal' although 'they may become normal some day', Robertson to Haig, 14 January 1916, no. 30, in Secretary of State for War File, WO 158/21, PRO. Robertson also told General Maxse that machine-guns were more important than men 'in the peculiar type of operations in which we are at present engaged', Robertson to Maxse, 11 March 1916, 69/57/7, Maxse Papers, IWM.

8 There was a general realization in the First World War that too much stress had earlier been placed on unchanging principles, summarized in Robertson's letter to Rawlinson in July 1916, when he wrote that the war was very peculiar, that Field Service Regulations (FSR) would have to be revised, and that 'principles, as we used to call them, are good and cannot be disregarded, but their application is a very difficult business, and I think that we still take these principles too literally'. In effect, principles by themselves meant little, Robertson to Rawlinson, 26 July 1916, 1/35/100, Robertson Papers, KCL.

9 Commander-in-Chief [Haig] to War Cabinet, 20 June 1917, WO 158/24, PRO; Haig, 'Future Use of Cavalry', 14 December 1927, 346, Haig Papers, NLS.

10 Haig, notes taken at lecture by Major Jackson, Chatham, 1896, 'Modern Forts', in 'Tactical Notes', 18, Haig Papers, NLS.

11 General Noel Birch to Edmonds, 8 July 1930, Cab 45/132, PRO.

12 Haig, 'Combat in Modern War', in 'Strategy II', 1896–7, 20, Haig Papers, NLS. It seems that some of these notes may be post-Staff College, perhaps soon after the South African war.

13 Haig, typed 'Introductory Lecture' included in 'Tactical Notes', 1896, 18, Haig Papers, NLS.

14 Haig, 'Notes on Waterloo Campaign', August 1896, 7, Haig Papers, NLS. See also Gerard de Groot, 'Educated soldier or cavalry officer? Contradictions in the pre–1914 career of Douglas Haig', *War and Society*, vol. 4, no. 2 (1986), pp. 51–69.

15 See, for example, R. Meyers, 'International paradigms, concepts of peace, and the policy of appeasement', *War and Society*, vol. 1, no. 1 (1983), p. 50; Kuhn, *Structure of Scientific Revolutions*, pp. 149–50.

16 Haig, '1870 Campaign' in 'Tactics', 17, 1896–7, Haig Papers, NLS.

17 ibid.

18 ibid.

19 ibid.

20 Haig, 'Cavalry Manoeuvres', no date, but between 1893 and 1899, 346b; and Haig, 'Tactics', 1896–7, 17, Haig Papers, NLS.

21 Haig to Evelyn Wood, 15 March 1898, and 7 September 1898, 6g, Haig Papers, NLS.

22 Haig to Hugo (his brother), 2 August 1900, Haig to Henrietta (his sister), 26 November 1899 and 22 February 1900, 6c, Haig Papers, NLS.

23 Haig (Inspector General of Cavalry, India) to Lieutenant General Sir Edward Hutton, 29 December 1903, 50086, Hutton Papers, BL. Also Haig to Edmonds (on the same day and on the same topic!), 29 December 1903, 2/4/1, Edmonds Papers, KCL.

24 *Field Service Regulations, Part I, Operations* (London: War Office, 1909), p. 11 and ch. 7; Haig to Kiggell, 14 July 1910 and 13 July 1911, 1, Kiggell Papers, KCL. See also John Gooch, *The Plans of War*, pp. 113–17. Exactly similar ideas can be found in Haig, 'Waterloo Campaign', 1896, 7; 'Military History Papers', 1896, 10; and 'Tactics', 1896–7, 17, Haig Papers, NLS.

25 For example in Haig, 'Military History Papers', 1896,10, Haig Papers, NLS.

26 Haig, *Report on Staff Tour (1910), held by the CGS, India* (Simla, 1911), pp. 26–7, 67, in 84, Haig Papers, NLS.

27 In 1910 in India, Haig felt the artillery should assist the infantry by a storm of shells at the moment of attack, but in 1913 he thought the artillery should destroy obstacles in front of the infantry assault, Haig, *Report on Staff Tour (1910), held by the CGS, India*, ibid., p. 26, and Haig, 'Aldershot Command General Staff and Administrative Staff Tours, June 1913,' p. 22, 91a, Haig Papers, NLS. Maxse to Tiny (Maxse), 20 September 1913 and 28 September 1913, Maxse Papers, WSRO.

28 Haig, Diary, 15 March 1916, WO 256/9, PRO.

29 Haig, Diary, Kiggell to Rawlinson and Gough, 2 August 1916, WO 256/11, PRO.

30 Haig, *Report of a Staff Tour (1911), held by the CGS, India* (Simla, 1911), p. 51 in 85, Haig Papers; and Haig, *Report of a Staff Tour (1910), held by the CGS, India* (Simla, 1911), p. 26 in 84, Haig Papers, NLS.

31 *Memorandum on Army Training 1910* (War Office, 1910), pp. 11, 7–9; Bidwell and Graham, *Fire-Power*, ch. 1; T. H. E. Travers, 'The offensive and the problem of innovation in British military thought', *Journal of Contemporary History*, vol. 13, no. 3 (1978), p. 531.

32 Haig, 'Tactical Notes', 1896–7, 18; Haig, 'Aldershot Command: Comments on the Training Season 1913', p. 6, 91b; Haig, 'Memorandum on Army Training in India, 1910–1911', 91g, Haig Papers, NLS. Haig did not fully realize that it was the artillery fire itself that should support infantry rather than that the guns themselves should be physically close to the infantry.

33 Haig, General Percin 'Reports on French Artillery Training 1910–1911', pp. 17, 18, 23, 75, for Haig's underlining; Major Radcliffe's Report, p. 42, for Haig's margin comment, 90, Haig Papers, NLS.

34 Colonel Fairholme to Haig, 19 May 1911, pp. 2–3, in 90, Haig Papers, NLS.

35 Haig, General Percin, 'Reports on French Artillery Training 1910–1911', pp. 72–3, in 90, Haig Papers, NLS.

36 Haig, *Report of a Staff Tour (1911), held by the CGS, India* (Simla, 1911), p. 52, in 85, Haig Papers, NLS. True enough in its own way, but Haig was throwing the baby out with the bathwater in refusing to emphasize anything but the offensive.

37 Haig, 'Strategy' (dated 1882 in the Haig catalogue but obviously after 1883, and very probably before 1896), 3, Haig Papers, NLS.

38 *Memorandum on Army Training 1910* (War Office, 1910), p. 7.

39 It was a characteristic of Haig that his basic ideas did not change, as Lord Esher noted in a letter to him, Haig, Diary, Esher to Haig, 1 June 1916, WO 256/10, PRO.

40 See T. H. E. Travers, 'Technology, tactics and morale: Jean de Bloch, the Boer War, and British military theory, 1900–1914', *Journal of Modern History*, vol. 51, no. 2 (1979), pp. 264–86.

41 Haig, Diary, 25 June 1915, 30 July 1915, 8.January 1916, 14 January 1916, 16 January 1916, 18 January 1916, 15 March 1916, 10 April 1916, 29 May 1916, WO 256/5–10, PRO.

42 Haig to Robertson, 29 May 1916, 1/22/41, Robertson Papers, KCL; Haig, handwritten note, dated 13 June 1916, in First Army Memo to GHQ, 6 June 1916, WO 158/185, PRO; R. H. K. Butler (GHQ) to GOC Armies, 27 May 1916, Fourth Army, WO 158/233, PRO.

43 Brigadier General John Charteris to Edmonds, 24 February 1927, Cab 45/120, PRO; 'General Staff Note on the General Military Situation', 5 August 1915, p. 2, WO 158/17, PRO; GHQ, 'A Paper by the General Staff on the Future Conduct of the War', 16 December 1915, p. 12, WO 106/308, PRO; Fourth Army, 'Tactical Notes', 11 April 1916, p. 2, 5201–33–70, Rawlinson Papers, NAM.

44 Haig, Diary, 20 May 1915, WO 256/4, PRO.

45 Haig, 'Strategy II', 1896–7, 20, Haig Papers, NLS. These sentiments were copied from the tactical and strategic works of Prince Kraft von Hohenlohe-Ingelfingen, published between 1887 and 1892.

[5]

The Personality of Douglas Haig and the Role of GHQ

Douglas Haig, appointed to command the BEF as Sir John French's replacement at the end of 1915, was an ambitious, politically conscious, and self-confident soldier. He was devoted and loyal to his family and friends, but his ambition and aloof character often overrode the interests of others. Although many have seen Haig's character as dominated by fixity of purpose, or by method and determination, or by the fetish of consistency,[1] others have simply and unkindly labelled Haig as stupid. Among these were Edmonds, Major General Sir Ernest Swinton (the tank supporter) and Haig's opponent, Henry Wilson. Edmonds remarked: 'I have to write of Haig with my tongue in cheek. One can't tell the truth. He was really above the – or rather, below the average in stupidity.' Swinton's opinion was that Haig 'was steeped in tradition and very industrious. His reception of a new idea like the Tanks was beneath contempt ... French was a stupid ill-educated man. Haig was a stupid man but better educated.' Henry Wilson, no friend of Haig's, frequently berated him in his diary; for example after a mix-up in August 1916 between Haig and Haking over whether the latter should attack or not, Wilson wrote, 'Haig is simply unintelligible and a d- - stupid man'. Wilson quoted others such as General Sir Walter Congreve and H. A. Gwynne (of Reuters) who had a low opinion of Haig, and cited Lord Esher who argued that Haig was simply 'a meticulous Staff Officer'. General Sir Archibald Murray offered another critical opinion, that Haig was 'a man of mediocre ability, slow to absorb, tenacious of what he had learnt; not a very pleasant man to deal with, though he tried to be pleasant'.[2]

However, a close reading of letters regarding Haig's childhood, and of biographers who knew Haig very well, such as Charteris (who was with Haig in India, at Aldershot, and was his chief of intelligence at GHQ in 1916 and 1917) and Sergeant T. Secrett, Haig's batman, reveal that Haig was a man who developed early in life such a sense of self-discipline and self-control that these qualities both guided and limited his abilities in the future. In this Haig was a true Victorian, following those nineteenth-century popular authors such as Samuel Smiles whose books stressed the self-disciplined character as the model to be attained. Another way of saying the same thing with reference to Haig, is to use David Riesman's phrase, 'inner-directed'. Riesman describes the inner-directed individual as one whose character and sense of goals and direction are implanted early in life by parents or elders, and who thereafter ceaselessly maintain and develop this character throughout their life by self-discipline – rather like a psychological gyroscope that, once set spinning, always points in the same direction and keeps the inner-directed personality 'on course'.[3]

During Haig's early life, it would appear that his religiously minded mother had a very considerable influence over his character. At an early stage of Haig's childhood she had already developed a strong belief in his future success, and she encouraged him in this belief. As a child he was already self-disciplined – for example he was seemingly able to cure himself of asthma by strict adherence to a diet, and he also learnt to contol his temper by self-discipline, so that this 'became a habit'. By 1881 he was a self-controlled young man who 'never idled'.[4] At school at Clifton, Haig was respected but a characteristic of the inner-directed personality now emerged, a difficulty in forming friendships, for 'few seemed to have become intimate with him'. This trait became noticeable, and Charteris remarked that as a young officer Haig was 'solitary, aloof and alone', so that 'Friendship in the ordinarily accepted sense of the term was almost unknown to Haig'. Secrett also observed that Haig tended to be aloof and unfriendly with subalterns and others, while Edmonds, who was at the Staff College with him, wrote that Haig was rough and abrupt with fellow officers at the Staff College, and had only one friend, Blair, from a Scottish regiment.[5] This characteristic was to have unfortunate repercussions in 1916 and 1917 in that Haig evidently found it difficult to communicate with others, just as senior officers and staff found it almost impossible to sit down and talk out problems frankly with him. There is no doubt that this situation did much to isolate GHQ during the offensives of 1916 and 1917.

At Sandhurst, Charteris noted that Haig was not popular and exacted strict discipline, as was possible for a Senior Under Officer, but Sandhurst apparently also completed the process of self-discipline, for there, according to Charteris, Haig learnt 'complete self-control'. This sense of self-discipline and of adherence to an inner-direction prevented Haig from easily accepting innovations in life style and behaviour, and Charteris described how the 'incongruous and grotesque irritated him – it was as if the unreasonable should ... be utterly extinguished'. When subordinates deviated from what Haig considered the correct path of conduct, Haig would hold 'himself perfectly rigid ... his eyes blazing, [and] he would administer reproof in tone so hard and words so forcible that even the most callous winced'. It was as if Haig's own inward self-control, outwardly expressed in his rigid stance, could bodily bring the miscreant to a similar self-discipline. Haig's batman, Secrett, confirms Charteris's picture: 'Anything indecorous always offended Sir Douglas Haig. In all emergencies he was neat and modest. Officers skipping about with scarcely any clothing on, and sometimes none at all, to take their morning tubs, always annoyed him.' Off-colour jokes 'offended him', and once when Haig noted a column of troops riding by, singing a ribald song, he left the house, galloped after the column and told the officer commanding, 'I like the tune ... but you must know that in any circumstances those words are inexcusable!' As might be expected, Haig also objected to other 'deviations' such as gambling, to which he had a 'rooted aversion', and he particularly disliked unconventional behaviour by women. 'Haig was such a stickler for the absolutely conventional way ...', wrote Secrett, 'He certainly did all he could to prevent a mixing of the sexes'.[6] It may also have been significant that Haig did not marry until he reached the age of 44.

A further characteristic of Haig's inner-directed personality was a concern with time and work. Charteris noted how, in India, Haig's days were exactly timetabled, starting at 10 a.m. and finishing at 10 p.m., 'when with clockwork regularity he sought his rest'.[7] He noticed the same characteristic when at GHQ in 1916, namely that Haig's 'day is mapped out with the regularity of a public school ... He is very upset if anything interferes with it'. In similar vein, Haig would take his two hours riding every day, whatever the crisis.[8] Parallel to such an outward structure was an inward organization also, relating to diet and health. Mention has already been made of his childhood dietary cure of asthma. Following this he undertook a water cure in 1895 due to an enlarged liver, perhaps at his sister's urging. Later on at Aldershot, Charteris claimed tht Haig became obsessed with the state of his health, and he devoted himself to a series of strictly enforced special diets – '"Sour milk," "whole meal bread" and "Sanatogen" each in turn had its trial.' By 1916 Haig had shifted to 'Panopepton', taking a tablespoonful every night before retiring, and also followed Dr Muller's exercises and 'deep breathing'.[9]

Haig's personality revolved around an almost obsessive need for order. His structured interior and exterior life due, it can be argued, to an early developed inner-directed character, meant that he was simply not receptive to basic changes in ideas or life style. Several contemporaries remarked upon the tenacity with which he clung to his ideas. For example Charteris stated that Haig was 'immensely tenacious of his own views', and that since he did little outside reading 'He had not a critical mind'. In fact Haig 'never argued, he had not the dialectic cut. "I don't agree with you. I think ... " then his own view.' Similarly Edmonds likened Haig's mind to a defective telephone, which needed shaking before it could function.[10] Haig's tenacity regarding his own views was also apparently reinforced in 1916 by a feeling that God was helping him: '*I feel* that every step in my plan has been taken with the Divine help – and I ask daily for aid ... I think it is this Divine help which gives me tranquility of mind'; and again 'I *do feel* that in my plans I have been helped by a Power that is not my own. – So I am easy in my mind'. These sentiments, however, do not so much reflect a divine mission as Liddell Hart and others suggest, instead the words strongly indicate a mechanism for alleviating stress and anxiety, and for the reinforcement of controversial views and decisions. The existence of this belief, however, contributed to Haig's sense of his own inward correctness at critical junctures, for example during preparations for the Somme.[11]

As already noted, Haig's personality prevented him from easily accepting innovation and change. This was a serious matter for the BEF after the end of 1915, but it is also important to notice that Haig's personality fitted in only too well with certain lessons from his Staff College training – the need for the Commander-in-Chief to be determined and display singleness of purpose, the need for unanimity at GHQ, and the rejection of advice from subordinates because of fear of undermining the authority of the Commander-in-Chief. These were all lessons from an earlier Napoleonic age when leadership in battle did require strong decision and willpower; but when applied at GHQ in 1916 and 1917, Haig's rigid personality and understanding of the role of the Commander-in-Chief, led to his own isolation, the isolation of GHQ as a whole from the rest of the BEF, and a lack of serious discussion of alternative tactics and strategy at GHQ or at conferences. Most senior officers were simply afraid of Haig and were not prepared to question him at conferences or make suggestions. Added to this sense of isolation was the clear Staff College concept that the Commander-in-Chief should set strategy and let subordinates carry out the offensive, and so a very significant vacuum opened up between Haig and his GHQ, and between Haig and his army commanders at the Somme and Passchendaele.

In practice, then, how did GHQ operate under Haig? First, there was the question of the Staff College emphasis on unanimity at GHQ, plus Haig's own personality. According to Gough, Haig picked 'yes-men' for GHQ, especially his Chief of Staff, Kiggell, who would 'neither represent contrary views to Haig nor decide between contrary views when representing Haig'.[12] According to another source, Kiggell was simply worn out, but Gough suggested that Kiggell was actually a weak character, and knuckled under to pressure.[13] Henry Wilson's frequent complaints about GHQ included criticisms that Kiggell was silent in Haig's presence, that Haig actually prevented Kiggell from visiting other units, and that Kiggell (and others at GHQ) knew nothing. Since Henry Wilson was reporting other officers' criticisms as well as his own observations, it seems likely that he was not far from the truth in his views, despite his well-known anti-Haig and anti-GHQ bias. As CGS in 1916 and 1917 Kiggell held a potentially important post. But he had only been appointed as CGS because Haig wanted to get him out to the front, and originally intended to replace him after three or four months, since by that time Kiggell would then be able to command a Corps. In other words, Haig was doing his old friend and War Office deputy a favour, and it seems that Kiggell responded with consistent and self-effacing support, even after the war. Kiggell himself was enigmatic about his role at GHQ, although he once wrote to Edmonds after the war saying that he could not urge a particular point (giving more initiative to officers) because he had no personal experience of the front and 'being *embusqué* at GHQ!' *Embusqué* means 'in ambush' or 'under cover', and probably describes his often silent role rather well.[14]

There is no doubt that senior commanders were afraid of Haig, and this obviously contributed to an uncritical unanimity at GHQ. Edmonds once commented on the status of General Sir Herbert Plumer in April and May 1916, 'Poor old Plum was in deadly fear of Haig at that time. Haig twice had him on the carpet threatening to send him home. I once said something appreciative of Plumer at Haig's table. He fired up at once and said "You would never have heard of Plumer if I hadn't sent Harington [Plumer's chief of staff] to him!" After Messines [1917] the old man [Plumer] put on side [*sic*] and stood up for himself.' Henry Wilson said much the same thing of Monro, GOC First Army: 'He is terrified of Haig and thinks if we don't constantly raid that Haig will be angry. Rawlinson, too, according to Foch, was afraid of Haig, and kept one eye on Haig and one on the Germans. And Edmonds suggested that Snow (GOC VII Corps) was more scared of GHQ and Haig than of the enemy.[15]

At the same time, fear of Haig and GHQ made some commanding officers and liaison officers tell Haig what he wanted to hear. It seems also that Haig could not easily tolerate criticism or suggestions. Edmonds remarks in his unpublished Memoirs that he could make suggestions to Robertson or Macdonogh, but not to Haig. Edmonds also recalled how in October 1917, Colonel Rawlins frankly told Haig that if the Passchendaele offensive continued, no artillery would be available for a 1918 spring offensive. Haig reportedly went white with anger and said, 'Col. Rawlins, leave the room'. When Edmonds agreed with Rawlins, Haig added: 'You go, too.'[16] In similar fashion, Gough claimed that Haig's conferences were too big and formal, and that army commanders only attended to hear Haig's plans, and not to discuss the plans or make suggestions.[17] Haig himself noted in his diary various occasions when army commanders came in to see him, and he inevitably recorded the conversations as one-sided. For example, when Plumer, then GOC Second Army, came in on 14 January 1916 to prepare for the army commanders' conference the next day, he told Haig what he intended to say, got Haig's criticisms, and automatically agreed to 'amend his statement accordingly'.[18]

It would only be fair to add that the same kind of system seemed to work at Army and Corps level, although at a lesser degree of intensity. For example, in the month of April 1916, Rawlinson explained the plans for the Somme to his Corps commanders. It would apper that Congreve in particular saw difficulties and was roundly criticized by Rawlinson for seeing too many problems. In consequence Congreve's task on the Somme was reduced and the more difficult attack given to Horne's Corps. Congreve was upset by Rawlinson's criticisms, and wanted to complain to Haig. The net result, however, was that when Rawlinson told the same Corps commanders in May 1916 how the attack was to go, he naively noted in his diary that 'there was little or no caviling or argument,' and then in June 1916 when he explained the new northward thrust of the forthcoming Somme attack, 'The Corps commanders took it very well and few questions were asked'. Congreve had evidently learned his lesson. In similar fashion, Aylmer Haldane recorded in his diary the behaviour of Allenby, his Corps and then Army commander. It appears that Allenby frequently became enraged and terrorized his officers, so that he was nicknamed 'The Bull'. Because one of his Corps commanders, Keir (GOC VI Corps), frequently opposed Allenby's wild attacks in the Ypres salient, Keir in turn was nicknamed 'The Toreador'. Keir was removed, but Allenby continued his furious ways, and Haldane remembered one of his typical bullish onslaughts on an officer in November 1916. Allenby had severely damned an officer, who responded, 'Very good, Sir'. Instead of leaving the matter, Allenby became enraged, and shouted, 'I want none of your bloody approbation'. Edmonds too thought Allenby rough in manner and speech, and unkindly recorded how Allenby had once shouted at and abused a soldier for not wearing the correct dress in the trenches only to discover that he was addressing a dead man.[19]

Returning to the case of Haig and GHQ, it would also only be fair to note that his staff and commanders *were* capable of changing Haig's mind, although it obviously had to be done very discreetly and with a careful avoidance of personal confrontation. Haig reports in his diary for 11 July 1916, that Rawlinson and Fourth Army had suggested a night attack for 14 July. Somewhat naively Haig wrote in his diary that he told Rawlinson the plan 'was unsound. He [Rawlinson] at once, in the most broad minded way, said he would change it.' Evidently, Rawlinson had no intention of accepting Haig's rejection, for he mounted a campaign to obtain Haig's consent to the night attack as well as the consent of the Corps commander who would carry out the attack, General Horne (GOC

XV Corps). Horne was won over by 10 p.m. on 11 July, and Haig by 11 a.m. on 12 July, although Haig insisted on having Mametz Wood and Trones Wood cleared before the night attack could go ahead.[20] Rawlinson (and Fourth Army) had evidently persisted in trying to convert Haig because Rawlinson thought the attack was of absolutely critical importance. On 13 July he wrote: 'Tomorrow is the most important battle of the war. God give us victory.' And the next day, after the attack, 'one of the greatest days of my life'.[21] Why did the normally difficult GHQ and Haig himself accept the Fourth Army plan for 14 July, in place of Haig's own rather poor plan? Judging by the subsequent Fourth Army operations report on 14 July, the arguments advanced by Rawlinson were calculated to appeal to Haig's sense of urgency, to his continuing hope for a decisive blow, and to his faith in the cavalry as a breakthrough weapon. Thus Rawlinson had stressed the importance of time, the enemy's poor morale, the need to take 'risks when the decisive moment arrived', plus the proposed use of cavalry in pursuit. In addition, Fourth Army used Major General Lawrence, a cavalryman at GHQ, to persuade Haig, although this took 'several days'.[22] Haig's acceptance of the plan had indeed been very reluctant, and perhaps because of this a night attack was not repeated at the Somme, despite the obvious success of the 14 July attack.

In summary, GHQ, together with Haig's personality and understanding of the role of Commander-in-Chief, learnt at Staff College, were so structured as to make change, innovation and suggestions difficult, although not impossible, particularly when the situation was critical and the dissenting approach was subtle. However, a more frequent criticism of GHQ, and in the end a more damaging one, was the apparent isolation of Haig and GHQ from the rest of the BEF. This was not a wholly new reaction since Sir John French's GHQ had previously been seen as unapproachable,[23] but the volume of criticism against the isolation of GHQ was such that the situation had obviously deteriorated. Haig's aloof and inner-directed personality seems to have been largely responsible for this, as illustrated by the remarks of visitors to his mess. For example, when Maxse, then GOC 18 Division, visited Haig for lunch on 17 October 1916, he remarked that Haig lived 'a very simple and rather retiring life', with just three of his GHQ staff in attendance, plus 'only one young A.D.C. to run his mess'. Maxse added that Haig 'avoids a crowd, [and] works very hard'.[24] The most vociferous critic of GHQ's isolation was Henry Wilson, and his adverse comments increased towards the latter part of 1916 as the Somme campaign lost direction and purpose. No doubt the animosity between Haig and himself influenced Wilson's comments, as well as his being passed over for promotion. On the other hand, Wilson's views were supported by others, and his comments were often reports of senior commanders who had encountered similar problems.

A typical diary entry from Henry Wilson on 1 September 1916 reports the conversation of Major General A. M. (Jock) Stuart, Director of Works in France, 'Haig is *very* optimistic though quite out of touch with the whole Army and even with his own Staff. Jock *never* sees him. *Kigg* knows nothing and decides nothing and Jock can get no decisions on any subject. I urged the importance of getting touch between GHQ and Corps by means of first class liaison officers . . . He [Stuart] agreed but said Haig was entirely opposed.' On 3 September 1916 Brigadier General G. G. Loch (GOC 168th Brigade) also agreed that GHQ was right out of touch with Corps. On 24 September 1916 'Uncle' (General Harper*) told Wilson that GHQ had no touch with the troops, no knowledge and no imagination. On 17 October 1916 Foch remarked to Wilson that Haig isolated himself and therefore made unnecessary enemies. On 24 October 1916, Congreve complained that he never saw Haig or anyone from GHQ. In November 1916 several entries complain of Haig's isolation, for example on 1 November 1916 Wilson wrote that Haig 'lives an isolated life completely out of touch with his Corps Generals and with the feeling of the Army; sees nobody, entertains nobody, knows *nothing* . . . Kiggell who never goes anywhere and has never seen anything; Butler who is rude and stupid and Tavish Davidson* who is a good Staff Officer but limited ability'. Finally, Wilson reported the comment of Major General (Tom) Holland (GOC 1 Division) on 13 November 1916, that Third Army felt GHQ to be completely out of touch and wholly out of sympathy with them. Wilson put the blame on 'Haig and GHQ who write nonsense and who are wholly inaccessible and who are therefore useless as guides, philosophers or friends'.[25]

Wilson's comments have to be viewed in the light of his feelings about Haig, but the quoted comments of many others in his diary, in addition to the general feeling that staff at GHQ never bothered to see the front for themselves,[26] gives the impression of a group who consciously or unconsciously had isolated themselves from the rest of the army. Liaison officers, who had the duty to inform GHQ of conditions at the front and in other units, either did not go to the front, or rarely did so – or being junior officers, did not have the influence to override Corps and Army staff officers.[27] The question of GHQ staff not visiting the front is an interesting one in the light of the postwar publicity over the story that when Kiggell and Lieutenant Colonel R. L. Aspinall did later visit the road to St Jean at Passchendaele, Kiggell became upset and allegedly said, 'Did we really order men to advance over such ground?'[28] The reason that GHQ staff did not visit the front in 1916 and 1917 seems to be partly because Haig had decreed in 1915, as GOC First Army, 'that no staff officer was to go nearer the trenches than a certain line'. This was because of the danger involved for difficult-to-replace staff officers. The order appears to have originated in October 1915 in GHQ under Sir John

French who, after three of his divisional generals had been killed, said that such senior officers should not visit the front.[29]

At the same time, it seems that Haig found his liaison reports sufficient, and in accordance with his Staff College perception that the Commander-in-Chief should set objectives and then leave subordinates to carry out the task, without interference. Hence it was not as important for Haig or GHQ staff to see the front as it was for, say, Corps and Division commanders and their staffs. Edmonds also suggests another reason for GHQ staff not visiting the front, and this was that Haig and his GHQ did not *know* Kitchener's New Army or feel strong emotional ties to the new units. There was therefore less interest in finding out conditions in these visits, and consciously or unconsciously, the conditions at the front were avoided. As Aylmer Haldane noted in April 1916, Plumer and Haig 'deliberately shut their eyes to facts which we at the front have to face'. According to Haldane, Plumer changed the subject or did not listen when casualties or unpleasant facts were mentioned, Allenby got angry, and GHQ's reaction was to try to find scapegoats when things went wrong. Finally, when Liddell Hart talked to J. F. C. Fuller after the war, the latter argued that GHQ did not improve until new staff officers like Dill,* Paget and Nethersole were appointed to GHQ in 1918 and went to the front to see for themselves.[30] This would imply that it was the age, past experience and training of the 1916 and 1917 GHQ staff that was at fault, and it is likely that this is part of the answer.

In fact the problem of senior officers not knowing conditions at the front, and not visiting the front, was not limited to GHQ. It is clear that Corps, Army and some Divisional commanders did not normally visit the front, and that a wide gulf separated Corps HQ from Divisional HQ, and again that a rift sometimes existed between Divisional HQ and Brigade.[31] These complaints were so frequent that it is evident that a basic problem in command structure existed in the BEF, from GHQ downwards. Haldane partly identified this structural problem when he wrote in August 1916 that Corps HQ acted as a kind of post office, with Divisions as mere tenants, so that Corps HQ did not seem to take responsibility for the front line or the rear lines, and as Divisions moved, there was no continuity. He complained again in October 1916, 'I am told that in the 3rd Corps, Pulteney and his BGGS Romer, never go to the trenches, so get little first hand information. What Corps commanders do all day ... I cannot imagine'.[32]

The problem was not solely one of inexperienced staffs. It was also due to the large increase in the size of the army, and to a traditional sense of army hierarchy whereby information and orders came down the chain of command, while lower-level reports from the front were often disregarded or treated with scepticism.[33] GHQ itself mistrusted the experience and skill of lower commanders, but were not in close enough touch with the rest of the BEF to rectify the situation. In fact, Liddell Hart in conversation with Gough and Lloyd George after the war came to the conclusion that GHQ did not actually command the BEF, but left Army commanders alone to do the actual planning and fighting. This was certainly in line with Haig's Staff College understanding of the non-interventionist role of the Commander-in-Chief, but it did create a vacuum in command. Aylmer Haldane supported this argument when in 1916, after the failure at St Eloi, he wrote, 'The fact is that GHQ is without a policy. The tail wags the dog, and Army commanders who have their own advancement in sight, submit schemes, instead of GHQ . . . so that what is ordered may fit in with the general policy. But there being no general policy except that of frittering away and trying to exhaust the enemy, GHQ seems to cling to any straw that offers.' Indeed, senior commanders did seem to be given *carte blanche* to a large degree; for example Haking's attack at Fromelles was criticized by a Captain on the staff of 182nd Infantry Brigade: 'The weakness of GHQ lay in not seeing that a Corps commander, left to himself, would also be tempted to win glory for his Corps by a spectacular success, and would be prodigal in using the Divisions that passed through his hands for this purpose.[34]

To be fair, GHQ did pursue an overall strategy after 14 July 1916 of wearing down and then the decisive blow, and GHQ's non-interference policy was at least one possible way of operating, but the overwhelming evidence available for 1916 and 1917 shows that Haig and GHQ's position in relation to the BEF can be summed up in the words 'poor communications'. As has been argued, some of the blame for this must rest with Haig himself. But it is also clear, as later chapters will show in regard to the Somme and Passchendaele, that Haig was often in a dilemma over which kind of offensive to pursue – set piece versus breakthrough – and that his indecision over this made it difficult for him to issue clear instructions to his army commanders, resulting in confusion and further poor communications. Also GHQ sometimes deliberately created confusion, particularly when dealing with politicians. This was the case when Charteris phoned from GHQ to Fifth Army HQ in 1917, with instructions to remove all able-bodied prisoners from the prisoner compound when Lloyd George visited, but to leave the remainder, so as to give a false impression of the general state of the German army. It seems also that Haig and GHQ overcame Cabinet doubts in June 1917 about the proposed Passchendaele offensive, by underestimating German strength and British troop requirements and overestimating French support.[35]

It has already been argued that Haig's personality, his Staff College training, and structural problems in the BEF were responsible for largely isolating GHQ from the rest of the army. But this isolation resulted, as might be expected, in conformist small-group decision-making. Irving Janis has shown how small-group decision-making can convert to a 'group think' conformity,[36] and this theory can usefully be applied to GHQ to explain how the process operated. Janis points out that three pre-conditions are necessary for 'group think' to operate. First, *insulation of the policy-making group*, which provides no opportunity for the members to obtain expert information and critical evaluation from others within the organization. A second feature is *lack of a tradition of impartial leadership*. In the absence of appropriate leadership traditions, the leader of a policy-making group will find it all too easy to use his or her power and prestige to influence the members of the group to approve of the policy alternative he or she prefers, instead of encouraging them to engage in open inquiry and critical evaluation. A third administrative or structural factor is *the lack of norms requiring methodical procedures for dealing with the decision-making tasks*.[37]

These 'group think' pre-conditions are evidently applicable to Haig and GHQ, and even more so in a hierarchical and 'personalized' army such as the BEF, where GHQ could exert tremendous influence. Hence those officers who actually did dissent found that they were charged with having the wrong attitude,[38] while those who kept to the official GHQ line found safety and advancement, as shown in Chapter 1.[39] There was also a later suggestion by Edmonds that innovation was even seen as something of a threat, thus further increasing the insulation of GHQ from the outside world. 'What one cannot hint – except very occasionally – is that the great ones resented suggestions and ideas, fearing perhaps that if they encouraged such things they might in the end lose their jobs.'[40]

Many factors therefore went into the isolation of GHQ and the Commander-in-Chief – some of them based on Haig's understanding of the role of the Commander-in-Chief – but the net result was a paralysis at the top, which prevented change, innovation and rational planning. In effect, there existed a command vacuum, which led to changes in tactics, ideas and training filtering upwards and sideways to avoid GHQ, rather than downwards from GHQ. For example, the *Official History* pointed out that it was not until 1917 that the General Staff at GHQ produced training manuals for general use, and there was a general complaint that GHQ never made any attempt to forecast and provide against variations in enemy tactics. Instead, out-of-date enemy pamphlets were translated and instructions issued based on these pamphlets.[41]

A typical comment regarding GHQ's attitude toward training and the establishment of training schools came from Brigadier General Kentish, who wrote in 1917, 'What has been done in the training line in France is due more to individual efforts of Army, Corps, Divisions and Brigade commands than to any clear direction from Higher Command (GHQ)'. Similarly, the driving force behind the creation of Army and Corps training schools came from individuals rather than GHQ, and the Army schools were created by the individual efforts of General Sir Charles

Monro.[42] GHQ apparently had little interest in the Army schools, while Haig actually ordered the abolition of Corps schools in favour of the Divisional schools. However, Haig's decision was unworkable and the order was later reversed. In general, GHQ did not seem to be concerned with large-scale training. 'It is curiously *stupid* how Haig and Kiggell ignore the schools', wrote Henry Wilson on 21 October 1916, and he had already complained in August and September 1916 of Haig's desire to close down the Corps schools. In late August he also commented that First Army School had not received a single paper from GHQ, nor a visit from Haig, Kiggell, Butler or Davidson.[43] It is also apparent that the evolution of ideas on attack and defence developed on an *ad hoc* basis among senior commanders. It is striking how often Henry Wilson noted in his diary the tips and 'wrinkles' on attack and defence that he obtained from visiting friends, including Foch.[44] This was a natural and useful development, but was in fact a casual and *ad hoc* method of learning ideas and tactics that necessarily took the place of a GHQ system that simply did not exist.

GHQ's lack of tactical direction is also illustrated by the fact that when Kiggell did issue GHQ's 'Training of Divisions for Offensive Action' in May 1916, the general emphasis on discipline, and the weight and impetus of the assault was traditional, while most tactical points were merely copies from Fourth Army's 'Tactical Notes' of April 1916. Moreover, GHQ's advice contained little instruction on the artillery, and did not emphasize counterbattery work. For that matter, Fourth Army's 'Tactical Notes' were also weak on the artillery, and infantry-artillery co-operation. It is also noteworthy that when Fourth Army attempted to learn lessons from the first weeks on the Somme by asking divisional commanders to write in with comments, there was a considerable reluctance actually to point out mistakes, and when Brigadier General Kentish did so, he was in turn criticized for being a critic! This seems to have been a very different process from that taking place in the German army after the removal of von Falkenhayn in 1916, when contrary opinions and suggestions were accepted and actually encouraged by the operations section of the German Army High Command (OHL), in order to develop appropriate tactics.[45]

The evolution of ideas, therefore, ran into the difficulties of the continuation of prewar army hierarchy as well as of GHQ remoteness. It was also important that Robertson (then CIGS), Maxse, and later Gough, all pointed out a serious flaw in the evolution of ideas that existed both at Fourth Army HQ and at GHQ in 1916, namely, the tendency always to stress principles rather than actual methods. Principles were easy to enunciate and required little imagination because they were traditional and generally accepted. But it began to be apparent in 1916 that principles still had to be applied on the ground, and that specific methods were required and not general principles. Thus, in July 1916, Robertson told

Rawlinson that principles were all very well 'but their application is a very difficult business, and I think that we still take these principles too literally'. Maxse also told Major General A. A. Montgomery in reply to Montgomery's request for lessons of the Somme, that methods were wanted, not principles, while Gough severely attacked Rawlinson's Fourth Army for using general principles that had no real application on the ground:

> Rawlinson and the Fourth Army had very little real capacity for command or tactical sense ... and that instead, under the influence of prudent general principles, which had no particular application to the situation before them, they let most valuable opportunities slip. Platitudes, rather than realities, were their guide.

Gough was being over-critical, but there was truth in this evaluation, and as though to deflect such criticism, Fourth Army's 'Tactical Notes' of April 1916 had concluded by stressing the need to adapt the principles of war to the new conditions.[46]

GHQ did indeed have a tendency to issue generalized instructions, particularly in July 1916, and to stress the demoralization of the enemy as a general principle of war. Typical of this aspect was a series of orders and letters from GHQ in early July 1916. For example, Kiggell's memo of 6 July 1916 from Advanced GHQ declared there was 'conclusive evidence of considerable loss of morale and confusion on the enemy's side', and stated that 'serious demoralisation may set in at any time, possibly tomorrow', therefore the Commander-in-Chief wanted commanders to watch closely for symptoms of serious demoralization among the enemy's troops. Two days later Haig wrote to his army commanders, telling them, 'It is of the highest importance that all commanders in touch with the enemy shall watch the state of his *moral* [sic] closely, and be guided in their actions by their judgement of it'. However Haig did admit that it was very difficult to estimate the enemy's morale, even when in close touch.[47] GHQ continued to stress the importance of breaking enemy morale until the end of July 1916, at which time there was a reversion to the principle of the 'wearing out' battle,[48] although there still continued to be a great emphasis on the state of enemy morale.

Even GHQ seems to have realized by the end of September 1916 that the general concepts of pressing the enemy, wearing down, breaking morale, drawing in reserves, the decisive blow etc., were vague, and that actual methods were far more useful. In an interesting defence of GHQ policies, Brigadier General Davidson (GHQ) wrote a Note on 25 September 1916, replying to criticisms of heavy Somme casualties. After an obligatory reference to the wearing-out battle leading to decisive results, Davidson admitted that the artillery knew the principles of mass artillery and the creeping barrage, but did not know how to apply those principles.

After a strange attempt to blame the New Armies for essentially being too brave, Davidson went on to admit that there had been times when 'great tactical principles have not been applied', thus resulting in casualties. Davidson really meant that realistic methods had not been used, and argued that improvization in war (i.e. applying new methods) was difficult.[49]

Perhaps it was as well that GHQ did not see its role as that of deciding on specific methods of attack and defence, since there was a general consensus that Haig himself did not understand some aspects of modern war. Edmonds was particularly hard on Haig, claiming that 'He [Haig] knew nothing about infantry or engineers, and could not understand artillery', and particularly criticized his tendency to decentralize the guns. On another point, Edmonds declared that Haig could not grasp technical matters, such as railways and the use of concrete. General Barrow* (MGGS First Army) also pointed out that Haig had trouble using technical innovations such as gas and tanks in the most useful ways.[50] Kiggell, too, had some problems with new technology. One example occurred on 3 February 1916, when he told Henry Wilson that in the event of *Flammen werfer* attacks the first defence line should be given up, and the support line strongly held instead. Rawlinson replied, enclosing Wilson's comments, which pointed out there was no attack expected, and that 'to be logical, we ought to fill in every front trench within 50 yards of the enemy's front line'. Therefore, Rawlinson declared, there was no need to move back. On 5 February 1916 Haig intervened on Kiggell's behalf and ordered machine-guns into the front trench, while still developing strong support trenches.[51] The conclusion then was that there was no need to retreat from the first line, even in the event of *Flammen werfer* attacks! On another topic, Kiggell (or perhaps Haig) was in difficulties about whether to use High Explosive (HE) or shrapnel for cutting wire. In fact HE was much more effective, but in April 1916, Kiggell wrote to von Donop (the MGO) regarding the latter's recommendation of 50 per cent each of HE and shrapnel, 'this recommendation was based primarily on the assumption that HE was as effective for wire cutting as shrapnel – an assumption which experience has proved to be wrong'. As a result, in May 1916, the army in France went back to 25 per cent of HE as against 75 per cent shrapnel.[52]

It was, in fact, in the artillery area that GHQ had most to learn. According to Colonel Rawlins, artillery tactical developments came from experience and not from GHQ, so that it was Corps and Division which developed ideas and tactics and not GHQ or Army. Again, this was not necessarily a bad thing, yet, as with infantry tactics and ideas, the evolution of artillery tactics from the ground up occurred because there was no system in place to guide the artillery arm. Worse than this, according to Rawlins, was the 'deep seated prejudice' in GHQ 'against any definite recognition of higher artillery command'. Rather than prejudice, it was more likely to be the ignorance of a cavalry and infantry dominated GHQ, for when Major General 'Curly' Birch was appointed to be artillery adviser to GHQ in June 1916, artillery doctrine was then evolved, tactics were developed by artillery officers, and accepted by the artillery arm.[53]

Another well-known problem at GHQ was the over-optimism of Charteris (in charge of GHQ intelligence), which did much to promote the isolated 'group think' syndrome of Haig and his staff. By the end of 1917 Charteris had lost his credibility, and Robertson went to GHQ to remove him and others.[54] Brigadier General Bonham-Carter* (Staff Duties and Training at GHQ) judged that Charteris indulged in *à priori* thinking,[55] and was therefore often wrong because of this. Fortunately there exists for 1916–17 detailed correspondence between Charteris and Macdonogh (DMI at the War Office), which reveals Charteris's approach to problems in this period.

Before the Somme battle commenced, Charteris was confident that the Russian offensive of early June 1916 against Austria would result in the Germans shifting several divisions from the west to Russia, although Haig himself was confused as to whether Charteris was arguing for German troops going to or from Russia![56] However, by 6 July Charteris was not sure which German divisions had gone to Russia, perhaps only three had gone. On 9 July Charteris now felt that only the 5th (German) Division had gone, but by 20 July it was clear that no German divisions at all had left the Western Front.[57] So much, therefore, for the overall strategy of two fronts attacking together in order to divert German reserves. However Charteris's major error during the Somme was always to assume that German morale was lower than it actually was. Because of this he and Macdonogh engaged in a fairly acrimonious correspondence, particularly when GHQ decided to do some propaganda work of its own, normally the province of the DMI at the War Office. In late July 1916 Macdonogh told Charteris to leave propaganda alone, and criticized Charteris for undue optimism in estimating the state of German morale as low.[58] Then in early August 1916, Charteris attached an intelligence report to a Haig memo, in which he evidently argued that German reserves available amounted to only 300,000 men. In contrast, Macdonogh estimated two million German men were available! Macdonogh wrote that Charteris's 300,000 was obviously a minimum and must refer only to men in Germany and not to those in Field Depots, while his own two million was a maximum estimate. Furthermore, while Charteris argued that the 1918 German class of recruits could not be available before January 1917, Macdonogh claimed that they could take to the field after four months training if urgently required, i.e. in mid-October 1916. Macdonogh concluded, 'I can therefore see no hope of exhausting the German reserves of personnel this year'.[59]

The argument between Charteris and Macdonogh was really about strategy. Charteris and Haig obviously hoped to work through the German reserves and then achieve the decisive blow they sought on the Somme, while Macdonogh was sceptical both as to the strategy and GHQ estimates of German reserves available. In fact Charteris's reply to Macdonogh in August 1917 really gave the game away – although he disagreed about the early arrival of the 1918 class, he admitted that the 1916 class had barely arrived at the Somme. Hence there was no chance of exhausting German reserves 'irretrievably' in 1916, and thus by implication GHQ's 'decisive blow' strategy was likely to be a failure. However, Charteris tried to paper over the failure in a confusing way by arguing that if the Somme battle was carried on, it would 'result in the German losses having outrun the resources which will be available up to the end of the year, altho' of course he [Germany] will rectify this by the early Spring [of 1917] with the 1918 classes and other reserves coming in'.[60] It was not clear therefore why the Somme battle should be continued, if it had no chance of success.

The simmering feud between Charteris and Macdonogh continued throughout the Somme, over the same two points of, first, German morale and, secondly, who was supposed to be doing propaganda work. Charteris's letters continued the rather confusing dialectic of strong optimism about low German morale (often couched in personalized terms), together with an admission that the battle probably could not be won in 1916. On 1 October 1916 Charteris wrote:[61]

> We are getting very optimistic here with regard to the fighting. There is no doubt that the German is a changed man when opposed to British infantry now. His tail is down, he surrenders freely, and on several occasions he has thrown down his rifle and ran away, and altogether there is hope that a really bad rot may set in any day. Do not think this means I am over sanguine. No one who has seen the ground here over which the men are fighting can be. Still, there is a possibility.

After another rebuke from Macdonogh about propaganda and overestimating the fall of German morale, Charteris returned to the attack with the same confusing combination of personalized optimism and admission of strategic failure:[62]

> the German, though he is very far from being a demoralized enemy, is most undoubtedly not of the same calibre as he was this time last year. The offensive has shaken him up in a way that is very difficult for anybody not here to realise. He is trying to conceal this from neutrals. I have certain fears that he may succeed in concealing it from our own people.

The feud between Charteris and Macdonogh was symbolic of the differences between GHQ and the War Office in London over the Somme battle and its continued difficulties. A neutral observer, Major General G. S. Clive, watched the development of the feud, and in his diary remarked that he sympathized with Macdonogh, and felt that Charteris was a difficult man to combat, and was on the spot. A little later, in early October 1916, Clive observed that Charteris was only interested in Macdonogh from his own point of view, implying that Charteris was not playing a straight game. It is interesting to note also that Butler at GHQ explained the feud to Clive by saying that the argument between Macdonogh and Charteris was really only Sapper jealousy, implying that the problems were personal rather than a real difference of opinion about the Somme.[63] Macdonogh was evidently sceptical of GHQ's conduct of the battle, and after the war told Edmonds that he was something of an Easterner, and thought that the British army too had been destroyed at the Somme.[64]

The War Office, Robertson and the War Cabinet, were all obviously finding it difficult to control Charteris and GHQ, and suspected that GHQ was not telling the full story of what was going on. After the war Gough argued that Charteris made statements which would please Haig, and that even Army and Corps intelligence officers knew how very unreliable Charteris's efforts were.[65] However, although Charteris obviously followed the GHQ 'line' in regard to the Somme, a greater problem was the intelligence system and the kind of intelligence that was gathered. Charteris himself claimed that Haig relied on Macdonogh for positive information only and not forecasts.[66] This meant that Charteris and GHQ intelligence was supposedly responsible for forecasts, but a perusal of Charteris's intelligence reports reveal an emphasis on the movements of enemy units and numbers; evaluation of the German press; and comments on German morale, derived from captured German prisoners and documents.[67] There was no analysis of enemy tactics or strategy apart from the translation of German documents and of French analyses, and no forecasting. Perhaps Charteris felt that this was not necessary, for GHQ really *was* waiting for German morale to break, yet the state of enemy morale was something that by its very nature could not easily be forecast, although Charteris continued in early 1917 to comment on falling German morale.[68]

Charteris's approach to military problems no doubt derived from a variety of sources, but his Indian Staff College papers of 1907 still exist, and show once again the tendency of officers to quote tags of principles from military thinkers such as Clausewitz and von der Goltz without really understanding them or thinking about their application. In his 1907 essay 'The Relative Advantage of Offensive and Defensive Strategy', Charteris, then a Sapper Captain, cited Clausewitz on defence and offence

117

and von der Goltz on the principle that the aim of all war is the imposition of the will of the victor on that of the vanquished. No doubt true, but how to do it? Charteris decided logically enough that only offensive action could lead to quick 'decisive results'.[69] A simple conclusion, but hardly useful in a battle situation, and in effect a continuation of the late nineteenth-century concept of decisive offensive action and the importance of morale. Another Charteris essay, also from 1907, entitled 'The Decisive Factor in War' came to the conclusion that time was the great factor in war, and he also strangely criticized the Boers for lack of military spirit, and their unwillingness to take risks.[70] Taken together – the concepts of time (the necessity for swift attacks), running risks, the importance of morale, and the desire to achieve decisive results – all these Charteris helped to apply nine years later at the Somme. However, the day had passed when these principles could easily be applied in such a straightforward manner.

Reviewing the role of Haig and GHQ, one is struck by the way in which Haig and his staff conceived of themselves as master planners who issued generalized instructions, but did not often get down to working out what was actually happening on the ground. There was not one simple reason for this, but several: Haig's own inner-directed personality, his training at Staff College, structural problems at GHQ, and so on, yet all seemed to revolve around the functional isolation of GHQ. Haig and his staff certainly did their best, but they were overwhelmed by the size of the army, by the difficulty of applying a late-nineteenth-century concept of war to the tactics of a different twentieth-century war, and by an inability to devise means for coming to grips with a changed style of war. In a strange way GHQ seemed to become or make itself largely irrelevant during the Somme and Passchendaele battles – rather like a Deist Being who set the clock running and then retreated to observe results. The ability to solve problems through discussion seemed to disappear, and so the battles of the Somme and Passchendaele proceeded with a momentum largely of their own. For a test case of this conclusion, it will be useful to look at the planning and execution of the Somme offensive and a later chapter will advert to this problem again in regard to the planning of the Passchendaele offensive.

Notes

1 General Sir James Marshall-Cornwall, *Haig As Military Commander* (London, 1973), p. 240; Captain B. H. Liddell Hart, *Reputations* (London, 1928), pp. 120–3; Bidwell and Graham, *Fire-Power*, p. 63. Still the best biography is that of John Terraine, *Douglas Haig: the Educated Soldier* (London, 1963). Recent interpretations have been less sympathetic, although often without Terraine's research. A psychoanalytic interpretation of Haig is

offered in Norman F. Dixon, *On the Psychology of Military Incompetence* (London, 1976), pp. 249–53, 371–92. Dixon's analysis is rather one-sided in attributing, for example, all the problems of Passchendaele to Haig's personality. As Marx might have commented, subjective conditions (Haig's personality) should be matched by objective conditions (the material and technical factors).

2 Liddell Hart, Talk with Edmonds, 8 December 1930, 11/1935/—[59], Liddell Hart Papers, KCL; Major General Sir E. D. Swinton to Liddell Hart, 17 March 1950, 1/259/217, Liddell Hart Papers, KCL; Henry Wilson, Diary, 18 August 1916, 15 September 1916, 29 September 1916, 28 October 1916, Wilson Papers, IWM; Archibald Murray to Spears, 11 May 1931, 10, Spears Papers, KCL.

3 David Riesman, *The Lonely Crowd*, Yale paperback edn (New Haven and London, 1961), pp. 15–16.

4 E. M. Haig (wife of William Haig) to Lady Haig, 7 April 1928, 322a (Childhood and Schools), Haig Papers, NLS.

5 Lady Haig, 'Notes for Bee' (Haig's brother), 322a, Haig Papers, NLS; John Charteris, *Field Marshal Earl Haig* (London, 1929), pp. 25, 44, 389; Sergeant T. Secrett, *25 Years with Earl Haig* (London, 1929), p. 54; Edmonds, 'Memoirs', ch. XIV, p. 266, Edmonds Papers, KCL.

6 Charteris, *Earl Haig*, p. 9; John Charteris, *Field Marshal Earl Haig*, 2nd edn (London, 1933), pp. 41–2; Secrett, *25 Years*, pp. 157–8, 159–60, 174–5, 207.

7 Charteris, *Earl Haig* (1929), p. 60.

8 John Charteris, *At GHQ* (London, 1931), p. 169; Liddell Hart, Talk with J. F. C. Fuller, who repeated the information from Brigadier General Cox (BGS, Intelligence), 1 October 1929, 11/1929/16, Liddell Hart Papers, KCL.

9 Haig to Henrietta (his sister), 23 April 1895, 6b, Haig Papers, NLS; Charteris, *Earl Haig* (1929), p. 65; Haig to Lady Haig, 9 January 1916 and 16 February 1916, 143, Haig Papers, NLS.

10 Charteris, *Earl Haig* (1929), pp. 36, 69; Charteris, *Earl Haig* (1933), p. 41; Liddell Hart, Talk with J. F. C. Fuller (quoting Edmonds), 1 October 1929, 11/1929/16, Liddell Hart Papers, KCL. In fairness to Haig, he did undertake a considerable amount of military reading, especially around 1910, and earlier at Staff College. Charteris meant that Haig never read a novel, or literature outside the military profession.

11 Haig to Lady Haig, 22 June 1916 and 30 June 1916. Haig first seems to have become aware of divine help in February 1916, Haig to Lady Haig, 15 February 1916. It is also noticeable that these references to God's assistance disappear as the Somme campaign lost its potential for a decisive result, 143, Haig Papers, NLS; Liddell Hart, *Through the Fog of War* (London, 1938), pp. 52–7; David Woodward, *Lloyd George and the Generals* (Delaware, 1983), p. 75.

12 Liddell Hart, Talk with Hubert Gough, 9 April 1935, 11/1935/72, Liddell Hart Papers, KCL.

13 Liddell Hart, Talk with Sir Charles Bonham-Carter, 12 December 1935, 11/1935/114, Liddell Hart Papers, KCL. Gough to Edmonds, 2 February 1944, Cab 45/33, 'Flanders 1917', inside Cab 45/140, PRO.

14 Wilson, Diary, 29 June 1916, 1 September 1916, 1 November 1916, Wilson Papers, IWM. Haig to Lady Haig, 24 December 1915, 143, Haig Papers, NLS; Kiggell to Edmonds, 16 June 1938, Cab 45/135, PRO.

15 Haldane, Diary, Edmonds to Aylmer Haldane, 17 March 1931 and 22 April 1916, Haldane Papers, NLS; also Wilson, Diary, 12 July 1916, and 22 June

1916, Wilson Papers, IWM; Liddell Hart, Talk with Edmonds, 23 April 1937, 11/1937/30, Liddell Hart Papers, KCL.

16 Liddell Hart, Talk with Edmonds, 1938, 11/1938/59, Liddell Hart Papers, KCL; cf. Edmonds, 'Memoirs', Ch. XXVI, p. 1, Edmonds Papers, KCL.

17 Gough to Edmonds, 27 May 1945, Cab 45/33 inside Cab 45/140, PRO.

18 Haig, Diary, 14 January 1916, WO 256/7, PRO.

19 Rawlinson, Diary, 6 April 1916, 10 April 1916, 17 May 1916, 22 June 1916, Rawlinson Papers, CCC; Haldane, Diary, 7 August 1916, 8 November 1916, also 7 November 1916, 27 November 1916 etc., Haldane Papers, NLS; Edmonds, 'Memoirs', ch. XIV, p. 270, Edmonds Papers, KCL; Lieutenant General Sir Ronald Charles also thought Allenby a disaster, and noted that Allenby made terrific scenes if soldiers were improperly dressed, Liddell Hart, Diary Notes, 2 February 1939, Talk with Lieutenant General Sir Ronald Charles, 11/1939/6, Liddell Hart Papers, KCL.

20 Haig, Diary, 11 July 1916, WO 256/11, PRO; Record of discussion over July 14 attack, Advanced GHQ, 13 July 1916, Fourth Army, WO 158/233, PRO.

21 Rawlinson, Diary, 13 July 1916 and 14 July 1916, 5201–33–26, Rawlinson Papers, NAM.

22 Operations of 14 July 1916, p. 6, 5201–33–69, Rawlinson Papers, NAM. See also the comments of Luckock and Montgomery on Haig's 'awful' plan, and the influence of Lawrence, Major General R. M. Luckock to Edmonds, 22 December 1937, and Field Marshal Sir Archibald Montgomery-Massingberd to Edmonds, 7 December 1937, Cab 45/135 and Cab 45/136, PRO.

23 In September 1915 Major General du Cane complained that GHQ was unapproachable except by mail, and this took weeks to get a response; reported by Rawlinson, Diary, 1 September 1915, Rawlinson Papers, CCC. See also Major General Sir Archibald Montgomery-Massingberd to Edmonds, 11 January 1926, Cab 45/121, PRO.

24 Maxse to (Tiny) Maxse, 17 October 1916, Maxse Papers, WSRO.

25 Wilson, Diary, 1 September 1916, 3 September 1916, 24 September 1916, 17 October 1916, 1 November 1916, 13 November 1916, Wilson Papers, IWM.

26 Wilson, Diary, 6 November 1916, quoting Woodroffe for Advanced GHQ, Wilson Papers, IWM; Shoulbridge to Maxse, 30 July 1916, 69/57/7, Maxse Papers, IWM; Brigadier General Antill to Hutton, 26 November 1916, 50086, Hutton Papers, BL; Haldane, Diary, 21 March 1917, in 13, Spears Papers, KCL.

27 Liddell Hart, Talk with Sir Charles Bonham-Carter, 12 December 1935, 11/1935/114; Talk with Major General C. C. Armitage, 15 May 1936, 11/1936/62; Talk with Sir Edward Grigg, 15 May 1936, 11/1936/63, Liddell Hart Papers, KCL.

28 Liddell Hart, Talk with General Edmonds, 7 October 1927, 11/1927/17, Liddell Hart Papers, KCL. There is some question about the authenticity of this story, although Edmonds believed it was true. The story is reported in Liddell Hart, *History of the First World War*, p. 336.

29 Haldane, Diary, quoting Brigadier General Cator (GOC 37th Brigade), 23 August 1916; and Haldane, 'Autobiography', vol. 2, p. 367, Haldane Papers, NLS.

30 Liddell Hart, Talk with General Edmonds, 7 October 1927, 11/1927/17, Liddell Hart Papers, KCL. Haldane, Diary, 6 April 1916, 20 April 1916, Haldane Papers, NLS. Liddell Hart, Talk with J. F. C. Fuller, 1 October 1929, 11/1929/16, Liddell Hart Papers, KCL.

31 Among many examples, Francis Edwards to Edmonds, 6 January 1937, Cab 45/133; R. Fitzmaurice to Edmonds, 7 November 1937, Cab 45/133; R.

Luckock to Edmonds, 25 January 1931, Cab 45/135; Charles Page to Edmonds, 1 June 1929, Cab 45/136; Colonel William Parker to Edmonds, Cab 45/136; Lieutenant Colonel Parry Jones to Edmonds, 13 October 1937, Cab 45/136; E. G. Wace to Edmonds, 30 October 1936, Cab 45/138; H. W. Higginson to Edmonds, 1 January 1934, Cab 45/134, PRO.

32 Haldane, Diary, 11 August 1916, 26 October 1916, Haldane Papers, NLS. It would seem, however, that Haldane had reasonable links with his Corps commander, Congreve, when he himself commanded 3 Division, Brigadier H. Potter to Edmonds, no date, Cab 45/136, PRO.

33 E. Woulfe Flanagan to Edmonds, 19 December 1934, Cab 45/133; Lieutenant Colonel Hole to Edmonds, 6 November [?], Cab 45/134; D. F. Anderson to Edmonds, 6 April 1936, Cab 45/132; H. H. Tudor to Edmonds, 2 December 1933, Cab 45/138; George Lindsay to Edmonds, 28 June 1937, Cab 45/135, PRO.

34 Liddell Hart, Lunch with Gough and Lloyd George, 27 January 1936, 11/1936/31, Liddell Hart Papers, KCL; Haldane, Diary, 6 May 1916, Haldane Papers, NLS; Captain Philip Landon to Edmonds, 2 April 1937, Cab 45/135, PRO.

35 Liddell Hart, Talk with Sir Wilfred Greene, 29 May 1937, 11/1937/46, Liddell Hart Papers, KCL. Greene, as liaison officer at GHQ, stated that he refused to carry out Charteris's order, although it was apparently carried out at Corps level; Leon Wolff gives a brief paragraph to this incident in his *In Flanders Fields*, Penguin edn (Harmondsworth, 1979), p. 222. Liddell Hart, 'Note on Passchendaele', 7 May 1936, 11/1936/57, Liddell Hart Papers, KCL. Cf. Woodward, *Lloyd George and the Generals*, pp. 168–9, 203.

36 Irving Janis, *Groupthink*, 2nd edn (Boston, 1982), ch. 8.

37 ibid., pp. 176–7.

38 Liddell Hart, Talk with Colonel C. Allanson, 19 August 1937, 11/1937/69, Liddell Hart Papers, KCL, referring to the slur against Broadwood. A comparable situation occurred in the United States, in regard to the Vietnam war where Janis points out that nonconformists were branded with losing their effectiveness, Janis, op. cit., p. 115.

39 For example, Edmonds claimed that General Horne owed his rise entirely to agreeing with GHQ everytime, Liddell Hart, Talk with Edmonds, 23 September 1929, 11/1929/15, Liddell Hart Papers, KCL.

40 Edmonds to Liddell Hart, 8 March 1932, 1/259/46, Liddell Hart Papers, KCL.

41 Edmonds, *Military Operations, France and Belgium, 1916* (London, 1932), p. 292; and Edmonds, *Military Operations, France and Belgium, 1918* (London, 1939), p. viii.

42 Brigadier General R. J. Kentish to Maxse, 22 February 1917, 69/57/7, Maxse Papers, IWM.

43 Wilson, Diary, 21 October 1916, and 11 August 1916, 6 September 1916, 28 August 1916, Wilson Papers, IWM; Haldane also complained about the abolition of Corps schools, Haldane, Diary, 24 October 1916, Haldane Papers, NLS.

44 Wilson remarked on 12 September 1916 that he got many 'wrinkles' from Foch on how to attack, and unofficial advice from other friends on various other occasions, e.g. Jimmy Shea (GOC 30 Division) on 14 August 1916. Wilson, Diary, 12 September 1916 and 15 August 1916, Wilson Papers, IWM.

45 R. J. Kentish to Montgomery (Divisional Reports on Somme fighting), 4 August 1916, 47, Montgomery-Massingberd Papers, KCL; and R. J. Kentish to Maxse, 22 February 1917, 69/57/7, Maxse Papers, IWM. For German practice, see below in Epilogue; also Timothy T. Lupfer, *The Dynamics of*

Doctrine: the Changes in German Tactical Doctrine during the First World War (Fort Leavenworth: Kansas, 1981), pp. 8–11 and *passim*.

46 Robertson to Rawlinson, 26 July 1916, 1/35/100, Robertson Papers, KCL; Maxse to Montgomery (Divisional Reports on Somme fighting), 31 July 1916, 47, Montgomery-Massingberd Papers, KCL; Gough to Edmonds, 16 June 1938, Cab 45/135, PRO; Fourth Army 'Tactical Notes', signed by A. A. Montgomery, 11 April 1916, p. 31, 5201–33–71, Rawlinson Papers, NAM.

47 Kiggell, 6 July 1916; Commander-in-Chief to Allenby, Gough, Rawlinson, 8 July 1916, 111 (Kiggell signed for Haig), Fourth Army, WO 158/234, PRO.

48 Kiggell, 2 August 1916, Fourth Army, WO 158/235, PRO.

49 Brigadier General J. H. Davidson, 'Note on the criticism that our casualties have been too heavy in proportion to the results gained', 25 September 1916, 4, Creedy–Kitchener Papers, WO 159/8, PRO.

50 Liddell Hart, Diary Notes, 13 September 1930, 11/1930/15; and Talk with Edmonds, 8 December 1930, in 'Facts', 7 February 1935, 11/1935/59, Liddell Hart Papers, KCL. Wilson, Diary, 4 April 1916, Wilson Papers, IWM.

51 Kiggell to Henry Wilson, 3 February 1916; Rawlinson to Kiggell, 3 February 1916; Haig to Monro, 5 February 1916, First Army, WO 158/185, PRO.

52 Kiggell (for Commander-in-Chief) to MGO, 19 April 1916, cited in Major General Sir Stanley von Donop (MGO), 'The Supply of Munitions to the Army' (1919), opposite p. 145, and p. 27, 69/74/1, von Donop Papers, IWM. In fairness, it would seem that GHQ had trouble getting CRAs (Commanders Royal Artillery) to draw HE as they mostly asked for shrapnel, ibid., p. 29.

53 Colonel Rawlins, 'A History of the Development of British Artillery in France, 1914–1918', pp. 88–9, 92, 103, 109, 115, MD/1162, Rawlins Papers, RAI.

54 Robertson to Henry Wilson, 16 December 1917, Correspondence with Robertson, 73/1/6, Wilson Papers, IWM.

55 Liddell Hart, Talk with Sir Charles Bonham-Carter, 12 December 1935, 11/1935/114, Liddell Hart Papers, KCL.

56 Haig, Diary, Charteris, 'Situation on the 18 June 1916', 19 June 1916, WO 256/10, PRO.

57 Charteris to Macdonogh, 6 July 1916, 9 July 1916, Macdonogh to Charteris, 20 July 1916, WO 158/897, PRO.

58 ibid., Charteris to Macdonogh, 21 July 1916; Macdonogh to Charteris, 23 July 1916, and 25 July 1916; Charteris to Macdonogh, 28 July 1916; Macdonogh to Charteris, 1 August 1916.

59 ibid., Macdonogh to Charteris, 8 August 1916.

60 ibid., Charteris to Macdonogh, 9 August 1916. Charteris also indicated in this letter that he had used the French army's GQG figures on reserves under special circumstances, i.e. to keep the French fighting at the Somme.

61 ibid., Charteris to Macdonogh, 1 October 1916.

62 ibid., Charteris to Macdonogh, 26 October 1916; and for Macdonogh's rebukes, Macdonogh to Charteris, 9 October 1916 and 24 October 1916.

63 Major General G. S. Clive, Diary, 6 September 1916, where Clive saw the two opposing sides as Kiggell and Charteris versus Macdonogh and Robertson, and 26 September 1916, where Clive thought the conflict was between the War Office belittling the BEF versus Charteris not playing straight, 2 October 1916 and 3 October 1916 (Sapper jealousy entry), Cab 45/201/2, PRO.

64 Lieutenant General Sir George Macdonogh to Edmonds, 19 July 1938, Cab 45/136, PRO.

65 Gough, Comments on 1945 Draft Chapter XVII, *Reflections*, referring to Passchendaele, in 'Flanders 1917', Cab 45/140, PRO.

66 Charteris to Edmonds, 22 May 1930, Cab 45/132, PRO.

67 Summaries of Reports Received [from GHQ], 1916, WO 157/8, WO 157/9, WO 157/10, PRO.
68 Charteris to Macdonogh, 3 January 1917 and 11 January 1917, WO 158/897, PRO.
69 Captain Charteris (RE), 'The Relative Advantage of Offensive and Defensive Strategy' (1907), Charteris Papers, WO 79/61, PRO.
70 ibid., Captain Charteris (RE), 'The Decisive Factor in War' (1907).

PART III

A Case Study:
the Somme, 1916

[6]

Preparing the Somme

In analysing GHQ and Fourth Army preparations for the Somme offensive, it is necessary to keep in mind the previous discussion, since a real understanding of the Somme must include prewar attitudes and technical developments, as well as the intellectual evolution of Douglas Haig, relations between GHQ and senior commanders, and the hierarchical, personalized system by which the army operated. Particular attention might be paid to Haig's Staff College ideas and his view of the role of the Commander-in-Chief; the 'detached' status of GHQ; prewar technical thinking, for example in regard to the artillery; the prewar cult of the offensive and stress on morale; and the two evolving 'pessimistic' and 'optimistic' concepts of battle. Finally, as a related undercurrent, there continued to flow the sense of two images or paradigms of war, the late nineteenth-century ideal and the technical ideal, which coexisted uneasily and whose adherents had difficulty mentally in coming to grips with each other.

For Douglas Haig the preparation for the Somme offensive revolved around one fundamental problem: how to apply the traditional principles to what was seen as a new and puzzling form of warfare. In particular, how could an offensive penetrate and break through three lines of defence in depth? In the summer of 1915, faced by the problem of the Second Battle of Ypres, Haig had come to the conclusion that it would be necessary to apply the Napoleonic Advanced Guard strategy of engaging the enemy along a very wide front, and then using the General Reserve to break through at a weak point. Speaking to Lord Haldane at the end of July 1915, Haig said that the war could be won 'by applying the old principles to the present conditions. Engage the enemy on a wide front, the wider the better, 100 miles or more, then after five or six days, bring up a strong Reserve of all arms, attack by surprise and break through where the enemy had shown that he was weak.'[1] This was the idea, learnt at Staff College by Haig, of forcing the enemy to use up his reserves, and then launching the decisive surprise below.

Although the idea of a large front was generally accepted, it was also understood that the particular problem was how to get through to the third and last line of defence, and to the guns, when the third line and sometimes the second line, were out of range and/or observation of one's own artillery. Moreover the distance to be covered was usually greater than could be achieved by the infantry in one rush. Major General G. S. Clive noted in his diary in late 1915 that he and Major General Sir Frederick Maurice had discussed the future 1916 offensive, and were in agreement over the necessity of wearing down the enemy's reserves before the decisive attack, because of the 'uselessness of trying to get forward with the attacking troops once the enemy have fresh reserves on their 2nd or 3rd lines, etc'.[2]

By the end of 1915, most General Staff and GHQ appreciations were focusing on the question of the use of the reserves (remembering the lessons of Loos), and of how to use up the reserves of the enemy. The general conclusion was that it was necessary to go back to first principles, use up the enemy reserves by a series of preparatory attacks, and 'then and then only the decisive attack which is to win victory should be driven home'.[3] In January 1916, the CIGS (Robertson) also concurred that in the modern battle the problem was one of how to employ the reserves. Robertson cautioned that there would not be one great battle, but prolonged fighting leading to some kind of breakthrough, even though this might not be decisive.[4] Robertson's cautions pointed to the problem of just how the enemy's reserves should be used up, while preserving one's own reserves, and whether this process would result in a decisive victory, or would simply be a lengthy process of attrition, followed no doubt by the crumbling morale of the enemy.

In January and February 1916, Douglas Haig, and the various levels of staff, struggled with this problem. It was generally agreed that there should be a three act offensive, consisting of 'wearing down' local attacks, followed by the preparatory attack, and concluding with the 'real decisive effort'.[5] In mid-January 1916, Douglas Haig himself thought in terms of a three act offensive: first, 'wearing down' operations starting in April 1916; then secondly, the preparatory action, which would draw in the enemy reserves 10 to 12 days before, thirdly, the decisive attack was launched. In other communications at that time to Robertson and Kitchener, Haig continued to think of a structured offensive, with a final mass assault where the enemy was weak, 'to break through and win victory'. However, he was careful to note that all the Allies should participate in the wearing out fight simultaneously.[6]

The stage seemed set for a long drawn-out, but clearly planned, campaign. Yet by the end of January and early February 1916, Haig had begun to suspect that the Allies, particularly the French, would not support the necessary wearing down operations; that these operations were not so easy to conduct without great loss to one's own troops; and that the public might very well lay the blame on him and GHQ for any reverses involved.[7] In fact, no one had seriously considered how these wearing down operations should actually work on a practical level, and Haig's memorandum to his GHQ staff in February 1916 showed that he was very uneasy over the likely success of wearing down tactics. He asked his staff, for example, how the wearing out fight would be carried out and how the enemy reserves would be used up, and he remarked that even large operations would not use up a large number of enemy divisions.[8] There does not seem to have been any specific answer to Haig's request for answers. Instead, on 14 February 1916, Haig met with General Joffre, the French Commander-in-Chief, and agreed that there would *not* be a lengthy wearing out fight before the main offensive, but instead a straightforward preparatory attack 10 to 15 days before the main offensive, in order to draw in the enemy reserves. (This was now the transformed role of the Napoleonic Advanced Guard.)

At this interesting stage in the planning, the German army attacked at Verdun, and changed the requirements of the Somme offensive. On 15 March 1915, Haig noted in his diary that because German reserves were being drawn into the Verdun melting pot, there was less need now even for the preparatory attack, and because the First Army had taken over the Tenth (French) Army front, there was not enough manpower for the First Army to mislead with a feint attack. On 10 April 1916, Haig made this view official, writing to Joffre that because of Verdun, preparatory attacks were no longer required, and that all forces should be devoted to the main offensive.[9] It is interesting to note that Haig had now removed both the wearing out fight and the preparatory attack from his original three act battle plan, although confusingly his chief of operations at GHQ, Davidson, was still writing in May 1916 about the preparatory attack followed by the main offensive.[10]

Somehow the traditional Staff College principles upon which the offensive was being planned had crumbled away, and Haig now seemed to shift to the idea of a straightforward breakthrough as reported by Rawlinson on 1 April 1916: 'D. H. is for breaking the line and gambling on rushing the 3rd line on the top of a panic.'[11] And in his 5 April 1916 comments on Rawlinson's scheme for the Somme, Haig declared that it was not sufficient to gain three or four kilometres and kill Germans, but that the idea was to get the Allies across the Somme and enable both forces to fight in the open.[12] From time to time Haig returned to the wearing out thesis, as he did at the Army commanders conference on 27 May 1916, when he requested that the other armies support the Fourth Army offensive by three days of wearing out operations just before the assault. According to traditional principles this would be the second or preparatory stage, but it actually only consisted of the use of gas, smoke and night raids.[13] In this case Haig had reverted again to his Staff College ideas, where the Commander-in-Chief should try to 'mystify and mislead' the enemy through minor operations.

It was clear, therefore, by the beginning of April 1916, that a very fundamental, and perhaps fatal change, had taken place in the Somme planning. The orthodox three act campaign had gone, and a rather strange mixture had taken its place. Most accounts, including those of Edmonds and Liddell Hart, have concluded that Haig now set out to plan a breakthrough, but that after the failure of 1 July 1916 he sought to conceal that he had ever wanted to achieve such a thing. In his severe fashion, Liddell Hart wrote that:[14]

> the offensive was only a few weeks old when the story was spread by officially inspired apologists that Haig was throughout aiming at a campaign of attrition and had not dreamt of a 'breakthrough'. This denial was vehemently maintained for years, long after the war; it forms one of the most elaborate perversions of historical truth that has come to light. The 'smoke screen', composed of particles of truth dishonestly mixed, was finally dissipated by the publication of the *Official History* in 1932.

Liddell Hart based his accusations on private discussions with Edmonds, whose earlier comments on the chapters and 'scenes' in Liddell Hart's *The Real War* (1930) included the observation that the wearing down business came *after* 14 July 1916, and that he had heard this from Lieutenant Colonel Luckock, GSO 1 to Fourth Army. Edmonds also told Liddell Hart that in the Somme planning, Haig had told the Cabinet in June 1916 that he would only wear down, but in fact really aimed at a breakthrough.[15]

Edmonds and Liddell Hart were actually correct, but the record is not quite so clear, partly because Haig himself was uncertain of what could be achieved, and partly because he had received a very evident warning from Robertson in late May 1916. Robertson clearly told Haig that he should not give the government cause to expect a great offensive with far-reaching results. Instead he should assist the Allies, bring on the French, and 'well strafe' the Germans. Robertson also wondered whether there was not a need for much more artillery. This warning fitted in with an entry in Rawlinson's diary a week earlier in which he reported that in London neither Kitchener, Lord Derby, nor the king wanted a big 'do', but only a methodical 'bite and hold' advance.[16] Haig appeared to take Robertson's caution to heart and wrote to him the next day (for Cabinet consumption) that his overall plan was first to train his divisions, build up reserves and resources, and wear out the enemy; secondly, to support the French with a resolute attack and exploit any success; and thirdly to put his troops in good position for the spring of 1917, and avoid the mud beyond the Pozières Ridge.[17] If true, this was a much more modest aspiration than the straightforward breakthrough plan.

Despite this official position, it seems that Haig did indeed hope for a breakthrough on the Somme,[18] regardless of his letter to Robertson, although he still left open the concept of shifting the offensive elsewhere. In fact, Haig's planning for the Somme in its final stages actually revealed the same weakness that his earlier First Army operations had shown at Loos on 25 September 1915. There Haig had simply hoped for the best, namely, that the use of gas would provide the breakthrough method, but he had not clearly thought out an alternative if the gas attack was to fail. Similarly, at the Somme, Haig's hope for the breakthrough was so strong that he had not clearly thought through alternatives in case of failure. And in reality there was not an easy alternative, for to mount a major offensive elsewhere would require considerable time and material preparation. Rawlinson's diary supports Haig's hope for a breakthrough, for in the entry of 19 June 1916 he wrote that if the Green Line (the first objective) was obtained, the idea was to put Gough and the cavalry through, and he repeated the same idea in his diary entry of 21 June 1916, while Haig's diary entry for 21 June 1916 showed that he expected to put the cavalry through on the capture of Pozières Ridge (roughly the Green Line objective). After the war Kiggell also wrote Edmonds that the idea had been to force the enemy from his entrenched positions, and follow up with cavalry if possible.[19]

But what if none of these were possible? What then? Haig's thinking provided no answers. It would seem that Haig's ideas still depended to a very large extent on his Staff College conception of a structured and decisive battle, yet already the three or four act battle had been reduced to two acts (the decision and the exploitation), the role of the transformed Napoleonic Advanced Guard had gone, and there was an unpleasant possibility that even the last two acts would not take place. Haig was confused, therefore, as his future discussions with Rawlinson over the nature of the Somme offensive would indicate. Meanwhile, for his part, Rawlinson was confident of gaining the Green Line objective, but doubted that a breakthrough would occur, since as he told his Fourth Army staff on 22 June, and then Lieutenant Colonel Wigram (private secretary to the king) on 26 June: 'I shall be agreeably surprised if we succeed in breaking through the line on the first day.' Instead, Rawlinson thought in terms of getting through the three lines of German trenches in two weeks or less, and he thought this even after the serious problems of 1 July 1916 were starting to become evident.[20]

Hence the strange mixture was in place – Haig wanted a breakthrough, but had not properly considered what to do if that failed, while Rawlinson did not really believe in the breakthrough (and in fact expected its failure), but hadn't considered what to do either if his methodical two-week advance failed to get through the German lines quickly enough. It is true that Rawlinson's later conception of the 14 July 1916 night advance and pre-dawn attack was a partial solution, but prior to 1 July, neither Haig nor Rawlinson were prepared to consider alternatives in the case of failure or even partial failure. On balance, Liddell Hart's accusations have some merit in regard to Haig, and certainly the concept of 'wearing out' only reappears at the end of July 1916. In fairness, however, it could be argued that 'wearing out' was not mentioned between 1 July and 30 July because GHQ thought the German reserves *had* actually been used up by mid-July, in other words the 'wearing out' phase was supposedly over.[21] Only when it was seen that the German reserves had *not* been used up did GHQ revert to the traditional 'wearing out' concept. And it should also be noted that there were others at the time who had not expected a breakthrough, for example the Brigade Major of 105 Brigade, who wrote in his diary on 2 July, that GHQ 'had no idea of breaking right through – they all had a limited objective'.[22]

However, this is to anticipate. Back in April 1916 Rawlinson had been called upon to produce a detailed scheme of attack. He found himself in a difficult position because he had expressed doubts about the western theatre from an early stage in the war, and the problem of exploiting success at Neuve Chapelle (March 1915) had caused him then to advocate a limited step by step advance, supported by artillery. Rawlinson had rejected the idea of rushing three lines of defence and pushing the cavalry through, as impractical, due basically to the power of the defence. Instead, after Neuve Chapelle, he advocated the pessimistic 'bite and hold' principle, as outlined in Chapter 3, which emphasized German losses rather than ground gained. The 'bite and hold' idea simply asked the troops to bite off enemy trenches and then annihilate the expected enemy counter-attacks.[23] While this idea made a good deal of sense, it involved three assumptions that were to prove fatal at the Somme.

Rawlinson's first assumption was that the most important tactic to consider was the process of consolidation ('hold') *after* capturing the front line trenches, in order to prepare for enemy counter-attacks. In other words, the actual assault on the enemy trenches received less emphasis than did consolidation. Thus, the final draft of the Fourth Army 'Tactical Notes' of April 1916 stated confidently: 'The capture of a system of hostile trenches is an easy matter compared with the difficulty of retaining it.'[24]

Rawlinson's second and parallel assumption behind the 'bite and hold' theory was therefore that gaining the first line of trenches was a relatively simple matter, although breaking right through the defence was either very difficult or impossible. Hence, in two or three letters before the battle of Loos, he always assumed that the first line of trenches could be taken whatever the defence. Writing to Major General Godley in August 1915,

Rawlinson noted that the German defences at Loos were very strong, and that without overwhelming artillery and unlimited ammunition, 'I much doubt if we shall get through more than the first line of trenches'. Again, to Colonel Fitzgerald, he remarked that gas together with artillery would 'make doubly sure of gaining at least the front line trenches', and he told Lieutenant Colonel Wigram that miles and miles of wire and trench work would likely bring the attack to a standstill before the second line could be penetrated.[25] It must be admitted, however, that both Neuve Chapelle and Loos seemed to support this assumption, which was also shared by some at GHQ and by other commanders. For example, GHQ repeated Fourth Army's sentence: 'The capture of a system of hostile trenches is an easy matter compared with the difficulty of retaining it'. And Major General Maxse rather rashly declared in April 1916 that 'any of us can take over the enemy's *front* line trenches without many casualties to ourselves. The artillery makes front line trenches an easy prey to an attack.'[26] (Hence the slow pace of the infantry assault on 1 July – there was no need to advance quickly.)

Thirdly, Rawlinson conceived of the assault ('bite') on the front (and second) line trenches as an artillery plan, in which heavy artillery and gas simply prepared the way for the infantry. When deep enemy trenches proved resistant to artillery bombardment, it did not occur to him to devise new infantry tactics, but simply to increase the weight of artillery or introduce gas and mines. Writing to Colonel Fitzgerald in June 1915, Rawlinson had noted the problem of deep trenches and dugouts, but thought that more ammunition would really bury the Germans and that gas would reach the deep dugouts. A few days later Rawlinson wrote to General Braithwaite: 'What we want is a favourable wind and plenty of good strong chlorine and bromine gas which will sink right down into the deep trenches – the only other thing is to mine them as the Japs did at Port Arthur but in Flanders water is a great trouble.'[27] Hence, artillery, gas, or mining would do the work, but not the infantry.

It is interesting to note, however, that on 5 June 1916, Rawlinson found out that one of 29 Division's trench raids had discovered deep dugouts between the German front and support lines with exits into both: 'This may be very difficult to deal with', he wrote.[28] Apart from a gas attack a few days later by 29 Division (on 26 June 1916), Rawlinson seems not to have worried further about this matter, and was able to tell Lieutenant Colonel Wigram on 26 June 'That we shall gain possession of the first system of trenches I have no doubt'. Evidently Rawlinson continued to think in terms of artillery warfare, for when it was clear that the opening three days of the Somme offensive had been a failure, he wrote again to Wigram: 'We are going to beat the Germans by heavy howitzers and heavy trench mortars as they are the only weapons which will smash him in his deep dugouts – with more of these weapons and with unlimited ammunition for them we shall be able to reduce our casualties considerably.'[29]

Although this was one possible solution, it is curious that as an infantryman Rawlinson did not think of altering the method of the infantry assault, especially as he had already in June 1915 and again in October 1915 recognized the problem of the enemy manning their trench parapets before the assaulting infantry could reach them. In fact in October 1915 Rawlinson had himself written that if the infantry did not advance to the assault the moment the preparatory smoke or gas had ceased (or presumably the artillery fire), 'they are practically certain to fail: for once the enemy is given time to man his defence with rifles and machine-guns, no assault is likely to succeed in getting across the 150 yards ... between the two [lines of] trenches'.[30] The answer must be that Rawlinson was thinking along traditional lines, and could not break free of these principles.

Taken together, the emphasis upon consolidation, confidence in obtaining the front lines of trenches, and the conception of an artillery plan leading to an over-reliance upon artillery and gas – all this caused Rawlinson to give a particular twist to his planning for the Somme. Especially was this the case in regard to the divergence of opinion between himself and Haig over the objectives of the Somme offensive. Rawlinson's pessimistic 'bite and hold' tactic had really emerged as an antidote to the over-optimism of Sir John French and his GHQ in 1914 and 1915, who had initially thought of sweeping breakthroughs. Rawlinson's reaction was to institute 'pessimistic' offensives and limited objectives, with 'bite and hold' assumptions, de-emphasizing the infantry, over-emphasizing the artillery, and hoping for lighter losses than the enemy.[31] Haig and his GHQ, on the other hand, held the opposite and more 'optimistic' view which emphasized the breakthrough role of the infantry (and cavalry), while paying less attention to the artillery. Thus, in his May 1916 paper on the 'Training of Divisions for Offensive Action', Kiggell saw success as coming through the sheer weight of the infantry assault, using such phrases as 'energy' and 'driving power', and advocated four lines or waves of assaulting troops. In the past, Kiggell too had seen failure as an infantry problem, and quoted the prewar FSR on the need for a vigorous offensive, rapidity, training, confidence, etc.[32] This cult of the offensive attitude anticipated heavy infantry losses and GHQ was at pains to point out that 'the nation must be prepared to see heavy casualty lists for what may appear to the uninitiated to be insufficient objectives and to have produced unimportant results'.[33] In a strange way, Rawlinson and his staff had learnt too much, while Haig and his staff had learnt too little.

Another curious fact was that neither Rawlinson's step by step approach, nor Haig's rush through to the guns really required a strategic objective. It did not actually matter where the offensive took place, as long as the enemy was there, the front was wide, the wire could be cut, the ground was suitable, and the artillery observation was good. This may explain why Haig described his Somme plan in early April 1916 as a 'manoeuvre', and why there was little discussion from the Corps commanders when the thrust of the offensive was radically altered in the final stages of planning (late June 1916) from a southward movement to assist the French, to an opposite northward movement. Indeed, Rawlinson casually recorded in his diary how on 22 June he had explained the new northward thrust of the offensive to his Fourth Army Corps commanders, who simply accepted the change with little comment.[34] Had strategy been a really significant factor, the discussion would hopefully have been more insistent. The lack of a strategic objective (apart, generally, from arriving at the high ground in front) also accounts for the fact that when it became clear the French would have a minor rather than a major role in the offensive, there was very little problem in altering the specific plans, from assisting the French in crossing the Somme north of Péronne, to gaining the high ground around Pozières.

The dialectic between Rawlinson and Haig between March and June in deciding on the specific tactics of the offensive reveal, as before, the 'pessimistic' principles of artillery warfare versus the 'optimistic' cult of the offensive. Rawlinson, supported by his Corps commanders, had in mind an infantry assault only as far as the artillery could support the infantry, without the guns having to be moved forward. Having captured various tactical points, the infantry would then consolidate and, with the artillery, await the expected counter-attacks. Haig, on the other hand, remembering his Staff College lessons, wanted 'to get the enemy out of the trenches', to instil a panic, and thus engineer a breakthrough, in other words, a success based on shaking the morale of the enemy – the old ideal of cavalry 'shock'.[35] Rawlinson had summarized his plan by stating:

> It does not appear to me that the gain of two or three more kilometres of ground is of much consequence, or that the existing situation is so urgent as to demand that we should incur very heavy losses in order to draw a large number of German reserves against this portion of our front. [This was a reference to Haig's earlier concept of the 'wearing out' fight.] Our object rather seems to be to kill as many Germans as possible with the least loss to ourselves, and the best way to do this appears to me to be to seize points of tactical importance which will provide us with good observation and which we may feel quite certain the Germans will counter attack.

The historian of the Somme, Farrar-Hockley, sees this statement of intention by Rawlinson as an attempt at 'covering himself against failure'.[36] In fact it was no such thing – long ago in 1915 Rawlinson had decided on the 'bite and hold' principle, and his proposed 1916 plan followed exactly these lines.

Upon the receipt of Rawlinson's plan in April 1916, Haig broadened the offensive to include Gommecourt in the north and Montauban in the south, and requested 'as wide a front as possible', obviously still thinking in terms of drawing in the enemy reserves along a very broad front, and then punching through in the central Thiepval–Boiselle–Pozières area.[37] Kiggell then drew up a memorandum in which he and Haig insisted on the offensive gaining as much ground in the first rush as possible, which was deemed to be a simpler task than the consolidation of ground gained. Rawlinson recorded in his diary on 14 April that Haig wanted to do the attack in one rush, and that XIII Corps should attack Montauban. Rawlinson felt all this was risky, and required an enemy panic in order to succeed. His revised plan of 19 April (actually prepared by his Chief of Staff, Major General A. A. Montgomery) held out for the 'bite and hold' principle by attempting to get through the enemy second line in at least two stages, relying on artillery support. Rawlinson also made use of Haig's mention of sustained operations, which seemed to support the concept of a 'bite and hold' approach. Finally, he again stressed artillery rather than infantry as the key arm, when he asked for a long and physically destructive bombardment rather than a short, and presumably demoralizing, surprise hurricane of fire. Rawlinson was also cautious enough to lay the final decision for a single rush, deep objective attack, on Haig's shoulders.[38] For his part, Haig's comments were that the objective was the Pozières–Combles Ridge; that it should be captured as quickly as possible; that there should be an intense surprise bombardment; and that, surprisingly, the question of a deep objective versus a shallow two-phase attack would depend on the number of tanks available. The questions of deep or limited objectives, and a long or short bombardment, were not resolved.[39] However, it was clear that Haig wanted a breakthrough (defined as getting through the enemy's three lines of defence, and following up with cavalry), and thought in terms of moving warfare checked only by awkward entrenched positions.[40]

By the middle of May, Rawlinson was confident that he had obtained Haig's agreement to a long bombardment and to a limited objective on the first day. Strangely enough, despite this agreement, Rawlinson still felt that he had agreed to Haig's basic plan, for on 23 May he recorded in his diary that Haig's unlimited offensive was a gamble, but that he (Rawlinson) would do it. However, he did not expect the assault to get beyond the first objective, the Green Line.[41] In effect, what had happened was that the final Somme plan was a mixture of limited objectives and unlimited offensive, a combination of Haig's and Rawlinson's ideas. This can be seen in the Green Line initial objective for the first day, which in the north and centre fitted Haig's ambitions – the German second line – but in the south, where Rawlinson felt Montauban to be a difficult target, was simply the German front line. But both commanders continued to act as though *their* plan was being put into effect, and this basic confusion must relate back to the problems of command as suggested in Chapter 5.

Nevertheless, Rawlinson and Montgomery continued to stress artillery preparation and the problem of consolidation. This latter point became even more important as Rawlinson feared for the discipline of the New Army troops, who did not have the same traditions as the Regular Army. There was need, therefore, for tenacity, determination and the 'strictest discipline, the moment a position has been gained'. As before, Rawlinson thought the first Green Line objective would certainly be gained, either on the first rush, or in the afternoon, or the next day, but he feared the German counter-attacks, and stressed consolidation more than the first assault.[42] Haig, on the other hand, through Kiggell, emphasized cavalry preparation, and how to exploit success when enemy morale and resistance broke down. Of course, the Commander-in-Chief was quite right in preparing for such an eventuality, but his mind tended to leap over obstacles and consider exploitation rather than the fight itself, for example when he told Robertson at the end of May that the cavalry force should not be reduced, since 'We ought therefore to be prepared to exploit a success on the lines of 1806'. The reference here was to Haig's Staff College notes concerning Murat's very lengthy cavalry pursuit after the battle of Jena.[43]

The contradiction between Rawlinson's step by step approach and Haig's 'push right through to Bapaume' attitude continued until the very eve of the offensive. Thus on 27 June Haig recorded in his diary that Rawlinson wanted to halt on the enemy's last line for an hour before proceeding, while Haig wanted the troops to push on ahead immediately.[44] However, Haig's more aggressive attitude received a strong boost from his chief of intelligence, Charteris, who in late June revealed only 32 German battalions opposite, with 65 in Reserve, and no serious defences behind the front line system. On this basis, success seemed hopeful, and Kiggell ordered the cavalry to push through to Bapaume, then strike north to take the trenches in reverse.[45] Even Henry Wilson, who had been extremely critical of the Somme plans, now began to believe in success, although he had little regard for Haig or his GHQ.[46] Both Haig and Rawlinson were now more confident, but neither had been overcome by a rush of optimism, as most historians have assumed.[47] Past experience at Neuve Chapelle and Loos had shown that the real problem was how to exploit success with the reserves, and in this regard Haig and Rawlinson seemed to be prepared. There remained two major questions in the few days before the battle commenced: would the artillery bombardment, the key to the offensive, really work? And what were the tactics of the fight going to be?

In his comments on the Somme, Liddell Hart remarked that 'it seems inexplicable that the bombardment should have been counted on to leave nobody alive in the opposing trenches'. In reality, neither Haig nor Rawlinson clearly understood the artillery, and Rawlinson's letter to GHQ on 21 June 1916 regarding artillery preparation makes interesting reading. He began by correctly stating that the enemy defences were 'very much more formidable' than anything previous, and that therefore heavy artillery was needed. Concentrated bombardments were required to destroy fortified localities (plus counter battery work), but the idea was to destroy the enemy's defences and *not* personnel, 'except incidentally, with field guns when he mans his parapets at the conclusion of the bombardment'. However, the point is that it was not important to Rawlinson whether the trenches were lightly or heavily manned.[48] Instead Rawlinson thought of classical siege warfare, in which defences rather than manpower were the target, and that prevention of enemy fire from the parapets, as the assault went in, was only incidental. Hence, Liddell Hart's comment does not really encompass Rawlinson's expectation of the bombardment's purpose and function, which was to 'systematically beat down the enemy's defences'.[49]

Fourth Army's 'Tactical Notes' of 1916 did not emphasize infantry–artillery co-operation, and said nothing about air–artillery co-operation, or about counter battery work. On the other hand, the Notes did indicate a preference for a kind of creeping barrage, but due to various problems, opted for fixed artillery lifts. In the event, Fourth Army produced a six-day wire cutting and bombardment plan, with the actual details of mines, and artillery lifts, left to Corps and Divisions. On 28 June, Fourth Army announced the postponement of the offensive and gave four roles to the artillery: (1) prevent enemy movement and work, (2) complete wire cutting, (3) counter battery work and (4) deception.[50] There was therefore some artillery direction from Fourth Army, but the General Staff at GHQ were reportedly not well-informed in regard to counter battery work and artillery support in holding a position. GHQ had been slow to realize the power of the artillery, and in any case were more interested in the infantry and cavalry than in the artillery. One sign of this was GHQ's 'Training of Divisions for Offensive Action' (8 May 1916) which barely mentioned the artillery, and only once referred to infantry–artillery co-operation. Another sign of this attitude, according to Colonel Rawlins, was the opposition of 'GHQ against any definite recognition of higher artillery command'. This situation was only altered in June 1916 – too late for the Somme – when Major General Noel Birch was appointed to GHQ as artillery adviser.[51]

Birch himself claimed that at the time of the Somme, Haig did not understand the artillery, 'poor Haig – as he was always inclined to do – spread his guns'.[52] Instead of guns and infantry concentrating, therefore, the guns were spread out evenly along the whole line. Also, where the Green Line objective included the German second line trenches, the wire there was distant enough to be difficult to cut. The lack of artillery tactical direction from above, particularly in regard to counter battery work (whose staff was still being organized during the battle), meant that Corps and Divisions had to devise their own tactics from experience, and these were often far from perfect. In fact the direction of the artillery – the most important element of the 1 July offensive – existed in a vacuum. Time and again, basic mistakes were made at Corps levels, for example Major C. N. F. Broad* (Fifth Army) later remarked that III Corps Artillery did not understand the barrage, and jumped from one trench system to another without searching the shell holes or destroying the concrete machine-gun posts.[53] Another example, among many, concerns the VIII Corps Artillery. Major J. H. Gibbon (460th Battery) remembered that he knew the 1 July attack in his sector was doomed when the GOC of VIII Corps (Lieutenant General Hunter-Weston) ordered the heavy artillery to lift off the front line enemy trenches ten minutes before zero, and the field artillery two minutes before zero hour. Having served in Gallipoli, Gibbon knew that the artillery should keep firing until after the infantry had left the trenches. He wrote to Hunter-Weston on the subject, but received no reply, perhaps because he was only of the rank of major.[54]

The severe problems of the artillery in tactical expertise and direction, in technology and sophistication, in simple knowledge and ability, and in the objectives chosen, boded ill for the infantry waiting to attack on 1 July. Not all the problems can be laid at the door of GHQ, or of Fourth Army, or of the General Staff, for as Major General Birch later wrote, 'In truth the problem of semi-siege warfare and the large concentrations of guns necessary for the work had never been studied by the General Staff in peace, nor by any of the leading gunners, or gunnery schools, so we had to learn our lesson in the pitiless school of war'.[55] But in at least one area, there was a curious lack of concern by GHQ and Fourth Army. That was over the key question of whether obstacles to the assault were properly destroyed prior to 1 July 1916, namely, wire and deep dugouts.

In the middle of May 1916, Kiggell had told Rawlinson that there must be a thorough artillery bombardment until commanding officers of attacking units were satisfied that obstacles were 'adequately destroyed'.[56] As long ago as September 1915, Major General A. A. Montgomery had noticed at Loos that the Germans had deep dugouts, 20 to 30 feet down, so that 'nothing can injure men in them'. On this problem, Montgomery advocated a long, slow, accurate bombardment over four, five or more days to break down defences and morale.[57] It remained to be seen whether this was a sufficient solution. Evidence gathered from trench raids in June 1916 during the preparatory bombardment, while somewhat conflicting, did reveal the existence of deep dugouts in the enemy front line system, and that these were often undamaged. For example, a Fourth Army intelligence interrogation of prisoners from the German 111th Reserve Infantry Brigade in the Fricourt area, taken on the night of 26/27 June, revealed that the 'dugouts are still good. The men appear to remain in these dugouts all the time and are completely sheltered.' Another prisoner taken on 26 June in the Ancre valley area from the German 26 Reserve Division said that only three men had been wounded so far from the bombardment, and that new dugouts were being made in the support lines. And a raid on 26 June in the Montauban area showed there were undamaged deep dugouts under the parapet, although with few men in them.[58] Despite some contrary evidence, it would seem that the bombardment was not having much effect on the deep dugouts, nor was the information obtained having much effect on GHQ or Fourth Army.

Part of the reason for the rejection of information gained during the period of the bombardment may have been because trench raids were seen by Haig, Rawlinson and others, as much for the purpose of raising morale as for obtaining information. On 28 June Haig claimed that VIII Corps had not carried out any successful raids (apparently forgetting the raid of 4/5 June by 29 Division of VIII Corps, which discovered the presence of deep dugouts), and noted that unless raids were successful, 'troops cannot be depended upon in the general attack'. Although the VIII Corps raids had problems because of uncut wire, this fact did not seem to alarm Haig, instead he wrote 'these offensive efforts raise the morale of our own men'. Rawlinson also criticized VIII Corps, and General Haking's remarks in May 1916 probably summed up the high command view of the function of trench raids when he said that no division could be considered a fighting unit until they had carried out a successful raid.[59] It was a sign of the detachment of GHQ and Fourth Army HQ from the realities of the situation, that trench raids actually had the opposite effect, for example Lieutenant Colonel Simonds (170th Brigade, 31 Division) wrote later: 'I know that at this time [end of June 1916] the orders coming from the Division to the Brigade CO's to carry out raids was most unpopular and was at the same time costly in personnel and besides was not good for the morale of the men.'[60]

If trench raids had discovered barely damaged deep dugouts just prior to 1 July, it was also clear that some of the German wire had not been well cut either. At the lower levels, Brigades and Divisions were sceptical, thus Charles Howard (93rd Brigade, 31 Division) reported that the Corps commander (Hunter-Weston) had been extremely optimistic, saying that the wire was blown away and the troops could walk in, but 'we could see it standing strong and well'. Others, such as a Second Lieutenant in 46 Division, were equally sceptical, in his case stating that the wire was not cut on a two Battalion front and that wire patrols had to go out and cut the wire, since the artillery were not 'competent to do it properly'. At the higher levels, between 27 June and 29 June, it was reported to GHQ by Corps that the wire in front of VII Corps was well cut or satisfactory, but that the wire in front of VIII Corps, to the south of VII Corps, was either not cut at all or not well cut. Strangely, Haig noted on 27 June that Rawlinson (and Gough) had been 'well satisfied' with the bombardment, yet Rawlinson wrote in his diary on 30 June that not all the wire had been cut, and the front line trenches had not been knocked about as much as he would have liked.[61] Apparently Rawlinson had not wanted to complain or to undercut the assumptions of the offensive.

Two other aspects of the Somme artillery preparation should also be mentioned – the use of gas shells and counter battery work. Remembering the gas fiasco at Loos, Rawlinson was reluctant to use cylinder gas, and decided that it was to be released only on the fronts not involved in the actual assault. Gas shells, however, were to be borrowed from the French, and were to be fired from minus 65 minutes on Z day (1 July) until zero hour, mainly by French 75s and 4.5 inch howitzers. Rawlinson wondered whether to use the 40,000 French prussic acid shells available, but Kiggell told him on 19 June to use the 60,000 phosgene shells, and wait for War Office approval on the prussic acid. There is no record of War Office approval. It is worth noting that the gas shells (no. 4 phosgene, and no. 5 lachrymatory) were not to be used against deep dugouts (of which Rawlinson was well aware), but against parapets at the time of the assault, and against enemy guns (counter battery work). In the event, only some 3 per cent of the guns on 1 July fired gas shells, mostly in the southern sector, in III, XV and XIII Corps. Information is scarce, but the gas shells apparently had to be borrowed from the French and may have been in short supply. In any case, it does not seem that the gas shells made much difference, although the potential for the use of gas against deep dugouts was high, as Haig noted in his comments on Rawlinson's Somme plan of 19 April 1916. It would seem that Haig deferred to Rawlinson and that Rawlinson wished simply to add gas shells to the bombardment, and hoped that something useful would result.[62]

It is clear that both GHQ and Fourth Army, despite their different views on the assault – rush through versus artillery plan – did not understand or attach enough importance to the vital counter battery work. This was not surprising, since the artillery itself did not fully appreciate the problem, and the general sophistication and understanding of counter battery work was only slowly growing at this time. For example, there was no efficient intelligence artillery system during the Somme, and it was only in late 1916 that a counter battery staff officer was appointed.[63] Consequently, when Charteris claimed in mid-July 1916 that Field Survey companies had located 60 per cent of the enemy's guns, he was being unduly optimistic, and even so, location did not necessarily mean destruction.[64] The poor results of counter battery work were seen up and down the line on 1 July from VIII Corps in the north to XV Corps in the south, where Lieutenant Colonel Reginald Har, of 17 Division RFA, claimed that counter battery work was weak in his sector at the time of the assault because when the artillery barrage was over, the artillery crews were tired and simply sat back.[65] On the other hand, it would appear that XIII Corps counter battery work (in the far south) was much better, due to the assistance of the French, the poor location of the German guns, and XIII Corps realization that howitzers should perform counter battery work. But in 56 Division of VII Corps, it would seem that the heavy artillery never did any counter-battery work at all, but simply fired on a distant line. Counter battery work was generally not successful, partly due to ignorance, and partly due to the lack of technical means to carry out the work properly. And yet counter battery work was vital to the success of the assault.[66]

The artillery preparation, on which all else depended, was in fact weak. The lack of technical means, the rigidity of the artillery plan, the confidence of gaining the first line of trenches, and preoccupation with the problems of consolidation and breakthrough, rather than with what the artillery was actually achieving, all spelled trouble. Did any Corps commanders, or GHQ, have doubts prior to the assault? It would appear that some of Rawlinson's Corps commanders *were* concerned, but most were silent. Rawlinson noted in his diary on 6 April 1916, that he had gone over the attack proposals with his Corps commanders, and had criticized Congreve for seeing too many difficulties. As a result, Rawlinson reduced Congreve's task, and gave Horne the more difficult sector of Mametz and Fricourt. (Ironically, Congreve was given the southernmost sector and his XIII Corps proved the most successful of all Fourth Army's Corps on 1 July.) When Rawlinson went over the altered attack proposals on 17 May, he naively wrote, 'There was little or no caviling or argument and I certainly carried the sense of the meeting with me'. The same consensus greeted Rawlinson's discussion of his Fourth Army 'Tactical Notes'. Then, on 22 June, when the Somme objective was swung to the north, as noted before, Rawlinson again somewhat naively remarked on the Corps commanders' consensus and lack of questions.[67] Perhaps the plan could not have been changed very much anyway at this stage of proceedings, but it is plain that opposition was not encouraged in Fourth Army.

Finally, of critical significance to the Somme planning was the vacuum in leadership that existed at the all-important *tactical* level. It has been argued previously in Chapter 4, that Haig's experience at Staff College led him to defer tactical battle planning to lower levels, indeed as early as 20 March 1916 he had told Lady Haig: 'I have nearly fixed everything up, and it is for the various subordinate comman[drs] now to gradually work out their parts of the business'. Similarly, GHQ was detached from the tactical battle-planning process, while Haig himself seems to have continued in two minds over the nature of the Somme offensive – whether to attempt an all out breakthrough or not. But in turn, Fourth Army actually left Corps to work out their own specific methods of attack (within the overall plan) on 1 July; and they in turn asked for plans from Division and Brigade staffs, and then attempted to co-ordinate them at Corps HQ.[68] In theory this system was democratic and functional, giving lower levels the chance to contribute, but in practice there was a lack of firm tactical direction, and the *ad hoc* system of working out what to do at various levels of command was confusing, just as the artillery at the Somme lacked tactical direction and guidance. In fact a 'learn as you go' system operated, with Corps and Division commanders giving each other tips on how to operate, and with ideas and tactics percolating upward from below.[69]

Such a system might have worked well, in that actual experience was used to deduce tactics. But it took a long time, was a costly way to learn, and often ran up against higher opposition, as a story by Brigadier General Jardine* (GOC 97th Brigade) relates. Jardine had been an observer at the Russo-Japanese war, and had seen the value of infantry following up close behind the artillery barrage. So at the last rehearsal before the attack of 32 and 36 (Ulster) Divisions on 1 July 1916, Jardine suggested to Rawlinson, who was in attendance, that the leading lines were not close enough to the barrage. '"How close should they be?" asked Rawlinson. "30 to 40 yards, and expect some casualties," replied Jardine. Rawlinson did not like the reply, and said "Oh, 30 to 40 yards!!?" "Well Sir, that's what the Japanese did." And his [Rawlinson's] reply was "Oh, the Japanese" in rather a sneering way.'[70] Ultimately Fourth Army HQ, and especially Major General A. A. Montgomery, filled the leadership vacuum in tactical guidance at the Somme, and although Corps and lower levels were allowed to choose their own methods of attack, it was Fourth Army's 'Tactical Notes' (issued in May 1916, and gone over by Rawlinson with Corps commanders on 17 May 1916) which dictated the overall style of the offensive. Furthermore, since Corps commanders were dissuaded from complaining, and since junior commanders like Jardine had little luck in changing Fourth Army's basic ideas (although Jardine was able himself to put 97th Brigade discreetly into No-Man's-Land and follow the barrage), then the ultimate responsibility for the tactical preparation of the Somme must rest with Rawlinson and Fourth Army HQ.

What were the tactical ideas of Fourth Army and of GHQ at this time? The initial ideas were supplied by Rawlinson in an undated manuscript that was jotted down prior to the issuance of the Fourth Army 'Tactical Notes' in May 1916. The underlying theme of his notes was that a methodical approach be taken to the problem of the infantry assault. The emphasis was on proper 'wave' intervals, specific objectives and the problems of reinforcements and counter-attacks. Rawlinson's methodical nature is clearly revealed, and he obviously felt that the 'energy' of the disciplined assault was more important than the rush forward: 'Assault must be delivered as one man – Waves of men going on at 50 to 100 paces distance is best method.' In only one instance was he prescient when he noted: 'Front line is the outside of the nut and the hardest part great care necessary to ensure that we succeed in breaking it.' However, he offered no ideas on how to break the line apart from the use of smoke and gas, for in the following sentence he wrote: 'When front line is broken endeavour to get to our distant objective as quickly as possible.' Interestingly, Rawlinson's emphasis on speed and quickness was always *after* the front line had been broken, and not before.[71]

The next and critical document was the previously mentioned Fourth Army 'Tactical Notes', presented as a final draft by Major General A. A. Montgomery on 11 April 1916. In this document, Montgomery laid a great deal of stress on the need for discipline in the army, since 'We undoubtedly started [the war] with the disadvantage of pitting an undisciplined nation against a disciplined one'. After this dubious but very Edwardian assertion, Montgomery went on: 'No opportunity, therefore, must be lost in inculcating discipline into the troops, whether in the trenches, on the march or in billets.' Montgomery then turned his attention to the officers, and in the only underlined sentence in the whole thirty-two page document, he wrote: '*Finally, it must be remembered that all criticism by subordinates of their superiors, and of orders received from superior authority, will in the end recoil on the head of the critics and undermine their authority with those below them.*' Having re-established the social and military hierarchy, Montgomery turned to the tactics of the offensive. Here he reverted to a very traditional approach, namely, the use of 'energy', and 'weight' and 'mass' to take the front line of trenches. Although he cautioned against using too 'thick' an attack, the whole tone of the document is conveyed in such sentences as 'the assaulting troops must push forward at a steady pace in successive lines each line adding fresh impetus to the preceding line', and in the assertion that although two and three lines of attack sometimes succeed, yet 'four or more lines have usually succeeded'.[72] This was in fact a prescription for heavy losses in the attack, and the concept goes back to the prewar cult of the offensive and the idea of succeeding through a decisive moral and physical blow, in which each line of troops should deliver 'the assault as one man'.[73]

In regard to the speed of the attack, Montgomery at one point mentioned celerity of movement, but generally recommended a steady pace. He, like Rawlinson, only saw speed of action as necessary *after* the initial objective had been captured. The document went on to discuss briefly infantry–artillery co-operation, the capture of woods and villages, the placing of headquarters, the use of contact patrols and balloons for communication purposes (but not for artillery observation), and the use of Lewis guns, machine-guns and mortars.

In general, Fourth Army's 'Tactical Notes' paid insufficient attention to the severe difficulty of the infantry assault across the fire-swept zone of open ground, and this apparently resulted from four factors, the first two of which reflected prewar thinking. First, there was the underlying theme that sufficient 'weight' and 'energy' would always carry a position, and secondly, Montgomery's 'social' feeling that it was more important to stress control[74] and discipline of one's own troops than worry about the enemy. Thirdly, there was the past experience of Neuve Chapelle and Loos where surprise and the artillery had successfully opened the way for the infantry, and lastly, there existed the current assumption that 'the capture of a system of hostile trenches is an easy matter compared with the difficulty of retaining it'.[75] In only two instances did Fourth Army's 'Tactical Notes' anticipate the future, once when Montgomery recommended that Lewis guns move into No-Man's-Land ahead of the infantry assault and deal with hostile machine-guns untouched by the artillery, as well as sweeping the parapet; and once when Montgomery proposed a virtual creeping artillery barrage.[76] Yet neither were used on 1 July 1916, mainly because the sheer organization and mass of detail surrounding the plans for 1 July seemed to iron out innovation – the structure was stronger than any deviations.

The last significant tactical document was GHQ's 'Training of Divisions for Offensive Action', dated 8 May 1916, under Kiggell's signature. This copied and repeated Fourth Army's 'Tactical Notes' in many aspects, looked back to the prewar cult of the offensive, and laid stress on the traditional concept of success through 'energy' and 'weight' in attack. The document stated: 'The depth of the assaulting column depends on the distance of the objective, and on the opposition that has to be overcome in reaching it. Its strength must be calculated so as to give sufficient driving power to enable the column to reach its objective and to provide sufficient remaining energy to enable the objective to be held when gained.' Kiggell also repeated the idea that four lines of attack usually succeeded in the assault, and ended the section by noting that 'All must be prepared for heavy casualties'. The conclusion of GHQ's document stressed discipline, morale, obedience, determination, and rapidity *after* the breakthrough. The underlying theme of this document[77] was the gradual breaking down of the enemy through successive waves or lines, and it is noticeable how frequently the verb 'push' is used, as in 'push on', which fully reveals the difficulty that GHQ had in conceiving of alternative ideas or tactics in the infantry offensive.

The conclusion to be reached on infantry tactics for the first day on the Somme is that they show how the late nineteenth-century ideal of war had bumped up against the new technology of war, but had not really engaged gears. It was as if one fundamental ideal of war had met another and had slid away from it without engaging in serious discourse. After the Somme, Fourth Army became dimly aware of this, or perhaps realized that their proposed tactics had been inappropriate, and so Rawlinson and Fourth Army staff sought to recall and destroy all copies of the 'Tactical Notes', but this they failed to achieve.[78]

Finally, as the sun rose on the fateful morning of 1 July 1916, what were the expectations of Haig and Rawlinson? Haig can best be described as cautious rather than optimistic, for the previous evening he had written to Lady Haig, essentially 'transferring' personal anxiety and responsibility to a higher Power: 'But whether or not we are successful lies in the Power above – But I *do feel* that in my plans I have been helped by a Power that is not my own. So I am easy in my mind and ready to do my best whatever happens tomorrow.' For his part, Rawlinson was more confident, although doubts about the artillery preparation were obviously nagging at his mind. Both men, however, were fearful of the behaviour and discipline of the New Army soldiers – in fact Fourth Army sometimes seemed more worried by their own men than by the enemy[79] – and both hoped for their own particular concept of the Somme to work. Haig hoped for demoralization in the enemy and a breakthrough, while Rawlinson hoped to obtain the Green Line, and then a fairly rapid step by step advance.

The Somme preparation had in fact involved the awkward integration of these two different concepts, the one the application of acts two and three of the prewar structured offensive; and the other the pessimistic 'bite and hold' artillery plan. But in neither case was there sufficient technical means or appropriate tactics, so that the offensive of 1 July foundered on the impossibility of applying Haig's optimistic and structured concepts to a new style of technical warfare, while Rawlinson's newer ideas also failed for technical reasons and because of his three fundamental but mistaken assumptions of consolidation, the ease of capturing the first line of trenches, and the conception of the assault as an artillery plan. Moreover, there were problems of hierarchy and of communication, which will become more apparent in the next chapter as the Somme offensive gradually evolved into a four-and-a-half-month ordeal.

Notes

1 Haig, Diary, 30 July 1915, WO 256/5, PRO; see also entry for 25 June 1915, WO 256/4, PRO, where Haig spoke of a thirty-mile front, drawing in of enemy reserves, and then the decisive surprise attack.
2 Clive, Diary, 25 November 1915, Cab 45/201/1, PRO.
3 'General Staff Note on the Situation', 30 November 1915, p. 10, WO 106/308, PRO.

4 'Note prepared for the War Committee by the CIGS on the Question of Offensive Operations on the Western Front', 5 January 1916, pp. 7–9, WO 106/308, PRO.

5 GHQ, 'Plans for Future Operations', 10 February 1916, WO 158/19, PRO.

6 Haig, Diary, 'Some thoughts on the Future', no date, but mid-January 1916; Haig to Robertson, 16 January 1916; Diary, 18 January 1916; Haig to Kitchener, 19 January 1916, WO 256/7, PRO. See also the three-stage offensive in GHQ, 'Allied Plan of Campaign', 16 January 1916, WO 158/19, PRO.

7 Major General Clive reported on 2 February 1916 that Haig would not consent to an *offensive d'usure* alone, weeks before the general offensive, Clive, Diary, 2 February 1916, Cab 45/201/1, PRO; Haig, Diary, 28 January 1916, WO 256/7, PRO.

8 'Questions from Commander-in-Chief', no date, but mid-February 1916, WO 158/19, PRO.

9 Haig, Diary, 14 February 1916, 15 March 1916, Haig to Commander-in-Chief French Army, 10 April 1916, WO 256/9, PRO.

10 Davidson (BGGS), 'Outline of Offensive Operations', May 1916, WO 158/19, PRO.

11 Rawlinson, Diary, 1 April 1916, Rawlinson Papers, CCC.

12 Haig, Diary, 5 April 1916, WO 256/9, PRO.

13 Haig, Diary, Army Commanders Conference at Third Army HQ, St Pol, 27 May 1916, WO 256/10, PRO.

14 Liddell Hart, *First World War*, p. 236.

15 Edmonds, comments on *The Real War* (ch. 5, 1916), pp. 15–16, in 9/8/2, Liddell Hart Papers; Liddell Hart, Talk with Edmonds, 31 October 1929, 11/1929/17, Liddell Hart Papers, KCL.

16 Haig, Diary, Robertson to Haig, 28 May 1916, WO 256/10, PRO; Rawlinson, Diary, 23 May 1916, Rawlinson Papers, CCC.

17 Haig, Diary, 29 May 1916, WO 256/10, PRO; and Haig to Robertson, 29 May 1916, 1–22–41, Robertson Papers, NAM.

18 It is not quite correct to argue, as Graham and Bidwell have done, that Haig normally attempted both a breakthrough and an attrition battle at the same time and place (in this case, the Somme). In fact, Haig initially wanted preparatory attrition followed by a breakthrough, and then by May and June 1916, hoped for a simple breakthrough only, Bidwell and Graham, *Fire-Power*, p. 71.

19 Haig, Diary, Kiggell to all Armies, 16 June 1916, Diary, 21 June 1916, WO 256/10, PRO; Rawlinson, Diary, 18 June 1916, 21 June 1916, Rawlinson Papers, CCC; Kiggell to Edmonds, 2 December 1937 and 25 January 1938, Cab 45/135, PRO.

20 Rawlinson to Wigram, 26 June 1916, 5201–33–18, Rawlinson Papers, NAM; Rawlinson, Diary, 29 June 1916, 2 July 1916, Rawlinson Papers, CCC; 'Report of the Army Commander's Remarks at the Conference held at Fourth Army HQ, 22 June 1916', Fourth Army, WO 158/234, PRO.

21 Kiggell to Rawlinson and Gough, 2 August 1916, Fourth Army, WO 158/235; Kiggell to Rawlinson and Gough, 12 July 1916, Fourth Army, WO 158/234, PRO.

22 Major General Milward, Diary, 2 July 1916, 6510–143–5, Milward Papers, NAM.

23 Rawlinson, 'Appreciation', 21 January 1915, pp. 9–10, 5201–33–64, Rawlinson Papers; Rawlinson to Kitchener, 24 October 1914, Rawlinson to Wigram, 25 March 1915, Rawlinson to Kitchener, 1 April 1915, 5201–33–17, Rawlinson Papers, NAM.

24 Fourth Army, 'Tactical Notes', 11 April 1916, 5201–33–70, Rawlinson Papers, NAM.

25 Rawlinson to Godley, 11 August 1915, Rawlinson to Fitzgerald, 29 August 1915, Rawlinson to Wigram, 3 September 1915, 5201–33–18, Rawlinson Papers, NAM.

26 GHQ, 'Consolidation of Trenches and Localities after Assault and Capture', 4 May 1916, 69/10/1, Butler Papers, IWM; Maxse to [Tiny] Maxse, 1 April 1916, Maxse Papers, WSRO. In this letter, Maxse advocated the 'bite and hold' principle along a forty-mile front, taking only the front line of defence, and inviting counter-attacks.

27 Rawlinson to Colonel Fitzgerald, 21 June 1915, Rawlinson to General Braithwaite, 25 June 1915, 5201–33–18, Rawlinson Papers, NAM.

28 Rawlinson, Diary, 5 June 1916, Rawlinson Papers, CCC.

29 Rawlinson to Wigram, 26 June 1916, Rawlinson to Wigram, 3 July 1916, 5201–33–18, Rawlinson Papers, NAM.

30 Rawlinson to Colonel Fitzgerald, 21 June 1915, 5201–33–18; Rawlinson, 'Notes on the Operations in the Neighbourhood of Loos between 25 September and 13 October, 1915', 18 October 1915, pp. 7–8, 5201–33–67; Rawlinson Papers, NAM.

31 A series of letters in May and June 1915 laid out this pessimistic reaction, e.g. Rawlinson to Earl of Derby, 26 May 1915, 5201–33–18, Rawlinson Papers, NAM.

32 Haig, Diary, Kiggell (GHQ), 'Training of Divisions for Offensive Action', 8 May 1916, WO 256/10, PRO.

33 Haig, Diary, GHQ, 'Memo on Policy for Press', no date or signature, but probably end May 1916, WO 256/10, PRO.

34 Haig, written comment dated 5 April 1916 in Rawlinson's Somme plan, 3 April 1916, p. 15, WO 158/233, PRO; Rawlinson, Diary, 22 June 1916, Rawlinson Papers, CCC.

35 Rawlinson, Diary, 31 March 1916, Rawlinson Papers, CCC; Kiggell to Edmonds, 2 December 1937, Cab 45/135, PRO; Haig, written comment dated 4 April 1916, in Rawlinson, 'Plan for Offensive by Fourth Army', 3 April 1916, p. 11, WO 158/233, PRO.

36 Rawlinson, 'Plan for Offensive by Fourth Army', 3 April 1916, p. 11, WO 158/233, PRO. A. H. Farrar-Hockley, *The Somme*, Pan edn (London, 1966), p. 66.

37 Haig, written comment dated 5 April 1916 in Rawlinson, 'Plan for Offensive by Fourth Army', 3 April 1916, p. 15, WO 158/233, PRO.

38 Kiggell, Rough draft memo, no date or signature, but between 5 April and 14 April 1916, WO 158/233, PRO. Rawlinson, Diary, 14 April 1916, Rawlinson Papers, CCC; Rawlinson (Fourth Army) to GHQ, 19 April 1916, WO 158/233, PRO.

39 Haig, handwritten comments, dated 23 April 1916, on Rawlinson (Fourth Army) to GHQ, 19 April 1916, WO 158/233, PRO.

40 After the war, Kiggell rejected the term 'breakthrough' as GHQ's aim, and wished to substitute the sentence 'Force the enemy from his entrenched positions'. However, Kiggell defined 'breakthrough' as sending troops and cavalry as far as possible into an ever-narrowing salient, while 'force the enemy from entrenched positions' meant sending the cavalry through as far as possible and judicious, i.e. to a good, defensive front. It seems that both definitions should be termed 'breakthroughs', Kiggell to Edmonds, 25 January 1938, Cab 45/135, PRO.

41 Rawlinson, Diary, 23 May 1916, Rawlinson Papers, CCC.

42 'Report of the Army Commander's Remarks at the Conference held at Fourth Army HQ, 22 June 1916', 24 June 1916, WO 158/233, PRO. Rawlinson's diary at this time (May and June 1916) emphasizes detail, training, discipline and precision rather than dash and speed.

43 Haig, Diary, Haig to Robertson, 29 May 1916, WO 256/10, PRO; Kiggell to Army Commanders, 21 June 1916, WO 158/233, PRO.

44 Haig, Diary, 27 June 1916, WO 256/10, PRO.

45 Kiggell to Army Commanders, 21 June 1916, WO 158/234, PRO.

46 Wilson, Diary, 22 June 1916, Wilson Papers, IWM.

47 Liddell Hart, *First World War*, pp. 237–8; Martin Middlebrook, *The First Day on the Somme* (New York, 1972), p. 71.

48 Liddell Hart, *First World War*, p. 238; Rawlinson to GHQ, 21 June 1916 (approved by D. Haig, 21 June 1916), WO 158/233, PRO.

49 Rawlinson to GHQ, 19 April 1916, p. 9, WO 158/233, PRO. Rawlinson also expected a moral effect, but this was secondary to the elimination of enemy defences.

50 Fourth Army, 'Tactical Notes', 11 April 1916, p. 24, 5201–33–70, Rawlinson Papers, NAM; Major General A. A. Montgomery, 28 June 1916, WO 158/233, PRO.

51 Brigadier Anstey, 'History of the Royal Artillery, 1914–1918', p. 114, 1159/12, Anstey Papers, RAI; Colonel Rawlins, 'A History of the Development of British Artillery in France, 1914–1918', pp. 92, 103, MD 1162, Rawlins Papers, RAI.

52 Noel Birch to Edmonds, 8 July 1930, Cab 45/132, PRO.

53 Noel Birch to Edmonds, 29 June 1938, Cab 45/132; Major General C. N. F. Broad to Edmonds, 11 June 1930, in Cab 45/132, PRO.

54 Major J. H. Gibbon to Edmonds, [?] February 1930, Cab 45/134, PRO.

55 Noel Birch to Edmonds, 8 July 1930, Cab 45/132, PRO.

56 Kiggell to GOC Fourth Army, 16 May 1916, WO 158/233, PRO.

57 Major General A. A. Montgomery, 14 December 1915, 'Battle of Loos – Lessons', p. 8, in 45, Montgomery-Massingberd Papers, KCL.

58 Report, 29 June 1916; Report, 27 June 1916; Fourth Army Intelligence Summaries, June 1916, WO 157/171, PRO. Major General Shea, Report on raid by 2nd Bedfordshire Regiment, 26 June 1916, 'Operation Orders Other Divisions, Trench Raids 27 June', 69/53/6, Maxse Papers, IWM.

59 Haig, Diary, 28 June 1916 and 29 June 1916, WO 256/10. PRO; Rawlinson, Diary, 6 June 1916 and 30 June 1916, Rawlinson Papers, CCC; Milward, Diary, 26 May 1916, reporting Haking's ideas, 6510–143–5, Milward Papers, NAM.

60 Lieutenant Colonel C. R. Simonds (170 Brigade, RFA, 31 Division) to Edmonds, 3 February 1930, Cab 45/137, PRO.

61 Charles Howard (93 Brigade, 31 Division, VIII Corps) to Edmonds, 6 November 1929, Cab 45/134, PRO; Ian Grant also reported that VIII Corps Staff were saturated with optimism regarding the preliminary bombardment, Ian Grant to Edmonds, 29 October 1929, Cab 45/134, PRO; Rawlinson, Diary, 30 June 1916, Rawlinson Papers, CCC; Second Lieutenant Downman (139 Brigade, 46 Division) to Edmonds, 12 July 1929, Cab 45/185, PRO. Reports by Third and Fourth Army to GHQ, and 'Appendix E', between 26/27 June and 30 June 1916, File 5, GHQ War Diary, 191, Haig Papers, NLS; Haig to Lady Haig, 27 June 1916, 144, Haig Papers, NLS.

62 Major General A. A. Montgomery to Corps, 17 June 1916; Rawlinson to GHQ, 17 June 1916; Kiggell to Fourth Army, 19 June 1916; A. A. Montgomery to Corps, 23 June 1916; 'Report of Army Commanders' Remarks at

the Conference held at Fourth Army HQ on 22 June 1916', 24 June 1916, p. 5, WO 158/233, PRO. Edmonds, *Military Operations, France and Belgium, 1916, Sir Douglas Haig's Command to the 1st July: Battle of the Somme* (London, 1932), pp. 79–80. Haig's comments in regard to deep dugouts were 'We must have gas shells for these', Rawlinson to GHQ, 19 April 1916, p. 9, WO 158/233, PRO.

63 Colonel Rawlins, 'A History of the Development of British Artillery in France, 1914–1918', pp. 20–4, 54, MD 1162, Rawlins Papers, RAI.

64 Charteris to Macdonogh, 13 July 1916, WO 158/897, PRO. Brigadier Anstey claimed that counter battery policy was wrong before the Somme, because it was not realized how heavy a fire was necessary to destroy enemy guns, Anstey, 'History of the Royal Artillery, 1914–1918', p. 110, 1159/12, Anstey Papers, RAI.

65 Lieutenant Colonel Hole (31 Division, VIII Corps) to Edmonds, 6 November [?], Cab 45/134; H. C. Rees (VIII Corps HQ) to Edmonds, 14 November 1929, Cab 45/137; Lieutenant Colonel Reginald Har (17 Division RFA, XV Corps) to Edmonds, 13 April 1934, Cab 45/134, PRO.

66 Anstey, 'History of the Royal Artillery, 1914–1918', p. 118, 1159/12, Anstey Papers, RAI; Colonel L. A. C. Southam (RA, 169 Brigade HQ, 56 Division, VII Corps) to Edmonds, 3 July 1929, Cab 45/137, PRO. For technical evolution of the artillery, see Bidwell and Graham, *Fire-Power*, ch. 6.

67 Rawlinson, Diary, 6 April 1916, 10 April 1916, 22 June 1916, Rawlinson Papers, CCC.

68 Haig to Lady Haig, 20 March 1916, 143, Haig Papers, NLS. Wilson, Diary, 28 June 1916, Wilson Papers, IWM; Colonel S. J. Scobell (X Corps HQ) to Edmonds, 23 June [?], Cab 45/137, PRO. Colonel Weber (GSO 1, 30 Division) complained that orders from Corps and above were only a summary of decisions taken at various conferences, and included the choice of methods selected by even Battalion commanders, Colonel Weber (GSO 1, 30 Division, XIII Corps) to Edmonds, 19 October 1933, Cab 45/138, PRO.

69 From Henry Wilson's diary it is apparent that GHQ treated training schools casually. It is also clear that Divisional and Corps GOCs learnt tactics from simply talking to each other, Wilson, Diary, 15 March 1916, 29 June 1916, 11 August 1916, 14 August 1916, 28 August 1916, 21 October 1916, Wilson Papers, IWM; an example of an artillery 'tip' from one CRA to another, in regard to the creeping barrage, is in G. W. Stander to Edmonds, 21 February 1930, Cab 45/137, PRO.

70 Brigadier General J. B. Jardine (GOC 97 Brigade, 32 Division, X Corps) to Edmonds, 13 June 1930, Cab 45/135, PRO.

71 Rawlinson, 'Infy Notes', 5 pages handwritten, no date, but prior to Fourth Army 'Tactical Notes', since he requests they be included in the latter, so early 1916, 5201–33–70, Rawlinson Papers, NAM.

72 Fourth Army 'Tactical Notes', 11 April 1916, pp. 2–3, 3–4, 6, 8, 5201–33–70, Rawlinson Papers, NAM.

73 ibid., pp. 6–7.

74 In the sections dealing with the infantry assault, this document constantly stressed the need to retain control of the troops as long as possible, ibid., pp. 2–3, 5, 7 ('the importance of retaining control by battalion and company commanders until the last possible moment'), and pp. 8, 11, and *passim*.

75 ibid., p. 13.

76 ibid., pp. 18, 24.

77 Kiggell, GHQ, 'Training of Divisions for Offensive Action', 8 May 1916, pp. 1–3, 5201–33–70, Rawlinson Papers, NAM.

78 Liddell Hart, Talk with General Edmonds, 7 October 1927, 11/1927/17; and 'Note on the CIGS, Montgomery-Massingberd', 1934, 11/1934/64, Liddell Hart Papers, KCL.
79 Haig to Lady Haig, 30 June 1916, 144, Haig Papers, NLS; Rawlinson, Diary, 30 June 1916, Rawlinson Papers, CCC. For example, 'Report of the Army Commander's Remarks ... 22 June 1916', 24 June 1916, p. 6, WO 158/234, PRO; and Fourth Army 'Tactical Notes', 11 April 1916, pp. 1–4, where Major General A. A. Montgomery made this apprehension very clear. On 14 July 1916, for example, Haldane put the New Army battalions in front of the attack in his division because they were less 'reliable', Haldane to Edmonds, 11 December 1929, Cab 45/134, PRO.

[7]

Action at the Somme, July–November 1916

At 7.30 a.m. on 1 July 1916 the long lines of the assault divisions started slowly forward, under the cover of a strong but diminishing morning mist, and with the support of smoke, artillery and overhead machine-gun fire. Despite the difficulties of the artillery, the German defenders all remarked on the effect of the sustained artillery bombardment, and on the bravery of the English soldier (the Germans did not use the word British). The war diary of Lieutenant Colonel Bedall, CO of the 16th Bavarian Infantry Regiment (in the southern sector, near Longueval) read, in part:[1]

> After a very intense bombardment of the entire Second Army front and under cover of the ground haze, the long-expected English offensive has set in. With an overwhelming superiority of artillery the English have maintained, for eight days, an infernally violent bombardment and this, in part, with guns of the heaviest calibre (28 cm) and with naval guns. This was directed on our trenches, and second and third lines, our billets and on the villages. It has set fire to and blasted into ruins almost all the hamlets behind our first line as far back as 15–20 km. This has enabled them at the outset to obtain partial successes South of the Ancre rivulet, but North of it our positions could be maintained except for a few unimportant alterations in the line.

Other German comments on this assault stressed the tenacity and courage of the British infantryman, although it was agreed that the officers and High Command (GHQ) lacked ability in certain situations. Lieutenant General von Stein (GOC XIV Reserve Corps) wrote: 'The individual English soldier is well trained and shows personal bravery. The majority of the officers, however, are not sufficiently thoroughly trained. They are lacking in ability to exploit a success and to follow it up quickly.' Lieutenant General Sixt von Armin (GOC IV Corps) said much the same, but added in regard to the employment of British cavalry later in July, that

152

1 Lieutenant General Sir Hubert
   Gough in March 1918.

2 Field Marshal Sir Douglas Haig.

3 Field Marshal Sir Douglas Haig with army commanders and Chief of Staff.
Generals Rawlinson, Byng, Sir Douglas Haig, Horne, Lawrence and Birdwood
in 1918. (Note the symoblic distance between Haig and his generals.)

4 Moving an 8 inch Mark V Howitzer into position during the Somme battle at Becordel, July 1916.

5 Brigadier General and staff officers studying a much needed map in Mametz Wood, July 1916.

6 Results of the assault on Bazentin Ridge, British and German wounded near Bernafay Wood, 19 July 1916.

7 Captured German machine gun post near Mametz, August 1916.

8 Battle of Pilckem Ridge. British soldiers in the newly dug support line after the first objective had been taken, 31 July 1917.

9 Battle of Pilckem Ridge. Three British Guardsmen looking at the body of a dead German in a shell hole, 31 July 1917. German defensive tactics at this time emphasized the use of shell holes rather than trenches in order to escape the preparatory bombardment.

10 German photograph of knocked out British tank, probably Mark IV, either late 1917 or early 1918. This tank has been more thoroughly destroyed than was normally the case.

11 German offensive of March 1918. Mark IV tank passing through Péronne, 23 March, 1918. Abandoned British canteen and burning store building.

12 German offensive of March 1918. Action at the Somme Crossings: Men of 20th Division and the French 22nd Division in hastily dug defence pits, Nesle sector, 25 March 1918.

13 German offensive of March 1918. Action at the Somme Crossings: Gordons in support watching the fighting, 24 March 1918, near Nesle. These are stragglers on 20th Division front and the photograph indicates how mobile the war had become.

14 A French party pass two dead British soldiers. Only one man spares them a glance. The photograph gives a sense of the war weariness of 1918.

this gave 'some indication of the tactical knowledge of the Higher Command'.[2]

Up and down the line on 1 July 1916, personal bravery was often not enough to guarantee success, except in the south where XIII Corps reached and took Montauban.[3] Full details of the casualties were not known for another two or three days, but the initial enthusiasm at GHQ continued for some days, as reflected in the almost daily letters between Douglas Haig and Lady Haig. These letters offer the best evidence for Haig's thinking at the time, since the correspondence was private and did not aim to influence any audience. On 1 July, he sent his wife a telegram at 10.55 a.m., 'Very successful attack this morning – captured portion of enemy second line on a front of 8,000 yards – we hold the hills about Longueval and hope to get the Cavalry through – All went like clockwork ...' Later that day, he wrote 'we have done well. But the fight is still going on and it will be a hard one. I'll try to get a message through to you tonight to let you know that we have done well, driving in the enemy on a front of 16 miles!'[4]

Haig's enthusiasm is understandable, although the references to the cavalry pursuit and the front of 16 miles reflect his continued traditional view of war. By 2 July, however, he was more cautious. 'Things are going well and I hope that, with perseverance and help from Above a considerable success may in time result.' On 3 July he found fresh hope that German reserves were running out, and on 4 July he thought the situation 'most favourable' and called upon 'God's help ... to turn it to account'. But by 5 and 6 July, Haig realized that progress was slow and that results might take some time, although he still believed 'that Strength is being given to me which will enable me to win'.[5] On 8 July he named a specific time by which he thought the offensive might succeed: 'In another fortnight [i.e. 22 July] with Divine help, I hope some decisive results may be obtained.' In the interim the hard fighting pleased Haig, and he wrote on 10 July, 'The battle is being fought out in lives which suits us'. Realizing that this did not sound quite right, he added, 'that is to say the enemy puts his reserves straight into the Battle on arrival to attack, thereby suffering big losses'.[6]

It is noticeable that from about 2 July onward Haig had seemingly abandoned the breakthrough hope and was thinking now of his Staff College lessons which called for acts two and three of the structured battle – the drawing in and using up of the enemy reserves, and then the decisive blow. Curiously, however, his own plans for the next proposed offensive, on 14 July, were initially piecemeal and on a narrow front, almost as though he did not believe his own declarations. Even more significant is that from the middle of July, his letters no longer speak of Divine help – a striking unconscious indication that Haig no longer felt hopeful of decisive results, and no longer needed to call on Divine assistance because the opportunity for a decision had really passed. Although the results of the 14 July attack pleased Haig – 'The best day we have had this war' – the tone of his letters had changed to accommodate the attrition warfare of slowly using up enemy reserves while waiting for enemy resistance to break. Thus on 17 July he admitted to Lady Haig, 'It is a hard fight and will last some time yet', and on 28 July, one of his staff told Lady Haig that miracles could not be expected now, and reverted to 'personalized' language about the Germans – a sure sign of frustration – 'the Bosche is as cunning as a monkey and as tough as a wild pig'.[7]

By the end of July, therefore, hopes for decisive results had been shattered, and Haig and GHQ were under attack both at home and at the front for poor tactics and heavy losses. Divisional commanders like Aylmer Haldane even felt that Haig would go.[8] What then had gone wrong on 1 July?

As long ago as November 1915, Haig's own First Army HQ had spelled out certain lessons of the artillery barrage. In regard to the assault, the report had stated, 'The great object to be attained, is to prevent the enemy from manning his trenches and placing his machine guns in position before our infantry can reach the hostile parapet'. The report suggested enfilade fire so that guns could continue firing after the infantry advanced to the assault. The artillery lift should not be sudden, and should lift a short distance at a time. Also it was agreed that 'Generally speaking the fire of the guns was lifted much faster than the advance actually moved'.[9] This report contained many of the solutions to the problems of the Somme barrage on 1 July, but the sheer size of the Somme offensive seemed to offset the need to learn and apply the lessons of the past. Or rather, the lessons tended to focus on the wrong problems, for example whether to have a long or short bombardment, and how to put in the reserves. These were important large-scale problems, but they overlooked the smaller-scale tactical problems that in the end proved to be the real difficulties.

Reading the reports of the Somme offensive on 1 July, one is struck by the great variety of mistakes and difficulties pointed out by the participants. These difficulties can be classified under three general headings: first, artillery preparation and counter battery work; secondly, the tactical handling of the assault; and thirdly, command structure and attitudes. Rather than attempt to cover the entire Somme battlefront, it will be more useful here to select one or two assault points – for example, Gommecourt and Serre/Beaumont Hamel.

Lieutenant General Sir Thomas Snow commanded VII Corps, and he was given two divisions, 46 and 56, to attack Gommecourt as a diversion to the main Somme assault. Indeed, probably because VII Corps' attack *was* only a diversion, Snow did not appear alarmed at German knowledge of his preparations, and in a postwar letter a senior officer of 46 Division wrote that Snow 'had purposely taken no particular care to keep the "secret" [of the Gommecourt assault] from the enemy'. On the other hand Major General Bols maintained that Snow had actually complained to Third Army about the problems facing VII Corps at Gommecourt (VII Corps was in Third Army), and the complaint was passed on to GHQ. After the war, Snow would write no more than that the Gommecourt salient proved stronger than he realized.[10] No doubt the initial error was Haig's insistence on the inclusion of Gommecourt in the Somme offensive as a diversion, although this was based on the reasonable grounds that the greater the width of the offensive, the better.

It would seem that Haig did not stop to consider whether Gommecourt itself was a feasible target for a diversion. He discounted the fact that the enemy artillery was out of range of all but the 60 pounders and the 6 inch and heavier howitzers, while the observation posts could not see behind Gommecourt wood, where an intricate trench system existed. Since the artillery was outranged, the counter battery work was poor, or even non-existent, according to one report. The artillery support for the assault was also weak, there being only sixteen 18 pounders and four 4.5 inch howitzers for each brigade. Accurate shooting off the map was not possible, due to the lack of meteor telegrams (giving wind speed at various heights) and of proper gun calibration, while survey techniques to locate enemy guns were still being evolved. Another difficulty related to the developing science of aerial observation for the artillery, which advanced rapidly during the Somme battle, but required parallel administrative structures, such as counter battery staffs and artillery intelligence officers. These necessary appointments were implemented too slowly, while in the air itself the Royal Flying Corps suffered very high casualties in attempting to counter superior German air fire-power and the newly organized German fighter squadrons. As a result the artillery was not strong enough for the assault, and the enemy guns could not be properly observed or reached.[11]

The two divisions of VII Corps advanced on Gommecourt at 7.30 a.m., attacking through clouds of smoke that actually confused the troops. 46 Division found much uncut wire, and were met by heavy German artillery fire at zero hour, in addition to enfilading machine-gun and small arms fire. Only small groups of 46 Division entered the enemy trenches, and were soon turned out. Later, 46 Division officers listed a variety of tactical problems, reiterating the difficulties of uncut wire, enfilade fire, 40-foot-deep German dugouts and the fact that the enemy knew where the attack was going to be directed. But a surprising consensus also emerged in regard to two other problems, namely, the lack of weight and determination in the attack, and the effect of rain on the trenches. Second Lieutenant Downman argued that there were not enough men in the attack, that the Battalions involved only contained 500 to 600 men each, and that only four Battalions attacked at 7.30 a.m. These Battalions were not supported, and later 46 Division attacks were not good either, wrote Downman, so why not attack all at once at 7.30 a.m.? Downman believed the problem was the half-heartedness of the GOC of 46 Division, Major General the Hon. Stuart-Wortley. An explanation for the lack of reserve support for the original assault was provided by Brigadier General Shipley of 46 Division, who said that the rain in the communication trenches delayed the rear waves in going across, and by that time the covering smoke had cleared away.

Meanwhile the other division involved, 56 Division, found the wire well cut, and despite heavy enemy artillery fire, were able to go through to the front line trenches, which they found destroyed and therefore of no value as protection. Pressing on, the remnants of 56 Division reached their first objective, and some even pushed forward to the second objective. But they had suffered heavy casualties from the enemy counter barrage, and were eventually bombed out of their gains. By nightfall they too were back in their start trenches. Although Gommecourt had been only a diversion, the idea had been to bite off the salient and then meet the counter-attacks and inflict heavy casualties. But two basic aspects of the assault had created the failure – in the first place, Gommecourt was a very strongly defended locality, and secondly, the lack of success of counter battery work. An artillery officer of 56 Division believed that the original orders were too optimistic and the enemy artillery was the chief reason for all the problems.[12] And, as in the entire Somme offensive on 1 July, had the artillery remained on the enemy trenches as the assault went in, instead of lifting off to shell the support trenches, all would have gone better.

As a result of the failure at Gommecourt, Stuart-Wortley was sent home. Was he a scapegoat for the senior commanders, Allenby, GOC Third Army, and Snow, GOC VII Corps? Many thought Stuart-Wortley a poor general. A typical complaint against him came from Brigadier General Frank Lyon (VII Corps Staff), who thought of him as old, as someone who never visited the front, and as an officer incapable of raising enthusiasm. Lyon went on to say that when the new GOC, Major General Thwaites, took over the division, he turned it into a good unit by 'keeping them at ceremonial drill of which he knew the value'. Lyon's judgement seems to suffer as a result of this remark but others, including J. F. C. Fuller, had little time for Stuart-Wortley or his staff.[13] However, it seems possible that Stuart-Wortley was at least a partial scapegoat, because although there was a consensus that he was a poor general, or at least half-hearted, and although there was a hint that some of 46 Division had been drinking quantities of rum before the assault, yet even a 'good' general would have had difficulty altering the outcome. In any case, Stuart-Wortley's name was put forward for 'degumming', and Haig let him go. According to Edmonds, Haig sacked Stuart-Wortley not so much because of his failure at Gommecourt, but because Stuart-Wortley had been corresponding with the king, and Haig was jealous of the fact. Thus, three factors may have come together to facilitate the removal of Stuart-Wortley: his poor reputation, the desire for a scapegoat and Haig's dislike of the man. Added to this equation was the fact that Haig did not often sack Corps commanders for inefficiency, both because this was getting too near the top, and because there were not many better Corps commanders around, and so Snow was safe.[14]

If Gommecourt had been a failure, what of the assault, directly to the south, on Serre and Beaumont Hamel, by Lieutenant General Sir Aylmer Hunter-Weston's VIII Corps? Apparently Haig had little confidence in Hunter-Weston, his staff, or the counter battery work of the Corps. Two days before the offensive began Haig noted the failure of VIII Corps trench raids, and after consulting with the officer commanding the artillery of VIII Corps, he came to the conclusion that Hunter-Weston and his officers were 'amateurs in hard fighting', although they thought they knew much because of having been in Gallipoli. In contrast, Haig's own experience was that 'Adversity, shortage of ammunition and fighting under difficulties against a superior European enemy, has taught us much'. Haig's suspicion of VIII Corps continued through the opening days of the offensive, so that on the evening of 1 July he wrote, 'I am inclined to believe from further reports, that few of VIII Corps left their trenches'. He was, of course, wrong, since VIII Corps had suffered casualties of 14,000 officers and men, but it is interesting to note that Haig's initial reaction to VIII Corps' failure did not focus on tactical shortcomings, but on the traditional areas of moral qualities and leadership. Rawlinson was equally uncomplimentary about VIII Corps on the eve of the battle, and both he and Haig seemed strangely irked by Hunter-Weston's previous experience at Gallipoli. In fact Hunter-Weston had not covered himself with glory in Gallipoli, so that Rawlinson's and Haig's estimate of his abilities was probably not far wrong – as one of the official historians wrote privately after the war, 'my own blood had boiled as I read of the ... results of Hunter-Weston's pig-headed tactics at Gallipoli'.[15]

For their part, Hunter-Weston and his VIII Corps staff appeared very optimistic before 1 July, in fact 'saturated' with optimism, according to one member of VIII Corps staff, especially in regard to the preliminary bombardment.[16] Ironically, it was on the artillery bombardment that Hunter-Weston later laid the blame for failure. The day after the assault he wrote to the CIGS (Robertson) claiming that the artillery had failed to knock out the trenches, that the counter battery work had failed against the German howitzers, and that his guns did not have enough howitzer ammunition, there being only one and one third howitzer shells per yard-run of fire trench. Much later, in 1929, Hunter-Weston blamed the failure of his Corps on the premature explosion of the mine at Hawthorn

Redoubt (at zero minus 10), and the poor artillery preparation. It 'was felt at the time', he wrote, 'that, with the inadequate artillery preparation, necessitated by the lack of guns and ammunition', the assault of both VII and VIII Corps against such good positions 'was an impossibility'.[17]

If Hunter-Weston felt this before 1 July, he kept it to himself, since at the time he actually said the opposite to at least two officers.[18] In addition, an artillery officer tried to get Hunter-Weston to agree to keep the heavy artillery firing on the enemy front trenches after zero hour instead of lifting off at ten minutes before zero, but the GOCRA (VIII Corps) said that Hunter-Weston could not be moved from his scheme.[19] At the time, therefore, Hunter-Weston seems to have been satisfied, and even optimistic about the artillery preparation and prospects for the assault, although the order for the heavy guns to lift at zero minus ten minutes was copied by all heavy artillery in VIII Corps, and this had a devastating effect on the entire Corps assault. The error seems to lie with Hunter-Weston himself.

Attacking on the left of the line, toward Serre, 31 Division found that the wire was not fully cut, and that they were enfiladed by machine-gun fire. Counter battery work had not knocked out sufficient German guns, which were heavily shelling No-Man's-Land. Brigadier General Rees, GOC 94th Infantry Brigade of 31 Division, wrote an interesting report at the time, regarding the advance of his Brigade:

> They advanced in line after line, dressed as if on parade, and not a man shirked going through the extremely heavy barrage, or facing the machine gun and rifle fire that finally wiped them out ... [Rees] saw the lines which advanced in such admirable order melting away under the fire. Yet not a man wavered, broke the ranks, or attempted to come back. He has never seen, indeed could never have imagined, such a magnificent display of gallantry, discipline and determination. The reports that he had had from the very few survivors of this marvellous advance bear out what he saw with his own eyes, viz. that hardly a man of ours got to the German front line.

Rees's report went on to lay much of the blame for the failure of his Brigade's assault on the German barrage.[20]

Rees's report is remarkable in that he evidently regarded the failure, indeed the destruction of his Brigade, in a positive light. This must be because at the time he was still applying traditional judgements to a new style of war. But thirteen years later his letter to Edmonds was understandably more analytic. He told Edmonds that the Somme offensive was marred by a huge mass of detail in the plans, which were rigid and deterred initiative and elasticity; that there was no attempt at surprise or deceit; and that the plan called for an equal assault all along the line, instead of the seizure of tactical points. Rees felt that the specific causes of failure were the lack of secrecy or deceit, the deep dugouts of the enemy, and the failure of counter battery work.[21] The CRA of 31 Division basically agreed with Rees, also noting the poor counter battery work.[22] It would appear, therefore, that the most basic cause of the failure of 31 Division was the enemy barrage, together with unimaginative tactics and enemy machine-gun fire.

Just to the south, 4 Division and 29 Division were not having an easy time either. The commander of 4 Division claimed at the time that his division had fought well, but was 'too keen' and had advanced 'too rapidly'. The very careful timetable had 'naturally' gone to pieces at the first check. 'Of course all were going for a big thing; but in a very optimistic vein, and for success everything has to go like clockwork.' The leading brigade of 4 Division had met machine-gun fire from the flanks, and was devastated by some sixty enemy artillery pieces that had not been found earlier by aerial spotting or other means. The timetable now called for the two follow-up brigades to go into the fight – and although Major General Lambton, GOC 4 Division, tried to stop them, it was too late. After the war, Lambton told Edmonds that Corps orders had decreed when the two brigades should advance, that it was too soon, and that they had got mixed up in the first assault wave.[23] In fact the problem was that observation and communication were so difficult that control over the battle was lost as soon as the first wave went in. And Lambton had been right – the timetable had called for optimistic results and could not easily adapt to anything else, for example when the Royal Warwickshire Regiment met wire that was not well cut, forcing the men to slow down and bunch up, they were then cut down by machine-gun fire. There had been no surprise, said the CO, and the final artillery barrage was not strong enough when the attack took place.[24] These complaints have a familiar ring to them, and the experience of 29 (Gallipoli) Division, also at Beaumont Hamel, was only a little different.

The 29 Division assault experienced one defect that the two other divisions of VIII Corps did not, namely, the firing of the mine at Hawthorn Redoubt, ten minutes before zero hour. Apart from alerting the enemy, the mine crater made the advance difficult, and the artillery barrage lifted ahead early because of the mine. Stokes mortars were used in the final barrage and had also been placed in No-Man's-Land before zero hour, but according to one participant, demonstrations at the trench mortar school had given an exaggerated idea of what the Stokes could do. In fact the mortar was inaccurate and the heavy shell led to ammunition supply problems. The consensus of reports by survivors of 29 Division was that the early firing of the mine at Hawthorn Redoubt, the too quick lifting and advance of the artillery barrage (ten minutes before zero hour and 100 yards in two minutes), the fact that the gaps in the wire were soon enfiladed, the failure of counter battery work, and instructions for the infantry to advance at a walk, all made failure inevitable.[25] In the end the key factor was the lack of understanding of the artillery barrage,[26] together with the linear infantry tactics which paralleled the rigid artillery time-table. Two flashes of inspiration had occurred before the attack, once when 29 Division suggested digging trenches towards the enemy, and once when an artillery officer suggested a slower artillery lift. The first idea was turned down by a conference that included the Commander-in-Chief (Haig), the CGS (Kiggell), Fourth Army (Rawlinson), VIII Corps (Hunter-Weston) and the 29 Division GOC (de Lisle*), on the grounds that it would give away the attack. The second idea was apparently disregarded.[27]

The problems of VII Corps at Gommecourt and VIII Corps at Beau-mont Hamel were repeated down the line on 1 July, with the exception of XIII Corps in the south. Here the strong artillery preparation, helped by the French artillery, as well as the good observation of enemy ground, the intelligent counter battery work, and the shorter distance to the enemy front line, all combined to aid the success of the well-trained 18 and 30 Divisions.[28] The major failure in the south was Rawlinson's subsequent decision not to exploit the success of XIII Corps, which had reached Montauban and Bernafay Wood by midday on 1 July. Rawlinson did not turn to account the advance of XIII Corps partly because he expected success and exploitation in the centre of the line and not in the south, partly because of problems in co-operating with the French, and partly because his whole conception of the offensive did not rely on break-throughs, but aimed at a slow and steady advance from objective to objective. This conception of siege warfare is evident from Rawlinson's diary entry for 2 July, in which he writes that he wanted to keep going for two weeks more because the Germans did not have many reserves to bring up, and therefore the whole line might slowly crumble. And as previously argued, Rawlinson's pre-Somme 'bite and hold' idea was simply to capture the front line trenches, then consolidate and meet counter-attacks. These 'bite and hold' ideas, together with the other reasons, fully account for Rawlinson's decision not to exploit at Montauban. Nevertheless, the same diary entry contains a note of caution – Robertson, writes Rawlin-son, had been telling Haig 'fairy tales' about Montauban – an obvious reference to criticism from the CIGS for not exploiting the Montauban situation. Haig was justifiably angry with Rawlinson for attempting to move the reserves against the unbroken Thiepval in the centre rather than against the shaky Montauban sector. Only Gough's refusal to renew the attack on Thiepval later in the day on 1 July saved many further casualties.[29]

Rawlinson's long letter to Lieutenant Colonel Wigram on 3 July also shows that he expected a siege-type battle, that he was mainly concerned about enemy counter-attacks driving his army from captured strong points, and that heavy artillery was still the key to victory. Notably, he did not call for new tactics, but for more artillery to reduce casualties:[30]

We are going to beat the Germans by heavy howitzers and heavy trench mortars as they are the only weapons which will smash him in his deep dug-outs. With more of these weapons and with unlimited ammunition for them we shall be able to reduce our casualties considerably. Anyhow we have shown the Boche that we can break his line on a wide front and I think we shall penetrate the second line if our ammunition holds out.

Rawlinson tended therefore to fall into the 'more and more' syndrome – if artillery had failed, then it was simply a question of more artillery and ammunition. At some point this would no doubt have worked, but on 1 July the British had neither the necessary weight of artillery, nor the technical ability or knowledge to use it effectively.

At this juncture, it will be useful to review three key elements of the 1 July offensive in turn: artillery, tactics, and the command structure. The key element of this offensive, on which Rawlinson and Fourth Army had relied so heavily, was the artillery. Yet a close study of the task set for the artillery shows that it was simply not capable of carrying out that task. In the first place, there were not sufficient heavy guns, for example only one 6 inch howitzer per 45 yards compared to the one to every 20 yards of the French.[31] There were no instantaneous fuses for high explosive shells (HE), so that shrapnel was used for wire cutting instead of the more effective HE.[32] In any case the General Staff, and the artillery generally, seemed to consider that shrapnel was best for wire cutting. Headlam*, GOCRA of XV Corps, advocated shrapnel, and the General Staff in June 1916 said that HE had 'practically no effect against wire'.[33] Von Donop, the MGO, also claimed that in 1916 'GHQ found difficulty in getting CRA's to draw HE as they mostly wanted shrapnel'. On the other hand, it would appear that Rawlinson was in favour of using HE against wire in late 1915. The evidence suggests that there was some confusion, caused in part by shell shortages and fuse problems, while the artillery remained undecided between the advantages of shrapnel and HE. There were also some artillery critics, for example Henry Wilson, who remarked after the battle of Loos, in which the gunners fired 380,000 rounds of shrapnel and only 40,000 rounds of HE, 'They [the gunners] are a stupid conservative lot and of the four arms they are the most behindhand'.[34] Shrapnel was also quite generally used against trenches and so John Keegan's comment on the artillery at the Somme that 'almost everyone in the BEF from GHQ officer to simple gunner had now come to realize that it was high explosive alone which did serious damage to the enemy' seems to be incorrect.[35]

Tactically, there was no true infantry–artillery co-operation, rather the infantry adapted to the artillery programme. Instead of fire *and* movement, the assault consisted of fire followed by movement. Although both the Fourth Army's 'Tactical Notes' and the General Staff envisaged something 'of the nature of a creep' before the Somme, the actual barrage on 1 July consisted of the siege-type 'batter down and advance' system, as previously argued.[36] And if some Corps and Divisions realized the necessity for a creeping barrage during the month of July – for example 9 Division on 14 July, and IX Corps Staff at the end of July, who declared: 'It is cheaper to lose men by our own artillery fire than to give the enemy time to bring his machine guns up' – yet in late July, Fourth Army was still ordering the artillery to lift at zero on to the further infantry objectives.[37] In reality, it was not until the battle of Flers–Courcelette on 15 September 1916, that the first official Fourth Army creeping barrage was ordered, advancing 100 yards every three minutes. It was also only on 14 July that the first official barrage map was issued, by XV Corps.[38]

The impression gained is one of understandable artillery confusion, with tactical lessons being learnt and applied at Division and Corps level.[39] No doubt this was one way to proceed, but the technical side of the artillery war required strong direction from above because the artillery sometimes resented changes in the way their guns were actually aimed and fired. For example, meteor telegrams were generally available before the Somme, but according to one artillery officer in the Fricourt sector on the Somme, Royal Field Artillery (RFA) officers in 1916 'refused to make an accurate use of the data then supplied in the range tables of their guns' to allow for meteorological conditions. So these changes were done by guess work and were unreliable in accuracy by 25 to 50 yards.[40] This artillery officer also claimed that the RFA could not do blind enfilade by precise map alignment, and generally neglected the meteor corrections then available. He related the story of his experience in early 1916 near Armentières, while with 21 Division RA. On the walls of his battery command post were meteor corrections for every wind change. A captain in the RFA came along and tore them down, saying, 'Not done in Field Artillery'.[41]

On the one hand, other officers stated that on 1 July meteor telegrams were not available, so that while the temperature was taken, the wind speed had to be guessed. Yet Brigadier Anstey*, in his unpublished history of the Royal Artillery, writes that meteor telegrams *were* available before the Somme.[42] The answer seems to be that the use or otherwise of new techniques in individual units depended on the ideas of individual artillery commanders from Corps HQ downwards. This impression is strengthened by the attitude toward predicted shooting (i.e. off the map and not by previous registration). Lieutenant G. P. MacClellan wrote that shooting off the map was possible at the Somme on 1 July, but that senior artillery officers who came from the Royal Horse Artillery (RHA) did not encourage the idea. One officer of 56 Division RA claimed that mapshoots were not possible, yet another from 36 Division RA did do predicted shooting off a 1/10,000 map. The pivot gun 'shot in' at zero point, and the other guns were then kept parallel, with the angle of sight measured off the map. However, there were no elaborate map boards or bearing pickets at that time. Corrections were also done for atmosphere, temperature and gun calibration.[43]

Other technical advances reveal the same *ad hoc* system,[44] and leave the strong impression that the demands made on the artillery at the Somme simply could not be met. For example, Captain E. R. Ludlow Hewitt recalls that although the pioneer work on air–artillery co-operation had been done by October 1915, there was little system or organization. Individual arrangements for ranging were made between battery commanders and the air observer using a clock code. The Somme perfected this system, but Ludlow Hewitt found that the gunners were very individualistic and each battery commander had his own ideas and 'intensely resented being interfered with'. The liaison officer between Fourth Army RA and 4th Brigade RFC also confirmed the initial resistance of gunners to air co-operation, while on the other hand many new developments did take place in 1916, such as the establishment of the counter battery HQ, a new zone or area call system, a central wireless station, directional wireless transmission, and so on.[45]

A Canadian pilot at the Somme, T. F. Williams, gives an idea of how artillery–air co-operation actually took place:

> Each battery had a number. It would be commissioned to respond to certain types of demand from the ground or the air. There would be a number of batteries assigned to zone calls which could be fleeting and urgent. Only the Recon. [Reconnaissance] types of aircraft had wireless. Scouts all had message bags which had colored streamers to be dropped at report centres at known locations where a white cross could be seen on the ground. The message might be a movement of enemy troops. The message might read – 500 fan e 28–16 B -c 8–6 (500 infantry going east on sheet 28; square 16 – sub square 8–6). For counter-battery shoots – one aircraft dealing with one battery – the aircraft would run out a 300 ft. aerial and be flying toward the target as he gave the signal to fire. He would observe where the most of the shells fell using the clock code and the distance in tens of feet by numbers. This would go on until the M-O-K. would come back. In the latter part of the war cameras were used in the before and after verification.
>
> It was the pilot of the two-seater who handled the wireless; the Observer-so-called who kept a look-out for the Huns.

T. F. Williams was generally sceptical of what was actually achieved at the Somme, believing that air–ground co-operation was still weak – 'It took the Battle of the Somme to bring the Services together – and he argued that the technical ability to deal with precise targets was then absent.[46]

Techniques to locate enemy batteries were still evolving at the Somme, but field survey methods tended to be 'active' – that is, if the enemy guns did not fire they could not easily be located, and the Germans employed 'sleeper' batteries that only opened up at critical times. Hence VIII Corps had spotted 55 enemy batteries before 1 July, but on that day 66 enemy batteries actually opened up.[47] The lack of heavy artillery, the lack of the instantaneous 106 fuse, the still evolving artillery intelligence system, the still evolving counter battery system (including counter battery staff and 'Active Hostile Battery Lists') – all these factors almost eliminated the likelihood of reasonable counter battery success on 1 July.[48] Some sense of the average success rate of counter battery work can be obtained from the later figures for the offensive of 15 September 1916, when 159 active enemy batteries had been located. Of these, 70 were engaged via air–artillery co-operation. Of these 70, 29 were silenced, for a success rate of only 41.4 per cent against the number actually engaged.[49]

Plainly, counter battery work was not more successful at the Somme on 1 July because technical ability, training and knowledge[50] had not developed to the point where significant success was possible, unless special circumstances favoured the artillery, as in XIII Corps. One other factor should be mentioned – the extremely high attrition rate of pilots and observers at the Somme, perhaps as high as 135 per cent over the four months of the battle.[51] A first-hand account by the young pilot Cecil Lewis in his book, *Sagittarius Rising*, shows that he had very little training or flight time before joining his squadron for the Somme, and that fatigue and tension were serious factors. When Cecil Lewis finally left France after four months of the Somme,[52] he

> climbed into the train at Amiens with a wonderful feeling of relief. While I had been on the job, screwed up to the pitch of nervous control it demanded, all had been well. In fact, the only effect of a long spell at the front seemed to be to make me more reckless and contemptuous of the danger. But now that tension had been relaxed, I realized how shaky and good-for-nothing I was. Eight months overseas, four months of the Somme battle, three hundred and fifty hours in the air, and still alive! Pilots, in 1916, were lasting, on an average, for three weeks.

If the ability of the artillery was the major reason for both the problems and the successes of 1 July, what of the tactics employed? The Chief of Staff of Fourth Army, Major General A. A. Montgomery, had interesting points to make about the assault when Edmonds began to prepare the Somme chapters of the *Official History* in 1930 (Rawlinson having died in

1925 and Haig in 1928). After complaining of the critical tone of the draft, Montgomery suggested that 'the writer does not seem to realise at all the advance in the "organisation of the battle" over 1915. The French came down often to find out what we were doing, as regards artillery especially, and copied many of our methods.' Montgomery criticized the lack of training and the scarcity of well-trained junior leaders, as he had already argued in November 1916, although he agreed in a letter in 1938 that employing small groups trained to use the ground would have saved lives.[53] Montgomery's Fourth Army GSO 1, R. W. Luckock*, wrote an exactly similar letter, also complaining about the tone of the draft, and also arguing that the organization of the battle was a 'prodigious' advance on anything done before, while the omissions of 1916 were dealt with in 1917 and 1918. 'If he [the author of the Somme draft] would rewrite the chapters on those lines it would give a much truer picture than does the present draft.'[54]

The defence by Montgomery and Luckock is interesting in that the two staff officers correctly argued that the Somme was an advance on the battle of Loos in terms of organization, as were the battles of 1917 and 1918 over the Somme. But organization does not win battles by itself, and the offensive of 1 July actually depended upon the correct use of tactics, both infantry and artillery. Despite Montgomery's assertion that the tactics employed were superior to those of 1915, this is not at all clear, nor do the planning and tactics of 31 July 1917 (Passchendaele) seem to be a great advance over 1916. Yet Montgomery's contemporary analysis of the tactics used was rather curious. The 1 July attacks had failed, he wrote in August 1916, for two reasons, one foreseen, one partly unforeseen. What had been foreseen was the violent enemy artillery barrage, and here the wide extent of the offensive and the counter battery work should have helped, but did not. This reveals that Montgomery did not really understand the state of the artillery's efficiency at the time of the Somme. The partly unforeseen aspect was the German system of deep dugouts. Yet his own experience in 1915 had clearly shown that the Germans did use deep dugouts, and trench raids before 1 July had actually discovered the deep dugout system. Montgomery added that in future, if artillery was available against enemy artillery and dugouts, then the Fourth Army's 'Tactical Notes' of April/May 1916 held good, but if not, then the assault should hurry across No-Man's-Land.[55] Clearly Montgomery (and Fourth Army) had run out of ideas in 1916, especially since a report issued by Fourth Army later that year turned around and declared that artillery actually could *not* destroy deep dugouts.[56]

Tactically, the Somme offensive had failed because of the artillery problems mentioned, because of the hybrid Haig–Rawlinson plan and because of Rawlinson's assumptions before the battle: (1) that capturing the first line of trenches was relatively simple; (2) that consolidation was therefore more important than the assault; and that (3) the artillery simply prepared the way for the infantry to walk in. The tactical difficulties described in the account of the assaults on Gommecourt and Serre/Beaumont Hamel almost all flowed from these pre-Somme assumptions. But behind these assumptions lay the 'bite and hold' lessons of 1915, and behind these again lay the prewar cult of the offensive, with Haig's emphasis on the structured offensive and the idea that an offensive had to be decisive in the Napoleonic sense, without clearly thinking what decisive meant in the context of 1916. In attempting to interpret these prewar concepts in terms of 1916, Rawlinson had opted for the newer 'pessimistic' approach of artillery warfare, while Haig had grafted on to the Somme plan his 'optimistic' cult of offensive expectations.

Finally, the command structure before 1 July had not worked efficiently because a communications gap had opened up between Haig and GHQ on one side and Rawlinson and Fourth Army on the other side. This GHQ isolation, described in Chapter 5, did produce a critical vacuum in command, and led to the confused 'mixed' Somme plan of Haig and Rawlinson. Rawlinson had qualms in approaching Haig, and could never sit down in a frank atmosphere of 'give and take' to thrash out differences and problems. Nor was this a problem for Rawlinson alone for a similar vacuum opened up between Haig and Gough in 1917 and again in 1918, as Chapters 8 and 9 will show. But in 1916 this communications gap was very serious for the 1 July planning in producing an offensive that was not only mixed in its aims, but in leaving a strong impression of an offensive that went forward of its own momentum as though the offensive itself had taken over from those that were supposed to plan it and participate in it. It should also be noted that the communications gap, described in Chapter 1, existed not only at the highest levels but throughout the various levels of command in the army, and contributed in large measure to the problems of the future operations of the Somme offensive.

Following, then, the disappointments of 1 July, the Somme battle subsequently fell into three stages. There was first the attempt in July to get through the remaining German reserves and lines of defence as quickly as possible, including the successful 14 July assault. Secondly, there took place the more methodical attempts during August and early September, to wear out the enemy with a view to launching a decisive blow in mid-September (again the transformed Advanced Guard concept). Then, thirdly, there occurred the winding down of the battle in October and November. The first stage required speed, and this accounted for the poorly prepared and often isolated attacks that month, while the second proceeded more slowly but equally optimistically. However, both stages operated on the same premise – the drawing in and using up of German reserves, and then the decisive blow. Again, only selected examples of the battle will be reviewed here rather than an attempt at a complete story.

The desire for haste in early July also related to the over-optimism of Fourth Army and GHQ, who felt that the enemy had few reserves left. Rawlinson on 2 July and Haig on 3 July both thought that the Germans were fast running out of reserves. This was confirmed by Haig's note of an interview at Fourth Army HQ on 2 July which declared that the enemy 'has undoubtedly been severely shaken and he has few reserves in hand'. Then Kiggell told Rawlinson on 8 July that German reserves were limited and could be overcome comparatively easily.[57] The net result was a number of battalions thrown into piecemeal attacks on 3 July, attacks which could well have been seen as logical at Corps or Army level, but which at battalion level often seemed foolish, wasteful and hurried. Rawlinson had ordered Gough to bring up reserves and attack north of the Ancre at Beaumont Hamel and Thiepval, but at Haig's insistence, Rawlinson reluctantly agreed to exploit XIII Corps' success in the south instead. Rawlinson's reluctance has been earlier explained, and also related to the fact that the area around Montauban was very congested, and because it was difficult to arrange a joint advance with the French, who shared the Montauban–Hardecourt front with XIII Corps. Even so, two brigades from X Corps and two from III Corps were to attack in the centre at Thiepval and Ovillers either as a diversion, or as part of Rawlinson's original plan. The attack was to take place in the early morning hours of 3 July, but neither Army nor Corps staff realized just how much time was needed for an attack to be planned and organized, including the absolute necessity in a night attack for prior reconnaissance. However, Rawlinson, under pressure himself, urged his Corps to attack as soon as possible, and they in turn pressed their Divisions and Brigades.

The result was that some orders came too late. For example one Brigade Major was explaining the plan at his Brigade HQ (75th Brigade, X Corps) on the evening of 2 July, when the commanding officer broke in to say that the Brigade had to commence its advance to the front line. There were complaints to X Corps staff, and the attack of 75 Brigade and the other Brigade in X Corps was postponed for three hours. These new orders postponing the attack apparently only reached the artillery halfway through their bombardment, which therefore did not properly support the assault. Meanwhile the III Corps attack on Ovillers went forward at the original zero hour, three hours before the X Corps effort, thus nullifying the joint attack concept.[58] One can sympathize with all parties involved, each trying to achieve the impossible. Subsequently Brigade staff tended to blame Corps staff. For example, Brigadier Solly-Flood of 35 Brigade in X Corps remarked later that his Brigade's attack was a first class example of incompetence on the part of the higher command and foredoomed to failure. Had we been given a few days to make arrangements and to get our assault trenches (which were then quite wrongly the fashion) nearer our objective, and had all attacks been simultaneous there would have been a reasonable chance of success.

As it was, there had been no administrative arrangements by X Corps, thus causing delays in troops arriving, and leaving no time for reconnaissance. Solly-Flood concluded: 'It was a damn bad show.' In fact, X Corps HQ came in for general criticism, with another officer complaining that they were inexperienced in any kind of war, let alone the new style of warfare: 'We used to say at the time that FSR appeared to be unknown to the higher staff.'[59]

It would seem that the greatest problem was simply that of inexperience, compounded by one-way communication from GHQ and Army to Corps, and from Corps to lower levels. There was also an understanding by senior commanders that if their units attacked successfully, their reputations would be enhanced, whereas if they did not press on, the reverse would occur.[60] On the other hand, failure was naturally resented. Thus the 3 July attack of III Corps' two brigades aroused the ire of Rawlinson, whose diary entry for 4 July reveals a rather simplistic critique of Pulteney* (GOC III Corps): 'He is not good at keeping his end up – I have little trouble with the other two [Corps Commanders] who are first rate and full of enterprise.'[61] Major General A. A. Montgomery simply believed that Rawlinson, 'being further back did not feel the draught so much and kept on pressing for an advance'.[62]

Montgomery's comment reveals the gap between an Army commander and his Corps commander, and shows why the Corps commander in turn would naturally press his subordinates. Major General Wace (GSO 1 32 Division) shows how this pressure worked between General Gough and Wace's divisional commander, Major Genral Rycroft, GOC 32 Division, which was in Gough's X Corps. Wace believed that X Corps' postponed attack on 3 July was a foredoomed failure since Rycroft had only been given plans for the attack at 9.45 p.m. the night before: 'it was another of Gough's mad ideas – Gough was furious then with our Division [for its failure on 3 July] and with Rycroft and me in particular. He "threw" the unfortunate Jenkins [GOC 75th Brigade, attached to X Corps for the 3 July attack, and apparently degummed] but couldn't fix the blame on us. Rycroft knew he'd "got it in for us", and when at Bethune we got orders to go back to the Somme in October he turned to me and said wryly this would be his undoing unless we went to Rawlinson's Army.' Wace added that Rycroft was 'terrified of Gough', and implied that 32 Division's mauling in the later 14–19 November 1916 assault was connected to the division's earlier 3 July failure.[63]

In similar fashion, the hurried attacks on the Mametz Wood area from 7 July on resulted in the dismissals of Major General Pilcher (GOC 17 Division), Major General Philipps (GOC 38 Division) and Brigadier General Oxley (GOC 24 Brigade). Both Lord Horne (XV Corps) and Pulteney (GOC III Corps) were feeling the pressure from Army level, and passed this pressure on to their subordinates. Subsequently the blame for the costly attacks on Mametz Wood in early July was placed on the shoulders of Major General Philipps, although really the system was as much at fault as the individual. Perhaps Philipps *was* a poor commander, and carried out his attacks one brigade at a time, with instructions not to press the attack if machine-gun fire was met.[64] But Colonel Price-Davies, in 38 Division, wrote later that communication was very poor within the Division, non-existent with the artillery, and Divisional HQ was seven miles away and difficult to reach. The attack of one Brigade in 38 Division on Mametz Wood on 8 July was aimed at an imaginary line through the wood, there was no time to line up for the jump-off and the key communication trench was blocked. Philipps did not cancel the attack, perhaps because on the previous day he had ordered the withdrawal of another Brigade of his Division after several fruitless attacks. But on 9 July Philipps was relieved of his command and by 12 July, 38 Division was finally in Mametz Wood.[65]

Some days later Fourth Army called for divisional comments on the July fighting, and among others Major General Kentish (GOC 76th Brigade, 3 Division) sent in some frank remarks concerning the problems of Mametz Wood. Kentish believed that the attacks there from 5–8 July had failed through lack of time to organize. To this Major General A. A. Montgomery pencilled in a thick question mark, and when Kentish argued that the continued attacks on Mametz were also failing because the troops were tired, Montgomery added two more question marks and the comment that '38th Div. had done nothing'. There was a similar attitude in GHQ when on 9 July Kiggell told Rawlinson that 38 Division had failed to take Mametz Wood with 'quite insignificant losses', and were unworthy of the traditions of the army. Yet when 38 Division finally left Mametz Wood on 12 July, they had lost nearly 4,000 men of all ranks, including seven Battalion commanders.[66] And when Robert Graves of the Royal Welch Fusiliers visited Mametz Wood on either 13 or 14 July he described a scene of carnage, far removed from the comments of Montgomery and Kiggell:[67]

> The next two days we spent in bivouacs outside Mametz Wood. We were in fighting kit and felt cold at night, so I went into the wood to find German overcoats to use as blankets. It was full of dead Prussian

Guards Reserve, big men, and dead Royal Welch and South Wales Borderers of the New Army battalions, little men. Not a single tree in the wood remained unbroken. I collected my overcoats, and came away as quickly as I could, climbing through the wreckage of green branches. Going and coming, by the only possible route, I passed by the bloated and stinking corpse of a German with his back propped against a tree. He had a green face, spectacles, close-shaven hair; black blood was dripping from the nose and beard. I came across two other unforgettable corpses: a man of the South Wales Borderers and one of the Lehr Regiment had succeeded in bayoneting each other simultaneously. A survivor of the fighting told me later that he had seen a young soldier of the Fourteenth Royal Welch bayoneting a German in parade-ground style, automatically exclaiming: 'In, out, on guard!'

The attitude of Montgomery and Kiggell was not necessarily callous, they were simply ignorant of details, and overly optimistic as to what could be achieved. The higher command literally did not know much of what was going on, and when it did there was also a natural desire to deflect blame elsewhere. For example, on 1 August 1916, Rawlinson was still blaming 38 Division for not occupying Mametz Wood earlier, and saying that Philipps should 'have been got rid of before'.[68] However, Rawlinson attached no blame to Lord Horne for failing to occupy Mametz Wood when it was empty on 3 July, or to himself for failing to exploit the success in the southern part of the line on 1 July. He was also critical of the loss of Contalmaison on 7 July, writing in his diary that the troops had only been shelled out, when in fact three companies of infantry from 24th Brigade had been bombed rather than shelled out when their own bombs and ammunition had run out. In reality 800 casualties were suffered in attempting to hold Contalmaison.[69] On 8 July Rawlinson told Haig that 24th Brigade had abandoned Contalmaison without just cause, and Haig approved of Brigadier General Oxley (GOC 24th Brigade) being sent home. On the same day Haig was also inquiring into the conduct of Major General Philipps and 38 Division at Mametz Wood, on the recommendation of Lord Horne.[70]

Fourth Army and GHQ were prepared to believe the worst of some of their men and officers, partly because of the high command's desperate anxiety to get through the German reserves and break out beyond. Rawlinson later told Lord Derby that if the night offensive of 14 July had been executed earlier, on 10 July (Haig's precondition for the offensive had been the capture of Mametz and Trônes Woods on the flanks, which delayed the assault for four days), then 'These four days would in all probability have enabled us to gain possession of the hostile third line of defence, which at that time was less than half finished, in the same rush and had this been done we could have passed the cavalry through and made a big haul of guns. It makes me very sick to think of the "might have beens" ...'[71] Rawlinson could have reflected that he himself had failed to order the occupation of Trônes and Bernafay Woods on 1 July when they too were empty. Instead, as with Mametz Wood, there were a series of rushed piecemeal attacks on Trônes Wood between 8 and 13 July, causing Major General Shea* (GOC 30 Division) to write that when his division was involved in assaulting Trônes Wood, 'so long as no other movement took place elsewhere, the capture and maintenance of this wood was not a feasible operation'.[72] However, the wood was half-captured by 13 July at great cost (one regiment suffered 75 per cent casualties),[73] and Rawlinson was then prepared to launch his 14 July offensive against the German second line, having partially secured Mametz Wood on the left and Trônes Wood on the right.

The concept of a night attack on a three-Corps front had originated in Fourth Army according to Major General Luckock, but the plan was opposed by Haig and most of GHQ. Luckock wrote that there was

> no doubt that D. H. and GHQ intensely disliked the 4th Army plan. – D. H. produced a dreadful plan big attack on a narrow front from which further operations were to be started. We all knew that owing to intense artillery fire, the subsequent ops. could never have been started. It was an academic plan that would have been given good marks at the Staff College.

Aylmer Haldane made the same criticism. Haig had wanted one Corps to attack alone on 14 July, followed by the other two Corps later on – which would have allowed the German guns to concentrate on the first Corps.[74] Most of GHQ, and Haig in particular, had certainly been opposed to the concept of a night attack, claiming that it was not possible because the troops were not highly trained or disciplined, the staff were inexperienced, and it was a difficult manoeuvre even in peace-time. Haig therefore told Rawlinson that the plan was 'unsound'.[75] But Rawlinson had no intention of giving up the idea, and by 12 July had persuaded first Lord Horne (commanding one of the Corps to take part in the attack) and then Haig to accept the idea of a night attack through the good offices of a supporter on Haig's staff, Major General Lawrence.[76]

In initially turning down the plan, Haig had also pointed out that the defence, including machine-guns, was very strong, the enemy artillery could bear on the ground in question, the attack supports would come under artillery fire even if the first wave got through, and so on. It seems to have escaped Haig's attention that the night attack was suggested precisely to overcome these problems, and it is noteworthy that in the discussion over the innovative plan, two features emerge. First Haig (and Horne) initially rejected the plan because it was 'unsound', i.e. not according to Staff College or routine methods; and secondly, Haig and GHQ mistrusted their troops and subordinates to carry out the attack.[77] Even when the plan was reluctantly accepted, Haig insisted on securing the two flanks at Trônes and Mametz Woods as a precondition. In other words, imagination and innovation were hampered because prewar ideas and mistrust of men and officers were stronger than the actual lessons being learnt from day to day.

According to Major General A. A. Montgomery the 14 July attack had been scheduled for the previous day but postponed due to a further delay in persuading Haig. Other reasons were the delays in taking Trônes Wood, and Lord Horne's desire to complete the wire-cutting.[78] In the event, the early hours of 14 July saw the preparations complete as the six assault brigades formed up in silence in No-Man's-Land, and then surged forward at 3.25 a.m., following a five-minute hurricane barrage. Rawlinson pinned great hopes on this offensive, hoping for a decisive victory, including a break through to the German third line of defence, and possibly even to 'fight a really decisive battle of Bapaume which should go near finishing the war'.[79]

Initially the offensive was very successful as the brigades took 6,000 yards of trenches of the German second line from Bazentin le Petit to Longueval. But, as on 1 July, misinformation and undue caution by the Corps commanders in failing to reinforce success cost the offensive dearly. Once again Lord Horne delayed, this time in declining to occupy High Wood because his flank at Longueval was not secure. Montgomery placed the blame for not occupying High Wood on both Lord Horne's Corps and 7 Division for not pushing forward, although 7 Division was actually not at fault. In any case the failure to exploit success along the line resulted in another two weeks of heavy fighting to take the line Pozières–Longueval–Delville, but Guillemont, Ginchy and High Wood could not be taken.

Kiggell wrote a defensive letter to the CIGS on the evening of 14 July acknowledging the slow progress, but stating that 'the Bosch was badly rattled on a good part of our front'. He claimed that a general front was maintained and isolated groups were not pushed forward – a reference to earlier criticisms from the CIGS in a letter dated 5 July 1916.[80] He conceded that artillery–infantry co-operation was weak (no doubt referring to the problems in co-ordinating XV Corps' early evening attack on High Wood on 14 July), but argued 'If they [the Infantry] do find fault [with the artillery support] I can only say they are impossible to satisfy because it has been most effective. Otherwise what had been done could not have succeeded.' However, Kiggell's letter is interesting because he stresses two aspects – the positive fact that the morale of the enemy was 'badly rattled' and 'we shook their nerves to pieces', and the negative fact that progress was slow. Kiggell obviously now had in mind the kind of offensive that first broke morale, which then led to a crumbling of the line and a rapid advance. But it was not to be: 'Future critics will show conclusively that we could and should have gone faster! I wish we could go and hear the S.C. [Staff College] lectures on the subject to the next generation – and have the lecturers here now to try their hand!' But speed was impossible, 'He sticks too tight in strong places which can't be rushed and must be dealt with methodically'.[81]

Essentially, two things were happening. First, it was beginning to dawn on GHQ and Fourth Army that they were in a battle of attrition, even though there were still optimistic noises about decisive results and getting right through the German lines of defence by the end of July.[82] And secondly, the CIGS, Robertson, held a very different point of view from both GHQ and Fourth Army as to the tactics of the battle. In several letters Robertson stressed the bite and hold 'pessimistic' point of view: that the advance should be methodical and step by step rather than rapid; that artillery and machine-guns should be used to gain objectives rather than men; that artillery should be concentrated rather than dispersed; that the aim should be limited to moderate objectives rather than break-throughs; and that there should be relentless methodical pressure on the enemy rather than attempts to gain ground. However, GHQ and Fourth Army seemed to be doing the opposite of what Robertson wanted, and he particularly tried to offset the influence of Haig by writing confidentially to Kiggell and Rawlinson, since he evidently felt that Haig was the prime culprit. On 5 July Robertson told Kiggell to pursue a deliberate advance and use artillery rather than men to get through defences, and requested that the letter not be shown to anyone. On 26 July he warned Rawlinson that he should watch out for man-power problems (i.e. wastage), and asked him to avoid following prewar books and lessons. 'FSR will require a tremendous amount of revising when we have finished with the Boche. Principles, as we used to call them, are good ... but their application is a very difficult business, and I think that we still take these principles too literally. I think you know what is in my mind.'[83] Judging by the tenor of Robertson's later remarks to Haig, he evidently meant that Haig was wasting manpower in attempts to push on rapidly and gain ground, in accordance with prewar FSR principles and the cult of the offensive.

Finally, a letter from Robertson to Haig on 29 July reported criticisms from London regarding the heavy casualties. Haig replied that he had no intention of going to the War Committee while the battle was still going on, and signed and dated his comments for 31 July 1916.[84] Haig may have felt defiant, but in fact Kiggell issued a GHQ order on 2 August calling for economy in men and reserves, so that when the 'wearing out' battle concluded, the 'last reserves' would be available for the decisive crisis of the fight in the second half of September. The central theme of the order, however, was economy and method, essentially Robertson's points. And Rawlinson's Fourth Army 'Appreciation' of 5 August claimed that the first phase of the Somme was over, and that careful economy in manpower was now necessary if the battle was to last another month or six weeks [i.e. to mid-September]. Rawlinson promised that manpower would be preserved either by siege warfare – sapping forward – or by using the heavy artillery to wipe out opposition before larger divisional assaults went in. Again the central theme was economy, but in the conclusion Rawlinson actually gave up hope for a decision in 1916, and pointed to victory in 1917.[85]

Behind the concepts and policies of Fourth Army and GHQ and the criticisms of the CIGS, lay the day to day reality during the last half of July of pressing the enemy without delay. Attacks were made on High Wood, Guillemont village, Longueval – Delville Wood, Pozières, and further north at Fromelles, where Lieutenant General Haking gained an unenviable reputation for incurring heavy casualties. Few of these attacks were successful, and most objectives were still being fought over in early September. One or two incidents show how difficult it was to co-ordinate and plan attacks – once again the gap between army commanders and battalion commanders was just too great to be bridged. Robert Graves recalls how the Royal Welch were assigned to be in reserve for the attack on High Wood on 20 July, and how the Colonel of the regiment addressed the company commanders at 2 a.m. for a 5 a.m. attack:[86]

I attended the meeting of company commanders; Colonel Crawshay told us the plan. 'Look here, you fellows,' he said, 'we're in reserve for this attack. The Cameronians and the Fifth Scottish Rifles are going up to the wood first; that's at 5 a.m. The Public Schools Battatlion are in support, should anything go wrong. I don't know whether we shall be called on; if we are, it will mean that the Jocks have legged it.' He added: 'As usual.' This was an appeal to prejudice. 'The Public Schools Battalion is, well, what we know it is; so if we're called for, that will be the end of us.' He said this with a laugh, and we all laughed.

We were sitting on the ground, protected by a road-bank; a battery of French 75's began firing rapid over our heads from about twenty yards away. There was an even greater concentration of guns in Happy Valley now. We could hardly hear the colonel's words, but understood that if we did get orders to reinforce, we were to shake out in artillery formation; once in the wood, we were to hang on like death. Then he said goodbye and good luck, and we rejoined our companies ...

[Graves continued] The Jocks did get into the wood, and the Royal Welch were not called on to reinforce until eleven o'clock in the morning. The Germans put down a barrage along our ridge where we were lying, and we lost a third of the battalion before the show started. I was one of the casualties.

The German batteries were handing out heavy stuff, six- and eight-inch, and so much of it that we decided to move back fifty yards at a rush. As we did so, an eight-inch shell burst three paces behind me. I heard the explosion, and felt as though I had been punched rather hard between the shoulder-blades, but without any pain. I took the punch merely for the shock of the explosion; but blood trickled into my eye and, turning faint, I called to Moodie: 'I've been hit'. Then I fell.

On another part of the line, there were three separate hurried and unsuccessful attacks on Longueval and Delville Wood on 19, 20 and 23 July and again, successfully, on 26 July. In one instance, XIII Corps ordered 9 Division (GOC Major General Furse) to attack early on 19 July. The commanding officer of a Brigade in 9 Division recalled that the attack was at very short notice – the order being given at midnight on 18 July for dawn on 19 July. There was no reconnaissance and no fire plan. The Brigade commander asked Furse, 'Is it absolutely necessary to carry out this attack tomorrow morning?' His reply was 'Corps has ordered it'. The Brigade commander realized that Furse didn't like it either, and placed the blame on XIII Corps, although ultimately the problem lay with the sense of urgency of GHQ and Fourth Army.[87] There was also a general complaint that there was no point in taking Longueval and Delville Wood at this time because they were overlooked by enemy-held higher ground, and in any case would only create a salient. Moreover there was not much point in trying to take the two places with one division while the rest of the army stayed inactive. Better to take the two at the next general advance, because even if they were taken separately, they could not have been easily held. On 19 July Aylmer Haldane complained of the salient and remarked, 'we are at the old game, which we seem to love, of nibbling a small bit, instead of waiting and launching a big attack'. Major General Furse himself felt at the time that the assault could only have succeeded with fresh infantry and intense artillery preparation.[88]

Indeed, through the hot days of August, Delville Wood continued to be contested, mainly it would seem, to straighten out the line. One regimental officer (Laton-Frawen) recalled how his unit was ordered by division to occupy the front line in Delville Wood on 21 August. His earlier reconnaissance showed the front line to be held in force by the enemy, so to save lives his Brigade commander told him to make any kind of attack and they jointly agreed on a feint or diversion. Even this was repulsed. Then division ordered the attack for 21 August, using the Stokes mortar for the preparation and assault. The attack went in, but received the mortar fire on their own heads, perhaps because of the practice of sending superfluous officers to mortar school (i.e. the less efficient officers that could best be spared). Laton-Frawen objected to side shows and line straightening such as these because they were costly and drew enemy fire from a two-mile front on to a few hundred yards.[89]

Haig's prewar principle of the 'wearing out' battle by the transformed Advanced Guard prior to a decisive result, meant continuous pressure on the enemy, as he wrote on 1 August, giving the enemy 'no rest and no respite from anxiety'. Thus the next stage of the Somme battle took place during August and early September – the wearing-out fight. In particular GHQ warned all commanders in touch with the enemy to watch for signs of demoralization, in case a collapse occurred. This was the reason, therefore, for all the sideshows and attempts to wear down the enemy with separate attacks.[90] It became a matter of faith to say that enemy morale was breaking, and that the Bosche was badly beaten. For example, Major General Maxse reported a conversation with Rawlinson and Fourth Army staff who were 'full of optimism ... they all believe we have beaten the Bosche badly this time ... I always find that the people behind are 50 per cent more optimistic than the people in front!' Indeed on 28 July Haig cheerfully told Lady Haig that a captured officer of the 5th Brandenburg Division had said 'Germany is beaten', and next month he wrote to Lady Haig, 'I think there is no doubt that the enemy's moral is suffering from our constant pressure'.[91] GHQ seemed to be applying prewar 'cult of the offensive' tactics to what was a fire-power attrition battle, while the remoteness of GHQ and Fourth Army made the battle very difficult to control or understand.

Sometimes Rawlinson himself seemed to doubt the wisdom of his actions, as on 22 July when he doubted the success of the attack planned for the next day, on Guillemont.[92] In a letter dated 1 August to Lord Derby, Rawlinson rather glumly wrote, 'I shall now have to get to work and have another go at the village. The task is now harder as the enemy have brought up a good many more guns, as well as some comparatively fresh Divisions.' Rather than suggesting different tactics, Rawlinson's letter went on to consider the might-have-beens of 1 July.[93] Indeed the subsequent attacks on Guillemont revealed so much lack of originality that there was finally a GHQ–Fourth Army conference on 9 August which acknowledged that there had been so many failures to take Guillemont that the method should be reconsidered! The solutions being considered were (1) larger numbers, (2) a fresh Corps and staff, (3) to review experiences, and (4) submit a new plan to Haig.[94] The GHQ–Fourth Army solutions were evidently not useful since Guillemont was not captured until 3 September after repeated attacks through August. Similarly frequent attacks were made on High Wood and Delville Wood into early September.

All this was part of the wearing-out battle, but many of the assaults seemed to be geared toward obtaining a straight line before the anticipated major offensive of 15 September. For example, the GSO 1 of 16 Division recalled that his division was ordered to attack the Quadrilateral area on 6 September, after two earlier failed attempts, so as to straighten out the line. Although this attack was partially successful, the division abandoned the ground gained when it sidestepped left before the attack on Ginchy on 9 September. In similar fashion a member of II Corps staff noted that successes were not followed up because 'we were always waiting till the line could be straightened'.[95] It would appear that traditional Staff College principles were being used instead of the practical methods Robertson wanted, although by late August and early September, attacks were being better co-ordinated, and time was now being given for preparation.[96]

Overall, the effort to co-ordinate an enormously expanded army efficiently was just too great. Even if the correct tactical decisions were being made at the higher levels, these could not easily be translated or co-ordinated at lower levels. Kiggell acknowledged this later when he wrote that Haig's idea had been to force the enemy from his entrenched positions, but that 'as time went on even that became more and more beyond our power owing to the labour at his [the enemy's] disposal and the rapidity with which he created new lines behind his front'.[97] Not only was the offensive failing strategically and tactically, but the command system was not working. There were serious liaison gaps between the infantry and the artillery, and on another level, the co-operation between different command levels of the army was very poor. Time after time Division complained that Corps would not listen or change the method or direction of the attack, or give enough time for preparation.[98] At lower levels the difficulty of organization was intensified, particularly by the very frequent complaints that Divisional and Brigade commanders did not personally come up to see the situation for themselves. In other words, there was first a gap in understanding and co-operation between Corps and Division, and secondly the same gap in understanding and co-operation between Division, Brigade, and lower units. A typical complaint was that of a Lieutenant Colonel Young, who argued that Brigade and Division HQs were so far in the rear that it was impossible for them to keep in touch with their troops, and anyway they just passed on orders and never emerged from their dugouts.[99]

Another interesting story of the gap between Brigade and lower units came from the future Major General A. I. MacDougall, who in July 1916 became Brigade Major to 64th Infantry Brigade. On 1 September 1916 MacDougall's Brigade was relieved when another Brigade arrived. According to MacDougall the commander of the relieving Brigade only went around the line until lunch-time, seeing only a fraction of the line, and one of the craters. MacDougall reported that it usually took six hours to investigate the line thoroughly, but at lunch-time the new Brigade commander went to the messes of both Battalions and drank the largest whisky and water MacDougall had ever seen. On 16 September, MacDougall went to visit another Brigade and found the Brigade HQ asleep at 7 a.m. But at 9 a.m. MacDougall's own troops had to go off to capture a particular trench in preparation for an attack, because the sleepy Brigade HQ had said the trench was in enemy hands, and the start line for the attack was 50 yards ahead of the same trench. However, the trench turned out not to be in enemy hands. MacDougall asked how a Brigade HQ could 'sleep in a dugout miles in the rear, neither knowing or caring where their men are or what they are doing. I was very glad to hear this Brigadier had been sent home.'[100]

Amidst these problems, Haig requested an offensive plan from Rawlinson at the end of August for mid-September, and Rawlinson complied on 28 August. Rawlinson's Fourth Army plan was initially for night attacks with infantry and tanks, but in a slow, methodical step by step advance, as the CIGS had earlier suggested. The plan was a curious amalgam of caution (the slow advance and doubts about the tanks) and innovation (use of infantry and tanks at night). Predictably Haig wanted boldness, and a rush through the third line of defence on the first assault, to capture the enemy guns. He wrote notes on the plan such as 'I think greater boldness should be shown at the outset', and then predictably he vetoed the night plan as not feasible.[101] In fact, the difference of opinion between Rawlinson and Haig was an exact re-run of their different opinions about the earlier tactics of both 1 July 1916 and 14 July 1916. As before, Haig wanted boldness and a final decision, but by means of an unimaginative day attack, while Rawlinson wanted a step by step advance and the protection of the night.

The one major innovation was the use of tanks, and here Rawlinson proved a cautious infantryman, wanting to keep them a mystery 'as long as possible', arguing that they could not cross open country in daylight, so therefore they should be used at night and then withdrawn. On the other hand, Haig thought of tanks as cavalry, as a shock weapon, and urged that 'they should be thrown with determination into the fight, regardless of cost!' As for the vulnerability of tanks in the open, during the day, Haig merely noted, 'But the country has valleys and covered and concealed approaches'. Haig summed up his ideas with a sense of urgency: 'So use tanks boldly, press success, demoralise enemy and try and capture his guns.'[102] Haig's feeling of urgency was carried over into his 'Notes on September Offensive', for his CGS, Kiggell, dated 29 August 1916. The central theme of this handwritten document was the desire for decisive results. Haig wrote, 'I wish the Septr. attack to be planned and carried out in such a way that it may be possible for our troops to achieve a decision if such a result is at all realizable!'[103]

There is no doubt that in July and August Haig recognized he was under pressure from the Cabinet and from the CIGS, Robertson. He attempted to defend himself in various ways, one being a letter sent by Kiggell to all Army commanders, acknowledging rumours of heavy casualties at the Somme, but arguing 'the actual truth is: our casualties for the month of July were, roughly, 120,000 over and above the ordinary trench warfare casualties in the preceding month ... while these figures are not to be made known publicly, Sir Douglas hopes that the truth can be made known quietly in conversation and that the false rumours which, he is told, are being circulated, can thus be corrected'.[104]

But even as Haig mustered his defence, he may not have known that Robertson was actually advising Kiggell (and Rawlinson) how to fight on the Somme, in terms that made it clear the CIGS disagreed with Haig's handling of the battle.[105] To Haig himself Robertson wrote a cunning letter, relaying to Haig the criticisms of the War Committee, but in fact making the same point that he had made to Kiggell and Rawlinson, and using the War Committee as his stalking horse: 'Being ignorant of what modern fighting means they [the War Committee] are rather impatient and apt to attach too much importance to gaining ground and do not pay sufficient attention to the effect that is no doubt being produced on the enemy by the pressure.'[106] As before, steady and careful pressure was required rather than Haig's boldness in seeking a breakthrough, and Robertson's letter was a veiled criticism of Haig's tactics by the CIGS himself.

Haig's replies were equally interesting. He appeared to follow Robertson's ideas in agreeing to maintain steady pressure on the enemy,[107] but in fact planned the ambitious and 'decisive' offensive of mid-September, using tanks as the surprise weapon. The urgency of Haig's emphasis on the decisive nature of the September offensive was partly due to the criticisms from Robertson and others, and partly due to the fact that this *was* the last throw of the dice for the Somme campaign. If the September offensive failed, so did the Somme battle overall, and the decision would have to wait until 1917 or later. There was also the possibility of Haig being replaced, just as Sir John French had been forced to resign. Henry Wilson thought that Robertson wanted Haig's job, and was trying to oust him by suggesting that Haig give up the Somme offensive, thereby admitting failure. But Haig refused to go to London, and weathered the storm.[108] By the end of August Robertson had failed to force his point of view on Haig, although he plainly told him that he saw the tanks as 'rather a desperate innovation', and appeared to have little faith in the planned September offensive.[109]

Undeterred, Haig instructed Kiggell to plan for a decision, if at all possible, and to aim at the quadrilateral Flers–Morval–Les Boeufs–Gueudecourt with a view to breaking through to Bapaume and then turning north-west towards Miraumont. Kiggell faithfully copied Haig's ideas in his orders of 31 August in which he demanded a decisive operation, relying on great boldness and utmost determination, and the exploitation of success within the first few hours, which was essential to victory. In this context, Kiggell hoped that the use of tanks 'may give great – perhaps decisive – results'. Kiggell expected a breakthrough, so it was 'necessary to impress all leaders that the slow methods of trench warfare are unsuited to the style of operations they will be called upon to undertake after the enemy has been driven from his prepared lines of defence'.[110] Despite the urgency behind Haig's ideas, both Gough (GOC Reserve Army) and Rawlinson told Kiggell that they could not comply with Haig's desire to secure the left flank before the offensive: Gough's reserve could not take Courcelette because it lay between two spurs, while Rawlinson thought it a waste of life to capture Martinpuich, also on the left flank, because the village could be outflanked and captured later as the general advance took place. Somewhat surprisingly Haig agreed with Rawlinson, but not with Gough; then on 14 September he apparently reversed his opinion and forcibly told Rawlinson that Martinpuich should be captured as soon as Courcelette was taken, and that the village's capture was not to be delayed by one day, even though it could then be encircled quite easily.[111] Haig was essentially sticking to the traditional Staff College offensive, with both flanks secured, but Aylmer Haldane for one did not expect decisive results since the enemy always seemed to recover from frontal attacks.[112]

The offensive was actually planned for 15 September, with zero hour fixed for 6.20 a.m. Forty-nine tanks were to take part, distributed evenly among the divisions scheduled to assault. Haig has often been criticized both for premature use of tanks, and for distributing them evenly and thinly along the line of attack. Both criticisms have the advantage of hindsight – but it was worth attempting a surprise with the forty-nine tanks available; also Haig visualized tanks being used to deal with unpredictable, unbroken and separated strong points, which was why they were evenly distributed along the line. Meanwhile the artillery and the infantry would actually achieve the breakthrough.[113] One interesting aspect of the September planning was Rawlinson's complete capitulation to Haig's ideas on the offensive, namely to act with boldness and go right through on the first day. It was very important, wrote Rawlinson in his revised plan, to force 'the battle to a decision at the earliest possible moment' as the Commander-in-Chief had requested. Rather abjectly, Rawlinson admitted his plan had not been ambitious enough for the Commander-in-Chief, and he was more than happy to change his tank tactics from tanks leading the infantry to tanks and infantry starting together, as Haig desired.[114] In fact, Haig was applying very considerable pressure on Rawlinson, almost daily in early September. Haig spoke frequently to the Fourth Army commander about the vital need for bold action and surprise, mentioning that the season for fighting was nearly over. It was clear that Haig himself saw this offensive as a final throw, and Kiggell's orders of 13 September 1916 were almost apocalyptic in their urgency and enthusiasm, demanding boldness and resolution to the utmost limits of endurance of the troops, and ending by declaring 'the situation is so favourable that it justifies and demands very bold and vigorous action'.[115]

Afterwards, Kiggell was to claim that neither he nor Haig were thinking of a breakthrough or a decisive victory,[116] but it was clear they were hoping for something very similar. However, most senior officers were sceptical of success. For example, 6 Division of XIV Corps were told of changes in their attack on Flers–Courcelette only on 13 September, and a staff officer recalled 'No one at HQ 6 Division had the least doubt that the prospects of success were very slender'. Similarly, Major General Du Cane was pessimistic on 14 September about his XV Corps attack the next day, saying that the orders were so long and detailed nobody understood them, and the artillery orders were impossible to follow. Haig was very optimistic but had miscalculated, thought Henry Wilson, and Major General Ivor Maxse of 18 Division discounted the prevailing optimism, although he felt the Germans were morally beaten, at least.[117]

The offensive commenced on 15 September with three Corps attacking, and a Canadian Corps in reserve. The artillery preparation had been largely successful, and the new creeping barrage enabled some objectives to be taken. Despite doubts about the tanks, they performed well, within their limits of durability, and Flers was taken, as was Martinpuich and Courcelette – the former with the assistance of tanks. Seven out of ten tanks reached the start line in the centre of XV Corps, and three out of the seven reached the village of Flers, where they led a cheering but disorganized mob of infantry through the streets. There were also reverses, as in the case of 47 Division's attempt to take High Wood. Enfilade fire from good cover prevented 47 Division from advancing, but there were other reasons too. One officer later argued that the confusion and casualties were caused by the formation employed by 47 Division, i.e. each company in each Battalion was to advance in a series of rushes – but there was no co-ordination, no reserve, and no move to the flanks to 'pinch' out the wood. Another officer claimed that 47 Division's advance down a forward slope, in daylight, in view of about 100 German forward observations officers would never have taken place had a senior officer of 47 Division come forward to look at the ground. Instead, out of sixty Commanding Officers higher than Battalion command, only one took a personal part in the battle. This analysis was supported by a regimental CO in 47 Division, who sadly remembered 47 Division's 16 September attack over the skyline, under shell fire, to an objective that was anyway held by the 6th London Regiment. The problem arose because neither Corps nor Division HQ came up to Brigade HQ in order to comprehend the situation.[118]

These separate analyses support the general theme of senior commanders' ignorance of the front, lack of co-ordination between levels of command, and the problems of an army that had grown too rapidly. The normal retribution followed when Haig degummed the GOC of 47 Division, and wrote in his diary, 'The 47 Division failed at High Wood on 15th September and the GOC was sent home! Barter* by name. Now Gorringe has taken over command ... I told him to teach the Division "Discipline and Digging".'[119] Lieutenant General Sir Charles Barter may have deserved his relegation, as did the CRA of 6 Division during 6 Division's difficult assault against the Quadrilateral strong point. It would appear that this attack did not succeed because of poor artillery support – either because of short shooting by 6 Division RA, or as Major General Wardrop claimed because the CRA of 6 Division did not follow orders. Cavan, GOC XIV Corps, ordered supporting fire on the Quadrilateral, and Wardrop passed the message on to the CRA of 6 Division. For some reason this officer did not follow orders, and later denied his error. Then he admitted it, and was immediately sent home.[120]

Once again, the system had not delivered the goods, and there was no means of exploiting and breaking out when considerable success did occur, such as at Flers. The artillery *was* wearing down the still strongly held German front defensive system, yet German defensive tactics were now starting to change. There was greater mobility, the defence took place from shell holes in *front* of the trenches, and more flexibility was allowed to local commanders. German defensive positions were also becoming very much more extensive in the rear, and were in fact almost impossible to break through given standard British frontal assaults, even with the benefit of tanks and the creeping barrage. It was not surprising then, that the problem of the communication and command system had still to be solved; nor was there sufficient flexible artillery co-ordination, or the ability of reserves to be at the right place at the right time. Essentially, once launched, commanders lost control of the battle and the initiative passed to the defence.[121]

GHQ had not appreciated German defensive changes and Kiggell, at least, was still limited by the prewar mental paradigm of the structured offensive. In a rather puzzled way he seems to have realized this, for in a letter written shortly after the 15 September offensive, he wrote:

> If the Germans had not had such endless systems of defence one behind the other they would have been thoroughly and completely defeated before now. They really have been defeated at least three

times over on the front of attack [meaning 1 July, 14 July and 15 September] but the conditions make it impossible to follow up a success rapidly ... with the result that they have been able to pull themselves together again in another prepared line of defence and bring up reinforcements.

However, instead of drawing conclusions in regard to a different method of attack and use of reserves, Kiggell opted for the same policy as in July, namely, pressing the enemy by means of hurried attacks. 'However, though they [the Germans] dig at a very marvellous pace, we have been advancing faster than they have been able to dig and the depth of defences behind them now is comparatively small.'[122] This was incorrect, and was a repetition of what had occurred after 1 July, and thus offered the same costly attacks.

However, the last turning point had now occurred in the Somme campaign. Whereas before the 15 September offensive, Kiggell had argued that only the severity of German discipline had been holding many of the German troops to their tasks, and Haig had been equally optimistic (according to Lieutenant General Haking, as reported by Wilson, Haig had said 'he will smash the Boche on the Somme next month'), now GHQ realized that the strategy of the wearing out battle and the decisive blow had not worked. There were still some defiant GHQ spirits such as Davidson, who on 25 September continued to maintain that the battle was in the wearing out stage and that decisive results could yet be obtained.[123] But GHQ's position was now one of implicit admission of impotence without explicitly admitting anything. Consequently, GHQ's letters from this period reveal a deliberate confusion. This is illustrated by a letter of 18 September from Charteris to Macdonogh.

Charteris started by admitting that there was not much change in the morale of the enemy, but then declared, 'I think the Germans are pretty far through now, and had we another two months before the winter weather set in, I should have no doubt at all about making them conform to our plans'. He was disappointed about the slow arrival of the Class of 1917, but expected to 'work through them pretty quickly ...'[124] After the comparative disappointment of the September offensive, his letter of 18 September shows that he had actually abandoned the doctrine of preparation, wear out, and decision, and now simply shifted to attrition warfare, hoping that the Germans would break before 'winter will forestall us'.[125] After the middle of September, there was no more talk of a decision as such, but simply that pressure must be kept up so that enemy morale (and material) would be reduced,[126] and underlying this again was the assumption that morale represented a quantum amount that could be reduced to zero, at which point the break would come. But morale, like a fever, could rise again if left unattended and should therefore continually be dealt with. Thus when the enemy was pressed, GHQ's own morale went up, in the same proportion as the enemy's morale was supposed to go down. Hence in early October, Haig declared that the enemy was showing 'unmistakable signs of deterioration', and had gone a long way to breaking point, so that the battle must continue. Charteris also announced on 1 October that 'we are getting very optimistic here with regard to the fighting' and 'there is hope that the rot may set in any day'. Yet, 'No one who has seen the ground here over which the men are fighting can be' very sanguine.[127]

This confusion carried over into the fighting. A typical example concerns a Brigade of 12 Division, which engaged in the battle for Le Transloy (7–30 October). The Brigade Major had bitter memories of this battle, which was fought in very poor conditions of rain and mud, and resulted in much loss of life. As a result of inadequate information on the enemy, the poor conditions, and senior commanders' ignorance of the state and position of their own troops, he declared that the Brigade HQ and downwards knew that success was impossible. Due to ignorance, 'higher formations frequently ordered attacks to take off from lines which were not held against objectives which could not be located on the ground', and so the artillery programme was inoperable. Generally, the Brigade Major felt that the conditions made fighting impossible – there were no landmarks, trenches were blown to pieces, and mud made communications difficult. The higher staff did not find out the real conditions, ignored lower reports, and issued impossible orders – nor were these orders given in sufficient time so that they tended to be verbal only. Hence the troops had no chance, and the Brigade Major concluded that Le Transloy was 'one of the most futile' of battles. Would official history conceal the story, he wondered?[128]

Time and again the same story was told in late September and October – HQs and GHQ either could not read their maps, or could not relate their maps to the shattered ground,[129] or attacks were made in weather and mud conditions that made success unlikely. One officer of 24th Infantry Brigade, under Lord Cavan as Corps commander, reported Cavan as addressing the Brigade: 'I give you my word, gentlemen, that unless the weather improves you will not be called upon to attack.' According to this officer, the weather got worse, and the attack went ahead.[130] The underlying theme of the period from mid-September to the end of October was pressure to attack, as in July, accompanied by the same lack of understanding and liaison between higher commanders and their troops. As before there was a yawning gap between Corps and Division HQs and again between Division HQ and Brigade HQ and the units that actually had to do the attacking. Examples of this abound. For instance, Major General Furse (GOC 9 Division) complained on 26 October of troops being hurried into action, 'all due to ignorance in certain quarters and lack of touch with commanders near the front who would soon explain why a reasonable amount of time is necessary . . . before launching the attack'.[131]

Thus the battle was winding down without much direction in late October, and Aylmer Haldane's diary confirms that with the failure of the 'wearing down' and 'decision' strategy, GHQ had simply run out of ideas. His significant diary entry for 22 October 1916 says of GHQ, 'It is evident that they have no clear plan except possibly that of attrition'; and again 'there is a complete lack of strategy in Haig's operations. He is playing the safe game of attrition at vast cost to the country in men and money. Unless he will take a grander view of the situation and encounter a few risks the war will be indefinitely prolonged.' Haldane suggested, as Haig had once done, that blows should be struck on other fronts, and the offensive shifted. Instead, wrote Haldane, there was 'Bludgeon work, as Wellington called it, hammering away at the same point is so much easier and safer and requires no skill or imagination as other schemes, which are far more productive and less expensive, do'.[132]

Why did Haig continue the battle during October and into November? One reason is that to the end of the battle in November, both Haig and Charteris continued hopefully to search for low German morale, although after the battle of Le Transloy, Charteris at least no longer talked of German morale breaking down in a decisive way. Indeed some observers like Major General A. A. Montgomery actually thought in October that German morale was rising.[133] It would appear that Charteris was feeding the ever optimistic Haig what he wanted to hear about falling German morale, and that various senior staff knew this, but did not know how to deal with the situation. Gough claimed later that Army and Corps commanders knew then how unreliable Charteris was, while Major General Clive at GHQ thought Charteris was simply wrong.[134] Haig was also under pressure from his critics in England, and from the French, who wanted the offensive to continue, because of the continuing fighting at Verdun and because if the offensive halted the Germans would have time to build a new series of defensive lines, and thus forestall the planned Allied spring 1917 offensive.[135]

However the major reason for Haig's continuing the battle seems to have been his own view, derived from his Staff College lectures, that the general who held on the longest would win. Sooner or later, he thought, the enemy would break. Haig had not meant to fight a lengthy campaign at the Somme, but by August he had committed himself, and now in October continuous pressure must be applied so that enemy morale might be kept at the state in which it might collapse. On 2 October Haig told Poincaré, the French President, that the enemy must be pressed continuously and not be given 'a moment's peace in which to recover his moral and to make good his shortage in guns and munitions'. By 13

October Rawlinson felt that the enemy had recovered from the last big attack, 'and must now again be shaken with heavy bombardment', although on 20 October he apparently told Henry Wilson privately that the Somme battle could not go on.[136] For his part, Haig on 6 October was keen to go on fighting all winter, and on 17 October was still full of confidence; but by the end of October and early November even he had apparently come to realize that the battle could not be won that year.[137]

Why then was the offensive still continued in November, with Gough's Fifth Army attacking Beaumont Hamel and the Ancre area in mid-November? The answer is complex and relates to postwar criticisms that Haig carried on the offensive longer than was necessary or feasible. On 5 November an attack had been planned for Lord Cavan's XIV Corps to assault Le Transloy, but there developed an upper level 'mutiny', headed by Lord Cavan, who on 3 November complained that the attack by his Corps, in fact 33 Division, should not go forward, given the exhaustion of his men, and the heavy enfilade fire likely across the lengthy route of attack. Among other complaints, Cavan courageously wrote:

> No one who has not visited the front trenches can really know the state of exhaustion to which the men are reduced. The conditions are far worse than in the first battle of Ypres, all my General Officers and Staff Officers agree that they are the worst they have seen, owing to the enormous distance of the carry of all munitions – such as food, water and ammunition.

Rawlinson supported Cavan's misgivings, and at a joint meeting of the French and British senior commanders at 2.30 p.m. on 4 November, it was agreed to cancel the main attack, but to maintain minor attacks. In other words, Haig agreed with XIV Corps' and Rawlinson's misgivings, although Foch was angry, and Major General Montgomery of Fourth Army was also very upset. Haig mollified Foch by promising that Gough's Fifth Army would make a big attack on 15 November astride the Ancre, in one big push if the ground was dry, or in a series of attacks if the ground was wet.[138]

It would appear that this was one of the few instances when commanders had the moral courage to resist the order to attack, and one of the few times in which high level commanders came up to the front to see for themselves. Lord Cavan related later how he and Rawlinson had gone beyond the wire early one morning (at 5.45 a.m. either on 3 or 4 November) and had slogged through the mud for 100 or 150 yards, and had realized that a general advance was impossible.[139] Not only did Haig agree to the cancellation of this attack, but on 8 November he gave instructions to Fourth Army to cease planning for any big offensives because 'weather and training requirements make a big offensive impossible'. Hence there would only be small local offensives to wear down the morale of the enemy and cause losses for another ten days before spring training commenced. Yet at the same time Haig was willing to let Gough's Fifth Army attack, astride the Ancre, go ahead in the middle of November as a relatively large offensive. If weather and training made it impossible for Fourth Army to attack, why would Fifth Army be allowed to mount a large offensive? Part of the answer seems to be in Haig's same order of 8 November to Fourth Army, which contained a note reading: 'A success by 15th would be very valuable as an argument at Conference against transfer of troops to Salonika.'[140]

This reference was to the Chantilly conference called by General Joffre to review the past year and plan for 1917. There was also a political conference scheduled for 15 November in Paris between the prime ministers of France and Britain. According to the future Field Marshal Sir Claude Jacob, then GOC II Corps, Haig's decision to let Fifth Army attack was so that he could say at Paris that he was still fighting. An ulterior motive may have been that Haig's own position was not secure, and rumours were spreading that he was going. Certainly Haig was under attack by Lloyd George, Winston Churchill, and Sir John French, although defended by the king. Other reports had it that Haig would be replaced by Ian Hamilton, although Lord Northcliffe once again came to the rescue as in July and broke up the intrigue.[141] Haig himself argued that the offensive had to go on because of pressure from the French, because Gough wanted to attack, and because of the situation in Rumania and Russia.[142]

In actual fact, there were two major reasons and one minor reason for the continuation of the offensive beyond its usefulness, and these are revealed in private correspondence between Kiggell and Edmonds after the war, and in postwar *Official History* documents. First, Kiggell maintained that although 'the later stages of the fight were hardly justified ... Gough was so keen and confident the Commander-in-Chief decided to permit them'.[143] There is other evidence that Gough persisted in pressing the offensive even though Haig was unsure, and various Corps and Divisional commanders and staff also protested at the continuation of operations. For example, one of the official historians wrote later, 'I first began to be suspicious of him [Gough] when I found that he had forced Jacob [GOC II Corps] to attack at Grandcourt in November 1916 against the latter's better judgement and more accurate information, thereby sharing a tendency to overrule the man on the spot and force him to submit to his own congenital optimism'.[144]

Secondly, Kiggell admitted that the offensive was continued because it might have a favourable effect at the Chantilly conference, and in particular a success at Beaumont Hamel would help Douglas Haig's sagging reputation at the conference. Thirdly, but of minor importance, Kiggell thought there was a tactical opening astride the Ancre. He wrote later to Edmonds:[145]

The full story is that, thinking there was a favourable tactical opening there, I suggested the attack to Sir Douglas, whereon he sent me to Gough for his opinion. At that time too I had heard rumours that Lloyd George meant to make trouble for D. H. over the Somme and the value of a good and 'cheap' success from that point of view, just before the Conference, came to me as an afterthought. Whether I mentioned this to Sir D. H. at the first I don't remember and much doubt – at any rate the responsibility for it is entirely mine and if it is to stand at all I hope that Sir D. H.'s mention of it to Gough, at any rate, will be omitted – as giving his enemies an opportunity of alleging that his decisions were influenced by such considerations, which would be entirely untrue and unjust ...

Whether the original idea had been Kiggell's or Haig's or Gough's, there is no doubt that the continuation of the offensive was largely the result of personal and political considerations, including Gough's own desire for a success which had so far eluded him. In addition, Gough was largely ignorant of conditions at the front and Haig, being impressed by Gough, was ready to let him proceed. Hence a number of factors came together to prolong the offensive although not many were of a purely tactical nature.[146]

After the war Kiggell was pleased to note that Edmonds had eliminated the offending sentences from the *Official History*: 'Very many thanks for your decision to omit the bit about the influence of Gough's success at Beaumont Hamel on the approaching conference.'[147] In fact Gough's offensive did achieve the capture of Beaumont Hamel, and Gough felt later that Fifth Army had fought the most successful battle of the Somme at Beaumont Hamel, beginning on 13 November, 'after days of pouring rain'.[148] Although he was pleased, his subordinates were not, and later reports indicated three problems: exhaustion due to the very poor conditions; muddle and disorganization; and Gough's incomprehension of the situation. One example relates to 19 Division, whose GOC had complained to Gough of the problems of attacking Grandcourt on 14 November, but the 'Army Commanding Officer and his staff had simply no conception of the conditions in the forward area'. The mud, water and cold soon reduced troops in a few hours to exhaustion. When Gough asked why 19 Division had not succeeded against Grandcourt, he was told of various problems relating to 58th Brigade in 19 Division, but he simply replied, '"But why in the world didn't Bridges [the GOC of the Division] leave the 58th Brigade in for another 24 hours?" This shows, I think, that he [Gough] had no notion of the physical strain on the troops of even a few hours in the line under such conditions.'[149]

Another example tells the sad story of 2 Division and 32 Division, and the results of terrible conditions and muddle. George Lindsay (2 Division

HQ) complained after the war that the ground was impassable for this November attack, as did the GSO 1 of 2 Division, and the GOC, Major General Walker. But Gough insisted, and the best and the bravest were killed, wrote Lindsay. The next day the troops were too tired to go through all the trench systems and attack, but were ordered to do so, with the same result. Many were lost, including 'stragglers' who turned back rather than attack.[150] A different perspective on this sector emerges when it appears that the immediate reason for the failure of attacks in the subsequent two or three days was that when 32 Division relieved Walker's 2 Division, the GSO 1 of 2 Division did not know where the front line was, and thus failed to tell 32 Division correctly where they were. As a result the barrage and assault by 32 Division on 18 November was not accurate, and the 'Divisional Commanding Officer [of 32 Division], GSO 1, and two Brigadiers (including our own very good Brigadier General Compton) were relieved, as an immediate result of the Division's failure'. According to another source, the number of officers degummed in 32 Division was actually seven, although the immediate cause of the disaster was probably 2 Division's misinformation.[151]

And yet the problems of the two Divisions were also the problems of an entire system that did not work. For example, the GSO 1 of 32 Division argued that the GOC of his Division, Rycroft, never actually commanded that day at the Ancre because Army told Corps what to do, and Corps told 32 Division what to do, usually chopping and changing plans, and so Rycroft had no say in the matter, particularly as he 'was terrified of Gough'. This had a poor effect on 32 Division, because, according to the GSO 1, Corps HQ Staff never came up to see how the Division was doing or to help, and certainly never came up to the front line. There seemed to be the same general feeling that Army and Corps were not properly in contact with Division and below, and that there were similar gaps between Division and lower units.[152] In other words, the articulation of the Army, the command structure, and the staff communication networks had largely failed.

In conclusion, there was first the problem of a command vacuum at the top. Haig and GHQ simply did not command properly, except in setting rather generalized strategy. In a discussion after the war, Liddell Hart, Gough and Lloyd George came to the same conclusion: the major problem was that GHQ left Army commanders alone to try to formulate their own plans.[153] The entire army resembled a floating and helpless whale, powerful in itself, but lacking co-ordination, proper purpose and articulation. The second major difficulty was that after each success or partial success, as at Montauban on 1 July, or on 14 July or in certain areas on 15 September, the ability to exploit success was not there. The break-in could not be converted into a breakthrough, as Liddell Hart argued in 1932.[154] Then thirdly, after the initial failures in early July, Haig and his GHQ could think of few alternatives to trying to press through the German lines of defence, and hoping that German morale would crumble and present an opportunity for a decisive attack. At the time, however, it is only fair to note that at least Major General Maxse thought Haig was correct. Thus Maxse wrote home at the end of the Somme on 15 November 1916: 'Haig has proved absolutely right in steadily and persistently and doggedly going for Bosch morale – in spite of criticisms by soldiers and politicians and those who expect "Sedans". I think he has the character to stick to his own views and methods.' But it was just those methods that Aylmer Haldane complained of in October and November 1916, 'It is evident that they [GHQ] have no clear plan except possibly that of attrition'. Haldane's critique seems cogent, and does not really contradict Maxse's views. Haig and GHQ had chosen one way to fight – it was not the only way, and not, in fact, the best way, but it was the least demanding intellectually, and if persisted in, would lead eventually to victory, although at heavy cost. As Haldane remarked at the prospect of another 'nibble' forward in December 1916, 'It looks like the old story – attrition – and nothing else'.[155]

Lastly, and perhaps most important, what happened at the Somme was really the application of prewar styles of thinking and operating to a technical reality that could not be so easily or quickly mastered. Haig and his GHQ were actually applying the prewar concept of the human-oriented structured offensive to the Somme, in hoping that wearing down tactics would lead to a German morale breakdown and the decisive offensive. But when this did not happen, GHQ was at a loss. At this point, a change in fundamental strategy was required, as occurred in the German army with its new defensive ideas in December 1916, and new offensive ideas in January 1918; but there was no structure or forum by which fundamental changes could easily be introduced into the BEF, except at GHQ, and there was no willingness in 1916 to look for radical changes. Consequently, the learning process at GHQ followed a cybernetic rather than an analytic pattern – that is to say, prevailing ideas were recycled and reaccepted by a small self-sustaining group, instead of external ideas and criticism being allowed to break the cycle.[156] The heroic efforts of all ranks at the Somme did have a dramatic effect on the German defenders (and thus forced the OHL into basic defensive changes), but the real tragedy of the battle was that the learning and decision-making process at very senior levels did not appreciably change as the BEF prepared for the battle of Passchendaele in 1917.

In fact, how would the British army try to adapt in 1917 and 1918? And what would the *Official History* have to say about the preparations for the controversial battle of Passchendaele, and then the German March 1918 offensive?

Notes

1 War Diary of Lieutenant Colonel Bedall, CO 16th Bavarian Infantry Regiment, 1 and 2 July 1916, 5201–33–68, Rawlinson Papers, NAM.

2 'Lessons Drawn from the Battle of the Somme by Stein's Groups', p. 8; 'Experiences of the IV German Corps in the Battle of the Somme during July, 1916', p. 5, 5201–33–68, Rawlinson Papers, NAM.

3 Details of the experiences of this day can be found in Martin Middlebrook, *The First Day on the Somme*; A. H. Farrar-Hockley, *The Somme*; and Lyn Macdonald, *Somme* (London, 1983).

4 Haig to Lady Haig, 1 July 1916; and Haig to Lady Haig, 1 July 1916, 144, Haig Papers, NLS.

5 Haig to Lady Haig, 2, 3, 4, 5 and 6 July 1916, 144, Haig Papers, NLS.

6 Haig to Lady Haig, 8 and 10 July 1916, 144, Haig Papers, NLS.

7 Haig to Lady Haig, 14 and 17 July 1916; E. G. Thompson (GHQ Staff) to Lady Haig, 28 July 1916, 144, Haig Papers, NLS.

8 Aylmer Haldane thought Haig would be replaced by Rawlinson before the end of the war, Haldane, Diary, 28 July 1916, Haldane Papers, NLS.

9 Advanced First Army HQ, 'Some Artillery Lessons to be Learnt from the Recent Operations in September–October, 1915', 7 November 1915, pp. 2–3, 5201–33–68, Rawlinson Papers, NAM.

10 Haldane, Diary, 13 March 1913, 3 May 1913, 69/36/1, Haldane Papers, IWM; Liddell Hart, Talk with Edmonds, 23 April 1937, 11/1937/30, Liddell Hart Papers, KCL; Brigadier General Shipley (139 Brigade, 46 Division) to Edmonds, 5 June 1929, Cab 45/187; Major General Sir Louis Bols to Edmonds, 31 May 1929, Cab 45/132; Lieutenant General Sir Thomas D'Oyly Snow to Edmonds, 9 January 1931, Cab 45/137, PRO.

11 Lieutenant Colonel J. H. Jones (VII Corps Heavy Artillery) to Edmonds, 3 June 1929, Cab 45/135; Colonel L. A. C. Southam (Territorial Artillery, 169 Brigade HQ, 56 Division) to Edmonds, 3 July 1929, Cab 45/137. The aerial side of artillery observation and other survey techniques have been ably covered in Bidwell and Graham, *Fire-Power*, pp. 101–15. Royal Flying Corps casualties at the Somme are discussed in Denis Winter, *First of the Few*, pp. 153 ff.

12 Colonel L. A. C. Southam to Edmonds, 3 July 1929, Cab 45/137; Second Lieutenant Downman (5th Sherwood Foresters, 139 Brigade, 46 Division) to Edmonds, 12 July 1929, Cab 45/185; Brigadier General Shipley (139 Brigade, 46 Division) to Edmonds, 5 June 1929, Cab 45/187; and also Brigadier General Sir Hill Child (46 Division Artillery) to Edmonds, no date, Cab 45/184; and an unidentified letter at the beginning of the 'W' section in Cab 45/187, PRO.

13 Brigadier General Frank Lyon (VII Corps Staff) to Edmonds, 10 June 1929, Cab 45/135; J. F. C. Fuller to Edmonds, 5 June 1929, Cab 45/133, PRO. Fuller also mentions drunkenness in 46 Division in this letter. On Stuart-Wortley's failure to visit the front before the attack, Charles Page to Edmonds, 1 June 1929, Cab 45/136; on 46 Division as a poor division, and Snow's desire to disband 2 Battalions of the Staffordshire Regiment (137 Brigade) for their problems, Lieutenant General W. Thwaites to Edmonds, 8 June 1929, Cab 45/138, PRO.

14 For Haig's alleged jealousy of Stuart-Wortley, and Haig's retention of Corps commanders, see Liddell Hart, Talk with Edmonds, 31 October 1929, 11/1929/17, Liddell Hart Papers, KCL. Martin Middlebrook believes that Stuart-Wortley was a scapegoat, *The First Day on the Somme*, pp. 238–40, 265–6.

15 Haig, Diary, 28 June 1916, 29 June 1916, WO 256/10 and 1 July 1916, WO 256/11, PRO. Rawlinson, Diary, 30 June 1916, Rawlinson Papers, CCC. W. B. Wood, 'Passchendaele 1917', no date but early December 1944, Cab 103/110, PRO.

16 Ian Grant to Edmonds, 29 October 1929, Cab 45/135; Charles Howard (93 Brigade, 31 Division) to Edmonds, 6 November 1929, Cab 45/134; and Lieutenant Colonel Charles Hole (31 Division) to Edmonds, 6 November 1929, Cab 45/134, PRO.

17 Hunter-Weston to Robertson, 2 July 1916, 1/21/27/1, Robertson Papers, KCL; Hunter-Weston to Edmonds, 12 December 1929, Cab 45/138, PRO; G. S. Clive, Diary, 5 July 1916, Cab 45/201/2, PRO.

18 Charles Howard (93 Brigade, 31 Division) to Edmonds, 6 November 1929, Cab 45/134, PRO. The other officer was Ian Grant, see above, note 16.

19 J. H. Gibbon (460th Battery) to Edmonds, [?] February, 1930, Cab 45/132, PRO.

20 Notes by Brigadier General Rees (GOC 94th Infantry Brigade, 31 Division), July 1916, 1/21/27/2, Robertson Papers, KCL.

21 Brigadier General H. C. Rees (VIII Corps HQ) to Edmonds, 14 November 1929, Cab 45/137, PRO.

22 E. P. Lambert (CRA 31 Division) to Edmonds, 1 November 1929, Cab 45/135, PRO.

23 W. Lambton (GOC 4 Division) to F. B. Maurice, 18 July 1916, 3/5/28, Maurice Papers, KCL; W. Lambton to Edmonds, 29 October 1929, Cab 45/135, PRO.

24 Lieutenant Colonel Dannerman (Royal Warwickshire Regiment) to Edmonds 23 December 1929, Cab 45/133, PRO.

25 Major C. J. P. Ball to J. H. Gibbon, no date, in Gibbon to Edmonds, [?] February 1930, Cab 45/132; J. F. C. Fuller to Edmonds, 24 January 1930, Cab 45/133; J. Hamilton Hall (CO 16th Middlesex Regiment) to Edmonds, 30 December 1929, Cab 45/134; Brigadier General H. Nelson (CO 1st Royal Dublin Fusiliers) to Edmonds, 18 December 1929, Cab 45/136; F. A. Wilson (1st Royal Dublin Fusiliers) to Edmonds, 17 June 1930, Cab 45/138, PRO.

26 Elles, the GOC of 87th Brigade, 29 Division told Edmonds that the real problem was they had not learnt how to use the artillery barrage, F. Elles to Edmonds, 3 February 1930, Cab 45/133, PRO.

27 J. F. C. Fuller to Edmonds, 24 Janaury 1930, Cab 45/133; Gibbon to Edmonds, [?] February 1930, Cab 45/132, PRO.

28 According to Brigadier Anstey, 18 Division adopted a form of moving/creeping barrage, while the counter battery work of XIII Corps generally was good, Anstey, 'History of the Royal Artillery', pp. 117–18, 1159/12, Anstey Papers, RAI.

29 Rawlinson, Diary, 2 July 1916, Rawlinson Papers, CCC; Liddell Hart, Record of conversations with Edmonds, 22 January 1931, 11/1931/3, Liddell Hart Papers, KCL.

30 Rawlinson to Wigram, 3 July 1916, 5201–33–18, Rawlinson Papers, NAM.

31 Edmonds, 'Memoirs', Ch. XXVII, p. 16, Edmonds Papers, KCL; Anstey, 'History of the Royal Artillery', op. cit., p. 135.

32 Anstey, 'History of the Royal Artillery', op. cit., p. 112; General Noel Birch to Edmonds, noting that there were no instantaneous fuses, 8 July 1930, Cab 45/132, PRO.

33 Major General Headlam (CRA XV Corps) thought that wire cutting by 18 pounder shrapnel was best because it swept the wire away but left the ground undamaged, 'Extract from Report by Major General Headlam on the Work of

the Artillery of the XV Corps', 6 July 1916, p. 2, B3, 'Secret Correspondence from and to the MGRA, GHQ, Part I, 1916–17', 1162/12a, Rawlins Papers, RAI; General Staff, 'Notes on Artillery', June 1916, p. 5, WO 33/756, PRO.

34 von Donop, 'The Supply of Munitions to the Army' (1919), p. 29, 69/74/1, von Donop Papers, IWM; Rawlinson to Colonel Fitzgerald, 14 October 1915, 5201–33–18, Rawlinson Papers, NAM; Henry Wilson, Diary, 29 September 1915, Wilson Papers, IWM.

35 John Keegan, *The Face of Battle*, Penguin edn (Harmondsworth, 1978), p. 238.

36 Anstey, 'History of the Royal Artillery', op. cit., p. 115; General Staff, 'Notes on Artillery', June 1916, p. 3, WO 33/756, PRO.

37 Brigadier General H. H. Tudor (CRA 9 Division) claimed that his division attacked on 14 July with 50-yard lifts every minute, using HE shell with delay fuses, H. H. Tudor to Edmonds, 7 March 1930, Cab 45/138, PRO; IX Corps Notes, 31 July 1916, 47, Montgomery-Massingberd Papers, KCL; A. A. Montgomery, Fourth Army to GHQ, 22 July 1916, WO 158/234, PRO.

38 G. W. Stander to Edmonds, 21 February 1930, Cab 45/137, PRO; Major General Alexander to Edmonds, 21 February 1930 in File 7, 'Creeping Barrage', 1159/7, Anstey Papers, RAI; C. Broad to Edmonds, 11 June 1930, Cab 45/132, PRO.

39 This is the burden of Anstey's complaint, although the appointment of Birch to be MGRA at GHQ in June 1916 began a slow process of improvement, Anstey, 'History of the Royal Artillery', op. cit., pp. 115, 119; Rawlins, 'A History of the Development of the British Artillery in France 1914–1918', pp. 88–9, 103, Rawlins Papers, RAI.

40 Major M. R. C. Nanson to Edmonds, no date, but c.1930, Cab 45/136, PRO.

41 Major M. R. C. Nanson to Edmonds, 1 March 1936, Cab 45/136, PRO.

42 E. A. L. Brownlow (36 Division Artillery) to Edmonds, 30 April 1930, Cab 45/132, PRO; Anstey, 'History of the Royal Artillery', op. cit., p. 112; Colonel L. A. C. Southam to Edmonds, 3 July 1929, Cab 45/137, PRO.

43 Colonel L. A. C. Southam to Edmonds, Cab 45/137; G. P. MacClellan to Edmonds, 8 August 1935, Cab 45/132; E. A. L. Brownlow to Edmonds, 30 April 1930, Cab 45/132, PRO. Another gunner maintained that the artillery was not then aware of the great difference that temperature and atmosphere had on the fall of the shell, A. A. Gricker to Edmonds, 9 March 1937, Cab 45/134, and yet another gunner indicated that predicted shooting arrived *after* the Somme, A. B. Clough to Edmonds, 1 December 1936, Cab 45/132, PRO.

44 Major General H. H. Tudor (CRA 9 Division) relates how he learnt from Ordnance in early 1916 how to pinpoint batteries on the map with precision, Tudor, 'Diary of the War 1914–18', 1916, p. 1, MD/1167, Tudor Papers, RAI.

45 E. R. Ludlow Hewitt to Air Vice Marshal R. Brooke Popham, 22 September 1926, Cab 45/120; R. Macleod (Liaison Officer, Fourth Army and 4th Brigade RFC) to Edmonds, 5 May 1937, Cab 45/136, PRO. Bidwell and Graham give a fuller and more detailed view of artillery evolution, Bidwell and Graham, *Fire-Power*, chs 1–8.

46 Private correspondence, T. F. Williams to Wayne Ralph, 25 February 1981, Calgary, Alberta.

47 Edmonds, *Military Operations, France and Belgium 1916, Sir Douglas Haig's Command to the 1st July: Battle of the Somme* (London, 1932), p. 425.

48 ibid., p. 122; Anstey, 'History of the Royal Artillery', op. cit., pp. 108, 119; Rawlins, 'History of the Development of the British Artillery in France', pp. 10, 21, 54–5, 116; draft letter, MGRA to all Armies, c. August–Septem-

ber 1916, B6, 'Secret Correspondence from and to MGRA, GHQ, Part I, 1916–1917', 1162/12a, Rawlins Papers, RAI. On problems of control, mainly between Division and Corps Artillery, Colonel Weber (GSO 1 30 Division) to Edmonds, 18 March 1930, Cab 45/138; and E. G. Wace (GSO 1 32 Division) to Edmonds, 30 October 1936, and 19 October 1933, Cab 45/138; Lieutenant Colonel Reg Harthoran (17 Division RFA) to Edmonds, 13 April 1934, Cab 45/134, PRO.

49 H. A. Jones, *The War in the Air*, new edn, Vol. 2 (London, 1969), p. 276.

50 For example, air observers were only supplied with the zone and squared method of location on 1/40,000 maps in June of 1916, ibid., p. 176.

51 ibid., Appendix 8, p 471.

52 Cecil Lewis, *Sagittarius Rising* (London, 1966), p. 154. Reprinted by permission of William Heinemann Limited.

53 Montgomery-Massingberd to Edmonds, 9 August 1930, and 19 June 1938, Cab 45/136, PRO. A. A. Montgomery, HQ Fourth Army, 10 November 1916, 'Notes on the Somme Fighting', 48, Montgomery-Massingberd Papers, KCL.

54 R. W. Luckock to Edmonds, 8 August 1930 (dated one day before Montgomery-Massingberd's letter to Edmonds in note 53), Cab 45/135, PRO.

55 A. A. Montgomery to [?], 28 August 1916, HQ Fourth Army, pp. 2, 3, 7, in 48, Montgomery-Massingberd Papers, KCL.

56 'The Artillery of the Fourth Army', Artillery Lessons of the Battle of the Somme, p. 2, no date, but *c.* November 1916, 48, Montgomery-Massingberd Papers, KCL.

57 Rawlinson, Diary, 2 July 1916, Rawlinson Papers, CCC; Haig, Diary, 'Note of Interview at Fourth Army HQ at Midday 2 July 1916', p. 2, WO 256/11, PRO; Haig to Lady Haig, 3 July 1916, 144, Haig Papers, NLS; Kiggell to Rawlinson, 8 July 1916, 1/6, Rawlinson Papers, CCC.

58 Lieutenant Colonel E. W. Snepp (Brigade Major, 75th Brigade) to Edmonds, 30 July 1930, Cab 45/137; Lieutenant Colonel T. G. Cope (CO 6th Battalion the Buffs, 37 Brigade, 12 Division) to Edmonds, 16 July 1930, Cab 45/132, PRO; G. S. Cotton (97th Brigade, [?] RA) to Edmonds, 8 August [?], Cab 45/137, PRO. Very similar complaints came from L. T. Miller (Brigade Major, 24th Brigade), who had to send off the 1st Battalion Sherwood Foresters to attack La Boiselle, in the dark, unaided, without maps or reconnaissance, Lieutenant Miller to Edmonds, 24 November 1930, Cab 45/136, PRO.

59 Brigadier General Arthur Solly-Flood (35th Brigade) to Edmonds, 26 November 1930, Cab 45/137; Major F. L. Watson (146th Brigade HQ) to Edmonds, 20 August 1930, Cab 45/138, PRO.

60 See Ch. 1, and Captain Philip Landon (182nd Infantry Brigade) to Edmonds, 2 April 1937, Cab 45/135, PRO.

61 Rawlinson Diary, 4 July 1916, Rawlinson Papers, CCC.

62 Montgomery-Massingberd to Edmonds, 7 December 1937, Cab 45/136, PRO. Montgomery-Massingberd's comment actually referred to the Longueval–High Wood situation, where Lord Horne, GOC XV Corps, was commanding, but the point to be made is similar.

63 E. G. Wace (GSO 1 32 Division) to Edmonds, 30 October 1936, Cab 45/138, PRO. Wace also complained that information went up to Corps, but there was no reciprocal effort from Corps, whose staff officers never visited at Brigade level, or went up to the front line.

64 Major G. P. L. Drake Brockman (38 Welsh Division) to Edmonds, [?] February 1930, Cab 45/132, PRO.

65 Colonel L. Price Davies (GOC 113th Brigade, 38 Division) to Edmonds, 6

March 1930, Cab 45/133, PRO; Edmonds, *Military Operations, France and Belgium 1916, 2nd July to the End of the Battles of the Somme* (London, 1938), pp. 31–2, 40, 49.

66 Kentish (76th Infantry Brigade HQ), 'Appreciation', 3 August 1916, pp. 4, 8, in 47, Montgomery-Massingberd Papers, KCL; Kiggell to Rawlinson, GHQ 9 July 1916, Fourth Army, WO 158/233, PRO; Edmonds, op cit., p. 54.

67 Graves, *Goodbye to All That*, p. 175.

68 Rawlinson to Lord Derby, 1 August 1916, 5201–33–18, Rawlinson Papers, NAM.

69 Rawlinson, Diary, 7 July 1916, Rawlinson Papers, CCC; Edmonds, op. cit. p. 34.

70 Haig, Diary, 8 July 1916, WO 256/11, PRO.

71 Rawlinson to Lord Derby, 1 August 1916, 5201–33–18, Rawlinson Papers, NAM.

72 Major General Shea (GOC 30 Division) to A. A. Montgomery, 10 August 1916, 47, Montgomery-Massingberd Papers, KCL.

73 Colonel Ripley (Northants Regiment) to HQ 54th Brigade, 7 August 1916, 'Battle of the Somme, 1916', 69/57/7, Maxse Papers, IWM.

74 Major General R. M. Luckock (Fourth Army HQ) to Edmonds, 22 December 1937, Cab 45/135, PRO. Haldane, Diary, 11 and 12 July 1916, Haldane Papers, NLS.

75 'Record of Discussion over Rawlinson's 14 July Night Attack', Advanced GHQ, 13 July 1916, Fourth Army, WO 158/234, PRO; Haig, Diary, 11 July 1916, WO 256/11, PRO.

76 Haig, Diary, 11 July 1916, WO 256/11, PRO; Luckock to Edmonds, 22 December 1937, Cab 45/135, PRO.

77 'Record of Discussion over Rawlinson's 14 July Night Attack', 13 July 1916, WO 158/234, PRO. In this same attack, Aylmer Haldane placed his 'unreliable' New Army battalions in front, to prevent them running away!, Aylmer Haldane to Edmonds, 11 December 1929, Cab 45/134, PRO.

78 Montgomery-Massingberd to Edmonds, 7 December 1937, Cab 45/136, PRO; Farrar-Hockley, *The Somme*, p. 182, note.

79 Rawlinson to Colonel Wigram, 13 July 1916, 5201–33–18, Rawlinson Papers, NAM; Rawlinson to Wully (Robertson), 14 July 1916, 1/21/28, Robertson Papers, KCL.

80 Robertson had told Kiggell that the method of advance should be deliberate and steady, and that the whole front should advance together, Robertson to Kiggell, 5 July 1916, 1/35/65, Robertson Papers, KCL.

81 Kiggell to CIGS (Robertson), 14 July 1916, 1/22/56, Robertson Papers, KCL.

82 Rawlinson, Fourth Army Appreciation, 18 July 1916, p. 14, 5201–33–18, Rawlinson Papers, NAM.

83 Robertson to Rawlinson, 26 July 1916, 1/35/100, Robertson Papers; and Robertson to Kiggell, 5 July 1916, 1/35/65, Robertson Papers; see also Robertson to Rawlinson, 15 June 1916, 1/35/99, Robertson Papers, KCL.

84 Haig, Diary, Robertson to Haig, 29 July 1916, WO 256/11, PRO.

85 Kiggell, Advanced GHQ, 2 August 1916, WO 158/235, PRO; Rawlinson, Fourth Army Appreciation, 5 August 1916, 5201–33–18, Rawlinson Papers, NAM.

86 Graves, *Goodbye to All That*, pp. 179, 180–1.

87 H. W. Higginson (GOC 53rd Brigade) to Edmonds, 1 January 1934, Cab 45/134; R. A. Chell (10th Essex Regiment) to Edmonds, 13 December 1933, Cab 45/132; Major J. K. Dunlop (53rd Brigade) to Edmonds, Cab 45/133, PRO.

88 H. H. Tudor (CRA 9 Division) to Edmonds, 2 December 1933 and 7 March 1930, Cab 45/138, PRO; H. H. Tudor, Diary, 15 December 1916, MD 1167, Tudor Papers, RAI; Major General Furse to Maxse, 14 August 1916, 'Battle of the Somme', 69/57/7, Maxse Papers, IWM; Haldane, Diary, 19 July 1916, Haldane Papers, NLS.

89 Laton-Frawen (8th Battalion, Kings Royal Rifle Corps) to Edmonds, 13 April 1934, Cab 45/133, PRO.

90 Haig, Diary, Haig to CIGS (Robertson), 1 August 1916, WO 256/11, PRO; Kiggell to Rawlinson, 8 July 1916, 1/6, Rawlinson Papers, CCC.

91 Maxse to Tiny (Maxse), 22 July 1916, Maxse Papers, WSRO; Haig to Lady Haig, 28 July and 20 August 1916, 144, Haig Papers, NLS.

92 Rawlinson, Diary, 22 July 1916, 5201–33–26, Rawlinson Papers, NAM.

93 Rawlinson to Lord Derby, 1 August 1916, 5201–33–18, Rawlinson Papers, NAM.

94 Fourth Army, 'Note of Interview at Querrieu at 11 a.m. 9 August [1916], between Rawlinson, Kiggell, Montgomery and Davidson', 166, WO 158/235, PRO.

95 Colonel F. C. Jackson to Edmonds, no date, Cab 45/135; F. P. Hosworthy to Edmonds, 29 July 1935, Cab 45/134, PRO.

96 R. Butler, Advanced GHQ, Secret, 'Training of Divisions for Offensive Action', 13 August 1916, 5201–33–70, Rawlinson Papers, NAM; F. P. Hosworthy to Edmonds, 26 August 1935, Cab 45/134, PRO.

97 Kiggell to Edmonds, 25 January 1938, Cab 45/135, PRO.

98 General Sir Reginald Stephens (GOC 5 Division) makes several points along these lines in two lectures he gave after the Somme, 'Lessons from the Recent Offensive Operations' [i.e. the Somme], c. September 1916, p. 8, and 'Artillery from the Infantry Point of View', c. late 1916, pp. 1–2, 69/70/1, Stephens Papers, IWM. Lieutenant General Jeudwine claimed that at Guillemont on 16 August, Congreve of XIII Corps ordered Jeudwine to renew the attack when it was impossible to do so and the Brigade was wiped out, Liddell Hart, Talk with Lieutenant General Sir Hugh Jeudwine, 1930, 11/1930/18, Liddell Hart Papers, KCL. One among very many complaints came from an artillery officer who claimed that the lack of co-ordination between Division and Corps caused the failure of attacks at the Ancre. Corps simply hoped that something good would turn up, R. Fitzmaurice (GOC [?] Brigade, 32 Division RA) to Edmonds, 7 November 1936, Cab 45/133, PRO.

99 Colonel William Parker (CO 24th Battalion) to Edmonds, 27 June 1935, Cab 45/136, PRO; Lieutenant Colonel Young (1/13 London Regiment, 168 Brigade, 56 Division) to Edmonds, 10 October 1929, referring to the fighting between 6 September and 9 October 1916. Young was then sent home after arguing with his Brigade commander, Cab 45/187, PRO.

100 Major General A. I. MacDougall, Diary, 1 September 1916, 16 September 1916, MacDougall Papers, IWM.

101 Rawlinson to Advanced GHQ, 28 August 1916, Fourth Army, WO 158/235, PRO (notes by Haig added in pencil and dated 29 August 1916).

102 ibid.

103 Haig to CGS (Kiggell), 'Notes on September Offensive', 29 August 1916, WO 158/235, PRO.

104 Kiggell to Army commanders, 6 August 1916, 5/31, Kiggell Papers, KCL.

105 Robertson to Kiggell (private), 5 July 1916, 4/3, Kiggell Papers, KCL; Robertson to Rawlinson, 26 July 1916, 1/35/100, Robertson Papers, KCL.

106 Robertson to Haig, 1 August 1916, 1/22/62, Robertson Papers, KCL.

107 Haig, Diary, Haig to CIGS (Robertson), 1 August 1916, WO 256/11, PRO; Haig to Robertson, 9 August 1916, 1/22/65, Robertson Papers, KCL.

108 Wilson, Diary, 5 July 1916, 10 July 1916, 12 July 1916, 20 August 1916, 29 August 1916, Wilson Papers, IWM; G. S. Clive, Diary, 2 August 1916, Cab 45/201/2, PRO.

109 Robertson to Haig, 29 August 1916, 1/22/72, Robertson Papers, KCL.

110 Kiggell, Orders, 31 August 1916, Advanced GHQ, WO 158/235, PRO.

111 Kiggell, 2 September 1916, 'September Offensive Discussion with Reserve and Fourth Army Commanders on 1 September 1916', WO 158/235, PRO; 'Report of Conversation between Commander-in-Chief and Rawlinson at Querrieu at 3.50 p.m.', 14 September 1916, WO 158/236, PRO.

112 Haldane, Diary, 10 September 1916, Haldane Papers, NLS.

113 Notes by Haig in Rawlinson to Advanced GHQ, 31 August 1916, WO 158/235, PRO; Kiggell, 'Note on use of tanks', Advanced GHQ, 5 October 1916, WO 158/236, PRO.

114 Rawlinson to Advanced GHQ, 31 August 1916, WO 158/235, PRO.

115 Haig, Diary, 10, 11, and 12 September 1916, WO 256/13, PRO; Kiggell, Orders, 13 September 1916, WO 158/236, PRO.

116 Kiggell to Edmonds, 25 March 1935 and 2 April 1935, Cab 45/135, PRO.

117 L. W. Savile (6 Division, XIV Corps) to Edmonds, 5 June 1935, Cab 45/137, PRO; Du Cane's conversation reported in Wilson, Diary, 14 September 1916, Wilson Papers, IWM; Maxse to Tiny (Maxse), 3 September 1916 and 7 September 1916, Maxse Papers, WSRO.

118 Major C. H. Fair to Edmonds, 15 May 1935, regarding High Wood and 47 Division, Cab 45/133; Colonel William Parker (24th Battalion) to Edmonds, 27 June 1935, Cab 45/136; William Newton to Edmonds, no date, regarding 16 September, Cab 45/136, PRO.

119 Haig, Diary, 2 October 1916, WO 256/13, PRO.

120 Bartholomew to Edmonds, 1 April 1935, regarding short shooting by 6 Division, Cab 45/132, PRO. General Sir Alexander Wardrop (CRA XIV Corps) to Edmonds, 20 January 1936, Cab 45/132, PRO.

121 G. C. Wynne, *If Germany Attacks*, pp. 103 ff. and 125 ff. Several participants noted that no one really controlled the offensive battle, e.g. R. W. Brims (RE) to Edmonds, 14 August 1934, Cab 45/132; and Major F. Watson (146th Brigade) to Edmonds, 5 July 1935, Cab 45/138, PRO.

122 Kiggell to Lieutenant Colonel Grant (HQ East Africa), 19 September 1916, 5/45, Kiggell Papers, KCL.

123 Wilson, Diary, 31 August 1916, also 29 August 1916, 1 September 1916, 15 September 1916, Wilson Papers, IWM; Haig, Diary, Kiggell to Rawlinson and Gough, 2 August 1916, WO 256/11, PRO; J. H. Davidson, 'Note on the criticism that our casualties have been too heavy in proportion to the results gained', 25 September 1916, 4, Creedy-Kitchener Papers, WO 159/8, PRO; Kiggell, Orders, Advanced GHQ, 13 September 1916, WO 158/236, PRO.

124 Charteris to Macdonogh, 13 August 1916 and 18 September 1916, WO 158/897, PRO.

125 Charteris to Macdonogh, 18 September 1916, WO 158/897, PRO.

126 For example, Haig, Diary, 30 September 1916, 2 October 1916, 13 October 1916, WO 256/13, PRO.

127 Charteris to Macdonogh, 1 October 1916, WO 158/897; Haig to CIGS (Robertson), 'Present Situation', 7 October 1916, WO 158/21, PRO.

128 D. F. Anderson (Brigade Major, 36th Brigade, 12 Division) referring to the battle of Le Transloy, 6 April 1936, Cab 45/132, PRO.

129 C. E. Hudson related the great confusion at Le Transloy, when maps at HQ

and the ground itself did not agree, Hudson to Edmonds, 28 February 1936, Cab 45/134, PRO. In 1917 Aylmer Haldane experienced the visit from GHQ of J. H. Davidson, who found it very different to look at a 1/1,000,000 map at GHQ and a 1/10,000 at Haldane's HQ. This was an admission, claimed Haldane, that revealed GHQ's ignorance of real conditions, Haldane, Diary, 21 March 1917 in 13, Spears Papers, KCL, and in Haldane, Diary, 21 March 1917, Haldane Papers, NLS.

130 G. E. Hill (2nd Lancashire Regiment, 24th Brigade, 8 Division) to Edmonds, 29 March 1936, Cab 45/134, PRO.

131 Haldane, Diary, quoting Furse, 26 October 1916, Haldane Papers, NLS. Other examples are G. F. Richards (25th Brigade) to Edmonds, 20 April 1936, Cab 45/137, and extracts from the Diary of F. H. Wallis (1/5 London Battalion, 169th Brigade), 7 October 1916 and 8 October 1916, in Cab 45/138, PRO.

132 Haldane, Diary, 22 October 1916, in 13, Spears Papers, KCL; and Haldane, Diary, 22 October 1916, Haldane Papers, NLS.

133 A. A. Montgomery, 'Causes of Non-Success', HQ Fourth Army, 13 October 1916, WO 158/236, PRO. In August, Montgomery had predicted the collapse of the enemy by autumn, 'if we only go on hammering at them as we are now', Massingberd to [?], 28 August 1916, p. 7, HQ Fourth Army, 'Notes on the Somme Fighting', 48, Montgomery-Massingberd Papers, KCL.

134 Gough's comments on ch. 17 of the 1945 draft of the *Official History*, 'Reflections, Flanders 1917', Cab 45/140; G. S. Clive, Diary, 26 September 1916, Cab 45/201/2, PRO. According to Henry Wilson, Douglas Loch and others thought Charteris to be a fool and out of touch with events, Wilson, Diary, 3 September 1916, Wilson Papers, IWM.

135 Wilson claimed that Lloyd George was hunting Haig and Robertson at this time, Wilson, Diary, 17 October 1916 and 22 October 1916, while Winston Churchill was also out to 'get' Haig, Wilson, Diary, 21 November 1916, Wilson Papers, IWM. For French pressure, see Edmonds, *Military Operations, France and Belgium, 1916, 2nd July 1916 to the End of the Battles of the Somme*, ch. 19, 'Retrospect'.

136 Cf. Chapter 4; also Brigadier General Charteris to Liddell Hart, 11 October 1935, 1/162/1, Liddell Hart Papers; and Edmonds's comments on Liddell Hart's *The Real War*, ch. 4, Scene 4, 9/8/2, Liddell Hart Papers, KCL. Evidence for a 'short' Somme is in Haig's July letters to Lady Haig, and Haldane, Diary, 22 October 1916, Haldane Papers, NLS; Charteris to Macdonogh, 1 October 1916, WO 158/897, PRO; Haig, Diary, 2 October 1916, and 13 October 1916, WO 256/13, PRO; Wilson, Diary, 20 October 1916, Wilson Papers, IWM.

137 Rawlinson, Diary, 6 October, 1916, 5201–33–26, Rawlinson Papers, NAM; Maxse to Tiny [Maxse], 17 October 1916, WSRO; Haig, Diary, 31 October 1916, WO 256/13, PRO; Charteris to Macdonogh, 26 October 1916, WO 158/897, PRO; Commander-in-Chief to Fourth Army, 8 November 1916, WO 158/236, PRO.

138 Lord Cavan (XIV Corps) to Fourth Army, 3 November 1916, WO 158/236; Rawlinson to Kiggell, 4 November 1916, Fourth Army, WO 158/236, PRO. For Montgomery's annoyance, Liddell Hart, Talk with Pope-Hennessy, 14, October 1933, 11/1933/23, Liddell Hart Papers, KCL. (According to Pope-Hennessy, Gathorne Hardy also had the moral courage to protest against the attack.)

139 Cavan to J. F. C. Fuller, 14 February 1933, WO 79/69, PRO.

140 Commander-in-Chief's instructions to Fourth Army, 8 November 1916

(initialled by Kiggell), WO 158/236, PRO. See also Farrar-Hockley, *The Somme*, pp. 247–8.

141 General Claude Jacob reported in Wilson, Diary, 11 November 1916, and regarding political attacks on Haig, 13 and 21 November 1916, Wilson Papers, IWM; Kiggell to Edmonds, 11 June 1938, Cab 45/135, PRO. Haldane, Diary, 26 November 1916 and 31 December 1916, Haldane Papers, NLS. Woodward, *Lloyd George and the Generals*, pp. 118 ff.

142 Haig, Diary, 12 November 1916, WO 256/13, PRO.

143 Kiggell to Edmonds, 4 June 1938, Cab 45/135; George Jeffreys to Edmonds, 23 October 1936, regarding complaints from Major General Bridges (GOC 19 Division), Cab 45/135; George Lindsay to Edmonds, 28 June 1937, regarding the complaints of Deedes (GSO 1 of 2 Division), Cab 45/135, PRO.

144 W. B. Wood, 'Passchendaele 1917', no date, but early December 1944, Cab 103/110, PRO.

145 Kiggell to Edmonds, 11 June 1938, Cab 45/135, PRO.

146 General Sir Hubert Gough, *The Fifth Army* (London, 1931), pp. 155–6; Kiggell to Edmonds, 4 June 1938, Cab 45/135, PRO; Edmonds claimed that Haig was infatuated with Gough, 'Memoirs', ch. XXVIII, 1917, p. 17, Edmonds Papers, KCL.

147 Kiggell to Edmonds, 16 June 1938, Cab 45/135, PRO.

148 Gough's comments on Edmonds's 1946 draft of ch. 19, 'Retrospect', p. 20, Cab 45/33, inside Cab 45/140, PRO.

149 George Jeffreys (19 Division) to Edmonds, 23 October 1936, regarding the battle of the Ancre, Cab 45/135, PRO.

150 George Lindsay (2 Division) to Edmonds, 28 June 1937, Cab 45/135, PRO.

151 E. G. Wace (GSO 1 32 Division) to Edmonds, 30 October 1936, Cab 45/138, Lieutenant Colonel H. J. N. Davis (CO 15th Highland Light Infantry) to Edmonds, 10 November 1936, Cab 45/133; Brigadier General Kentish (14th Brigade) to Edmonds, 19 December 1936, Cab 45/135, PRO.

152 E. G. Wace to Edmonds, 30 October 1936, Cab 45/138 (see Wace also for removal of Divisional artillery to Corps control); and Lieutenant Colonel A. H. Burne to Edmonds, 4 May 1930, Cab 45/132; for Brigade-Division gap, F. Bicknell (63rd Brigade) to Edmonds, 7 January 1937, Cab 45/132, PRO.

153 Liddell Hart, 'Lunch with Gough and Lloyd George', 27 January 1936, 11/1936/31, Liddell Hart Papers, KCL.

154 Liddell Hart, 'Some Lessons of the [Great] War' (for the Kirke Committee), p. 22, 11/1932/55b, Liddell Hart Papers; and for France and Belgium 1915, and Somme 1916, p. 2, 11/1932/66, Liddell Hart Papers, KCL.

155 Maxse to (Tiny) Maxse, 15 November 1916, Maxse Papers, WSRO; Haldane, Diary, 22 October 1916, in 13, Spears Papers, KCL, and in Haldane, Diary, 22 October 1916, and 13 December 1916, Haldane Papers, NLS.

156 For an explanation of cybernetic and analytic, see T. H. E. Travers, 'Learning and decision-making on the Western Front, 1915–1916: the British example', *Canadian Journal of History*, vol. 18, no. 1 (1983), pp. 93 ff.

PART IV

Remembrance
and
Recrimination

[8]

The *Official History*, the Somme, and the Planning of Passchendaele

The preparations for the battle of the Somme, and the events of the battle, have been described in some detail. But the Somme campaign, and those that followed, should also be seen in a wider context, because the history of the British army on the Western Front is also the history of the writing of that story. The battles of the Somme and Passchendaele, the work of Haig and his GHQ, the quality of commanders, the application of tactics and technology – all these have become fixed in the imagination by the early critics and historians of the war – and now can only be properly approached and understood in the context of that history. Perhaps the most important of the early histories of the Western Front was the British *Official History*, important because the official historians eventually came to know as much or more about the Western Front than any historians before or since, and because the story the official historians told has heavily influenced the controversies that have continued to swirl about the Western Front to this day. However, when the British official historians got down to work after the First World War, the full story of the Western Front did not always emerge. This was in part because the *Official History* tended to avoid specific criticisms and tried to tell the story as a straightforward narrative. Awkward passages were either relegated to footnotes or appendices, or simply omitted altogether. In addition, the official historian, Brigadier General Sir James Edmonds (known as 'Archimedes' to his friends) was quite clear about his role as a historian, which was to tell the story, but not to be too critical. Edmonds had been at Staff College with Haig, and after a health breakdown in 1914 had been rescued by Haig and placed on his GHQ staff as an engineer. After the war Edmonds was often privately critical of Haig, for example in letters to Liddell Hart, but he felt obligated to him and he became increasingly favourable to Haig and GHQ. In fact Edmonds felt himself to be 'but a

G.S.O. writing a military account of a modern campaign with the assistance of friends'. He believed he had 'the views of my comrades to consider', and he told Major General Maxse when writing about Maxse's role that he had amended one criticism, and elsewhere had 'toned down or omitted anything that seemed harsh'.[1] Apparently Edmonds also omitted facts when requested by senior commanders, one alleged example being the leadership of Brigadier General A. W. Currie at Second Ypres,[2] and another when Kiggell asked that Edmonds leave out the previously mentioned material about the reasons for the last Somme offensive in November 1916.[3]

The practice of the *Official History* was for a first draft to be prepared and then sent out for comments to the officers involved. In regard to the volumes on the Somme, this occurred in 1930, two years after Haig's death, and five years after the death of Rawlinson, GOC Fourth Army at the Somme. Fourth Army's next key staff officer involved in 1916 was Major General A. A. Montgomery, chief of staff to Rawlinson at the Somme. The first draft of the Somme volume dealing with planning for the battle did not appeal to Montgomery or to his GSO 1, Major General Luckock, to whom Montgomery passed on the draft. Both of them took the same line, that planning for the Somme in 1916 had been a great advance over 1915, and that it was only too easy to be critical after the event. Montgomery wrote: 'I don't like the tone in which this volume is written at all ... the writer of this volume is much too wise after the event, which is so very easy.' Moreover, 'The writer does not seem to realise at all the advance in the "organisation of the battle" over 1915. The French came down often to find out what we were doing, as regards artillery especially, and copied many of our methods.' Luckock followed Montgomery's criticism, saying that 'I am sure it [the draft] was not written by General Edmonds – not only is the tone entirely different to the earlier volumes, but the English is not of the same standard'. Luckock went on to argue that the organization of the Somme was a 'prodigious' advance on anything done before, and that a 'fair-minded writer' would point this out. He wanted the chapters rewritten, and added the comment that the writer of the draft constantly contradicted himself in order to belittle Rawlinson, implying that Haig was, in contrast, being treated too well.[4]

Judging by the volume which was actually published in 1932, dealing with the planning of the Somme to 1 July 1916, the comments of Montgomery and Luckock had some effect, for the evaluation of Fourth Army is favourable, although somewhat critical in regard to Fourth Army's tactical instructions for the battle. There is some blame attached also to Haig for being over-optimistic, but in general the tone of the volume was conciliatory. At this point Montgomery became CIGS (1933–6). When he saw the draft of the second volume, covering the period from 2 July to the end of the Somme, he strongly criticized the draft

as again being 'wise after the event', and he and Luckock defended
Rawlinson in their letters, while criticizing GHQ.[5] This evaluation seems
to have had an influence, since Montgomery was able to write to Edmonds
in June 1938 saying that 'the absence of the "wise after the event" superior
tone is most refreshing'.[6] Actually this volume was a strong defence of
Haig and GHQ, particularly in regard to casualty figures on the Somme,
which Edmonds manipulated in order to show the battle in a better light,[7]
while Fourth Army emerged relatively but not entirely unscathed.
Edmonds seems to have followed a strategy in this volume of moderating
the tone and removing specific criticism, and of defending Haig and his
GHQ. He allowed the blame for attrition warfare to fall on external
factors such as the French, the battle of Verdun, the standard of training of
the new officers and men, the equipment, etc., while obliquely blaming
Fourth Army staff for errors rather than GHQ.

This strategy or approach intensified with the Passchendaele volume,
except that here the personal rivalries involved, the sheer length of time
taken in producing this volume (1939–48), and the controversial conduct
of Gough as Fifth Army commander at Passchendaele, all made the
process more tortuous. The Passchendaele volume was the last to appear
(1948), after those on Arras and Cambrai, and involved an astonishing
sequence of changes in interpretation, particularly over the planning of
the battle. In reviewing the evidence concerning the planning of the battle
up to 31 July 1917, three major areas of controversy emerged. First, did
Haig and his GHQ Staff tell Gough, GOC Fifth Army, clearly what kind
of offensive it was going to be – a step-by-step advance, or a breakthrough? Secondly, did Haig and his GHQ Staff tell him clearly the
direction or line of the offensive, and the width of the offensive, particularly in regard to attacking and seizing the whole Gheluvelt plateau?
And thirdly, who was actually in charge of planning the Passchendaele
offensive? Ultimately, was it Haig and his GHQ or was it Gough and his
Fifth Army Staff? This last question in particular was to bedevil the
writing of the *Official History*.

The answer to the first question is 'No' – Gough did not know clearly or
understand what kind of offensive it was going to be. In fact he assumed
that it was to be a breakthrough. Indeed Haig had decided at a meeting on
28 June 1917 that it was going to be a breakthrough, but then became
more cautious in the next few days and appeared to revert to a step-by-
step advance. Also, why would Haig appoint a thruster like Gough to
command the offensive, rather than the cautious Plumer who knew the
ground very well, unless he did want to aim at distant objectives and a
breakthrough? Essentially, Haig and his staff wavered between a breakthrough and a step-by-step advance, and sometimes included both as
aims, but they did leave Gough with the impression that a breakthrough
was required.

The answer to the second question is 'Yes' – Haig did try to impress on Gough that the whole Gheluvelt plateau should be captured. Haig told him this very firmly on 28 June, and on 30 June Haig's pencil comments on the Fifth Army plan read 'Capture the Passchendaele–Staden Ridge'. This message was repeated in GHQ orders for 5 July, and again in Fifth Army orders of 8 July.[8] In fact, Gough and his Fifth Army staff did not put enough emphasis on this point, and did not realize their critical mistake in not strengthening the right of Fifth Army until later. On the other hand, the dividing line between Fifth and Second Armies made it difficult for Gough to include the southern edge of the Gheluvelt plateau in his plan of attack, and one of the official historians, Pope-Hennessy, told Liddell Hart that Gough had wanted a wider front for the Fifth Army offensive, but had been afraid to insist on this extension, for fear of Haig's reaction. Another version, from Brigadier Broad, had it that both Gough and Plumer (GOC Second Army) were cautious about the attack because the front was not wide enough, but that Haig had said the front could not be extended because of the French frontage to the north.[9] Apparently, Gough realized this mistake during August and insisted that Haig call a conference in which Plumer's Second Army (on Gough's right) was assigned the task of capturing the whole plateau. To this Plumer very reluctantly agreed.

Lastly, the answer to the third question is that ultimately Haig did have the overall responsibility of time, place and strategy, leaving Gough to work out the tactics to fit in with the general concept.

It will now be useful to review the actual process of writing the Passchendaele volume of the *Official History*, while keeping in mind the three major issues outlined above. As will become apparent, the volume went through no less than four major changes in interpretation, all of which related to drafts that alternatively blamed either Gough or Haig for the failures of Passchendaele, and these failures principally involved the three issues already discussed. Before turning to this story within a story it should be noted that of the main characters involved, Haig had died in 1928 and could not defend himself, although his DMO in 1917, Sir John Davidson, was alive into the 1950s and did intervene to defend Haig on some, but not all issues. On the other hand, Gough, as GOC Fifth Army, was alive until 1963, and was the chief critic of the various draft versions of the Passchendaele volume.

The first draft of this volume was started by Captain G. C. Wynne and Captain Cyril Falls in 1939. Shortly after, in October 1939, Captain Falls left to join the staff of *The Times* and Wynne was therefore responsible for the first draft, which characterized Haig as fully responsible for the planning of the less than successful 31 July Passchendaele offensive. This was *viewpoint 1*, which was then replaced by *viewpoint 2* in 1943 when Edmonds ordered Wynne to rewrite the first draft 'so as to transfer the responsibility [for the direction of the opening battles] to General

Gough'. Wynne obediently did so, and Edmonds approved the revised chapters as 'excellent in every way'.[10] At this point (April 1943) Wynne was assigned to North Africa, but reappeared in early 1944, when work on the *Official History* resumed. Wynne then decided to interview Gough. However, just before this interview took place Wynne received a letter from Edmonds, dated 17 February 1944, which was strongly critical of Gough. 'Let Gough have his say, but you have the last word, and I am certain that you have got to the bottom of the affair ... Gough was out to fight and get forward. He had no idea how to conduct the action Haig required and would not take advice.'[11] Edmonds's dislike and bias against Gough is partially revealed here, and this bias remained consistent throughout the drafting and discussions of the 1917 volume.

For his part, Wynne also disliked Gough, but was able to retain his objectivity and shift his opinions when other evidence was presented. This started to appear when Gough was given drafts of various chapters to read and comment on in early 1944. Predictably the anti-Gough tone of these drafts (*viewpoint 2*) elicited a major rebuttal from Gough, who complained of the 'carping criticism' of the draft. Specifically, he argued that Haig had failed to mass nearly enough force to achieve the results he envisaged, so that the front of the 31 July 1917 attack was too narrow and was in any case directed too far north; and he argued that Haig's instructions to him were to capture the Passchendaele ridge and advance rapidly on Roulers:

I have a very clear and distinct recollection of Haig's personal explanations to me and his instructions when I was appointed to undertake this operation. He quite clearly told me that the plan was to capture the Passchendaele ridge and to advance as rapidly as possible on Roulers. How many miles does Roulers lie behind what was the German front? – 40 miles? I was then to advance on Ostend. By the time I had reached and taken Roulers, Haig considered that the Fourth army on the coast would have advanced sufficiently to cover my left, and combine with me, in clearing the coast. This was very definitely viewing the battle as an attempt to break through and moreover Haig never altered this opinion till the attack was launched ... He confirmed this general idea on several occasions.

Finally, Gough also argued that the draft chapters set forth 'almost as a principle, the abrogation of authority and responsibility of commanders to command, by the frequent references that are made to Haig disapproving of my plans, and yet not interfering to alter them. This is quite a new light on Haig's character, and one which I fail to recognise. I doubt whether he would be very pleased!'[12]

Surprisingly, Edmonds made a mental somersault and responded to Gough's criticisms by saying, 'I thoroughly agree with you about the carping criticism in Wynne's narrative. I have already told him that a narrative of events is required, not criticism. He will have to rewrite the greater part of the story. Part of the explanation is that Wynne fell into the [anti-Gough and pro-Haig] hands of Tavish [Sir John] Davidson ...'[13] However what Edmonds actually meant was that the anti-Gough bias would remain regarding the three major issues, although the critical tone or style would be removed, as had happened with Major General A. A. Montgomery and the Somme volumes. This is clear from the next set of chapters sent to Gough regarding the Langemarck battle on the left of Fifth Army. Gough was not placated and wrote:

> Speaking generally, I should call these 7 chapters a vicious distortion of the facts. It seems to me that they are deliberately written with the object of absolving Haig, and, almost more so, GHQ, from all responsibility, by placing every possible reason for failures on my shoulders. Even my corps commanders are pictured as great soldiers who from first to last, foresaw all difficulties, recognized how they could be avoided, and only yielded to my direction under the most violent protests!

Two accompanying letters from Gough's chief of staff, Major General Neill Malcolm, bitterly termed the draft 'a farrago of malicious nonsense', and commented 'Wynne makes me tired ... Haig decided that he wanted a break through and Charteris was always telling him that the Germans were on the point of cracking. The break through was the policy.'[14]

In his margin notes on the draft chapters, Gough also emphasized that GHQ 'made the initial error in the choice of the battlefield and then in not organizing the extension to cover the whole plateau. The Second Army ought to have been ordered to take part in the battle from its commencement' (i.e. to emphasize the right wing). Gough also pointed out that it was he himself who was responsible for calling the conference which in August compelled GHQ to stress the right wing and encompass the whole Gheluvelt plateau in the continuation of the offensive. Gough had personally initiated this change of direction by asking to see Haig on this question, and the result was the August conference chaired by Kiggell (Haig being in London), at which Plumer was ordered to take over the battle. Plumer testily protested that 'he had been in a salient for over two years and he was not going to put himself into another'. Nevertheless, on his return to France, Haig confirmed that Plumer was to take over and overruled him on the change of direction of the offensive. In his critique, Gough also denied that Lord Cavan and other corps commanders had implored him before the start of the offensive to allow II Corps to 'bang through' on the right: 'Quite untrue. My corps commanders never made any such suggestion – much less "implored" me to do this. If Cavan now says this I say *he has invented the story*. Nonsense.' Despite Gough's typically forthright statements, he appears to be wrong on this question. Percy Beddington, who was GSO 1 of a division in the 31 July offensive, and later became Gough's chief of staff of Fifth Army, and was a strong postwar supporter of Gough, wrote later, 'I felt that his [Gough's] only fault [on 31 July 1917] ... was in attacking with insufficient strength on the right of the 8th Division, he wanted 2 [more] Divisions – and those about his best there on July 31st'. Gough should have strengthened the right of his offensive, but did not, perhaps because he did not fully recognize the critical significance of the plateau edge at the time, and perhaps because he was apparently afraid of approaching Haig with the idea of widening the whole offensive.[15]

Edmonds handed over these criticisms of Gough to Wynne, who wrote that his interpretation was based on evidence from Haig's diary, that Lord Cavan had indeed offered to punch through with his II Corps on the right of the plateau (as indicated in letters at the time), that the intelligence information came from Charteris's book, and so on. Wynne added, 'I have naturally no bias whatever against Gough or the Fifth Army – but both Pilckem and Langemarck were thoroughly bad in their planning, and even the *Official History* should admit as much – and Gough must lump it. He should have been sacked for them without a pension.' Yet, despite this, Wynne was prepared to shorten the chapters and meet some criticisms. However, as a parting shot he added, 'He [Gough] did at least graciously admit in his comments on the Pilckem chapter that Haig's big mistake was to select him (Gough) for the job – a point which must go in to the last chapter'.[16] It did, but the *Official History* does not contain the story behind the August 1917 Gough–Plumer–Kiggell conference, and the new change of direction.

One last series of draft chapters was sent to Gough, which he returned to Edmonds on 7 June 1944. Gough repeated his earlier defence, declaring again that Haig's 'plan did envisage a breakthrough' and he particularly resented the suggestion that on 28 June 1917 Haig and Gough had had lunch together, at which time Haig had instructed Gough to make sure of taking the whole Gheluvelt plateau. Gough denied this, although Haig's diary shows that the lunch did take place and recorded the conversation as Haig telling Gough to make sure to take the whole plateau. However, Gough now argued, 'No such advice was given to General Gough. If it had been, surely a conference and a discussion on the plan should have taken place? No such discussion did take place.'[17] Actually, this advice *was* given to Gough, there *was* a small conference on 28 June 1917 to discuss the change, and it was incorporated sufficiently into Fifth Army plans to please Haig, but Gough did not apparently pick up Haig's full meaning. And as previously argued, Gough did not appreciate the full significance of attacking over the whole plateau, nor did he wish to raise with Haig the fundamental issue of revising the width of the whole offensive. Thus in

1944 Gough simply repeated his earlier defence: 'it was General Gough who went to Sir D. H. [in August 1917] and demanded that this plateau should be assaulted on its whole front, which entailed the participation of the Second Army. Hence the conference between General Gough–General Kiggell (representing Sir D. H.) and General Plumer at Cassell.' However, by then, August 1917, it was too late to remedy the earlier mistake.[18]

In early December 1944, therefore, the Passchendaele drafts were holding to *viewpoint 2*, making Gough responsible for the problems in the planning of Passchendaele, although Wynne had been told to tone down his open criticism of Gough. At this time the official historians seemed united in feeling that Gough 'was at last getting his deserts', and that he had caused the 'disasters' at Passchendaele by 'adhering to his own plans for breaking the German lines over the whole of the Fifth Army front in preference to Haig's views'.[19] All's well that ends well it would seem, but the story now takes a strange twist, for Captain Wynne then interviewed Sir John Davidson, Haig's DMO, 'and obtained from him confirmation of his original belief that responsibility for the direction of the early part of the campaign rested with Sir Douglas Haig and not with General Gough. He [Wynne] took account of this in his final revision: and, so far as concerns the attribution of responsibility, reverted in his final version of the volume to the basis of his original draft.'[20] This then is *viewpoint 3*, a reversion to *viewpoint 1* in that it held Haig responsible for the planning of Passchendaele, but differing in that Wynne remained critical of Gough in many ways, although now absolving him from major responsibility for the planning of the 31 July offensive.

Edmonds saw Wynne's new draft, and was predictably annoyed. In fact he called for a 'careful re-editing' of the new draft, which produced a reaction from Wynne, fearing that Edmonds 'intends to revert to the "middle" stage [*viewpoint 2*] at which responsibility was attributed to General Gough'. This conflict between Wynne and Edmonds threw the other official historians into obvious difficulties, and there was general agreement that Edmonds would be biased against Gough. For example, one official historian remarked that 'as far as Pilcken [*sic*] and Langemarck are concerned, the General's [Edmonds's] feelings got the better of him and made him transfer the responsibility from the shoulders of Haig (where Captain Wynne had originally placed it) to Gough with unfortunate results'. Norman Brook, an official historian and later Secretary to the Cabinet, attempted to mediate:

> I am not happy at the thought of leaving General Edmonds to revise this Volume as he thinks fit, without the restraint imposed by the criticisms of a colleague. We know that General Edmonds has strong feelings about General Gough's conduct of this campaign: and some

of his remarks recorded in these papers suggest that he is unlikely to approach the task of revision in an unbiased mood. Moreover, I fear that, whatever restraint he has exercised in his past writings, he has not always been able to resist in recent years the temptation to introduce strong personal views into his historical work. I recognise that the same criticism has been directed . . . against Captain Wynne's work on the Passchendaele Volume but it must be borne in mind that these are criticisms of earlier drafts in which, according to his statement, he was writing to the direction of General Edmonds.

Brook therefore suggested that Wynne and Edmonds meet, and Wynne bring to Edmonds's attention the new information he had obtained from Sir John Davidson.[21]

Wynne and Edmonds did in fact meet, and although Wynne believed that Edmonds now accepted the revised views of Sir John Davidson,[22] in fact Edmonds went ahead revising and editing Wynne's text, while Wynne himself continued to complete his draft, including the final 'Reflections' chapter. This chapter was sent to Gough, and received severe and very extensive criticism from Gough on the three main points at issue – breakthrough or not, the whole plateau or not, and who was in command. Gough does not seem to have recognized that Wynne was in fact trying to help him, especially in the section that showed Haig and GHQ wavering between one plan on 28 June 1917 (breakthrough) and another on 5 July 1917 (step-by-step – capture the plateau and only then advance); and in the section showing that Haig had essentially accepted the Fifth Army breakthrough plan.[23] Gough also added three new criticisms of Haig and GHQ that now seem justified; first, and perhaps most important, that Haig chose a very poor battlefield – in fact 'the worst possible for an offensive operation'. Secondly, that 'Haig's staff was never a strong team', i.e. Charteris, Davidson, Lawrence and Kiggell. Thirdly, and this was one of the root causes of the problems at Passchendaele (and at the Somme):

There were not enough discussions, between the H.Q. Staff and the Army Commanders concerned – when we could sit round a table with all the maps before one, and really thrash out the problems. Haig's conferences were too big and too formal and Army Commanders only attended to hear Haig's plans, never to discuss them.

Gough defended his own weak point, the failure to make sure of the whole Gheluvelt plateau, by blaming GHQ:[24]

The front of the attack – the actual front allotted to me was entirely G.H.Q.'s. I – ignorant of the features of the ground – was brought on to it, and was told to attack with my right at X – and my left at Y – As you point out later on – it was a mistake appointing me to command this operation – Plumer knew the ground from A to Z . . . But if I had to undertake it – the whole front of the Second Army should have been placed under my command – It was GHQ who was entirely responsible for the attack in the first instance.

Gough therefore admitted he was not the man for the job, but defended himself with some justification by saying that Haig should have thrown in the Second Army in order to make sure of capturing the whole plateau. Gough also repeated his comments regarding the August 1917 conference:[25]

the attack on the Gheluvelt plateau across its whole breadth was insisted on by me – by the 5th Army – the 5th Army front did not cover half the plateau – we were forced to fight on a comparatively narrow edge of it ... the 2nd Army looked on – I recognised that this could not go on ... I asked for a conference with Haig to lay these ideas before him.

However, he did not say why he had not insisted on this change of direction in July 1917, before the offensive, rather than in August 1917. A subsequent interview between Wynne and Gough on 31 May 1945 reveals that Gough had spread his divisions along the start line in the then orthodox manner, and had made no special provisions for the Gheluvelt plateau, indicating that he had not grasped the need to alter traditional methods to take account of the obvious significance of the high ground.[26]

In regard to the question of a breakthrough or a step-by-step advance, Gough stuck to his story that although the *Official History* draft of the Passchendaele chapters frequently referred to GHQ plans

for a battle of attrition – a slow step-by-step advance – *None* of these plans were ever brought to my notice. Have they been drawn up 'after the event'? It is curious that if such plans existed that the C.G.S. or some representative of 'operations', did not constantly visit me to discuss all the pros and cons.

Gough could only remember two visitors, Davidson and Haig, both of whom proposed far-reaching operations, especially Haig, who according to Gough, 'very clearly made it plain to me that the object of the operation was to "break through" – Take Roulers if possible the first day and then march on Ostende'. Gough's memory, at least in regard to GHQ visits, seems to be faulty here, since Wynne noted on the draft, in pencil: 'The GHQ plan was handed to Gough by McMullen [GHQ Staff] on the 14 May [1917] – It says so on the cover.' Wynne later repeated this assertion, and indeed the fact of the McMullen visit seems to be incontrovertible. However, the McMullen plan itself was not clear-cut in regard to the choice of breakthrough or step-by-step advance, and so one is left again with the conclusion that Haig and GHQ were imprecise in their plans, and that Gough was not given absolutely clear instructions, in fact Gough was left with the strong sense that a breakthrough was required. Moreover, as Wynne pointed out to Edmonds, Haig's earlier instructions were 'to wear out the enemy, but at the same time have an objective'. No doubt Gough interpreted this to mean that the objective was primary, but in any case the instructions do seem deliberately ambiguous.[27]

Wynne's 'Reflections' chapter shows that *viewpoint 3*, although swinging back to blame Haig for the original planning, also continued to be critical of Gough. In order to resolve some of Gough's assertions, Wynne met again with Gough on 31 May 1945, and covered some of the key points in conversation. On the three major issues, Gough first denied lunching with Haig on 28 June, the occasion when Haig had strongly emphasized the great importance of the Gheluvelt high ground. Gough said that Haig had never suggested modifications to the Fifth Army scheme, and 'doubted the authenticity of Haig's diary and thought that parts of it ... must have been written up subsequently'. Secondly, on the question of a breakthrough, Gough said that the Fifth Army scheme for a breakthrough had been based entirely on Haig's own verbal instructions. Wynne then asked a key question, which would have considerably enhanced Gough's reputation had he answered in the affirmative:

I [Wynne] asked General Gough if he could remember a conference held [on June 28] by Sir D. Haig on Br.-General Davidson's memorandum of the 25th June which criticized the Fifth Army scheme, and at which General Plumer is said to have been present. General Gough said that to the best of his knowledge no such conference took place, and that he was quite sure General Plumer took part in no discussion on the Fifth Army scheme before the campaign opened. I said that Sir John Davidson had commented that this particular conference was 'burnt into his memory' and that General Plumer's advice to go right through to the Passchendaele ridge on the first day had swayed Haig to allow the Fifth Army scheme to stand.

Here then was solid evidence that at the end of June 1917, one month before the offensive started, Haig had given a clear-cut go-ahead to a breakthrough plan! Even if Haig and GHQ were to backtrack and vacillate in July, as in fact they did, Gough could at least point to a crucial conference where the Fifth Army breakthrough scheme had been officially approved by Haig in the presence of Plumer and Davidson. Apparently Gough was not present at this conference and he foolishly replied that:

Plumer was a wily old fox, and would quite likely have urged such a course knowing that he would be in no way responsible for the job; but although in that sense the story rang true he [Gough] personally had no recollection whatever of any such meeting or conversation, and he did not believe it. (As there is now no other evidence than Davidson's memory to support the story I [Wynne] have omitted it from the text.)

Gough had unwittingly damaged himself here, but he did succeed in having a footnote deleted that stated that Lord Cavan had urged Gough to concentrate his maximum resources on the right of Fifth Army against the Gheluvelt plateau ('Pure invention' said Gough). Then, thirdly, Wynne assured Gough that the text would say that Gough was not a free lance and that he had acted under the direct orders of Haig.[28] In this interview, Gough was sometimes wrong on factual matters, but it must be recalled that he had few documents to refer to, while the events were now twenty-eight years in the past, and Gough was in his seventy-sixth year.

Wynne now believed that the final draft was settled, and in June 1945 he completed his revisions, according to *viewpoint 3* (anti-Haig with some criticisms of Gough). However, Edmonds was not satisfied and wrote that 'careful editing of the volume is required ... I have drafted a preface and am putting together the final reflections [chapter], those drafted by Wynne being quite unsuitable'.[29] This cold comment signalled the eruption of a bitter and personal feud between Wynne and Edmonds until the completion of the Passchendaele volume. Edmonds remarked that Wynne 'has gravely deteriorated ... since he returned from N. Africa', and that 'Captain Wynne is lacking in military judgement and is indolent and careless. I have no further use for him.'[30] Then Edmonds wrote to another official historian (A. M. R. Topham), in January 1946, accusing Wynne of falsifying documents, of showing a bias against everyone (Haig, Robertson and Gough!) and of making a large number of mistakes, adding 'Wynne's behaviour has been strange for some time (he was 4 years a prisoner of war in 1914–18) and got a shock when he went to N. Africa in April 1943 ... I will tell you more and give you specimens of the dear lunatic's stuff when we meet next'.[31] Edmonds's point seemed to be that Wynne's time as a prisoner of war had unhinged him – as Edmonds wrote: 'The moral is, never employ an ex-POW'.[32]

Once more the official history group strove to mediate, with Wynne claiming that Edmonds's revisions of the final Passchendaele volume would be 'pro-Haig', and that Edmonds had tended to an extreme GHQ view of the major battles of the war, in particular Passchendaele.[33] Some of the official historians tended to side with Wynne, as did Sir John Davidson.[34] But Wynne knew the final version of the *Official History* would be Edmonds's, and so he requested that his own name be deleted from the list of authors of the volume (in fact all names were removed except for Edmonds's as completer and editor), and it was indeed Edmonds's final version that went to the press.[35] The published volume is in fact *viewpoint 4*, for Edmonds makes it unashamedly clear in the final

'Reflections' chapter on Passchendaele that Haig gave way to Gough 'as regards distant objectives and the neglect of the Gheluvelt plateau'. In other words, the *Official History* is once more strongly pro-Haig, for Edmonds argues that the fatal plan for 31 July 1917 was really Gough's and not Haig's; that Gough attempted a breakthrough against Haig's advice; and that he neglected the Gheluvelt plateau against Haig's advice. On the last point Edmonds is clear that Gough did not follow Haig's instructions regarding the plateau – and there is considerable justification for this particular criticism. However, the final result reflects very clearly Edmonds's long-held anti-Gough prejudice and his by now strong pro-Haig bias. At the same time, his behaviour during the writing of the volume shows that he was becoming more and more autocratic, particularly in his high-handed dealings with the unfortunate Wynne.[36]

Strangely enough, the final correspondence between Gough and Edmonds on 7 April 1946 shows that Gough thought Edmonds's chapters were 'an immense improvement on Wynne's', although in fact Wynne was far more favourable to Gough than was Edmonds! Gough however still objected to the Gheluvelt plateau problem, and claimed that Haig made him 'attack across only half the plateau when the right should have been extended by at least the front of two divisions'. Edmonds now thought that Gough was 'satisfied with Passchendaele', although it seems more likely that Gough had finally been worn down by the long drawn-out arguments over the various drafts and viewpoints, since the final volume was definitely very unfavourable to him. Edmonds had revised the rather stringent tone so that while the substance clearly remained critical of Gough, the tone did not, and thus Gough felt it was written 'in a fair and friendly spirit'.[37]

What can be concluded from this analysis of the *Official History* versions of the Somme and Passchendaele? First, that Edmonds, as *the* historian of the *Official History*, did exhibit a growing bias in favour of Haig and his GHQ, starting with the 1938 Somme volume, and concluding most clearly with the 1948 Passchendaele volume. He also displayed a growing autocracy, if not eccentricity, as the Passchendaele volume went through various drafts. It must be remembered, however that he was in his late eighties by then, and seemingly determined to have his own viewpoint accepted. Secondly, Edmonds did sometimes bend to postwar criticism by senior commanders (Montgomery, Maxse, Kiggell and even Gough) of drafts of the *Official History*. Of course the drafts were sent out to be criticized, and amendments were to be expected, but the *Official History* did follow a policy of avoiding specific criticism, and several very revealing passages were excluded.

Thirdly, because Haig had learnt at Staff College that the Commander-in-Chief should not interfere with his Army commanders in the tactical planning of offensives,[38] there existed a kind of dual command system or vacuum in leadership. At the Somme, the direction of the offensive had been shared between Haig/GHQ *and* Fourth Army, and similarly, during the planning of Passchendaele, there were two alternative (and changing!) sets of plans for the offensive, those of Haig/GHQ, *and* those of Fifth Army. This gave Edmonds and the *Official History* the opportunity and choice of blaming *one* of the command structures while exonerating the other. This had happened to some extent in regard to criticism of Rawlinson and Fourth Army in 1916,[39] but more clearly in regard to Edmonds's shifting the responsibility of planning the Passchendaele offensive from Haig and his GHQ to Gough and Fifth Army. In this respect, the Passchendaele volume did go through four very remarkable, if not scandalous, chronological changes in viewpoint: (1), anti-Haig by Captain G. C. Wynne in 1939; then (2), anti-Gough by Wynne on Edmonds's orders between 1943 and 1944; then (3), anti-Haig, but still partly anti-Gough, by Wynne (between 1944 and 1945) after seeing Sir John Davidson; and lastly (4), pro-Haig and anti-Gough by Edmonds in his revisions from 1945 until the text was published in 1948.

There is no doubt in regard to Passchendaele, that this *Official History* version is plainly wrong. Broadly speaking, Gough should be absolved for attempting a breakthrough – he was led by Haig to emphasize this, and was even specifically told on 28 June 1917 to try for a breakthrough. Subsequently it was not made abundantly clear to Gough that a step-by-step advance was required and not a breakthrough. This was all the more important in that Gough was known to be slow to accept advice, as Edmonds had once pointed out to Wynne. Gough remains at fault in not immediately recognizing the critical importance of the Gheluvelt plateau, for not reacting to Lord Cavan's suggestions about strengthening the right wing, and for not accepting Haig's clear instructions regarding the necessity of capturing the whole Gheluvelt plateau (even if he had been nervous in asking for a southern extension). On the other hand, the *Official History* does not mention Gough's request for a conference in August 1917 to remedy the problem, nor the structural problem of how Gough was to cover the whole plateau, when the boundary of his Fifth Army did not. Also, it was Haig and his GHQ staff who were at fault for not clearly settling these problems, and for not sitting down with all the parties to thrash out properly the differences and problems, particularly because Haig's choice of Passchendaele as the ground on which to launch an offensive was a very poor one. Ultimately then, the planning of Passchendaele was the responsibility of Haig and his GHQ. Yet the *Official History* version does unequivocally blame Gough and Fifth Army for the three major issues of type of offensive, width and direction, and planning responsibility.[40]

This story of the way that the *Official History* version of events came to be influenced by the participants, but particularly by Edmonds himself, is significant, since the *Official History* became the starting point for many of the heated arguments that still continue to generate controversy over the battles of the Somme and Passchendaele. The official historians had the opportunity then, and the knowledge, to set the record straight, but they did not do so. If this was how the years 1916 and 1917 were treated, would the *Official History* approach the dramatic events of March 1918 in the same manner?

Notes

1 Edmonds to Liddell Hart, 9 November 1934 and 4 February 1935, 1/259/94 and 1/259/109, Liddell Hart Papers, KCL; Edmonds to Maxse, 16 October 1934, Maxse Papers, WSRO. Liddell Hart's opinion was that Edmonds dug out facts well, but did not cross check, and his interpretations were sometimes wrong because he sat first in GHQ and then among his files, and so did not have personal knowledge of what had happened, Liddell Hart to Maxse, 28 November 1934, Maxse Papers, WSRO.

2 Liddell Hart alleged that Brigadier General Currie ordered the Canadians to retire at Second Ypres, but they refused, and Currie then had this deleted from the 1915 volume of the *Official History*, Liddell Hart, 'Facts', 7 February 1935, 11/1935/59, Liddell Hart Papers, KCL. It has been possible to confirm this confident statement from only one other manuscript source, namely Edmonds, 'Canadian Comments on "1915" (France) Vol. 1', 1 December 1926, Appendix I, p. 33, in Cab 16/52, PRO. Also a close reading of the *Official History* volume for Second Ypres would appear to reveal the bare bones of the story on 24 and 25 April 1915, J. E. Edmonds, *Military Operations France and Belgium 1915: Winter 1914–1915: Battle of Neuve Chapelle: Battle of Ypres* (London, 1927), pp. 219–20, 227, 247. When the GOC of the sector, Major General E. S. Bulfin, distributed praise for defence of this particular portion of the line, he strongly commended the 8th Durham Light Infantry but did not refer to the 2nd Canadian Brigade. A possible final piece of evidence concerns the fact that 28 Division orders on the evening of 25 April singled out the 2nd Canadian Brigade as the only unit having to remain under the orders of 11th Infantry Brigade; ibid., pp. 249, 251 (note 2), 396 (Appendix 25). Goodspeed, however, has nothing but praise for Currie during these events, *The Road Past Vimy*, p. 37.

3 Kiggell to Edmonds, 11 June 1938 and 16 June 1938, Cab 45/135, PRO. Cf. Chapter 7 regarding the comments of Kiggell, and Haig's decision on the Gough offensive in November.

4 A. A. Montgomery to Edmonds, 9 August 1930, Cab 45/136; R. W. Luckock to Edmonds, 8 August 1930, Cab 45/135, PRO. It was in a later letter that Luckock took the gloves off and criticized Haig's own plan for 14 July 1916, as 'dreadful', R. W. Luckock to Edmonds, 22 December 1937, Cab 45/135, PRO.

5 A. A. Montgomery to Edmonds, 7 December 1937, Cab 45/136, PRO.

6 A. A. Montgomery to Edmonds, 19 June 1938, Cab 45/136, PRO.

7 Liddell Hart and G. C. Wynne calculated the German casualties at the Somme

as considerably less than the British and French casualties, approximately 500,000 as against 624,000. However by various means Edmonds calculated the German total casualties at the Somme as 600,000 in volume 1 of the Somme, *Official History*, but changed even this to 680,000 in volume 2. The details of these calculations can be found in Liddell Hart, 'Note on the British *Official History* Estimate of German Casualties on the Somme, 1916', 23 November 1938, 11/1938/139; 'Talk with G. C. Wynne', 24 November 1938, 11/1938/140; and 'Comparison of Casualties in the Battle of the Somme', no date, 11/1938/142, Liddell Hart Papers, KCL. Cf. Woodward, *Lloyd George and the Generals*, p. 117.

 8 Neill Malcolm to Corps commanders, 30 June 1917 and 8 July 1917, Fifth Army, WO 158/249, PRO.

 9 Liddell Hart, Talk with Pope-Hennessy, 14 October 1933, 11/1933/23; and Liddell Hart, Talk with Brigadier Broad, Assistant in 1917 to General Uniacke (Fifth Army), no date but *c.* summer 1934, 11/1934/46, Liddell Hart Papers, KCL.

10 Norman Brook, 'Minute', 17 April 1945, Cab 103/112; and 'Passchendaele volume', undated but *c.* end January 1946, Time line record, entry for 1943, Cab 103/112, PRO.

11 Edmonds to Wynne, 17 February 1944, Cab 45/140, PRO.

12 ibid., Gough to Edmonds, 18 March 1944.

13 ibid., Edmonds to Gough, 24 March 1944.

14 ibid., Gough to Edmonds, 3 May 1944; and Neill Malcolm to Gough, 29 April 1944 and 7 May 1944.

15 Gough comments in margin, ch. 12, p. 3a, ch 13, p. 2 and ch. 14, p. 16, Cab 45/140, PRO; Percy Beddington to Gough, 13 August 1934, Cab 45/192, PRO; Liddell Hart, Talk with Pope-Hennessy, 14 October 1933, 11/1933/23, Liddell Hart Papers, KCL.

16 Wynne to Edmonds, 9 May 1944, Cab 45/140 PRO.

17 ibid., Gough to Edmonds, margin notes, 7 June 1944.

18 ibid.

19 W. B. Wood, 'Passchendaele 1917', no date but *c.* December 1944, Cab 103/110, PRO.

20 Norman Brook, 'Memorandum', 17 April 1945, Cab 103/112, PRO. See also M.T.F. to Sir Gilbert Laithwaite and Norman Brook, 'Passchendaele 1917', 29 March 1945, Cab 103/112; and 'Passchendaele volume', Time line record, Cab 103/112, PRO.

21 M.T.F. to Sir Gilbert Laithwaite and Norman Brook, 'Passchendaele 1917', 29 March 1945, Cab 103/112; Norman Brook, 'Memorandum', 17 April 1945, Cab 103/112; and Norman Brook to Wynne (Confidential), 19 April 1945, Cab 103/112, PRO.

22 'Passchendaele volume', Time line record, entry for 9 June 1945, Cab 103/112, PRO.

23 Gough to Edmonds, 27 May 1945, and margin comments on orginal draft, pp. 3–4, Cab 45/140, PRO. Gough's comments on this 'Reflections' chapter were very extensive and very critical, and he added a new criticism of Haig, namely that the battle should never have been fought at Passchendaele, but preferably at Cambrai.

24 Gough to Edmonds, 27 May 1945 and draft, p. 15, back of p. 29 and p. 5b, Cab 45/140, PRO.

25 ibid., draft, p. 5b.

26 Wynne, 'Notes on Interview between General Sir H. Gough and Captain G. C. Wynne: 31 May 1945', Cab 45/140, PRO.

27 Gough to Edmonds, 27 May 1945, and draft margin comments, p. 2, Cab 45/140; Wynne to Edmonds, 16 February 1944, Cab 45/140, PRO.

28 Wynne, 'Notes on Interview between General Sir H. Gough and Captain G. C. Wynne: 31 May 1945', Cab 45/140, PRO.

29 'Passchendaele volume', Time line record, entries for 9 June 1945, July 1945 and September 1945, Cab 103/112, PRO.

30 Edmonds to Murrie, 16 November 1945, and Edmonds to Joint Secretary, Official History Committee, 11 January 1946, Cab 103/112, PRO.

31 Edmonds to A. M. R. Topham, 8 January 1946, Cab 103/112, PRO.

32 Edmonds to Brook, 15 April 1946, Cab 103/112, PRO.

33 Norman Brook, 'Note for Record', 27 March 1946, Cab 103/112, PRO.

34 Eastwood to Brook, 9 March 1946; Norman Brook, 'Note for Record', 10 May 1946; Topham to Eastwood and Brook, 11 April 1946; A. B. Acheson, 'Note for Record', 28 August 1953; all in Cab 103/112, PRO.

35 Norman Brook, 'Note for Record', 10 May 1946, Cab 103/112, PRO.

36 J. E. Edmonds, *Military Operations, France and Belgium, 1917, Vol. 2, 7 June–10 November, Messines and Third Ypres*, completed and edited by Brigadier General Sir James E. Edmonds (London, 1948), p. 383, and see also pp. 127–31, 182, for anti-Gough conclusions, and pp. iii ff., 106, 182, 382, 385, for strong pro-Haig conclusions.

37 Gough to Edmonds, 14 April 1946; and Edmonds to Brook, 16 April 1946; (and cf. Brook to Sir Edward Bridges, 17 April 1946), Cab 103/112, PRO.

38 Haig, 'Strategy II', 1896–7, 20, Haig Papers, NLS.

39 J. E. Edmonds, *Military Operations, France and Belgium: 1916, 2nd July 1916 to the End of the Battles of the Somme*, pp. x ff., 553 ff., 571–2, for strong defence of Haig and GHQ.

40 See above note 36, for references to Edmonds's *Official History* criticisms of Gough and Fifth Army.

[9]

The German Offensive of March 1918, the *Official History* and the Problem of Command

One of the more controversial events of the war concerned the German offensive of 21 March 1918 (Operation Michael), which managed to penetrate 40 miles through the British front and capture over 1,000 square miles of ground before the opening phase of the operation ended on 5 April 1918. Fifth and Third Armies, which had opposed the German advance, had fallen back in retreat, often in confusion, but eventually the line had held, and the Germans were checked 10 miles short of Amiens. Several books have reviewed this battle,[1] and it will not be the intention of this chapter simply to recount the story of the battle or to repeat material available elsewhere, but to investigate specific aspects which remain partly or wholly unexplained.

Many questions come to mind. Was the German offensive expected? What were the assumptions behind Haig and GHQ's planning for the defence of the line? What was the relationship between GHQ and Gough's Fifth Army, which bore the brunt of the offensive? Did GHQ understand the plight of Fifth Army as the battle developed? Did Haig and his GHQ have to make a difficult choice and essentially support Third Army to the detriment of Fifth Army? (Gough was later to argue that Haig and his GHQ did in fact sacrifice Fifth Army.) Within Fifth Army, why did XVIII Corps make the critical decision to retreat as far as the line of the Somme on 22 March? Partly as a result of XVIII Corps' decision, Fifth Army's southern line crumbled. Later Gough was relieved of his command – but were there underlying reasons for this? Who was responsible for another critical Corps problem – the decision to delay withdrawal of V Corps from its defence of the Flesquières salient? Finally, did the *Official History* tell the real story of these difficult days, particularly in regard to the performance of the command structure in retreat? Edmonds and his assistants had the best and most detailed information available before or since on these two weeks. It is interesting, therefore, to see what conclusions were drawn by the *Official History*.

It is useful to start with Edmonds and the *Official History*, since this interpretation has strongly influenced historians ever since. As it happens, the first volumes for 1918 were published before the 1917 volumes, in fact between 1935 and 1937, before Edmonds had developed his strong antipathy to Gough; but he was respectful of Haig and his GHQ, and seemingly biased against General the Hon. Sir Julian Byng, GOC Third Army. It was in relation, however, to the 1918 material that Edmonds told Liddell Hart he 'had the views of my comrades to consider', and that his '1918' interpretation was that of a soldier. Edmonds added that the real business of war was not to be found in written documents, but was done by talk or dumb signs, and that the moral of the battle was to look out for General Staff and commanding officers in peace-time and see that they were trained for their jobs.[2] Edmonds was implying that some commanders and staff had had their problems due to inexperience or poor training, and that he would offer a favourable interpretation of the battle. It is understandable that Edmonds would not be critical of his comrades, but as he later told another official historian, Norman Brook, 'the whole truth cannot of course be told'.[3]

Edmonds did have difficulty with several episodes, and one of these concerned the question of manpower. There was no doubt that the War Cabinet decision of January 1918 ordering the British army to take over part of the French front, without compensating reinforcements, thinned the British defences. The decision to reduce the number of battalions per division from twelve to nine was also unfortunate, but the greatest problem for Haig and GHQ was that either Lloyd George, or the War Office, led by the CIGS Robertson, was reluctant to send manpower drafts to the Western Front. According to a recent book by David Woodward, the story told afterwards by GHQ and the *Official History* that Haig had been specifically denied manpower drafts by Lloyd George, was untrue. Even though Winston Churchill told Edmonds of Lloyd George's remark that 'he was not going to be Haig's butcher', nevertheless, Woodward argues, it was Robertson and the War Office, and not Lloyd George, who held back the general reserve in Britain. This was partly because Haig had said that he could hold on for eighteen days in the event of a German offensive, and this would give time for reserves to be transported to the front. Although Woodward exonerates Lloyd George as the denier of manpower to Haig in early 1918 (in fact Haig got 174,000 men instead of 334,000), nevertheless Woodward argues that as a general policy Lloyd George did attempt to control Haig by controlling manpower.[4]

It was no secret that Lloyd George was deeply suspicious of Haig, and it was as a result of Haig's visit to the War Cabinet on 7 January 1918, that Lloyd George privately referred to Haig as 'wooden-fisted, club-footed, and without imagination'. The key question discussed was that of manpower, and here Robertson reported that Haig

> found himself in a cleft stick ... He knew that the PM [Prime Minister] had taken strong exception to the continuation of the Passchendaele operations – and as a matter of fact the GS [General Staff] had also considerable doubt as to the wisdom of continuing them. Therefore, in discussing the situation he had to try and convince the PM that the operations had resulted in serious loss to the enemy, while he also had to prove his need for men, the enemy still being very powerful. It was not easy to be consistent in these two arguments. Moreover, Haig was notoriously inarticulate ...

Subsequently, Haig was asked to put his views on paper, but unfortunately these differed from his previous verbal arguments. Apparently in the War Cabinet on 7 January 1918, Haig had been asked whether he would attack if he was a German general – and he had replied he would only attack small portions of the front. But two days later in writing, he maintained that a major German attack *would* take place on the Western Front. Lloyd George threw the paper on the table, and asked what was to be thought of a man who totally changed his opinion over the space of two days![5]

The net result was that when 76 German divisions attacked through the early morning mist on 21 March 1918, they were faced with only 14 divisions in Third Army, 12 infantry and 3 cavalry divisions in Fifth Army, and with 8 divisions in GHQ reserve. Evidently the manpower policy of either Lloyd George or Robertson and the War Office had much to do with this imbalance, especially on the weakest front, that of Fifth Army, which had to defend a 42 mile line – the longest sector – with the fewest divisions. But again, who was responsible for manpower decisions? After the war Edmonds argued that the problem of the army in 1918 had been one of manpower. If the army had then had more divisions in reserve, thought Edmonds, the German defeat could have been settled in March 1918 by a counterstroke.[6] However Edmonds was apparently not sure who actually controlled the sending of reinforcements to France. He asked General Sir Robert Whigham* (Deputy CIGS from 1916–18), what the true story was, since Lloyd George had told Edmonds that it was nothing to do with him and that Robertson could have sent more men to France had he so wished. Lloyd George also claimed that after the German offensive of 21 March he personally ordered more troops to France. 'What is the truth?' Edmonds asked.[7]

Unfortunately, Whigham's reply does not seem to be extant, but Robertson's long letter to Edmonds of December 1932 gives support to Woodward's argument that Robertson himself was largely responsible for the lack of drafts. In this letter, Robertson went on to say that Lloyd

George was very poor on manpower (i.e. sending reinforcements to the Western Front), and that he himself had been removed by Lloyd George in February 1918 for three reasons – manpower, support of Haig, and support of the 'Westerner' viewpoint against Lloyd George's 'Easterner' viewpoint. However, despite Robertson's explanation of his dismissal, the real controllers of manpower after Passchendaele appear to have been Robertson and the War Office and not Lloyd George.[8]

Related to the question of manpower was the vexed issue of the creation of a general reserve of thirty British and French divisions, as suggested by Lloyd George and Henry Wilson in February 1918. However, Haig refused to support the idea – a decision that was soundly condemned at the time by Henry Wilson, and subsequently by Liddell Hart. Although the resulting defensive battle of 21 March–5 April would have been very much easier for Haig with the resources of such a large reserve, nevertheless there was the crucial question of who would control this reserve? If Haig had to wait for a decision from Versailles on the disposition of the reserve when the German offensive started, then it would probably be better for GHQ to control its own reserve. On the other hand, Haig's argument that he could only produce two divisions for the combined reserve, instead of the eight or nine requested, was evidently an excuse, since GHQ actually had several divisions in reserve![9] Whether Haig was right or wrong in his decision is hypothetical, although he was perhaps a little hasty in turning down the idea so quickly.

Another question of some significance is whether the German offensive of 21 March was accurately anticipated in weight and direction, and whether sufficient precautions were taken, given the question of manpower and the extent of the line to be defended. There is considerable doubt that the overwhelming nature of the German offensive was expected, although after the exit of Russia from the war at the end of 1917, and the transfer of German divisions from the Russian front, together with the German realization that time was running out, it seemed likely that there would be a major German effort somewhere on the Western Front, and most probably at a point of juncture. In regard to direction, the German attack was initially aimed at the British–French junction, but was amended to extend north almost as far as Arras – a frontage of some 50 miles! Thus both Fifth and Third Armies would be involved defending their sectors, and this was known to GHQ by early March, but German deception measures and the difficulty of obtaining clear-cut evidence had persuaded GHQ in their weekly summary of intelligence dated 10 March 1918 that there might be three smaller attacks, mostly to the north – in the Hill 70 sector; in the Neuve Chapelle –Bois Grenier sector; and in the Arras–St Quentin sector, but not south of St Epéhy, which was roughly at the junction of Third and Fifth Armies. It was also expected that the French would a face a major attack. By the last weekly summary of intelligence before the offensive, dated 17 March, the major attack was now expected in the Arras–St Quentin sector, with a lesser attack in the Bois Grenier–Neuve Chapelle area, and an attack on the French sector. Then on the eve of the attack it was agreed that both the Third and Fifth Armies would be attacked, with a supplementary attack in the north, and a major attack on the French. But it was still not known if the Arras–St Quentin attack would be the major offensive.[10]

It can be seen that GHQ was slowly moving its estimate of the British area to be attacked to the south, although still not far enough south. This was mainly because it had earlier decided there would be more logic and far greater danger if the German offensive attacked further north, and drove to the Channel ports, only some 50 miles from the front line. Thus GHQ had prepared to meet the major offensive in the Flanders area to the north, and only anticipated a preliminary attack perhaps in the Vimy Ridge or Flesquières salient areas further south. However, it felt able, if necessary, to fight in the Third and Fifth Army areas, thinking of a gradual withdrawal until reinforcements arrived for that southern sector. Nevertheless, GHQ actually continued to concentrate its attention *to the north*. This is why GHQ intelligence in March still did not foresee an attack extending south of St Quentin, and explains why, when XIX Corps was put into the line as a reinforcement, it was put in *above* St Quentin, between VII and XVIII Corps. This focus on the north also explains why the Fifth Army line was thinly held, and contradicts the subsequent GHQ explanation that there was enough space behind Fifth Army for the German offensive to lose its momentum – after all, GHQ had earlier imagined only a very gradual withdrawal in the south, giving plenty of time for reinforcements to arrive.

Essentially Haig and his GHQ had been slow to accept that the major offensive would come in the south, and the later explanation about the open space behind Fifth Army was really a *post facto* way of saving face. It is also the case that Haig clearly underestimated the strength of the German attack. This point emerges very clearly in his diary, where on 2 March Haig wrote that he was only afraid the front was 'so very strong that he [the German] will hesitate to commit his Army to the attack with the almost certainty of losing very heavily'. Again, on 18 March, Henry Wilson reported that Haig had told the king that he could smash any German attack. The day before the German offensive, on 20 March, Haig told Lady Haig that he was quite willing to come over to England, on the eve of the attack, to see her and his newborn son, since all questions of reserves and support troops had been settled, but he would not do so simply because people would 'talk'. Even so, he expected to be over nine days later! Then on 22 March, he wrote that he still expected a big attack to develop in the north towards Arras.[11] It is quite clear that Haig was over-confident about the German offensive and that he was still thinking about Arras and the north of the British line even after the German offensive had concentrated on the Fifth as well as the Third Army fronts.

This thesis is reinforced by a postwar letter from Major General J. G. Dill (BGGS Operations GHQ) to Edmonds, in which Dill relates why Haig kept his reserves mainly in the north:[12]

> I expect you remember some of the small fry at GHQ were anxious to get more reserves down from the north (particularly when the front of attack became fairly evident), which was thought to be somewhat over-stocked as the result of the aftermath of Passchendaele.
>
> Sir D. H. was very firm about this and said that these reserves would not be required in the early stages of the battle but later when local reserves had been used up. He pointed to our long drawn out offensives as an indication of what was to be expected.
>
> Sir D. H.'s reasons for keeping so many reserves in the north may have been wrong, but, as events turned out, it was a Godsend that they were kept out of the initial stages of the battle and thus available when the force of the German blow had spent itself. Do you agree?

On GHQ's behalf it can be argued that the northern sector was important because of the nearness of the Channel ports to the German line, and the danger of the British army being split in two. Yet there was an equal and probably greater danger of a rupture occurring between the junction of the British and French forces in the south. In fact this danger became so acute that when on 24 March General Pétain contemplated a possible withdrawal of the French forces away from the British, in order to cover Paris, thus opening up a gap between the two Allies, Haig called for political assistance from London, and offered to put himself under the command of Foch. According to Wilson, who saw Haig the next day, Haig was so alarmed he told Wilson that unless the 'whole French army' came up the British might be beaten. Clearly, Haig and GHQ had underestimated both the weight and direction of the attack and the serious potential of a break between the French and British forces, especially if the Fifth Army was forced away from the French in the southernmost sector of the British line.[13]

Other lesser explanations are possible for GHQ's concentration on the centre and north of the line, and its readiness to leave Fifth Army in a weaker position than the other Armies. One was the arrangement of the respective French and British Commanders-in-Chief on 7 March 1918 for mutual reinforcement in the case of attack. These reinforcements would be easiest for Fifth Army to receive since it was located next to the French, yet GHQ must have known that the French would not move their reserves if they also expected to be attacked, and in fact the last intelligence summary before the offensive began still indicated an attack was likely somewhere on the French front. Strangely enough, the first draft of the

Official History apparently neglected to mention the Anglo-French plan for mutual reinforcements at the juncture of Fifth Army and the French Sixth Army, although this was remedied in the published version. Perhaps this initial omission reflected Edmonds's scepticism of the value of the plan.[14]

Other possible explanations for Fifth Army's weakness were the belief that the Germans would not attack through the marshes in the south of Fifth Army's front, and the hope that the extent of the area behind Fifth Army was such that the Germans could advance for several miles before doing any great harm. Curiously, Haig only once mentioned this to Gough, and then in private conversation in the back of a motor car on 7 March 1918, so these thoughts were never set out clearly on paper for Gough to use in planning his defence. Perhaps this vagueness was partly due to the normal Haig–Army commanders communication problem, but it must have been mainly because of Haig and GHQ's over confidence as to what the Germans might achieve, and because of Haig and GHQ's emphasis on the northern Arras sector. Taking all factors into account, however, the 'open space behind Fifth Army' argument bears all the marks of a *post facto* rationalization by GHQ, and subsequently by the *Official History*. In any case it still overlooked the obvious danger of a Franco-British rupture.[15]

In view of the above, it is not surprising that there existed a divergence of opinion between Fifth Army and GHQ in regard to defensive plans and reserves in the two or three months preceding the German offensive. Both Gough and his chief of staff, Lieutenant Colonel Percy Beddington, were more and more convinced that a major offensive was brewing on Fifth Army front, and were increasingly concerned at the thinness of their line (one division per 6,555 yards as opposed to one division per 4,900 yards in Third Army) and particularly at their lack of reserves (one division per 18,000 yards as opposed to one division per 8,100 yards in Third Army). The reserves picture was actually much worse for Fifth Army, since one out of two divisions in Fifth Army reserve was cavalry, and both Fifth Army Corps reserve divisions were cavalry, while a cavalry division was only equivalent in strength to one infantry brigade. Understandably, Fifth Army complained to GHQ in early January 1918, then again on 1 February and 12 March (the January letter being known privately and somewhat contemptuously at GHQ as Fifth Army's 'scream letter'). Then on 19 March, Gough's attempt to have the two GHQ reserve divisions (20 and 50) moved closer to the line, was curtly rebuffed by Major General Lawrence at GHQ. Later on, Gough told Edmonds that 'G.H.Q. had very adversely affected the conduct of the operation by the delay in moving these [Reserve] Divisions forward before the Battle began', since they came up tired and with no time for reconnaissance.[16]

In the event, 50 Division in GHQ reserve was some 25 miles away behind the Somme and when it was put in, according to Gough, it was only given to one of his Corps for 24 or 48 hours 'thanks entirely to the stupid obstinacy and pedantry of Sir D. H. and GHQ'. In regard to the other GHQ reserve division behind Fifth Army (20 Division), this was given to Maxse's XVIII Corps. Maxse later wrote, 'I was allotted the 20th Division too late to do more than hustle it into a previously recced. position on a wide front, instead of using it for a planned counter-attack from a flank, as I had hoped'. In defence of GHQ it must be said that these two divisions were released immediately, and that 20 Division was in action by the evening of 21 March (taking seven hours to come into the line) and 50 Division had arrived in XIX Corps by the next day. More puzzling was GHQ's policy on 21 March when five divisions from the northern armies were sent to assist the south, but Davidson's order was that the first four divisions would go to Third Army, while Fifth Army would have to wait three days for their reinforcements. What had happened was that GHQ on that day was still thinking of the St Quentin-Arras sector, and was not yet properly in touch with the seriousness of the battle in the south.[17]

But this is to get ahead of the story. In arranging for Fifth Army defence before the offensive, GHQ sent Fifth Army a memo entitled 'Principles of Defence' on 4 February 1918, saying that it was better for Fifth Army to fight east of the Somme, but to fall back on the line of the Somme if necessary. Then on 9 February 1918, GHQ sent a further letter of instruction to Fifth Army, amending the previous principles, and now saying that Fifth Army should join with Third Army in defending the Péronne bridgehead, but if necessary to fall back slowly on the rear defences of Péronne and the Somme. Nevertheless, it was still preferable to fight to the east of the Somme.[18] GHQ was obviously doing its best to grapple with a difficult problem, yet Fifth Army's puzzle now was how to prepare to fight in three places (Péronne bridgehead; east of the Somme; the rear defences of Péronne and the line of the Somme) and to fortify the Péronne bridgehead. Labour was short for the digging of defences, and the rear two defence zones of the new three zone, defence-in-depth system, were hardly constructed. According to Edmonds, Haig had paid little attention to these defensive lines in late 1917, saying to Edmonds, who was the sapper in charge of such matters, 'Your old back lines aren't going to be any use'.[19] Moreover, in early 1918, where Fifth Army had taken over the French lines, these were found to be in very poor state. Hence Gough can be excused a certain sense of bitterness regarding GHQ support for Fifth Army, although GHQ naturally had its own priorities. Gough said later that his greatest mistake had been in not seeking an interview with Haig himself before 21 March, instead of dealing with Lawrence and Davidson who, claimed Gough, had no influence with Haig in 1918 in regard to military decisions.[20] Like others, Gough was intimidated by Haig, and felt reluctant to sit down and really thrash matters out. There was again exactly the same problem of communication between Gough and Haig as had occurred during the preparation of the Passchendaele offensive.

In fact, according to Farrar-Hockley, author of a biography of Gough, one of Gough's greatest problems was the bias against him in GHQ, which led to the neglect of Fifth Army needs. Gough's difficulties with GHQ in 1918 carried over into a postwar feud with Davidson, and with GHQ's version of events, which is not surprising, given Gough's subsequent dismissal after the March offensive. The most extreme example of this was a private statement by Gough to Edmonds in 1945:[21]

> I considered that Haig failed to realise the direction of Ludendorff's offensive, and piled all his reserves behind or within reach of the IIIrd Army, though the information at V Army's HQ – plainly showed that the attack was coming south of the Bapaume–Cambrai road, not north of it – In addition, between you and me and though I never say so, I am convinced that Haig was in such a temper by being forced by L. G. [Lloyd George] to extend his front southwards, that he abandoned the V Army in order to let the consequences fall on L. G. [Lloyd George] and the French.

Gough's view cannot be substantiated, except in regard to the direction of the offensive, and Edmonds does not appear to have responded directly to this accusation, although he did tell Liddell Hart that the inner conflict of March 1918 was the question of British and French frontage.[22]

In any case, Gough's anticipation of the German offensive seems to have been reasonably accurate from about 12 March, while an XVIII Corps raid just before it commenced had resulted in prisoners who accurately pinpointed the attack for 21 March, with the bombardment due at 4.40 a.m. This information was passed to GHQ and other armies and corps on 20 March by Beddington, but as he admitted the actual weight of the attack was not known and underestimated. Gough himself (and GHQ) accepted this and other information and expected the attack to be on 21 March.[23] Most other units were expecting the offensive, although the actual date did not seem to be known at lower levels, and one officer in V Corps said afterwards that the attack was unexpected, and even that a friend from GHQ had written on 19 March to say that an offensive was not expected! Haig himself seems to have been well aware of the impending offensive, although unsure as to the weight and weapons systems of the attack, and confident of halting any breakthrough.[24]

Despite the anticipation of the offensive, Gough knew his position to be weak, and when the combination of early morning mist, German hurricane bombardments, and 'blitzkrieg' rolling infantry tactics started to crumble the forward zone of Fifth Army on 21 March, Gough's worst fears were realized. The southernmost and most thinly defended area of Fifth Army, held by III Corps, started to give way. By the end of the day III Corps and 36 Division of XVIII Corps were fighting at the rear of their battle zones, and in fact falling back to the line of the Crozat canal on Gough's orders. Later that evening at 11 p.m., Gough spoke to Lawrence at GHQ, giving details of Fifth Army's difficulties, including the retreat also of parts of 16 Division. It would seem that Gough gave Lawrence a more optimistic picture than was actually the case, but Lawrence's comment that the Germans were not likely to 'come on again' the next day, showed that GHQ was not in touch with the battle. Edmonds felt privately that Lawrence was not good as a CGS and was slow to act, while the initial calmness at GHQ must have worried Gough, although Haig did agree immediately to Gough's request for Fifth Army retirements.[25]

After the war Gough expressed the opinion that GHQ was simply not capable of commanding the battle, and was actually abandoning Fifth Army:

> why GHQ entirely neglected the Fifth Army even in the very early stages – why they reinforced the Third Army with all those air squadrons and nearly every infantry division they could – why they never took any steps to get in touch with us by coming to see me personally and thus understand the desperate nature of the problem and the task they had set the Fifth Army – why they did, or did not do these things beats me – I consider it was because neither Lawrence nor any of his underlings had the faintest conception of how to command in battle.

Gough complained particularly about GHQ's lack of contact with Fifth Army: 'If I, in the midst of that terrific storm, could have gone round my four Corps commanders and covered 60 miles – surely to heaven, Lawrence or his deputy, or even Haig, should have come to me, even if it had been in the middle of the night?'[26]

Haig and Lawrence did visit Gough, although the former did not arrive until the afternoon of 23 March, and the latter not until the afternoon of the following day. In fairness to GHQ it had the whole of the British line to control, although the initial crisis was evidently on Fifth Army's front, and a postwar letter from Davidson to Edmonds does reveal a defensive attitude toward the criticism that GHQ did not visit Army HQs and was out of touch. Davidson writes:[27]

> I would like to emphasize again the desirability, even necessity, for referring to General Lawrence's visit to the 5th Army Headquarters on Sunday afternoon, the 24th March. [It *was* referred to in the *Official History*.] It is important, as Lawrence proceeded direct from there at Haig's request to meet him [Haig] at Byng's Headquarters at

8 p.m. the same evening. There is no doubt that Lawrence and Haig
were that evening when they met at Byng's Headquarters at 8 p.m. as
fully acquainted as they could be with the position on the 3rd and 5th
Army fronts at the time.

However, the *Official History* does make it clear, without actually saying
so explicitly, that GHQ *was* out of touch with the battle in the initial
stages.

For example, when XVIII Corps withdrew rather precipitously on 22
March, the *Official History* wondered why GHQ did not reinforce the
gap created on the left of the Corps. Then, also on 22 March, at
11.30 p.m., GHQ told Third Army to conform to the left of Fifth Army,
and to withdraw to a particular line. But as the *Official History* notes,
Third Army was *already* on that line, and mostly beyond it! Then again, at
5 p.m. on 23 March, GHQ issued orders to Fifth Army to hold the line of
the Somme at all costs, and pivot on Péronne, and keep close touch
between Third and Fifth Armies. In this case, the *Official History* remarks
that no assistance was given by GHQ apart from moving one division
towards the left of Fifth Army. Yet at just this moment, the line of the
Somme was being lost and the right of the Péronne bridgehead was
already being evacuated. As a last example, the *Official History* states that
GHQ should have ordered V Corps in the Flesquières salient to retire, and
the French should have been asked to help the centre of Fifth Army – but
neither order was sent by GHQ. Other evidence reinforces the impression
that GHQ was out of touch. Haig's diary shows surprise at the rapid
course of events – and it was only during his visit to Gough on 23 March
that Haig realized Gough's army was evidently no longer following the
defensive plan set down for it. Even on 24 March, according to Aylmer
Haldane (now GOC VI Corps), GHQ believed that the Germans only had
twenty divisions left for use, and that German losses were so high that
these divisions could not be put into the line.[28]

At the start of the German offensive, therefore, Gough had some cause
for complaint that GHQ was not up to date with the battle,[29] and that
Fifth Army's problems were being taken too lightly. It seems that GHQ
was still mentally focusing on the north and centre of the British line,
thinking that the attack in the south was preliminary only, and underestimating the weight of the German offensive. To repeat, the rationale that
Fifth Army was deliberately left weak because of the ample space behind it
in comparison with the north and centre of the line, seems to be largely
post facto, given Haig's overconfidence before the battle; Dill's letter
regarding the keeping of reserves in the north; Lawrence's attitude about
the position of the reserve divisions before the battle and his remark on the
temporary nature of the German offensive late on 21 March; Davidson's
orders regarding reserve divisions after the battle was under way; GHQ's

initial lack of personal contact with Fifth Army; and GHQ's relative slowness in coming to grips with the seriousness of the battle. Put plainly, GHQ did not anticipate what happened and was slow to adjust to rapidly moving events. In defence of GHQ, it was partially relying on French reinforcements, while Haig could have expected that Fifth Army would have held on longer to its territory. However, the effect of mist and fog, of intelligent German 'blitzkrieg' tactics, the weight of the German attack, and the difficulties of the thin British line, were all too much.

As the story of 21 March and the following days has been told elsewhere,[30] it will be useful to focus here only on certain aspects that do not seem to have emerged before in regard to the period from 21 March to 6 April. Reviewing the private letters sent to Edmonds after the war, which Edmonds naturally did not reproduce in the *Official History*, there seem to have been several common themes in the reactions of Fifth and Third Armies to the German offensive. First, there were command and staff problems, partly structural, partly due to loss of communications, and partly due to leadership problems when exhaustion, constant retreats, nervous tension, and wild rumours began to take their toll. Secondly, moving warfare in retreat was not anticipated or co-ordinated, and perhaps could not be, due to lack of reserves and German tactics, so that when retreats started to take place, the defensive system collapsed. This led, thirdly, to a greater degree of chaos than the *Official History* or subsequent accounts have allowed. None of what follows here is intended to reflect unkindly on the participants involved. The stress of battle (including the accumulation of four and a half years of warfare for some) amply accounts for the problems of some individuals and units.[31]

One theme among many Fifth Army letters to Edmonds was the feeling that the army could have done 'better', and puzzlement why this was not so. One officer wrote that the *Official History* draft read as if 'Mist and Masses' overcame Fifth Army, but 'most of us did badly and feel that if only we could fight it over again with our experience behind us we could do much better'. An artillery officer in Fifth Army asked rhetorically, 'why didn't we do better?' He placed the blame on the effects of Passchendaele, the failure of the forward zone on 21 March, leading to the hasty retreat of some divisions and their HQs who could not deal with moving warfare, and lastly, that the shortage of army reserves and the early decision to retire must have affected some divisional commanders. In Third Army, in contrast, there was a feeling that lack of confidence *before* the offensive began influenced later events. A junior officer in XVII Corps wrote that the morale of the BEF was not good, that the bombing and shelling of back areas had put the 'wind-up' of higher commands, who deluged units with paper on how to deal with tanks, planes, etc., instead of giving the infantry confidence. Another officer in V Corps argued that the army suffered from an encirclement complex, that the retreat really began in

January 1918 with the new defence-in-depth system, and that cheerful anticipation of the attack was wanted rather than fear. Finally, an officer commanding a machine-gun unit claimed correctly that there were rumours before 21 March that the Fifth Army GOC wanted to retire in the event of an offensive, while the Third Army GOC would stand firm, but that everyone down to private soldiers knew the troops on their flank would retire, so that rumours of these divergent policies weakened the junction of Third and Fifth Armies.[32]

In actually describing this battle, it will be convenient to start in the southernmost sector, and work northwards. Thus in Fifth Army, in the south, the enemy first started to break through on 14 Division's front. One officer of the division blamed this on the system of commissioning men from the ranks and then sending them off on one technical course or another to get rid of them, presumably rendering them less effective as leaders. Another staff officer, from the neighbouring 36 Division, complained that 14 and 36 Divisions had different strategies, the former to hold in strength and the latter in depth. Both divisions feared for their flanks, and when Fifth Army was appealed to, in order to settle the dispute over tactics, the two divisions were told to settle their own problems. Although Fifth Army was blamed for this decision, especially when 14 Division did give way and left 36 Division with an open flank, nevertheless Fifth Army was following GHQ's policy of allowing lower units to settle their own tactics. In the event, it would seem that 14 Division held their forward zone too strongly, and the performance of the division resulted in the degumming of 14 Division's GOC, Major General Sir Victor Couper, on 22 March, and his replacement by Major General W. H. Greenly.* However, this change in command was not a great success, because once the retreat started 14 Division's staff apparently ceased to 'function', to the understandable annoyance of Greenly. Unhappily Greenly himself broke down under the strain, and had to give up command of the division on 1 April.[33]

This division was in the southernmost Corps of Fifth Army, and the next Corps to the north was XVIII Corps, where a misunderstanding in staff work led to most serious results on 22 March. Gough had issued orders to all Corps on the evening of 21 March, saying that a withdrawal to the line of the Somme river was permissible, but only if *necessary*. XVIII Corps' GOC apparently took this to mean that a withdrawal was ordered, and at approximately noon on 22 March issued orders to this effect. This meant that XVIII Corps left its neighbour 'in the air', and resulted in a broken line and a subsequent German breakthrough in this sector. XVIII Corps' order dated 22 March was subsequently missing from the files, and it was not fully evident at the time why the order was issued. After the war, a staff officer of XVIII Corps HQ laid the blame partly on Fifth Army for issuing the order, and partly on XVIII Corps for 'slavishly' passing on the order. Why was there a fetish for retirement in line, asked this officer, because once started, 'the virus spread'. After the war, Edmonds laid the blame entirely on XVIII Corps, which naturally elicited the response from XVIII Corps' GOC, Maxse, that he was 'shocked to see that the official historian has selected me for the role of "scapegoat" in one of the greatest battles of the war'. Maxse argued that the XVIII Corps retreat was step by step, was planned, and was not left to chance. With some justice, Maxse also pointed out that Fifth Army was left on a flank without reserves, British or French, and that 20 Division was allotted too late from reserve to be of much use, and that when the French did arrive in support they had neither guns nor ammunition for infantry and machine-guns.[34]

Thus far the story seems clear, but still does not answer the question why the XVIII Corps retirement order of 22 March was issued. The XVIII Corps analysis of the March offensive suggests that the army commander, Gough, may have sanctioned the retreat in a conversation at 4 p.m. on 21 March; that both flanks of the Corps were 'in the air' by twelve noon on 22 March; that the rear zone defence line was not prepared and could not be held; and that the troops of XVIII Corps were exhausted and their front had been stretched from 16,000 to 22,000 yards. This document was XVIII Corps' reasonable defence of its actions, but in a private letter to Edmonds, Maxse admitted that although Lloyd George, Henry Wilson and Foch were all seeking scapegoats, only the official historian [Edmonds] had actually detected him! What this specifically meant was only revealed in 1937 in a private conversation when Edmonds told Liddell Hart that Maxse had actually been away from his Corps HQ from 22 to 24 March. These were the crucial days of XVIII Corps' abrupt withdrawal to the west of the Somme thus creating serious gaps for Fifth Army. The absence of the GOC XVIII Corps seems partly to account for the confusion at Corps HQ and the issuance of the XVIII Corps order to withdraw to the Somme. Edmonds kept this information out of the *Official History* in order not to be harsh and damage the reputation of an otherwise excellent officer, who in May 1918 was appointed Inspector General of Training.[35]

To the north of XVIII Corps was XIX Corps, which had particular trouble keeping in touch with the withdrawing XVIII Corps. As the confusion of the retreat increased, divisions began to lose cohesion, so for example, by 26 March, 66 Division, commanded by Gough's chief of staff in 1917, Neill Malcolm, simply ceased to function as a unit. The confusion had been caused by the lack of reserves and the piecemeal use of the one reserve division, as well as the fact that each division only knew what it was doing and not what its neighbour was doing. By 27 March, 66 Division HQ had disappeared and the enemy was through the gap between the division and its neighbour.[36] The next Corps to the north of Fifth Army was VII Corps, commanded by Lieutenant General Sir Walter

Congreve, VC. In this Corps, 16 (Irish) Division began to give way, mostly because, like the equally unfortunate 14 Division to the south, it had been ordered by its GOC to hold the forward zone in strength. Consequently when the enemy came around the flanks, the division found itself in trouble and retreated. On the other hand Congreve said later that some elements of 16 Division had not fought well, but admitted that the whole division had been too long in the line. Other complaints were that the division had political problems with its men, but in particular that the casualties sustained on 21 March crippled the division for the rest of the battle. The withdrawal of most of this division to the rear of the battle zone soon began to have the usual effects, for by 22/23 March, 16 Division staff did not know which division was on their right, and instead tried to keep in touch with a completely different division, whom they thought had moved up to their right![37]

The problems of VII Corps in retreat are graphically illustrated by the experiences of one officer, Brigadier General Sandilands, GOC 104th Infantry Brigade, in VII Corps, from 25 to 27 March. The story of this officer covers just two days, but shows how a withdrawal can very quickly turn into mass confusion. The account of this officer is significant enough to be given at length in Appendix I. It starts with the curious fact that he was given leave on 19 March, perhaps because his Brigade was in 35 Division of GHQ reserve. However, the GOC 35 Division did not apparently believe an attack was imminent and gave Sandilands permission to depart. While on leave Sandilands received an order to rejoin his unit on 25 March, which he attempted to do, but took two or three days to locate his brigade.[38] Sandilands's long account is significant in showing that some divisional commanders were apparently not expecting the offensive, in graphically describing the very great confusion of many units, in revealing the difficulty of co-ordinating an army in desperate retreat, and in catching some key actors during the crisis – Gough, Congreve, Wilson, and Lord Milner.

Sandilands's narrative takes us ahead of the story, since an equally difficult situation had now developed in VII Corps' neighbour to the north, V Corps. This corps, in Third Army, under Byng, was commanded by Major General Fanshawe, and had the unenviable task of defending the Flesquières salient. This salient had been formed by the Cambrai tank offensive of November 1917, and the defence of this ground on 21, 22 and 23 March matches the story behind XVIII Corps' withdrawal as a hitherto hidden element in the conduct of the overall battle. The defence of this salient had been laid down in two memos from GHQ on 13 December 1917 and 10 March 1918. The first memo said that salients were unsuitable for a defensive battle but that if a heavy attack developed, the idea was to delay the enemy and then fight in the battle zone at the rear of the salient. The second memo required that the forward zone of the salient be defended only as a false front in sufficient strength to check raids. The real battle would be fought in the battle zone at the rear of the salient.[39]

When the German offensive began, it soon became obvious that the enemy intention was to pinch out the salient. However, in the late evening of 21 March, Byng ordered V Corps to withdraw only some 4,000 yards to the intermediate defence line of the salient. This was partly because Gough's report to GHQ on Fifth Army was over-optimistic that evening, and partly because the centre of the salient apparently contained a strong defensive line. In retrospect this order was a mistake, since V Corps remained in a rapidly closing trap, while GHQ's last memo before the battle had clearly been to regard the salient only as a false front. Consequently as the situation deteriorated, Byng was forced to issue a series of hasty orders to extricate V Corps, all of which could have been avoided with an earlier organized withdrawal. Thus at 1.15 p.m. on 22 March, V Corps was ordered to withdraw that night to the front of the battle zone, then that same evening V Corps was ordered to withdraw even further, and finally at 12.45 a.m. on 23 March there came a third order, confirmed at 7.20 a.m., for V Corps to withdraw further still. These last orders had all come within 12 hours, and as a result the division on the right flank was unable to fully comply with the erratic retreat, so that a gap opened between this division and its neighbour. However the official Third Army version of events gives little sense of the difficulties of V Corps, and at times seems to be contradicted by V Corps' own account in regard to the reasons for the various withdrawals.[40]

Byng was later criticized for not withdrawing V Corps sooner from the Flesquières salient, and for holding the salient at all, since part of the German preparation for the attack between 10 and 16 March had been to drench the salient with mustard gas, creating severe casualties. The *Official History* recorded that the retention of the salient was a mistake because 'it led to the useless sacrifice of a great proportion of the infantry of the 2nd Division and part of that of the 63rd (Naval) Division, when the enemy shelled the salient with mustard gas – the loss, one may say, of a division. This later caused serious difficulties, from consequent lack of reserves, at the junction of the 3rd and 5th Armies.'[41]

How did Edmonds and the *Official History* come to the conclusion that Byng was to blame for the Flesquières problems, rather than Fanshawe, GOC V Corps? or indeed GHQ? The question is significant, for when V Corps did leave the salient, it was forced to retreat northwest, away from VII Corps to the south, thus creating a gap and a severe crisis, comparable to XVIII Corps' withdrawal. Initially, the *Official History* draft of the early stages of the March battle, written in 1926, seemed to blame Fifth Army for most problems. This interpretation was strongly resisted by Fifth Army and its supporters, for example, Congreve, who told Edmonds that the real blame for the constant gaps between his VII Corps and V

Corps, was 'the retention of the Cambrai [Flesquières] salient, from which the Vth Corps never recovered. Its retirement was forever Northwest instead of being Southwest, as ordered to conform to the dividing line of the two Armies, which ran Southwest.'[42] Congreve stoutly defended Gough, and by 1932, having read the many letters from participants, Edmonds seems to have come to firm conclusions about Byng's culpability in regard to the Flesquières salient.

In 1932 Edmonds wrote to Gough: 'The base of the trouble seems to me to be that GHQ or Third Army hung on too long to the Flesquières Salient. So when the garrison did at last clear out it was forced Northwest, away from the Fifth Army and a gap between the Armies was created.'[43] Then in 1934 when Macdonogh asked Edmonds who was responsible for V Corps being in the salient, Edmonds wrote back in very plain language: 'Byng the bungler was mainly responsible for clinging to the salient. I will exonerate Fanshawe who is merely stupid.' Later still, in his unpublished memoirs, Edmonds declared that unfortunately Haig had chosen Byng for the earlier Cambrai tank assault – describing the latter as a man with no military talent.[44] Consequently, it is not surprising that the published *Official History* version of the Flesquières salient *debâcle* tended to exonerate Gough, Fifth Army and Fanshawe, and to blame Byng, and that the first of the 1918 volumes contained a special preface defending Gough.[45]

Predictably Byng wrote to Edmonds at great length, defending himself against the charges in the 1934 *Official History* draft of not giving up the Flesquières salient earlier, and subsequently of not keeping in touch with Fifth Army. Byng admitted that it would have been better to retire to the base of the salient on 21 March, but asked what would have been the effect on the troops of this retirement? More specifically, Byng argued that on the evening of 21 March he understood the situation in Fifth Army to the south was more favourable than it actually was; that he had visited Fanshawe that afternoon and felt the position of V Corps could be re-established; that there were good reasons for holding the salient, such as observation; and that if Third Army, and V Corps especially, had failed to keep in touch with Fifth Army, and VII Corps in particular, it was because Fifth Army had temporarily disappeared! Byng also felt that Third Army was treated unfairly in the draft chapters, and remarked on the general tone of adverse criticism which read as though it was intended to belittle Third Army for the sake of defending Fifth Army.[46] Byng's protests were to no avail, and the *Official History* was published with Gough defended, Byng criticized, and Fanshawe exonerated. It can be argued that Edmonds was critical of Byng partly in order to defend Gough; partly because Byng was a cavalry man against whom Edmonds had an established bias; and partly because Edmonds had a poor opinion of Byng following his conduct of the later stages of the Cambrai tank battle. On the other hand, it is the case that Byng *was* slow to extricate V Corps, and must take some responsibility for the problems of the salient.[47] (Ironically, as shown in Chapter 8, Edmonds's defence of Gough in the 1930s was to be replaced with criticism a few years later when the Passchendaele volume emerged.) Meanwhile the other key player at Flesquières, Fanshawe, was degummed on 25 April 1918 at Byng's insistence, leaving some suspicion that he might have been selected as the scapegoat for the Flesquières salient battle and its aftermath. (This was actually Fanshawe's second removal, the first being after the defence of the St Eloi craters in 1916 as outlined in Chapter 1.)

Regardless of responsibility, the aftermath of the Flesquières salient battle was disastrous, and a gap opened up between VII Corps and V Corps on 23 and 24 March and again on 26 March. The problem for Haig and Byng on 23 and 24 March was whether to try to hold Fifth and Third armies together, or whether to retire Third Army away from Fifth Army, in order to preserve the rest of the BEF, and essentially abandon Fifth Army. This would be necessary if the French army retired on Paris, thus making Fifth Army vulnerable on both flanks. On 23 March, according to Fanshawe, the decision was still not made, but the next day Haig sent an urgent message to the CIGS in London requesting a meeting regarding Pétain's possible decision to retreat on Paris (Pétain himself fearing correctly that Haig might retreat to the coast). By the evening of 25 March Haig apparently told Byng not to rely on the French or on Fifth Army:[48]

> Sir Douglas Haig made it quite clear that the BEF had now to safeguard itself and that no help could be expected from the South [i.e. the French]. He made it quite clear that any further withdrawal must be in a North West direction and the Third Army must safeguard the right flank of the BEF by swinging its own right back. Sir Douglas Haig also took it for granted that no help was to be expected from the remains of the Fifth Army.

In other words, Haig was prepared to sacrifice Fifth Army, as Gough suspected, and to retreat away from the French. It was a hard decision, but probably correct in regard to saving the BEF. Fortunately, the Doullens meeting of 26 March between Haig, Lord Milner, Henry Wilson (now CIGS), and their staff with Poincaré, Clemenceau, Foch, Pétain and their staff, resolved British–French differences, and placed the direction of the battle under the overall command of Foch. This was the meeting that Brigadier General Sandilands had encountered Wilson and Milner hurrying to attend at 11 a.m. on 26 March, and it was a measure of London's distance from, and apprehension about the events taking place, that Wilson had to ask Sandilands whether Amiens was safe to drive through on his way to Doullens, although Amiens was then many miles behind the front.

Sandilands was not to know that with the Doullens conference, and the decision regarding Foch, the crisis was nearly over; nor could it be known that there would be a postwar controversy over whether it had been Haig or Wilson that had suggested the conference and the handing over of overall command to Foch.[49] And of course it was not apparent to V Corps, having desperately extricated itself from the salient, that the crisis was in the process of being resolved. Instead the chaos and confusion seemed worse than ever.[50] Inevitably in mobile war the standard chequerboard communications system, designed for static war, became obsolete, and could not easily adapt. This situation was particularly evident in regard to counter battery work and corps control of the artillery, since neither could easily operate in a retreat.[51] Time and again, divisions and brigades in V Corps lost touch with each other, as when V Corps on 24 March apparently did not know where two of their own divisions were. Similarly, further down the V Corps line of communications, the CO of a regiment wrote of the 'extraordinary confusion and lack of orders. Personally I received no orders from my Brigade (99th) from 9 am on 23 March until 7 am on 25 March, and then again I received no further orders until 9 pm that night.'[52]

Despite these problems V Corps somehow survived German attacks on 27 and 28 March, and again on 5 April. Meanwhile, further to the north, IV Corps (GOC Lieutenant General Sir George Harper) and VI Corps (GOC Lieutenant General Aylmer Haldane) appeared to suffer from command problems in the early stages of the retreat, particularly on 26 March, when a rumoured German breakthrough at Hebuterne created considerable chaos. The panic surrounding these rumours shows how easy it was for the most seasoned and reliable commanders and staff, already tired and exhausted, to give way to suggestions that in other circumstances would be readily dealt with. The German advance on this front involved nineteen German divisions, which used the early fog and a heavy artillery preparation on 21 March to batter down the defences of little more than four British divisions. In places, entire battalions essentially disappeared, and it is not surprising therefore that the future General Sir Frederick Pile, then serving with the artillery in 40 Division, VI Corps, reported that the chaos was indescribable, that 'lots of people' should have got the sack, that Corps commanders were wringing their hands, that the CRA of 59 Division was in a panic, saying the Boche had broken through, and so on. Even allowing for a certain amount of postwar hyperbole, Pile was probably accurate in revealing the kind of situation that had not been seen in the BEF since late August 1914.[53] Other incidents on this day also tended to show, as was the case later at Hebuterne, that it was the higher command structure that often weakened under stress – perhaps the uncertainty of not knowing exactly what was happening, in addition to the responsibility of having to deal with it, proved too much. Understandably the *Official History* made little mention of surrenders or command breakdowns, and instead concentrated on an exceedingly complex narrative of interlocking units and their stands and retreats. The result was a text that was dense and impenetrable, which thus concealed the actual breakdown of the command structure.[54]

According to the postwar narrative of Sir Frederick Pile, his Corps commander was in a poor way on 22 March, when a heavy German offensive commenced in their sector. Then the next day, the heavy artillery was transferred from Corps to Division, resulting in considerable chaos, and finally on 26 March his own CRA got up late and could not be got on a horse to look at his brigades until 10 a.m. Pile and his CRA met the GOC of 40 Division on that day, and he reported rumours of a German breakthrough with tanks at Hebuterne, and said that Corps had claimed the situation could not well be worse. Then, according to Pile, the Corps commander and his HQ left rapidly for another location, some fifteen miles from their original HQ. They left so rapidly, wrote Pile, that the BGGS was left behind and the flag on the Corps commander's car was still covered up. The VI Corps sign was a bulldog, noted Pile, and added rather unkindly, that it should be changed to a greyhound![55]

Other reports mention how the rumours of the German 'breakthrough' at Hebuterne on 26 March spread quickly and produced disorganization. One CO remarked that panic over the alleged breakthrough spread quickly, and caused gaps between units, and another observer recalled that he met a demented Major General on 26 March who 'cursed him for an idle fellow' and said that the Germans were in Hebuterne and their tanks over the ridge.[56] In defence of VI Corps, the CO of the 2nd Battalion of the Cheshire Regiment recalled that on that day the false rumours regarding Hebuterne actually arrived from Third Army, and that Third Army called the VI Corps commander and told him that Corps HQ were to move out at once.[57] The *Official History* confirmed that instructions were received by VI Corps from Third Army to shift headquarters back northwestwards, but added a new twist to the story by stating that Third Army had itself learnt of the Hebuterne 'breakthrough' from IV Corps! According to the *Official History*, VI Corps staff tried to re-establish order, and ordered 31 Division (GOC Major General Bridgford) to go back with his HQ and organize the situation.[58]

However, Bridgford told a somewhat different story. He thought that Third Army had initiated the story of Germans breaking through, but agreed with Pile in recalling that VI Corps HQ had left 'very hurriedly'. Bridgford phoned VI Corps to see if the breakthrough story was true, and an officer said 'yes', and that they (VI Corps HQ) were off now. So 31 Division was left out of touch with VI Corps and with the heavy artillery that the division needed, which was controlled by Corps. Bridgford remarked that he was kicked out for having left his HQ, which he could not locate, and concluded by saying that VI Corps 'upped it and left us in the soup' and then laid the blame on him.[59]

The truth seems to be that Third Army learnt of the German 'breakthrough' from IV Corps, and then told VI Corps HQ to leave. But in the process, Third Army evidently instilled a sense of panic in VI Corps HQ, who consequently left in such a hurry that proper arrangements for defence were not made. Somewhat naturally the *Official History* version skated over this material without revealing the underlying story, and did much the same thing with the initiators of the Hebuterne rumours, IV Corps. The IV Corps story is different from VI Corps in that it was particularly vulnerable on both flanks, and there were massive attacks against IV Corps on 22 March and then again on 23 March. After a defensive battle of retreat on 24 March, IV Corps was again attacked by an overwhelming force of fifteen German divisions the next day, which succeeded in creating a gap between the Corps and the rest of the line to the south.[60] It is not hard to see therefore, why IV Corps was exhausted on 25 and 26 March and open to suggestion of German breakthroughs.

The state of mind of IV Corps HQ was not assisted by problems among its divisions, for according to a brigade commander, 51 Division simply ceased to operate as a unit from 23 March, and on 25 March made no effort to stand but conducted a dour, deliberate and selfish retreat. Every day 51 Division retreated and left its neighbours 'in the air', argued this officer, while the GOC IV Corps apparently feared other divisions in his Corps were in the same pessimistic state of mind.[61] Another officer confirmed that 51 Division was inactive, and that on 25 March, at a divisional commanders conference, the GOC of 51 Division, to the surprise of all present, declined to put his division in the line, saying that the men were exhausted and demoralized and could not be trusted to stand.[62] Then another division in IV Corps, 2 Division, also got into trouble on 25 March. According to a staff officer, 2 Division was in great confusion on that date, since part of the division was over the Ancre river and part was not, and the GOC did not know what was happening. To make matters worse, V Corps was also withdrawing across IV Corps' line of retreat, and a large gap was created.[63] It was not surprising, therefore, that IV Corps was in a state of confusion the following day, 26 March, when the return of early morning mounted patrols plus the movement of some Ford tractors near Hebuterne, gave some staff officers the false impression that German cavalry and tanks were advancing through Hebuterne. The senior staff officer of IV Corps recalled that his HQ simply did not know what was happening that morning, and complained to Edmonds that the *Official History* draft tried to make out that IV Corps *did* know the real situation![64]

The *Official History* version of the Hebuterne incident played down the panic and confusion, and suggested that the confidence of the front line troops of the two Corps involved was not affected. This version of events also tended to paper over command breakdowns at Divisional and Corps levels (particularly the latter), and therefore did not tell an important part of the story of the German offensive of March 1918. The moral of the story is not that there needs to be criticism and blame, for after all the German offensive *was* successfully stopped eventually before reaching Amiens, but rather to show how a mood of confusion and even panic was communicated as high as Corps and Army level, and then redirected downwards again in a reciprocal and mutually reinforcing fashion – in fact a feed-back loop system. The *Official History* might have reflected on the problems of command during the retreat, but did not do so, although the *History* did defend the one army commander, Gough, who was degummed as a result of the March/April retreat. It was ironic that Gough, whom all agreed remained calm throughout those tense March days, and who fought the battle in retreat as well as could be done, with initially limited GHQ support and reserves, should be the man chosen as scapegoat for the ground lost in retreat.

Why was Gough picked as the man to blame? Privately, Edmonds told one of the official historians that Gough was sent home 'because Henry Wilson wanted to be Military Representative [to the Supreme War Council] at Versailles, where Rawlinson was, and "Rawly" would not quit unless he returned to an Army Command; so Henry [Wilson] who had Lloyd George's ear at the time – he later lost it by slapping Lloyd George on the back – engineered Gough's removal'.[65] As it turned out, Rawlinson was transferred from Versailles to take over Fifth Army command, but Edmonds must have been mistaken in saying that Wilson wanted to return as Military Representative to Versailles, since he remained as CIGS – instead Wilson appointed one of his friends to the position! Publicly, the *Official History* dared to say that the proposal to remove Gough on 28 March was made by Sir Henry Wilson who did not want a strong man like Rawlinson as Military Representative at Versailles, and was looking around for a post to which Rawlinson might be transferred, i.e. to command Fifth Army.[66] Judging by Henry Wilson's diary, Gough's removal was urged by Lloyd George and Lord Milner as well as by Wilson, and since Rawlinson was not thought to be performing well in Versailles, the switch could be made without too much trouble when Fifth Army was perceived in London to have retreated too far and too fast.[67] It is of interest also to see that Haig's own position was in considerable danger after the March offensive, with Lloyd George, Lord Milner, Henry Wilson and Sir John French keen to remove him. However, Haig was saved by Lord Derby, who threatened to resign in the event of Haig's dismissal.[68] Thus Haig was saved, and went on to become the victor of 1918, while Gough was sent home and subsequently denied a hearing.

In conclusion, what aspects of the March 1918 offensive have now emerged as significant? And which aspects did the *Official History* conceal as well as reveal? First, it is clear that Haig and his GHQ were very overconfident about their ability to halt any German offensive, and that this optimism spilled over into their treatment of Fifth Army. In addition, there does seem to have been a bias against Gough and his army, on the part of GHQ, although Gough did fight a cool and well organized battle of retreat, apart from XVIII Corps' departure across the Somme. Secondly, Haig and GHQ clearly focused too long on the north and centre of the line, and ignored the very real possibility of a rupture of the French and British forces further south. Subsequently, Haig and GHQ, and later the *Official History*, argued that the weakness in Fifth Army's southern part of the line was justified because of the open areas behind Fifth Army, which would eventually dissipate the energy of the offensive. This did actually occur, but the argument was *post facto*, since the real reason for the thinness of the line in the south was that Haig and GHQ believed the German offensive would strike further north and aim at the Channel ports. In the event, this mistake was responsible for much of Fifth Army's problems, and could have had very serious repercussions in allowing the German offensive to drive a wedge between the French and British armies. Thirdly, Haig and GHQ appeared to take approximately three days to 'catch up' with the battle, and Haig only realized the seriousness of what was happening around 23/24 March. Much of this early confidence of Haig and GHQ obviously related to the fact that genuine strategic breakthroughs were thought to be well nigh impossible, particularly against the new defence-in-depth concept, but GHQ did not take into account the confusion into which an army in retreat might fall. Fourthly, Haig and his GHQ did not seem to realize that the French would be slow to send reserves to support the British line, given that the French themselves expected an attack, and would naturally keep the reserves for themselves. Haig and his GHQ also obviously expected a much slower British retreat, which would have given time for reserves to be transferred from other parts of the line.

Turning to the *Official History* version of these events, this contained a defence of Gough that seems justified, and a *post facto* defence of Haig's decision to keep Fifth Army relatively weak that seems rather less justified. The *Official History* blamed the War Cabinet for keeping the Western Front short of troops and exonerated Robertson for this policy, for which he seems to have been responsible. It is possible however that Haig and his GHQ did have sufficient resources to fight against admittedly heavy odds. The *Official History* only obliquely referred to Haig and GHQ's lack of control of the battle in its early stages, and Edmonds was careful to conceal the worst of the errors committed by GHQ and the high command structure. This is the case with XVIII Corps' problems, and to a lesser degree with the Hebuterne incident. Edmonds was, however, starting to display his growing penchant for fixing on certain commanders to blame (as he was later to blame Gough for the failures of Passchendaele) and in this case he selected Byng as the culprit of the Flesquières salient battle. One can feel some sympathy with Byng, but despite his recent defence in Jeffrey Williams's book, *Byng of Vimy*, it does appear that Edmonds was correct – Byng was too slow in evacuating the salient.

Overall, then, the *Official History* evaluation of the March offensive exonerated Gough, skated over Haig and GHQ's performance, and pinned down Byng on the problems of the salient. The *Official History* was weakest in overlooking Haig and GHQ's attitudes before the offensive and in the early stages of the battle (including the by now familiar inability of Haig and his army commanders to communicate with each other), and did not reveal the 'feed-back loop' of confusion and even panic at Corps and Division command levels during various critical stages of the retreat. As an officer of 8 Division summed up: 'at times the chaos was indescribable and the sudden change from trench warfare to quickly moving events of open warfare conditions proved to some extent beyond the capacity of the existing organisations.' However, lest the impression be left that all the confusion existed on one side only, it is worth recalling what a German prisoner said to an officer of the Irish Guards. This prisoner stated that before the March offensive his commanding officer told them: '"Do you see that star ... Now march." And he [the prisoner] said we just cut our way through any wire we came to and went on until we lost ourselves.'[69]

The German offensive of March 1918 was followed by further offensives in the spring and early summer, but these turned out to be the last German throw of the dice. Soon after, the French, British and American forces launched their own surprisingly successful attacks, which mercifully led to the end of the First World War.

However, before bringing this long story to an end, it will be useful to refer briefly to the later events of 1918, and then outline some general conclusions regarding the reaction of the British army to the emergence of modern warfare in the period 1900 to 1918. To be valid, these conclusions must themselves be put in context by a comparison with French and German military reactions to the same problems faced by the British army. In short, the key question is, was the British experience unique?

Notes

1 Apart from the detailed volumes of the *Official History*, the most useful books are Barrie Pitt, *1918 – The Last Act* (London, 1962); John Toland, *No Man's Land: 1918 The Last Year of the Great War* (New York, 1980); Martin Middlebrook, *The Kaiser's Battle* (London, 1978); A. Farrar-Hockley, *Goughie* (London, 1975), ch. 12; and Jeffrey Williams, *Byng of Vimy* (London, 1983), ch. 11.

2 Edmonds to Liddell Hart, 9 November 1934; and Edmonds to General Sir Robert Whigham, 2 January 1935, Cab 45/185, PRO.

3 Edmonds to Norman Brook, 7 February 1950, Cab 103/113, PRO. At another point, Edmonds told Liddell Hart that 'he could not tell the truth frankly in an official history but hoped that it would be evident to those who could read between the lines', Edmonds, cited in Brian Bond, *Liddell Hart: A Study of his Military Thought* (London, 1977), p. 82.

4 Edmonds to Acheson, 22 July 1950, Cab 103/113, PRO; David Woodward, *Lloyd George and the Generals*, pp. 236 ff., 290, 336, and ch. 12.

5 Robertson to Edmonds, 1 December 1932, pp. 7–8, Cab 45/193, PRO; Haig, Diary, 14 March 1918, in Robert Blake (ed.), *The Private Papers of Douglas Haig 1914–1919* (London, 1952), p. 292.

6 Edmonds to Liddell Hart, 9 November 1934, Cab 45/185, PRO.

7 Edmonds to General Sir Robert Whigham, 2 January 1935, Cab 45/185, PRO.

8 Haig to Lady Haig, 5 February 1918, in Blake, *Private Papers of Haig*, p. 283; General Sir William Robertson to Edmonds, 1 December 1932, pp. 4, 5, 13, Cab 45/193, PRO. For Lloyd George's tactics, see Woodward, *Lloyd George and the Generals*, *passim*. J. E. Edmonds, *Military Operations, France and Belgium 1918, March–April: Continuation of the German Offensives* (London, 1937), pp. 470, 474. Apart from Robertson's reference to the valid need for troops for the Italian front, there was also Robertson's criticism of Haig for wasting troops in continuing the Passchendaele offensive, Robertson to Edmonds, 1 December 1932, p. 7, Cab 45/193, PRO.

9 Wilson, Diary, 23 February 1918, 6 March 1918, 9 March 1918, 29 March 1918, Wilson Papers, IWM; Liddell Hart, *History of the First World War*, p. 386. Woodward, *Lloyd George and the Generals*, p. 261, argues that control of the proposed general reserve was a crucial point.

10 J. E. Edmonds, *Military Operations, France and Belgium 1918, the German March Offensive and its Preliminaries* (London, 1935), pp. 107–9.

11 ibid., pp. 93–4; Haig, Diary, 2 March 1918 and 22 March 1918, and Haig to Lady Haig, 20 March 1918, in Blake, *Private Papers of Haig*, pp. 291, 294, 296; Wilson, Diary, 18 March 1918, Wilson Papers, IWM.

12 Major General J. G. Dill to Edmonds, 5 December 1932, Cab 45/192, PRO.

13 Haig to Edmonds, 26 November 1920, 'Not for Publication', Cab 45/183, PRO. Edmonds apparently left out a page of criticism of Pétain in regard to this episode, writing mischievously to Macdonogh that he often put things in drafts only, so that discreet people would see them!, Edmonds to Macdonogh, 27 June 1934, Cab 45/185, PRO; Wilson, Diary, 25 March 1918, Wilson Papers, IWM.

14 Major General Sir John Davidson to Edmonds, 10 August 1934, Cab 45/184, PRO.

15 Cf. Farrar-Hockley, *Goughie*, p. 265.

16 Lieutenant Colonel Beddington to Edmonds, 14 November 1932 and 13 August 1934, and Gough to Edmonds, 29 July 1934, comments on draft chapters, Cab 45/192, PRO; Middlebrook, *Kaiser's Battle*, pp. 127–8; Farrar-Hockley, *Goughie*, pp. 270–1.

17 Gough to Edmonds, 22 May 1923, 1/2, Edmonds Papers, KCL; Maxse to Edmonds, 7 October 1934, Cab 45/193, PRO; XVIII Corps Diary, p. 14, WO 95/953, PRO; Middlebrook, *Kaiser's Battle*, pp. 207–8; Edmonds however says that GHQ ordered three divisions late on 21 March to go to Fifth Army from Second and First Armies, Edmonds, *Military Operations 1918, the German March Offensive*, p. 253.

18 ibid., pp. 97–8; cf. Liddell Hart, *History of the First World War*, p. 387.

19 According to Major General E. G. Wace, GHQ was not particularly interested in labour, wishing instead to get men into the fighting line, and was more interested in maintenance. It left the QMG branch actually to direct the labour, E. G. Wace to Edmonds, 6 January 1933, Cab 45/193, PRO. Liddell Hart, Talk with Edmonds, 6 May 1929, 11/1929/7, Liddell Hart Papers, KCL.

20 Gough to Edmonds, 5 March 1951; Gough also thought Lawrence a century behindhand in strategical thoughts, Gough to Edmonds, 15 April 1953, 1/2, Edmonds Papers, KCL.

21 Gough to Edmonds, 27 May 1945, Cab 45/140, PRO; Farrar-Hockley, *Goughie*, p. 267. Gough made the same accusation in 1935 to Liddell Hart and Lloyd George, Woodward, *Lloyd George and the Generals*, p. 291.

22 Edmonds to Liddell Hart, 4 February 1935, 1/259/109, Liddell Hart Papers, KCL. The only sentence in the *Official History* that may obliquely refer to the difficulties between Haig and Pétain, occurs when Edmonds wrote: 'One feels at the back of one's mind that he [Haig] was determined the French should take back this front, and that Pétain was equally determined he would not do so.' Edmonds, *Military Operations 1918, Continuation of the German Offensives*, p. 486.

23 Beddington to Edmonds, 4 August 1934, 6 August 1934, and 13 August 1934, Cab 45/192, PRO; Edmonds, *Military Operations 1918, the German March Offensive*, pp. 109–10. XVIII Corps Intelligence Summaries for 18 and 20 March 1918, WO 95/953, PRO.

24 Edmonds, *Military Operations 1918, the German March Offensive*, p. 110; among those who expected the attack were Lieutenant Colonel Henderson (GSO 2 'I', XIII Corps), to Edmonds, no date, Cab 45/185, PRO; Captain Wimberley (1st Queens Own Cameron Highlanders) to Edmonds, no date, Cab 45/187, PRO, who said that from 15 March on they [Third Army] were told to expect the attack next day; E. L. Malone (7th Royal Fusiliers, 190th Brigade, 63 Division, V Corps) to Edmonds, 28 January [?], was the officer with the friend at GHQ who did not anticipate the assault, Cab 45/186, PRO. Haig's conversation with a counter battery intelligence officer in early March 1918 indicated that Haig expected an offensive based on strong artillery and tank components, but that any breakthrough would be contained before it reached Corps HQs. Haig was also well aware of the importance of locating and counting the number of newly arrived German batteries as an indication of the date of the offensive, H. H. Hemming (ed.), *Artillery Survey in the First World War* (Field Survey Association: London, 1971), pp. 20–1.

25 Edmonds, *Military Operations 1918, the German March Offensive*, p. 208; Farrar-Hockley, *Goughie*, p. 283; Liddell Hart, Talk with Edmonds, 24 June 1929, 11/1929/89; and Liddell Hart, Talk with J. F. C. Fuller, 1 October 1929, 11/1929/16, Liddell Hart Papers, KCL. Apparently Henry Wilson also doubted the German offensive was real, Woodward, *Lloyd George and the Generals*, p. 286.

26 Gough to Edmonds, 29 July 1934, Cab 45/192, PRO.

27 Major General Sir John Davidson to Edmonds, 7 September 1934, Cab 45/192, PRO; Edmonds, *Military Operations 1918, the German March*

Offensive, p. 367. Middlebrook is incorrect therefore when he states that Haig did not visit Gough at all, and that Lawrence arrived on the fourth day, i.e. 25 March, Middlebrook, *Kaiser's Battle*, p. 279.

28 Edmonds, *Military Operations 1918, the German March Offensive*, pp. 301, 322, 368; Haig, Diary, 22 and 23 March 1918, in Blake, *Private Papers of Haig*, p. 296; Haldane, Diary, 24 March 1918, Cab 45/185, PRO.

29 R. Sutter (III Corps) told Edmonds that after the second day, III Corps never got an order from GHQ (or Fifth Army) and so the whole retirement was carried out according to previous plans, R. Sutter to Edmonds, 6 March [?], Cab 45/193, PRO.

30 Apart from the *Official History*, the best accounts are Middlebrook, *The Kaiser's Battle*; Toland, *No Man's Land, 1918*; and Pitt, *1918– The Last Act*.

31 One of the great unwritten stories of the war concerns the effect of 'shell shock' – battle stress – on individuals. One can calculate that around one-third of all casualties suffered from 'shell shock' in one form or another at some time or another. Part of the reason that this story is unwritten is that the relevant Ministry of Health and other files in the PRO are closed, in many cases until the year 2024.

32 Maxwell Morrison [?] to Edmonds, 2 August 1927, Cab 45/193; Major van Straubenzee (Artillery) to Edmonds, 10 July 1928, Cab 45/193; Charles Reid (8/10 Gordons, 44th Brigade, 15 Division, XVII Corps) to Edmonds, 8 March 1928, Cab 45/186; Major R. H. Rippon (Royal Fusiliers, 5th Brigade, 2 Division, V Corps) to Edmonds, 27 July 1927, Cab 45/186; Lieutenant Colonel Buchanan-Dunlop (CO machine-guns, 2 Division, V Corps) to Edmonds, 11 June 1927, Cab 45/184, PRO.

33 Alan Regnott [?] (14 Division) to Edmonds, 8 March 1927, Cab 45/193; Major G. C. S. Hodgson (GSO 2, 36 Division) to Edmonds, 1 December 1926, Cab 45/193, PRO. Cf. Middlebrook's criticism, *The Kaiser's Battle*, pp. 326–7; E. Harding Newman (GS 14 Division) to Edmonds, 28 March 1927, Cab 45/193, PRO; Middlebrook, op. cit., pp. 327–8.

34 XVIII Corps Diary, 'The German Attack on the XVIII Corps Front, from 21 March–27 March, 1918', pp. 16, 18, 19, WO 95/953, PRO. Edmonds, *Military Operations 1918, the German March Offensive*, pp. 266, 276, 301; Major C. G. Ling (XVIII Corps Staff) to Edmonds, [?] August [?], Cab 45/193, PRO; Major General Maxse (GOC XVIII Corps) to Edmonds, 7 October 1934, Cab 45/193, PRO.

35 Maxse to Edmonds, 5 July 1953, and Edmonds to Maxse, 16 October 1934, Maxse Papers, WSRO; Liddell Hart, Talk with Edmonds, 11 November 1937, 11/1937/88, Liddell Hart Papers, KCL. Cf. also Edmonds, *Military Operations 1918, the German March Offensive*, pp. 266, 276, 301.

36 Edward Riddell (8 Division) to Edmonds, 10 February 1928, Cab 45/193, PRO.

37 Gough said that Congreve had previously written, declaring that 16 Division was unreliable due to politics undermining its morale, Gough to Edmonds, 3 May 1944, Cab 45/140; Lieutenant General Sir Walter Congreve (GOC VII Corps) to Edmonds, 6 January 1927, commenting on 16 Division's poor performance, Cab 45/192; Colonel Ramsay (48th Brigade, 16 Division) to Edmonds, no date, regarding German flanking tactics, Cab 45/193; L. C. Jackson (GSO 1, 16 Division) to Edmonds, 25 January 1927, concerning divisional recruiting problems and casualties, Cab 45/193; Colonel Jackson (GSO 1, 16 Division) to Edmonds, 11 February 1927, regarding confusion about 66 and 50 Divisions, Cab 45/192, PRO.

38 Brigadier General Sandilands (GOC 104th Brigade, 35 Division, VII Corps) to Edmonds, 14 August 1923, Cab 45/192, PRO.

39 Edmonds, *Military Operations 1918, Continuation of German Offensives,* p. 476; Kiggell to Army Commanders, 13 December 1917, and Lawrence to Third Army, 10 March 1918, in Edmonds, *Military Operations 1918, Appendices* (London, 1935), pp. 28–9.

40 Edmonds, *Military Operations 1918, the German March Offensive,* pp. 249–50, 322; Third Army, 'Short Account of Operations of 3rd Army from 21st March to 30th April 1918' seems to suggest a wholly successful withdrawal on 23 March and that the withdrawal was due to the need to conform to VII Corps on the right, p. 3, WO 95/749, PRO. On the other hand V Corps' account suggests that the withdrawal on 23 March was simply due to army orders, and that it was difficult for 17 Division and impossible for 47 Division to comply with, while the latter failed to conform to VII Corps on the right, at about 7.30 p.m., V Corps, 'Account of Operations on V Corps Front From March 20th to April 30th', pp. 4–5, WO 95/749, PRO.

41 Edmonds, *Military Operations 1918, the German March Offensive,* pp. 322, 377; *Military Operations 1918, Continuation of German Offensives,* p. 476. Cf. Williams, *Byng of Vimy,* ch. 11, for a defence of Byng and criticism of Fanshawe (GOC V Corps), for being too slow in withdrawing his Corps.

42 Edmonds, *Military Operations 1918, the German March Offensive,* pp. 322, 377, and *Military Operations 1918, Continuation of German Offensives,* p. 476. Congreve to Edmonds, 6 January 1927, Cab 45/192, PRO. A day earlier, Congreve had complained of the Lloyd George 'myth' about Fifth Army running away, and that he had 'suffered very cruelly' from being in Fifth Army, and wanted to see the drafts of the *Official History,* Congreve to Edmonds, 5 January 1927, Cab 45/192, PRO.

43 Edmonds to Gough, 21 November 1932, Cab 45/192, PRO.

44 Macdonogh to Edmonds, 26 July 1934, Cab 45/186, and Edmonds to Macdonogh, 27 July 1934, Cab 45/185, PRO; Edmonds, 'Memoirs', ch. XXIX, Edmonds Papers, KCL.

45 Edmonds, 'Preface', *Military Operations 1918, the German March Offensive;* and see Beddington to Edmonds, 13 August 1934, congratulating Edmonds on the preface, Cab 45/192, PRO.

46 Byng to Edmonds, 18 August 1934, Cab 45/192, PRO.

47 Williams's recent defence of Byng is an echo of Byng's own defence some fifty years earlier, although with greater criticism of Fanshawe, and with a reasonable protest about the then Edmonds–Gough axis, Williams, *Byng of Vimy,* pp. 236–8. For Edmonds's cavalry bias, in regard to Byng, see Edmonds's 'Memoirs', ch. XXIX (and regarding Gough as cavalryman), ch. XXVIII, Edmonds Papers, KCL.

48 Byng to Edmonds, 18 August 1934, Cab 45/192, PRO. See also Haig to Edmonds, 26 November 1920, 'Not for Publication', Cab 45/183, PRO, regarding Haig's view of Pétain's attitude on 24 March 1918.

49 The answer seems to be that it was Haig who wanted Wilson to come over and confer, and Haig who suggested that Foch be supreme commander, although Wilson afterwards claimed it was his idea, Duff Cooper to Edmonds, 24 March 1935, Cab 45/184; and Edmonds to Duff Cooper, 25 March 1935, Cab 45/185, PRO. Woodward states that Haig summoned Wilson, and that Haig accepted Foch as supreme commander to get rid of Pétain, *Lloyd George and the Generals,* p. 287.

50 Brigadier General Yatman (17 Divison, V Corps) to Edmonds, no date, Cab

45/187; Hugo de Pree (GS, 63 Naval Division, V Corps) to Edmonds, 9 May 1930, Cab 45/184, PRO.

51 Lieutenant Colonel Aston (Signals) to Edmonds, 3 October 1937, Cab 45/184; Lieutenant Colonel Haining (Artillery) to Edmonds, 4 July 1927, Cab 45/185; and Haldane, Diary, 28 March 1918, Cab 45/185, PRO.

52 Colonel E. M. Birch (47 Division) to Edmonds, 9 June 1927 and 24 August 1930, Cab 45/184; Lieutenant Colonel Stafford (60th Rifles, 99th Brigade, 2 Division, V Corps) to Edmonds, 13 August 1927, Cab 45/187, PRO. A similar story comes from G. R. Dubs (140th Brigade, 47 Division) to Edmonds, 6 January 1927, in which Dubs relates that his Brigade lost touch with 47 Division HQ and with their neighbours, 26th Brigade, Cab 45/184, PRO.

53 F. A. Pile (40 Division Artillery, VI Corps) to Edmonds, 25 October 1926, Cab 45/186, PRO.

54 Postwar reports are likely to be somewhat more accurate than March 1918 unit diaries, which the editor of the *Official History* declared to be often made up days later from hearsay, Edmonds, 'Value of Documents', in 'Reflections on the *Official History*', Cab 44/428, PRO.

55 F. A. Pile (40 Division Artillery, VI Corps) to Edmonds, 25 October 1926, Cab 45/186, PRO. Major General Solly-Flood said that VI Corps HQ was in a bad way earlier on 23 March, A. Solly-Flood (42 Division) to Edmonds, 20 November 1930, Cab 45/187, PRO.

56 Lieutenant Colonel Heathcote Digby [?] to Edmonds, 17 July 1930, Cab 45/184; Harold Lea (Third Army) to Edmonds, 15 February 1931, Cab 45/185, PRO. The demented Major General was unnamed.

57 Lieutenant Colonel A. Stericke (CO 2nd Battalion Cheshire Regiment) to Edmonds, 1 January 1931, Cab 45/187, PRO.

58 Edmonds, *Military Operations 1918, the German March Offensive*, pp. 523, 530. The VI Corps commander, Haldane, noted in his Diary entry for 26 March 1918 that the GOC of the Guards Division, Fielding, had complained of being out of touch for six hours, but Haldane defended himself against this charge, Haldane, Diary, 26 March 1918, Cab 45/185, PRO.

59 Major General Bridgford (GOC 31 Division) to Edmonds, 28 January 1931, Cab 45/184, PRO.

60 Williams, *Byng of Vimy*, pp. 217 ff.

61 Major General T. Astley [?] (GOC 57th Infantry Brigade, 19 Division) to Edmonds, 23 August 1929, Cab 45/187, PRO.

62 Major General G. Jeffreys (GOC 19 Division) to Edmonds, no date, Cab 45/186, PRO.

63 Lieutenant Colonel Jervis (GSO 2, IV Corps) to Edmonds, 15 September 1931, Cab 45/186, PRO.

64 Major General A. Symons (GSO 1, IV Corps) to Edmonds, 30 March 1931, Cab 45/187, PRO. Edmonds, *Military Operations 1918, the German March Offensive*, p. 523.

65 Edmonds to Acheson, 30 July 1950, Cab 103/113, PRO. Edmonds repeated this assertion in his 'Memoirs', ch. XXX, p. 18, Edmonds Papers, KCL.

66 Edmonds, *Military Operations 1918, Continuation of German Offensives*, p. 28, note 1.

67 Wilson, Diary, 3 March 1918, 6 March 1918, 24 March 1918, Wilson Papers, IWM. (Wilson's friend was Sackville-West.) Woodward, *Lloyd George and the Generals*, pp. 289, 292.

68 Wilson, Diary, 24 March 1918, 29 March 1918, 3 April 1918, 4 April 1918, 5 April 1918, Wilson Papers, IWM. Woodward notes that the whole Cabinet

was against Haig, but a better general could not be found, *Lloyd George and the Generals*, p. 292.

69 R. W. Brooke (8 Division) to Edmonds, 15 May 1927, Cab 45/192; H. R. Alexander (Irish Guards) to Edmonds, 4 February 1937, Cab 45/184, PRO.

EPILOGUE

1918 and the Franco–German–British Armies in Comparison

The German assault did not end in March 1918 of course. There were three more major offensives in April, May and July – and still to come were the triumphant 100 days of August, September and October 1918 leading to the November armistice. By the middle of 1918, there were serious manpower shortages, despite the arrival of American forces, but there were corresponding increases in the mechanical means of war, such as Whippet and Mark V Star tanks, and low flying ground attack aeroplanes, armed with bombs and machine-guns. The successful Amiens offensive of 8 August 1918 was notable for the use of these machines of war, for efficient counter battery artillery work, for the use of new Mark III wireless sets, for innovative tactics (the use of aeroplanes to drown the noise of tanks coming up to the start, no preliminary bombardment, and a rolling start with infantry and artillery action commencing at zero hour), and above all, for the idea of co-operation of all arms.

Some of these co-operative ideas were found to be awkward, if not incompatible, such as cavalry co-operating with Whippets, or special air squadrons operating with cavalry as well as with tanks. Also, two of the newer arms, aeroplanes and tanks, were very vulnerable, so that 40 aeroplanes were lost on 8 August 1918, and tank losses were so high that less than 40 of the 414 that started on 8 August 1918 were available four days later. However, the basic ideas of combining arms, and of allowing machines of war to find their own internal logic and tactics, were correct.

Perhaps even more important was the way in which the proponents of the human battlefield paradigm were starting mentally to engage the technological paradigm, although fundamental conceptions of war were naturally hard to change. A good example was the attitude of Rawlinson, the GOC Fourth Army for the 8 August Amiens offensive. He stressed the co-operation of tanks and other arms, but he still felt that the Tank Corps was there primarily 'to assist the infantry'. Then in his summary of the battle of Amiens, Rawlinson reverted to very traditional language: 'To

250

sum up, the Battle of Amiens has shown that our Imperial and Dominion Forces have lost none of the fighting qualities of the Anglo-Saxon race owing to the set-backs which they suffered earlier in the year. It has shown the enemy that his much vaunted offensive has failed to reduce our moral [*sic*] . . .' Again, 'Our own reserves are by no means all we could wish, but in this battle the moral of our troops has risen in a most encouraging degree, whilst that of our enemy has fallen proportionately'. And reverting to a manpower orientation, Rawlinson concluded: 'Had we another 15 or 20 good fresh divisions available we could hunt him out of France before the campaign of 1918 is brought to an end by the approach of Winter.'[1] It was almost as though this proponent of the pessimistic 'bite and hold' concept could not switch to the optimistic breakthrough concept without invoking the latter's emphasis on morale and manpower. Just at the moment when the combination of weapons was pointing to the clear arrival of the technological battlefield, Rawlinson wished to revert to the psychological battlefield! A similar attitude was expressed after the war by Haig in his Rectorial Address to the University of St Andrews in 1919, which was full of references to moral qualities, national character, and team games as the keys to victory.[2]

On the other hand, by 1917 and 1918 there were many officers who had detected the internal logic hidden within weapons such as machine-guns and tanks, and who realized that these and other weapons were significant in that they were both separate entities and yet primarily useful as they correctly interacted with other arms.[3] And it must not be forgotten just how far and fast mental changes had to travel from the prewar decade when officers still resolutely insisted that the 'same principles apply as were in force 100 years ago'[4] to 1918, less than ten years later, when warfare had become a fundamentally different undertaking.

Indeed the most striking phenomena of August 1914 from the British army's point of view was that the officer corps, by and large, had embarked for France believing that the war would be short in duration, tactically simple, and structured in well-understood stages. Battles would be swift and decisive, command would be centralized, and victory would come when the main enemy force was destroyed, or at least forced to retreat. The army with the right offensive spirit would prevail, based upon discipline and morale. Of course there was the awkward business of increased fire-power, but this could be overcome by discipline and morale, even if casualties were likely to be rather heavy. Neither Napoleon nor Clausewitz would have found much that was strange in this,[5] although Napoleon would have placed more emphasis on surprise, and on the combination of arms. But like Haig, Napoleon would have been content to run a centralized system and to decide strategy, although unlike Haig, he would have been involved in directing battle tactics.

From 1914 on, therefore, the story of the Western Front was really the attempt of senior officers to come to mental grips with a war that had escaped its pre-ordained boundaries and structures. It was a war that had 'got away', so to speak, and the groping towards enlightenment of the 1914–18 period was a continuous attempt to overcome prewar conceptions of a simple and understood form of war, and to find new theories or structures to encompass the new technical warfare.

This reaching towards enlightenment was hampered by the personalized army system, by the continuing influence of the cult of the offensive and the psychological battlefield, by the persistence of associated ideas concerning morale and manpower, by the structure of command whereby Haig and GHQ became isolated and created a vacuum, and by the tenacity with which Sir John French and then Haig clung to an earlier paradigm of war.[6] It is consistent that Haig's Staff College ideas were retained and applied in the planning and execution of the Somme (although somewhat transformed), and it is noticeable that the personalized army system of command, together with problems of communication, produced difficulties throughout the Somme campaign. It is also significant that the technological reality of the war split prewar offensive ideas into 'pessimistic' and 'optimistic' schools of thought, whose adherents failed to resolve their differences throughout the war, even in 1918. The problem of a lack of communication between Haig, GHQ and Army GOCs, continued to produce a command vacuum, and thus severe difficulties at Passchendaele and in March 1918. Finally, the 'personalized' army system seemed to operate again after the war, as the *Official History* volumes came to be written with an increasing slant in favour of GHQ.

Fundamentally, then, the British army was actually fighting two wars during 1914–18, a hidden internal war and an external 'real' war. The hidden war took place within the external war, and pitted the power of prewar ideas and the power of a prewar army structure, against the encroaching reality of a 'modern' technological war. Senior British officers began to accept the technological reality, but could not go on to propose appropriate solutions because the power of prewar ideas (the cult of the offensive, the psychological battlefield, the effect of late nineteenth-century Staff College training), and the strength of the prewar army structure (the hierarchical and personalized system) largely prevailed over the need to find a means of discussing, thinking through, and accepting basic changes in warfare. In other words, attitudes that were primarily social prevailed over the underlying and remorseless evolution of the technical means of warfare, and resulted in a strangely centralized, ordered and structured view of warfare.

In this the British officer corps was really a faithful reflection of middle and upper class Edwardian society, which also wished to retain Victorian moral certainties and social structure.[7] What is striking about senior British army officers before and during the First World War was their ready acceptance of new weapons, but their emotional difficulty in coming to mental grips with the tactical and command changes implied by the new or improved technology. As Thomas Kuhn suggests, the transfer from one paradigm to another is an emotional shift and not strictly a mental change, hence the emotional attachment to prewar ideas and army structure was simply too strong for most senior officers. The simple Victorian certainties of morale, character and social hierarchy were not so easily changed, therefore, not even by the harsh lessons of the war. Young 'unindoctrinated' officers, however, found it easier to make the emotional shift to a new technological paradigm, as Thomas Kuhn predicted, but even so the postwar period showed how difficult it was for fundamental conceptions of war to change. Perhaps the real difficulty was that the period 1900–18 marked a transitional phase for the British army between two conceptions of war, in which the newer technological paradigm had not fully emerged as a clear alternative to the prevailing human-oriented battlefield.[8] And so British officers and men found the Western Front to be a cruel killing ground, whose contours proved too difficult for most to perceive clearly, or to understand, or to which they could adapt.

A final conclusion cannot properly be reached without comparing the British experience with that of other nations. Was the British approach unique or not? A useful comparison can be made with the armies of France and Germany, since the former seemed to evolve in similar ways to the British while the latter made a remarkable series of changes starting in 1916, which involved a fundamental shift in perceptions of warfare.

From approximately 1900 on, the French army suffered from criticism and measures by the Radicals which were designed as reforms, but actually served to lower confidence and severely decrease efficiency.[9] This was not the case in Britain, but as in the British army the promotion system, for example, became disjointed, and often depended upon social connections rather than merit. In this way the French army worked on the same 'personalized' system as the British, although dominated to a greater extent by political influence. Low pay and poor prospects also drove many good officers from the French army, and it was generally recognized that many senior French officers and staff were incompetent and often physically unfit. As a result the French army had also to invent a new word on the outbreak of war to describe the degumming of officers – *limoger* or *limogéage* – to denote the exile of incompetents to the town of Limoges. It was also reported that the French Commander-in-Chief in 1914, General Joffre, was more of a figure-head than a leader because of his lack of ideas about modern warfare. Apparently maps and papers had to be placed in his normally bare office when important visitors or photographers arrived. Hence it was really Joffre's staff that directed strategy, and this is somewhat reminiscent of Sir John French's leadership, although Joffre's calm hand in the early weeks of the war did much to steady the French army.

Another aspect which revealed similarities between the French and the British was the prewar cult of the offensive. As in the British army, the pre-1914 French army really lacked a doctrine of war. This was partly because any one specific doctrine was thought to stifle initiative, and partly because neither the *Ecole de Guerre*, the general staff, nor Joffre as chief of the General Staff, seemed capable of formulating a doctrine. The result was a doctrinal vacuum, into which stepped Colonel de Grandmaison, General Langlois, Brigadier General Foch and others, who stressed the theory or spirit of the offensive at all costs. Indeed in 1913 Colonel de Grandmaison drew up the handbook *La conduite des grandes unités* which officially enshrined the tactical and strategic cult of the offensive.[10] As in Britain, this cult of the offensive seemed partly to be a substitute for a lack of doctrine, and partly to overcome the new fire-power that threatened to shatter the offensive. But here again the example of the Russo-Japanese war was similarly invoked, as in Britain, to re-emphasize the importance of morale, the bayonet and offensive spirit. However, French thinking was different from British ideas in that the French argued that the offensive spirit was also required in order to overcome German material and numerical superiority, of almost two to one in terms of officers and men in 1913. But, as in Britain, there was a feeling that modern warfare required individualism and high morale rather than automatic discipline, and the best tactic for patriotic soldiers with high morale was the offensive.[11]

The French cult of the offensive was not accepted without opposition, and just as in Britain where officers like Major McMahon formed a minority fire-power school of thought, so in France a similar fire-power minority was headed by Colonel Pétain. Pétain argued that fire-power made the attack extremely difficult, but suggested that 'Pour éteindre le feu qui le décime il faut désormais que l'assaillant réponde aux projectiles par des projectiles plus puissants, qu'il multiplie ses canons, en un mot qu'il ait recours à la puissance du feu, cette nouvelle divinité du combat moderne'.[12] Pétain had the right idea, although his concept of fighting fire-power with fire-power could and did lead easily to the later idea which divorced fire-power from the infantry advance, 'artillery conquers and the infantry occupies' – as was attempted by both Britain and France at the Somme. But in France, before 1914, and despite the protests of Colonel Pétain, and of Generals Maud'huy, Fayolle and Debeney at the *Ecole de Guerre*, the cult of the offensive was eagerly accepted, especially by younger officers, perhaps as much because it was simple and resolved the prevailing tactical confusion as for other reasons.

One other prewar similarity between Britain and France is worth noting, the lack of heavy artillery, and the poor co-ordination of artillery and infantry. As with most prewar armies, the French did not develop their heavy artillery, partly due to confusion over tactics, partly because of the emphasis on manoeuvre, and partly because funds and manpower were not forthcoming. Except by the fire-power school of thought, it would also appear that artillery tactics and infantry–artillery co-operation were not stressed in France, so that matters like counter battery work, infantry support, and artillery registration beyond the visual, were downgraded in favour of sheer mobility. On the other hand, the experience of the Balkan wars converted French officers to the cause of heavy artillery, and in 1913, two hundred and twenty 105 mm 'longs' were ordered. Nevertheless, as Joffre's 'Tactical Instructions' of 24 August 1914 indicated, infantry–artillery co-operation at the beginning of the war was very poor in the French army. It was also the case that the French machine-gun tended in training to be relegated to 'special' roles, as in Britain, or even rejected altogether by officers such as General Sarrail.[13]

At the outbreak of war in 1914, after the initial French retreat, there took place the miracle of the Marne, the defensive line was stabilized, and French tactics tried to come to grips with the trench deadlock. The spirit of the offensive still prevailed in the French army, and attacks were reportedly undertaken to satisfy the general staff's belief in the offensive. Together with this attitude went the corresponding belief that ground should not be given up, and if lost, should be immediately retaken. Underlying these offensive and defensive attitudes was the idea, common to all armies in the early stages of the war, that ground was the benchmark of success or failure, and thus the earth itself was invested with emotional content. This was particularly the case with French tactics since it was French territory that was in the hands of the enemy.[14]

The French attacks of 1915 tended to rely heavily on the artillery and to use up men and material, especially during the post-offensive 'nibbling' in Artois and Champagne. As with the British army, attacks began to assume a stereotyped pattern of lengthy artillery preparation followed by the infantry offensive, and then a costly series of follow-up attacks. Ideas were badly needed, but here the French senior staff structure appeared similar to the British, in that criticism and ideas were not always welcome at the higher levels. Thus Captain Laffargue's paper *L'Etude sur l'attaque* (1915), which broke new ground, was well received in the German army, but not in the French GQG, while General Nivelle and the GQG appeared impervious to criticism or scepticism before the Chemin des Dames offensive of April 1917.[15]

On the other hand, as in the British army, new ideas did sometimes emerge at the top in order to deal with the trench deadlock, and the fearful losses in men and material. While Kitchener, Rawlinson and others conceived of the 'bite and hold' idea, Foch and Pétain in late 1915 also sought different solutions, but Joffre apparently remained true to the large-scale, decisive offensive concept. Foch advocated a quick succession of limited objective attacks, with good artillery preparation, aimed at a slow and methodical advance. Pétain also thought of a methodical approach, but one that was somewhat similar to Haig's early ideas on the Somme preparation. Pétain wanted first a general push along the whole Franco-British line for several months until material and moral superiority was gained (similar to Haig's preparatory attacks), then either two or three breakthrough attempts on 20 kilometre fronts, or one large breakthrough offensive on a 50 to 60 kilometre front (Haig's decisive offensive). But here Pétain differed from Haig in maintaining that the real objective was not so much the breakthrough, but an attempt to get the enemy in open country so that attacks could be launched on one or both open enemy flanks, thus achieving a Napoleonic-type decision. Typically, Pétain wanted to rely on fire-power superiority to achieve his desired aim, while Foch was concerned about decentralizing the heavy artillery, and in using air observation to create effective counter battery work. However, neither Foch nor Pétain were to be allowed to try their hands at different strategies, for in December 1915 Joffre outlined strategic ideas that maintained the single rush-through, deep-objective, highly centralized, decisive offensive that Haig would like to have tried fully at the Somme.[16]

The battle of Verdun prevented a major French offensive in 1916, then Joffre was replaced, and in April 1917 General Nivelle was given his chance at the Chemin des Dames. Nivelle was an artillery officer, whose plan for the 1917 offensive was based on the normal large-scale preparatory attack, but then he called for a quick switch to another front, and the use of a fast-moving rolling barrage, and small-group infantry tactics, stressing speed and avoidance of strong points. These were good ideas, in advance of British tactics later on at Passchendaele, but for various reasons, including the German capture of Nivelle's battle plans, French rolling barrages that were too fast, French supply shortages, better German artillery observation, and well-concealed German machine-gun nests, the offensive failed. The heavy French casualties of the offensive resulted in French army mutinies, and Pétain was brought in to control this difficult situation. Following his successful restoration of French morale, Pétain conceived of new offensive tactics in October 1917. These stressed the dislocation of the enemy front with limited attacks over short periods of time but on widely separated fronts. These ideas were applied, but it was not until mid-1918 that large-scale French offensives could resume.[17]

Meanwhile, in early 1918, the French were slower to adopt the German elastic defence-in-depth system than the British. Pétain favoured the new system, but Foch apparently did not, judging by his June 1918 instructions, which ordered a foot-by-foot defence of territory. Pétain's subordinate, General Duchene, commanding Sixth French Army, either would not, or could not, adopt the new system, and suffered a severe reversal at the same Chemin des Dames in May 1918. By July 1918, however, Pétain had impressed the new defence-in-depth system on to the French army, and it was successful in holding the German offensive of mid-July 1918. Foch had now become Allied Commander-in-Chief, and from late July 1918 following, his successful offensive strategy consisted in launching several successive Allied offensives with limited objectives, which would loosen and unravel the German front, rather than aim at breakthroughs. Such was the result, although British and American co-operation with the French was not without its problems.

Despite differences due to the political structures of the two countries, the British and French armies appeared to operate with the same personalized and overly hierarchical structure. Degumming and *limogéage* were common, and the same pressure by GQG and GHQ to launch attacks was evident. In addition, the same prewar cult of the offensive, lack of doctrine, poor infantry–artillery co-operation, and devaluation of firepower, led to the same early difficulties in the war. During the war, however, the British army appeared to be more flexible tactically, and certainly helped keep the French army in the war in 1917. In March 1918 both armies had trouble adapting to the defence-in-depth system, but an agreement on offensive tactics and strategy from mid-1918 onward made the final victory possible.

Like other European armies, the German army in 1914 was dominated by the cult of the offensive, in this case both tactically and strategically (the Schlieffen Plan). The prewar German army was far more politically conscious than the British army, and the German cult of the offensive certainly possessed deeper political, social and intellectual roots than in Britain or France.[18] Social Darwinian thinking, for example, served to stress offensive ideas, as well as moral virtues such as character and will-power.[19] In the German army, however, the strategic and tactical offensive was not a substitute for lack of doctrine, since the offensive manoeuvre against the flank, leading to envelopment, was official doctrine. The frontal offensive was avoided in favour of flank assault and envelopment partly because of the emphasis on rapid manoeuvre and partly to avoid the fire of modern weapons. On the other hand, the German army was similar to other armies in stressing aggressive infantry tactics and the importance of high morale and bravery in battle as the keys to success. And like other armies, the German army undervalued machine-gun tactics and infantry–artillery co-operation. However, the need to subdue defensive forts in the opening stages of the Schlieffen Plan did result in a better supply of heavy artillery than in the British or French armies.[20]

Defensively, the German army was ill-prepared for the stalemate of late 1914. General von Falkenhayn's emphasis on densely-packed and rigid defences, and the retaking of every foot of lost ground, was symptomatic of a traditional way of thinking that was similar in the French and British armies in the early stages of the war. Parallel to this way of thinking in the German OHL went the familiar custom of degumming/removing commanders who failed to retake lost ground.[21] Offensively, the fast manoeuvre of 1914 was replaced by the indecision of 1915 when von Falkenhayn shuttled forces around without achieving a knock-out blow in either the East or the West.[22] By early 1916 when von Falkenhayn had finalized the Verdun attrition plan (Operation *Gericht*), the German army had come to rely on heavy artillery as the battle winner. As with other armies the solution to the tactical *impasse* had become artillery fire and then infantry movement. Von Falkenhayn's attrition plan at Verdun failed, and his insistence on strong front line defence at the Somme led to heavy casualties from British and French artillery. Von Falkenhayn was therefore removed in August 1916 and replaced by Field Marshal von Hindenburg, who brought with him Lieutenant General Ludendorff as Quartermaster General. Ludendorff and the operations section of the OHL visited units and solicited reports, opinions and criticism from front line units – a conspicuously different process from that in the British army. As a result, a new German policy regarding defensive tactics was revealed – the elastic defence-in-depth system. This was enshrined in two sets of regulations: *The Principles of Command in the Defensive Battle in Position Warfare*, 1 December 1916; and *The Principles of Field Construction*, 13 November 1916. Essentially, the defence was now to have three zones, the outpost, battle, and rear zones, with the artillery behind the protective line at the rear of the battle zone. Counter-attack forces were poised to fight in all three zones, and machine-gun strong points were located principally in the battle zone, although some were also located in the outpost zone. The principles of the new defence system were elasticity, fire-power and depth – the first emphasized regaining the initiative through counter-attacks when the enemy offensive had bogged down, and the second stressed that the key to the defence was fire-power – machine-guns and artillery – not men. Along the way one very important change had been made to the third principle, namely, that ground now need not be held at all costs, instead the depth of the position was to be used tactically (e.g. reverse slope positions) to defeat the enemy offensive.[23]

In other words, ground and the front line were stripped of their emotional content, and a new conception of war emerged, which focused on flexibility, function and technology rather than rigid defensive and offensive tactics. Although the elastic defence-in-depth system evolved in conception through the remainder of the war, the principle of tying tactics to results rather than pre-determined emotional content was decisive. The same cannot be said of French and British defensive tactics until late 1917 and early 1918, when both armies converted, often erratically and without complete understanding, to the more flexible defence-in-depth system. It is true that the German army had usually been on the defensive on the Western Front after 1914, and thus had more reason to develop defensive tactics than the French and British armies. However, although French and British offensive tactics from 1915 onward had been evolving quite rapidly due to the experience of frequent offensives, there was not the same fundamental change to a new technological understanding of war that seemingly took place in the OHL and the German army both defensively and offensively from late 1916 onward.

In May 1915, a French army officer, Captain Laffargue, wrote a pamphlet entitled *L'Etude sur l'attaque*. This was distributed to French army units by GQG, as was the custom in the French army with particularly useful and innovative ideas. Apparently the British army did not translate and distribute this pamphlet. (This was because many pamphlets were written by enterprising British officers, and the practice was for the War Office, GHQ, or relevant HQ to encapsulate individuals' ideas in official tactical pamphlets that were then issued according to their estimated value and the inclination of senior staff.) However in the summer of 1916 a copy of Laffargue's pamphlet was found by the Germans when they captured a French trench, and this was translated and distributed by the OHL. The difference between the three countries' appreciation of this pamphlet was that the OHL alone issued the pamphlet as an official training manual, because the OHL staff recognized that Laffargue's ideas had solved some of the basic problems of the attack. In other words, the operations section of the OHL proved more perceptive than GHQ or GQG in the area of offensive tactics.[24]

Laffargue's ideas stressed speed and sudden close fire-power support to enable the assault to go through the enemy front line, and that this assault should achieve deep penetration to disorganize enemy defences and to reach the enemy artillery. The assault force would press rapidly ahead by a system of fire-power and infiltration, identifying and leaving strong points to be dealt with later by succeeding waves. The assault force would be led by specially trained, aggressive *groupes des tirailleurs*, some fifty yards ahead, essentially storm troops, armed with light machine-guns, grenades and gas bombs to deal with machine-guns that threatened to halt the assault. (Perhaps Laffargue was thinking of the French irregular *tirailleurs* of the Franco-Prussian War.) Machine-gun units would follow in close support of the *tirailleurs*. Laffargue's plan depended on surprise (the sudden close support of the mortar, aerial torpedo and artillery barrage in depth and the quick assault); fire-power (maximum use of fire-power by all units); open warfare fighting skills; and the creation of an elite group of storm troopers to break open the crust of the front. If used on a wide front, thought Laffargue, this method of attack would achieve a break-through.[25]

The German counter-attack at Cambrai in November 1917 utilized many of Laffargue's ideas, although disregarding his emphasis on line formations and instead using small columns of heavily armed storm troops to achieve infiltration. On 1 January 1918 these methods were encapsulated in *The Attack in Position Warfare*. The central concept was the attack in depth, with the emphasis on disruption and demoralization rather than destruction. The sudden artillery rolling barrage was to be carefully co-ordinated with the infantry, so that the latter controlled the former, and not vice-versa, as was the case in the British and French armies. Infiltration, speed, envelopment and disruption were the tasks of the three waves of the storm battalions as they sought weak points and maximum penetration. Once again, as in the defence-in-depth system, 'ground' was not the centre of attention, but rather the use of tactics to demoralize and disorganize the defence. Parallel to this went another fundamental change. The decisive physical destruction of the main enemy army was not contemplated, as had been the aim of the traditional French and British paradigm of war, rather German strategy now emphasized large-scale disruption of the enemy front, leading to breakthroughs and the collapse of the enemy.

Initially successful, the German attacks of 21 March 1918 and those of succeeding months actually led to such difficulties in the German army that an armistice was eventually requested. Despite innovative tactics in defence and offence from 1916 following, the German army was defeated. The question to be asked, however, is why the OHL and the senior staff of the German army appeared to be more innovative and willing to change than their counterparts in the British and French armies? This problem is especially puzzling since the social and political horizons of the German officer corps seemed to be more conservative, mentally isolated and traditional than was the case in Britain and France. It might be expected, therefore, that von Falkenhayn, the OHL and senior staff would be resistant to basic changes, and this apparently was the case until 1916. Then, however, Ludendorff and Hindenburg presided over a fundamental alteration in the understanding of war, in which winning and losing ground was stripped of its emotional content, and that same emotional content was transferred on to small groups of men using aggressive defensive and offensive tactics.[26] These tactics were innovative, and geared to success with minimal losses rather than to predetermined conceptions. Generally speaking, these new tactics were not be found in the French and British armies. Why was this? Why was the German army more innovative?

There appear to be a number of possible answers, none of which are mutually exclusive. Four main arguments will be advanced, although these do not exhaust the possibilities. First is the argument that the German army contained a number of outstanding staff officers and tacticians, for example, Colonel von Lossberg, Captain Geyer, Colonel Bruchmuller, Colonel Bauer, and so on. These officers were given encouragement by the leadership of Hindenburg and especially by Ludendorff. This argument is obviously a variant of the 'Great Man' theory of history, and focuses on the achievements of particular individuals.[27] A second argument supersedes or perhaps complements the first, namely that the German army was able to innovate because the introduction of new tactics and ideas was really a collective or corporate effort, with a tolerance for dissent and discussion at the highest levels.[28] Very similar to this is the thesis of Colonel T. N. Dupuy, who states that the German army performed well because of 'institutionalized military excellence', meaning primarily the work of the German General Staff.[29] A third argument goes beyond the first two, and concerns the old idea of scarcity as the mother of invention. According to Norman Stone and Michael Geyer, the Allies (France and Britain) followed a policy of 'abundance' of resources, while Germany was forced to follow a policy of 'scarcity'. Thus the German army was compelled toward innovation and army reform due to a lack of manpower and resources.[30]

A fourth and final argument derives from Michael Geyer's stimulating discussion of the relationship between army, ideology and society. According to Geyer, the problem was not only 'scarcity' versus 'abundance', but a much more fundamental change in the war around 1916. This was the arrival of German 'machine culture' as a result of the appearance of technocrats in the OHL, led by Ludendorff, who espoused the maximum use of arms and the escalation of violence. In other words, the optimal use of weapons and the functional organization of violence, together with the enlistment of ideology, to achieve the greatest efficiency of the German army. Following the arrival of Hindenburg and Ludendorff, the emphasis was placed on machines rather than men, and on function and tasks rather than on established units or hierarchy. Ludendorff's technical rule led to the full rationalization of machine war, and also required ideological mobilization in the army and at home. This kind of machine war proved innovative and effective for the German army, and it was revolutionary in that the German army had radically shifted direction away from a century of hierarchy and subordination, towards the pure organization of weapons – away from the eternal 'laws' of war and towards a focus on available means and specific tasks.[31]

Geyer's thesis is an extension and encapsulation of the previous three arguments, but dispenses with the perhaps romantic view of the achievements of individual staff officers and of the OHL after 1916, and includes an important emphasis on the effects of technological change, and its resulting ideologies. In fact, if Geyer is correct, it may be concluded that German staff officers and the OHL converted to a technological paradigm of war around late 1916, while British and French staff officers generally did not make that same conversion. In contrast to Ludendorff and the OHL, Haig and his GHQ tried to adapt resources, men and technology to the traditional paradigm of war rather than the other way around. Thus the British army bypassed reform of the hierarchy and changes in basic ways of waging war, and instead concentrated on the application of ever-greater resources to the battlefield. The British army's reaction to the emergence of modern warfare was therefore a conservative reflex, perhaps because full accommodation to machine warfare would have required social and hierarchical changes with unforeseen consequences. In this the British army was not unique, being similar to the French army, while the German army embarked on an entirely new conception of war and ideology that was soon to have grave results in the reorganization of German society.[32]

Notes

1 Rawlinson to Wigram, Allenby, Monro, Cavan, Cobbe, 28 August 1918, pp. 13–14, 5201–33–20, Rawlinson Papers, NAM.

2 Haig, 'A Rectorial Address', St Andrews, 14 May 1919, 71/13/1, Lieutenant Colonel J. H. Boraston Papers, IWM. This is not to argue that the two concepts are mutually exclusive, but the key is the attitude which the individual emphasizes in his mental outlook.

3 It was natural that converts to the technological battlefield should primarily be those involved with such weapons, e.g. Major General G. M. Lindsay, First Army machine-gun officer, who characteristically transferred to the Royal Tank Corps after the war. Lindsay's Notes and Lectures from 1915–19 on the Machine-Gun are important, and can be found in 73/60/1, General Lord Horne Papers, IWM.

4 Hubert Gough to Roberts, 10 March 1910, 7101–23–221, Roberts Papers, NAM. However Lord Esher was already calling for motor traction and the disappearance of the horse in 1910, and criticizing the General Staff for shrinking 'from the responsibility of thinking out novel tactical excercises', Esher to Roberts, 1 January 1910, 7101–23–221, Roberts Papers, NAM.

5 Clausewitz's ideas were very similar to British ideas in 1914 in regard to basic concepts of morale and the decisive offensive against the main enemy force, Michael Howard, Clausewitz (Oxford, 1983), pp. 25–6, 36, 41, 44–5, 61.

6 Sir John French has not been properly evaluated in this book, but his prewar frame of mind may perhaps be gauged by a letter he wrote to Roberts in 1904: 'nothing can make me alter the views I hold on the subject of cavalry ...' French to Roberts, 6 March 1904, 7101–23–30, Roberts Papers, NAM. A valuable and balanced view of Sir John French can be found in Richard Holmes, The Little Field Marshal: Sir John French (London, 1981).

7 Samuel Hynes, The Edwardian Turn of Mind (Princeton, 1968), p. 86. A somewhat similar argument occurs in Martin van Creveld, Command in War, pp. 161, 166, 168.

8 Bond, *British Military Policy*, ch. 1; Bidwell and Graham, *Fire-Power*, pp. 146, 150; C. L. Mowat, *Britain Between the Wars 1918–1940*, paperback edn (London, 1968), p. 1; N. Branson and M. Heinemann, *Britain in the 1930s*, Panther edn (London, 1973), p. 17.

9 Much of the following section relies on the excellent analysis by Douglas Porch, *The March to the Marne: the French Army 1871–1914* (Cambridge, 1981).

10 General Sir James Marshall-Cornwall, *Foch as Military Commander* (New York, 1972), pp. 55–6. On the cult of the offensive, see also the articles by Stephen van Evera, 'The cult of the offensive and the origins of the First World War', and Jack Snyder, 'Civil-military relations and the cult of the offensive, 1914 and 1984', in *International Security*, vol. 9, no. 1 (1984), pp. 58–146.

11 Cf. Douglas Porch, *The March to the Marne*, ch. 11, 'The spirit of the offensive'.

12 Jacques Isorni, *Philippe Pétain*, Vol. 1 (Paris, 1972), p. 53, note.

13 The GQG's 'Instructions on Tactics', 24 August 1914, quoted in Major General Sir Edward Spears, *Liaison 1914: a Narrative of the Great Retreat*, 2nd edn (London, 1968), pp. 517–18. See also Porch, *The March to the Marne*, ch. 12, and p. 249; Alistair Horne, *The Price of Glory: Verdun 1916* (London, 1963), pp. 13, 15.

14 Eugène Carrias, *La Pensée Militaire Française* (Paris, 1960), p. 305; Porch, *The March to the Marne*, pp. 218, 253; Alistair Horne, 'Pétain', in Field Marshal Sir Michael Carver (ed.), *The War Lords* (London, 1976), pp. 63, 69; Lupfer, *Dynamics of Doctrine*, p. 3.

15 Carrias, *Pensée Militaire Française*, p. 305; Wynne, *If Germany Attacks*, pp. 54–7; Lupfer, *Dynamics of Doctrine*, p. 33.

16 Marshall-Cornwall, *Foch as Military Commander*, pp. 177–9; Isorni, *Pétain*, pp. 72–3.

17 Carrias, *Pensée Militaire Française*, p. 306.

18 Martin Kitchen, *The German Officer Corps: 1890–1914* (Oxford, 1968), pp. 98–114, 224; Michael Geyer, 'The German Practice of War: 1914–1945', forthcoming in *Makers of Modern Strategy*, Princeton, 1986. I am very grateful to Michael Geyer for allowing me to read his manuscript before publication. See also Stephen van Evera and Jack Snyder in *International Security*, op. cit.

19 Kitchen, *The German Officer Corps*, pp. 30, 127.

20 Lupfer, *Dynamics of Doctrine*, pp. 1–2; Wynne, *If Germany Attacks*, pp. 319–20; Colonel T. N. Dupuy, *A Genius for War: the German Army and General Staff, 1807–1945* (Englewood Cliffs, NJ, 1977), pp. 131, 144.

21 Wynne, *If Germany Attacks*, pp. 100, 103; Geyer, 'The German Practice of War', p. 12; Lupfer, *Dynamics of Doctrine*, p. 7.

22 Von Falkenhayn appears to have 'solved' the need for innovative ideas in 1915 by shifting the focus of the German effort to the East, Norman Stone, 'von Falkenhayn', in Carver, *The War Lords*, pp. 113, 116.

23 My interpretation follows but summarizes in different form those of Lupfer, *Dynamics of Doctrine*, ch. 1, and Wynne, *If Germany Attacks*, Pt 2.

24 Wynne, *If Germany Attacks*, pp. 57–8.

25 ibid., pp. 54–7; Lupfer, *Dynamics of Doctrine*, pp. 38–9.

26 Eric Leed makes many brilliant proposals regarding the emotional content of the war in his book *No Man's Land: Combat and Identity in World War I* (Cambridge, 1979). However, his consideration of the breakdown of the offensive personality does not seem altogether congruent with German tactics and results after 1916, ibid., pp. 102 ff., 156 ff.

27 This seems to be the thesis of G. C. Wynne, who focused on the work of Colonel von Lossberg as the key factor in innovation, Wynne, *If Germany Attacks*, p. 84 and *passim*. Most accounts of the German army or the Western Front will mention these names as significant factors, for example, Colonel Eugène Carrias's almost exclusive emphasis on Hindenburg and Ludendorff in his *La Pensée Militaire Allemande* (Paris, 1948), pp. 336 ff.
28 Lupfer, *Dynamics of Doctrine*, pp. 8, 11, 57.
29 Dupuy, *A Genius for War*, pp. 177, 180.
30 Norman Stone, 'Ludendorff', in Carver, *The War Lords*, p. 79; Michael Geyer, 'The German Practice of War', addition to p. 18. Cf. also Wynne, *If Germany Attacks*, pp. 319–21, where the OHL is accused of ignoring technical innovation and mass production.
31 Michael Geyer, 'The German Practice of War', especially pp. 1–28.
32 ibid., *passim*.

Maps

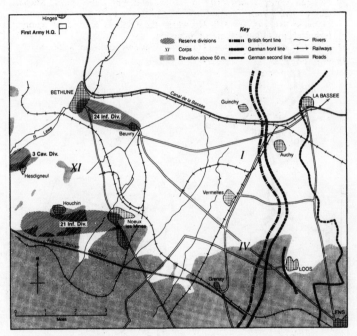

1 Position of the Reserves at the battle of Loos, 25 September 1915.

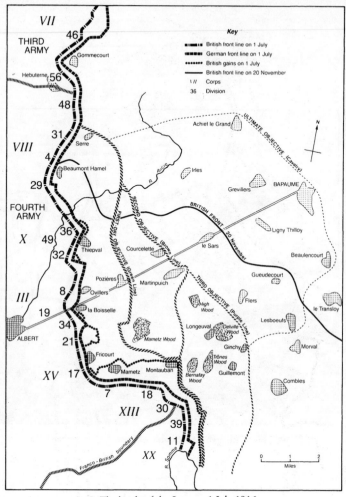

2 The battle of the Somme, 1 July 1916.

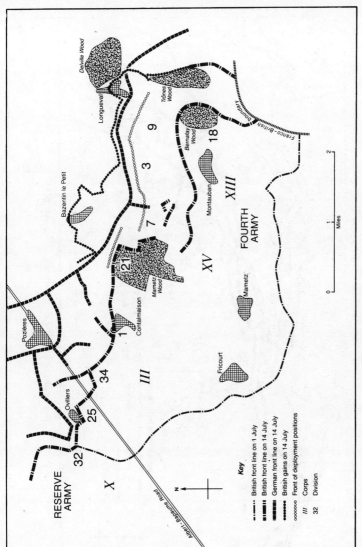

Key

- British front line on 1 July
- British front line on 14 July
- German front line on 14 July
- British gains on 14 July
- Front of deployment positions

III Corps

32 Division

3 The British offensive at the Somme, 14 July 1916.

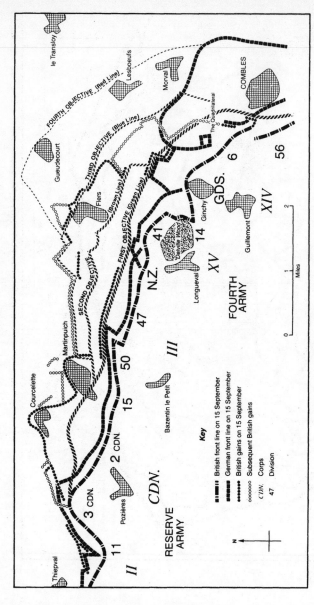

4 The British offensive at the Somme, 15 September 1916.

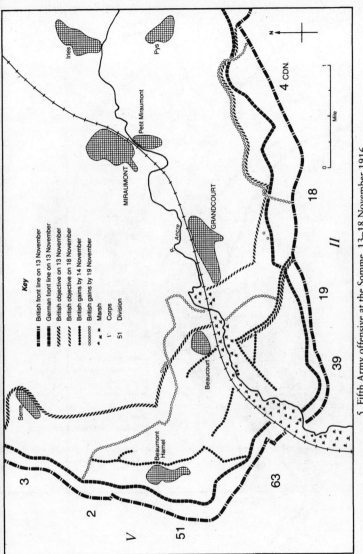

Key

- ▮▮▮ British front line on 13 November
- ▰▰▰ German front line on 13 November
- ▨▨▨ British objective on 13 November
- ▧▧▧ British objective on 18 November
- ••••• British gains by 14 November
- ∘∘∘∘∘ British gains by 19 November
- ▨ Marsh
- ⨯—⨯ Corps
- 51 Division

Serre

3

2

V

51

63

Beaumont
Hamel

Beaucourt

39

GRANDCOURT

19

II

18

4 CDN.

R. Ancre

MIRAUMONT

Petit Miraumont

Irles

Pys

N

0   ½   1
Mile

5 Fifth Army offensive at the Somme, 13–18 November 1916.

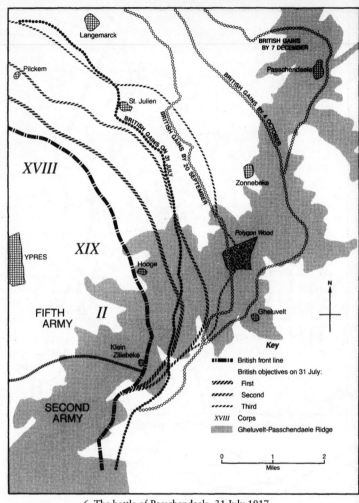

6 The battle of Passchendaele, 31 July 1917.

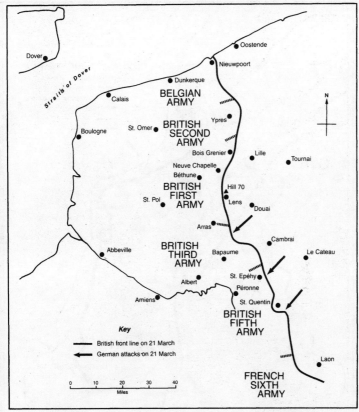

7 General situation before the German offensive of 21 March 1918.

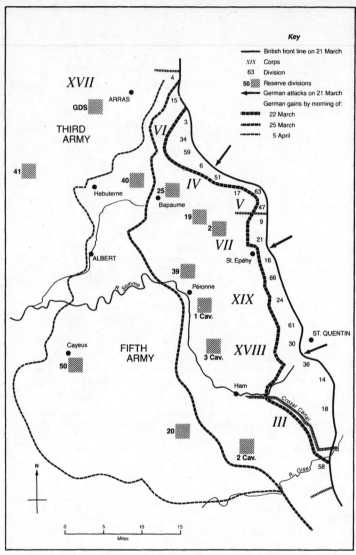

8 The German offensive, 21 March 1918, and position of British forces.

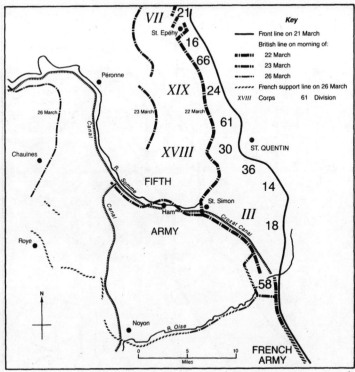

9 Retreat of XVIII Corps, 21–26 March 1918.

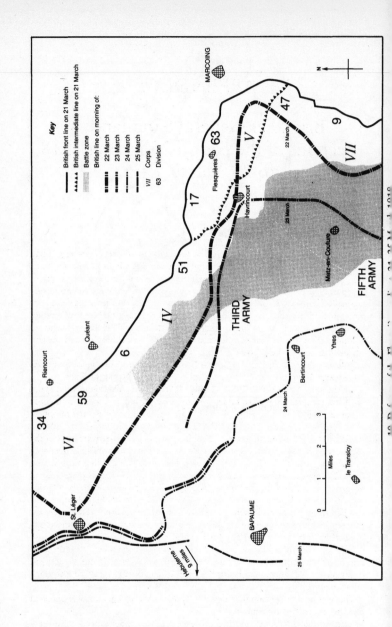

Key

British front line on 21 March
British intermediate line on 21 March
British line on morning of:
   22 March
   23 March
   24 March
   25 March
Battle zone
VII Corps
63 Division

N

MARCOING

Flesquières 63

17   V

Havrincourt

51   47

22 March

9

IV   THIRD ARMY   *VII*

Quéant   6

23 March

Metz-en-Couture

Riencourt

59

34   *VI*

St. Léger

Hindenburg 9 miles →

Bertincourt

Ytres

FIFTH ARMY

24 March

BAPAUME

le Transloy

25 March

0 1 2 3
Miles

19 Defence of the Flanders position 21–25 March 1918

APPENDIX I

Brigadier General Sandilands's account of the period 25 March 1918 to 28 March 1918

I arrived at AMIENS about midnight and found the town like a cemetery. It had been heavily bombed the night before and there was not a light or a person to be seen anywhere. I had never been to AMIENS before and I walked about for the best part of an hour trying to find someone, who could tell me what was going on.

Finally I came on to the Officers Club and found a few officers inside, one of whom by a bit of luck knew me by sight as being a Brigadier in the 35th Division. He assured me that he had seen several men of the Division being evacuated wounded from Amiens that morning and they had all stated that they had been hit somewhere near MARICOURT.

This was the first clue I got as to where my Brigade was likely to be found. As there was nothing more to be done that night, I went to bed in the Club.

On the morning of March 26th, I started off again trying to find out what to do, but I still completely failed to find any responsible person in Amiens, who could tell me anything worth hearing. The whole place was full of the wildest rumours.

About 9 a.m., I heard that the 5th Army Headquarters had come back to AMIENS. I induced the Manager of the Officers Club, who in private life was the Manager of the HOLBORN Restaurant, to take me out in a Ford van in the hopes of locating General Gough's Headquarters. This we succeeded in doing, finding them in a suburb of Amiens, in a state of great confusion. The whole place was full of lorries, motor cars and motor bicycles. Outside a very unpretentious villa was the Army Flag. I went into the house and found a room full of officers of comparatively junior rank, some of whom I knew personally. I also noticed an officer with his mouth wide open, sitting on a chair and a Doctor prodding at one of his teeth, but I did not pay any particular attention to him.

Feeling rather cheerful myself, I said to the assembled company 'What on earth are you all running away for like this'. My remark was received in dull silence, and to my horror the officer with his mouth open sprang up and said 'What the Hell are you doing here'.

This was no less a person than General Gough, with whom, like most people, I had had one or two encounters.

I replied that I had just returned off leave and was endeavouring to find my

Brigade and thinking that perhaps discretion was the better part of valour, I retired hastily from the room.

No one at Army Headquarters had any clear idea where the 35th Division was at 10 a.m. on March 26th, nor did they know which Corps it was in at the moment.

As there was nothing else to do, I just hung about outside Army Headquarters waiting for something to turn up.

About 11 a.m. a large limousine drove up, out of which to my astonishment stepped Sir Henry Wilson, followed by Lord Milner in an overcoat and a bowler.

Sir Henry Wilson, who knew me personally, asked me if I thought it was safe to drive through Amiens and I told him as far as I knew it was perfectly safe, as I had not heard the slightest sound of shelling or bombing the whole morning.

I naturally assumed that he was looking for the 5th Army Headquarters and told him that General Gough was inside the villa, at the gate of which we were standing.

He replied 'Oh he is here is he? Well good morning' and both he and Lord Milner got back into their car and drove off. I thought at the time 'That's the end of Gough'.

I suppose that Sir Henry Wilson and Lord Milner were on the way to the great DOULLENS conference, but I have no idea where they had come from that morning.

About mid day a Staff Officer told me definitely that the 35th Division were in General Congreve's Corps, whose H.Q. was at VADENCOURT (??) and that I was to go there at once, but he was sorry that they could not send me there in a car.

Vadencourt was about 10 miles away and he could offer no solution as to how I was to get there.

I fell back on my friend the Manager of the Holborn Restaurant and induced him to drive me out there in his Ford van, after having stood him the best lunch I could, at Les Gobelins.

I arrived at Corps Headquarters at about 2.30 or 3 p.m.

I had never seen General Congreve before and was quite shocked at his appearance. He struck me as being absolutely down and out and incapable of any clear thinking. He was evidently suffering from want of sleep and both mental and physical fatigue.

I was also amazed to find Sandy Ruthven (Lt-Colonel H. A. Hore Ruthven V.C.) in the capacity of a BGGS.

He had been a personal friend of mine for 20 years or more. I knew him to have completely failed to pass into the Army through any orthodox channel and regarded him as a thorough, good sporting, hard riding man with a minimum of intellect. To my mind it was a monstrous appointment. He certainly was quite cool and collected, but had not the slightest idea as to what was going on or what he was going to do next.

Both General Congreve and Ruthven were very glad to see me, as a man who was quite fresh and who had had a good deal of experience in rotten shows.

They told me a certain amount of what had happened and held a very gloomy view as to the immediate future.

Finally they told me they would send me straight to my Divisional Headquarters at HENNENCOURT (?) and that I was to deliver the following message to General Franks:

> The 35th Division is to come back as soon as possible to the line of the ANCRE and on no account to risk being implicated in a battle with the Boches, as there was no means of giving them any assistance with other troops.

They repeated this over and over again. Perhaps I ought to have made them write it down, but I did not as it was quite easy to understand and I paid no special attention to it as being anything except an ordinary operation.

I remember saying to Sandy Ruthven in the end 'Look here Sandy, I am not a bloody fool, I can deliver a message without making a mess of it'.

I should say that I left Corps Headquarters at about 4 p.m. and arrived at 35th Division Headquarters within half an hour of that.

My progress was considerably impeded by masses of troops coming back, artillery, infantry, engineers. There were no signs of a panic such as I had seen at LOOS, the men were marching along in platoons and companies with their own officers.

Occasionally I stopped and asked them where they were going to and they all said either that they had been relieved or were going back to some line either Red, Blue or Green.

I did my best to make them stop and assured them that there were no lines in the sense of prepared trenches or even wire. But it was of course impossible for one man to deal with masses of troops who evidently were under the impression that they were doing what was right, so I gave it up, thinking it best to get to my own people as quick as possible and hang on to them.

I arrived at 35th Division H.Q. at about 4.30 p.m. I went straight into General Franks' room and said I had a message to give him.

He was telephoning at the time and told me to go out of the room and wait outside until he had finished.

This surprised me, as he was in the habit of consulting me about fighting, especially with infantry.

I gathered afterwards that he was at that time being relieved of his command by General Congreve for refusing to obey an order.

After a few minutes, I was called back into the room and gave my message as already quoted above.

General Franks replied that he had received orders from the Corps to return to the BRAY position.

I said that there must be a mistake, as I had only left Corps H.Q. about ½ an hour ago and they had told me most emphatically that the 35th Division were to come back to the Ancre. General Franks said 'That is what we were ordered to do and have been doing all day, now the Corps has changed their orders and told me to go back to Bray.

'As an Infantry Officer do you think it possible that men who have been fighting a rear guard action and retiring for about 8 miles, could now turn round and advance again towards the position they were originally holding in the morning?'

I replied 'No, it would be madness to attempt it and I should refuse to do it'.

'That is what I have done', said General Franks, but he did not tell me that he had been relieved of his command.

The withdrawal of the 35th Division must form an important part in the Official History of the March Retreat, as it undoubtedly affected the subsequent operations.

What follows should be read in conjunction with the 35th Division and 104th Brigade War Diaries, as I did not arrive on the scene until 4.30 p.m., March 26th.

Who gave the order for the 35th Division to come back? The view was taken that General Franks had done so and that the Corps knew nothing about it.

I do not believe this to be the case. As can be imagined the question formed the subject of great discussion throughout the Division and the view taken by all of us was that General Franks had been made a scapegoat.

My Brigade (104th) were on the BRAY–ALBERT ROAD on the morning of March 26th, full of fight and not in the least bit rattled. The position was a very strong one and they were quite confident that they could easily repel an attack.

I was told afterwards that General Congreve had visited them that morning and had told the acting Brigadier that he would have to come back to the line of the Ancre that day and that if there was any danger of being cut off, they were to make their way as best they could across the SOMME and join the 5th Army.

This came to them as a great surprise, as they could see no reason at all for retiring from such a strong position.

Although I am of course not able to prove it, I believe that there can be no doubt that the order for the retirement came from the Corps, possibly the Corps may have received it from the Army.

What I am prepared to swear to is that about 3.30 p.m. or 4 p.m. on March 26th, I received instructions in the presence of General Congreve and his BGGS, Sandy Ruthven, to tell General Franks to get his Division back to the Ancre as soon as possible, and that by the time I got to Divisional HQ at about 4.30 p.m. General Franks had been told to turn round and advance again towards MORLANCOURT, which in my opinion would have ended in disaster.

The only cardinal mistake which General Franks made was to give orders for all transport including 1st Line, to get back across the Ancre as soon as possible before the retirement began.

His AQMG who was an Infantry Officer ought to have kept him straight over this and pointed out that 1st line transport is just as much part of a Battalion as the men's rifles and boots.

The result of this was that the Infantry were without food all day and ran short of ammunition.

General Franks of course refused to obey an order, but this is provided for in F.S. Regulations, when the Commander on the spot knows that the situation will not admit of its been carried out.

It was rumoured at the time, that the withdrawal of the 35th Division was discovered at the DOULLENS Conference, and that it was FOCH himself who gave the order for it to return to Bray.

Although what follows is of no historical importance, it may help to throw some light on the general confusion which reigned at that time.

278

General Franks told me that I ought to find my Brigade (104th) coming into BUIRE at about 6 p.m, so I went off there in a car from Divisional HQ.

Lavieville was simply blocked with troops of all sorts & we had the greatest difficulty in getting along the road at all. There were no signs of panic, but officers even including senior ones, Colonels & Majors, were just standing about in a hopeless sort of way, doing nothing.

I got to BUIRE at about 6 by which time the village was being heavily shelled, but I could find no signs of any British troops, except a very young R. E. officer and a few sappers trying to blow up a bridge.

I told them to clear out as I could see no reason why the bridge might not be of considerable assistance to us later on. I hung about in Buire for about ½ an hour and as I still could not see any British troops and was not too sure where the Germans were, I went back to Lavieville.

The confusion there was if anything worse than it had been an hour or so before, I found the 9th Divisional H.Q., but they could not give me any reliable information.

Just as it was beginning to get dark, one of my Brigade runners came up to me from out of the crowd and told me that he was lost. He had been sent back to bring the Brigade Transport to Buire, but he had no idea where it was and of course I too had not the slightest idea.

Within a quarter of an hour of this, by an extraordinary fluke, we came across the whole of our Brigade Transport amidst a mass of wagons, limbers and artillery of all sorts.

I got hold of them and led towards Buire as I still had some hope that my Brigade might have arrived there and I also thought it might also start some others going towards the enemy instead of doing nothing or going back.

By another bit of luck I came across the whole of my Brigade Signal Company after having gone about a mile. I fell them in too and we all went together towards Buire.

It was pitch dark when we got within about ½ a mile of Buire so I told all my men to halt and go to sleep while I went into the village.

When I got there I found the whole place crowded with troops and I could hardly believe it when I found they were my own Brigade. This must have been about 8 p.m.

They were very tired and dispirited but when the news spread that I had turned up with the cookers and ammunition, an extraordinary change came over them.

Within an hour they had all had their dinners and been given ammunition, and most of them were fast asleep. There was not a sound at the time, not a shell or a machine gun firing, so I left them alone for an hour or two, while I went off to find out whether there were any other troops about.

I got as far as Ribemont when I found remnants of the 21st Division, but the thing which confused me for a long time, was the number of Divisions which appeared to have stragglers all over the place.

By this time on the Western Front, if one asked an officer or a man what he belonged to, one usually said 'What Division do you belong to' and he replied such & such a Division.

From the various Divisions mentioned, I began to wonder whether things were not much worse than I had previously supposed. It was only when I found a complete party of about 50 Sergeants together, that I found out that all the Schools of Instruction, Courses etc, had been closed down and those attending sent up to do the best they could to fill up the break in the British Front.

I got my Brigade out on a good line East of the ANCRE near TREUX, before daylight.

Next morning (March 27th) at 10 a.m. we were attacked, but we easily disposed of the enemy.

On March 28th we were attacked three times at 6 a.m., 10 a.m. and 1 p.m., but we never gave way a yard.

The attacks were nothing special, rather feeble in fact, but anyhow it gave me the feeling that my men were all right and that it would take a pretty stiff attack to shake them.[1]

Note

1 Brigadier General Sandilands to J. E. Edmonds, 14 August 1923, Cab 45/192, PRO.

APPENDIX II

Biographies of senior officers

ALLENBY, Sir Edmund Henry Hyman (Field Marshal, Viscount Allenby of Megiddo). 'The Bull'. Born 1861. Educated Haileybury, Sandhurst. Joined Inniskilling Dragoons 1882. Bechuanaland and Zululand Expeditions 1884–5. Adjutant 1889–93. Staff College 1896–7. Brigade-Major, 3rd Cavalry Brigade 1898. South Africa, promoted Colonel, commanded regiment and later a column 1899–1902. CO 5th Royal Irish Lancers 1902. GOC 4th Cavalry Brigade 1905. Major General and Inspector General of Cavalry 1909–14. GOC of Cavalry Division, GOC V Corps 1915, GOC Third Army 1915–17. GOC Egyptian Expeditionary Force 1917–18. High Commissioner for Egypt 1919–25, obtained recognition of Egypt as a sovereign state in 1922. Created Viscount 1919. Died 1936.

ALTHAM, Sir Edward (Lieutenant General). Born 1856. Educated Winchester, Oxford. Joined The Royal Scots 1876. Bechuanaland Expedition 1884–5. Intelligence Division, War Office 1897–9 and 1900–4. PSC 1900. AAG for Intelligence, South Africa 1899–1900. General Staff, South Africa 1906–8. In charge of Administration, Southern Command 1914. IGC (Inspector-General Communications) Dardanelles 1915 and Egyptian Expeditionary Force 1916. QMG India 1917–19. Colonel The Royal Scots 1918–34. Died 1943.

ANSTEY, Edgar Carnegie (Brigadier General). Born 1882. Educated Wellington College, Woolwich. Commissioned in RA in 1900. Attended Staff College 1914. Brigade Major in Dardanelles. First World War, GSO 1 in France. 1920–2 Chief Staff Officer to armaments Sub-Commission. Instructor, Senior Officers School, Belgaum, India 1925–8. Brigadier, RA, Western Command, India 1925–8. Brigadier, RA, Western Command, India 1931–2. Brigadier, General Staff, Western Command, India 1932–5. Retired pay 1935. Military correspondent, *Daily Sketch* and *Sunday Times* 1942–4. Died 1958.

BARROW, Sir George De Symons (General). Born 1864. Entered Connaught Rangers 1884. ISC (Imperial Service College) 1886. Promoted Captain 1895. ADC to Commander-in-Chief, East Indies, 1899. Served Waziristan 1894–5, and China 1900. DAQMG, India 1903. DAAG Staff College 1908. General Staff Officer 1914. Served in First World War, promoted Major General. MGGS First Army. GOC Peshawar District 1919–23. GOC Eastern Command, India 1923–8. Retired 1929. Died 1959.

BARTER, Sir Charles St Leger (Lieutenant General). Born 1857. Educated abroad. First commissioned in 1875. PSC. Instructed at Royal Military College

281

1884–9. DAAG, War Office 1889–94. Military Secretary to Governor of Cape Colony and High Commissioner of South Africa, 1894–5. Participated in Ashanti Expedition, 1895–6, the Tirah Campaign, 1897–8, and the Boer War 1899–1901. First World War, GOC 47 Division. Sent home in 1916. Died 1931.

BIRCH, Sir James Frederick Noel (General). Born 1865. Educated Marlborough, Woolwich. Joined RA 1885. 1894 ADC to GOC Woolwich district, 1894. Ashanti expedition 1895–6. South Africa RHA battery, promoted Major, commanded battalion 1900–1. Commanded riding establishment, Woolwich 1905–7. Promoted Lieutenant Colonel 1912, CO 7th Brigade, RHA until 1915. Brigadier General, CRA 7 Division, later CRA I Corps under Haig. 1916–18, MGRA GHQ under Haig. Promoted Major General 1917, Lieutenant General 1919. Director of Remounts, 1920–1. Director General of Territorial Army 1921–3. MGO 1923–7. Retired 1927. Died 1939.

BIRDWOOD, Baron William Riddell (Field Marshal, Baron Birdwood of Anzac and Totnes). Born 1865. Educated Clifton, Sandhurst. Joined Royal Scots Fusiliers 1883. India, 1885–99, 12th Lancers, 11th Bengal Lancers, Viceroy's Bodyguard. Promoted Captain 1896. South Africa, DAAG to Kitchener, 1899–1902. Promoted Colonel 1905. 1909–12 commanded Kohat Independent Brigade. Secretary, Indian Army Department, 1912–14. First World War, Lieutenant General, GOC Australian and New Zealand troops in Egypt. Gallipoli 1915–16. GOC I Anzac Corps in France and combined Australian Corps 1916–18. Promoted General 1917. May 1918, GOC Fifth Army. 1919 created Baron. Commanded Northern Army, India 1920–4. Field Marshal 1925. Commander-in-Chief India until 1930. Died 1951.

BONHAM-CARTER, Sir Charles (General). Born 1876. Educated Clifton College, Sandhurst. PSC. Served in South African War 1900–1. Participated in First World War 1914–17, BGGS, SD and Training, GHQ. Promoted Major General 1926. Director of Staff Duties, War Office, 1927–31. GOC 4 Division 1931–3. Promoted Lieutenant General 1933. Director General of Territorial Army 1933–6. Appointed Governor and Commander-in-Chief of Malta 1936–41. Promoted General 1937. Retired 1940. Died 1955.

BRIDGES, Sir George Tom Molesworth (Lieutenant General). Born 1871. Educated Newton Abbot College, Woolwich. Joined RA, 1892. South Africa, served with Imperial Light Horse, promoted Captain 1901, commanded 5th and 6th West Australian Mounted Infantry. Promoted Major 1902. Commanded Tribal Horse, Somaliland, until 1904. Staff College 1905–6. 1907, Military Intelligence at War Office, Instructor at Cavalry School. Major with 4th Dragoon Guards, 1908. 1910–14, Military Attaché (Belgium, Netherlands, Denmark, Norway). Lieutenant Colonel 4th Hussars, 1914. GOC 19 Division 1916–17, promoted Major General. Mission to USA 1917, 1918. GOC 19 Division, 1917–18. Lost leg at Passchendaele. 1919 Chief of British Military mission, Army of Orient (Salonika). 1920, aided in evacuation of White Russian Army, in Greek–Turkish War, Smyrna. Governor of South Australia, 1922–7. Died 1939.

BROAD, Sir Charles Noel Frank (Lieutenant General). Born 1882. Educated Wellington, Cambridge. Entered RA 1905. First World War, Tank Corps 1916. 1924–7, Commandant Tank Gunnery School. DSD 1927. Commanded armoured brigade in exercises, 1931. BGGS Aldershot, 1931–4. Brigade Commander India 1935–7. GOC Aldershot 1929–40. GOC Eastern Army India 1940–2. Retired 1942.

BUTLER, Sir Richard Harte Keatinge (Lieutenant General). Born 1870. Educated Harrow, Sandhurst. Joined Dorsetshire Regiment, 1890. Promoted Lieutenant 1892. Captain 1894. South Africa, distinguished service with 5 Division's mounted infantry. Promoted Major. PSC 1906. GSO 2 at Aldershot 1911. Lieutenant Colonel 1913. First World War, CO 2nd Lancashire Fusiliers, GOC 3rd Brigade. BGGS I Corps, 1915. Major General, Deputy Chief of Staff, First Army under Haig, June 1915–18. GOC III Corps, 1918. GOC of a Division on the Rhine and later GOC I Division at Aldershot, 1919–23. Promoted Lieutenant General 1923. GOC Western Command 1924–8. Died 1935.

BYNG, the Hon. Sir Julian Hedworth George (Field Marshal, Viscount Byng of Vimy). Born 1862. Educated Eton. 1883 joined 10th Hussars. Soudan 1884. Promoted Captain 1889. Staff College 1894. Promoted Major 1898. Raised and commanded South African Light Horse, 1900–1. Commanded 10th Hussars 1902, 2nd Cavalry Brigade (Eastern Command) 1905, 1st Cavalry Brigade (Aldershot) 1907, Territorial East Anglian Division 1910. Promoted Major General 1909. First World War, GOC 3 Cavalry Division (Ypres) 1914, Cavalry Corps 1915, and IX Corps (Suvla) 1915. GOC Canadian Corps 1916–17. Captured Vimy Ridge, April 1917. GOC Third Army 1917–19. Promoted General 1917. Governor General of Canada, 1921–6. Viscount 1928. Field Marshal 1932. Died 1935.

CAVAN, Frederick Rudolph Lambart (Field Marshal, the Earl of Cavan). Born 1865. Educated Eton, Sandhurst. Joined Grenadier Guards 1885. ADC to Governor General of Canada 1891–3. Served in South Africa 1901. Retired 1913. Recalled 1914. GOC 4th Guards Brigade, GOC Guards Division (Battle of Loos), 1915, GOC XIV Corps (Somme and Third Ypres) 1916–17. Took XIV Corps to Italy, 1917. Succeeded as GOC of British troops in Italy, March 1918. Piave River crossing. ADC to the king, 1920–2. Commander-in-Chief, Aldershot 1920–2. Head of War Office Section of British Delegation at Washington Conference, 1921. Promoted General 1921. CIGS 1922–6. Field Marshal 1932. Died 1946.

CHARTERIS, John (Brigadier General). Born 1877. Educated Merchiston School, Woolwich. Entered Army 1896. Promoted Captain 1905. Staff Captain 1909–10. Headquarters, India. 1910–12, GSO 2. AMS (Assistant Military Secretary) to GOC at Aldershot, 1912–14. First World War 1914–17, DSO. 1916–17, Brigadier General, Intelligence, General Headquarters. Promoted Colonel 1917. 1918, Deputy Director General, Transportation. DQMG India 1920. DA and QMG Eastern Command, India 1921–2. Retired 1922. MP for Dumfriesshire 1924–9. Author, *Field Marshal Earl Haig* (1929), *At GHQ* (1931), *Haig* (1933). Died 1946.

CLIVE, Sir (George) Sidney (Lieutenant General). Born 1874. Educated Harrow, Sandhurst. Joined Grenadier Guards in 1893. Served in Nile Expedition 1898 and in South African War, 1899–1902. Promoted Captain 1900. Attended Staff College 1903–4. GSO War Office, 1905–9. Served First World War 1914–18 at GQG and GHQ. British Military Representative, League of Nations, Geneva, 1920–2. Appointed Military Attaché 1924–7. Promoted Major General 1924.

Director of Personal Services, War Office 1928–30. Military Secretary to Secretary of State for War 1930–4. Promoted Lieutenant General 1932. Retired 1934. Died 1959.

CONGREVE, Sir Walter Norris (General). Born 1862. Educated Harrow, Oxford, Sandhurst. Entered Army 1883. Joined Rifle Brigade 1885. Promoted Captain 1893. Served in South Africa 1899–1902, VC earned at Colenso. Promoted Major and Lieutenant Colonel 1901, Colonel 1908, commanded School of Musketry, Hythe, 1909. Major General 1915. GOC 6 Division, 1915, GOC XIII Corps 1916 (Battle of Somme), GOC VII Corps 1918. Transferred to GOC X Corps. Promoted Lieutenant General 1918. GOC British forces in Egypt 1919–23. General 1922. GOC Southern Command 1923. Governor of Malta 1925. Died 1927.

DAVIDSON, Sir John Humphrey (Major General). Born 1876. Educated Harrow, Sandhurst. Joined KRRC (King's Royal Rifle Corps) 1896. South Africa 1899–1902. Entered Staff College by nomination, 1905. GSO 3, Military Training Directorate of new General Staff, 1908–10. Brigade Major, 5th Infantry Brigade (Aldershot). Instructor, training and tactics, Staff College, 1912–14. First World War, GSO 2 (Intelligence) III Corps, 1914. Operations Officer to Sir Douglas Haig, 1915. DMO, GHQ, 1915–18. Promoted Major General 1918. Conservative MP, Fareham, 1918–31. Various directorships. Died 1954.

De LISLE, Sir Henry de Beauvoir (General). Born 1864, son of Richard de Lisle. Educated Jersey, Sandhurst. 1883 joined 2nd Durham Light Infantry (Gibraltar). In Egypt with Mounted Infantry, 1885–6. Promoted Captain 1891. Staff College 1899. In South Africa, raised and commanded 6th Mounted Infantry and 2nd MI Corps, 1900, commanded independent column of mounted infantry 1900–2. Promoted Major 1902, Lieutenant Colonel 1906. Commanded 1st Royal Dragoons 1906–10. Promoted Colonel 1910. General Staff, Aldershot 1910–11. First World War, GOC 2nd Cavalry Brigade, I Cavalry Division, 29 Division, XIII Corps, and then XV Corps. Promoted Major General and Lieutenant General in the field. GOC Western Command, 1919–23. Retired 1926. Wrote books on polo. Died 1955.

DILL, Sir John Grier (Field Marshal). Born 1881. Educated Cheltenham College, Sandhurst. Joined 1st Battalion in South Africa, 1901. Promoted Captain 1911, Brigade Major to 25th Brigade, 1914. Staff College, 1914. GSO 2 to Canadian Corps in 1916. Promoted Major 1916. GSO 1 to 27 Division 1917. Chief of operations branch, GHQ 1918. Promoted Colonel 1920. Army instructor, Imperial Defence College, 1926–9. Chief General Staff Officer, Western Command, India 1929–30. Promoted Major General 1932. Commandant Staff College 1931–4. DMO and Intelligence, War Office 1934–6. GOC Aldershot Command 1937–9. Second World War, GOC I Corps 1939–40. ADC to the king. CIGS 1940–1. British military representative, Washington 1941–4. Died 1944.

Du CANE, Sir John Philip (General). Born 1865. Joined RA 1884. Promoted Captain 1893. South Africa, 1899–1902. Promoted Major 1900 and Lieutenant Colonel 1902. 1905–7 DAAG Staff College. GSO 1, Army HQ 1908–10. CRA 3 Division, 1911–12. Staff Officer to Inspector General of Home Forces 1913–14. First World War, BGGS III Corps, 1914. Promoted Major General

1915, MGRA GHQ. Given special appointment, Ministry of Munitions, 1916. GOC XV Corps, 1916–18. British Representative with Marshal Foch 1918. MGO 1920–3. GOC Western Command 1923–4, and British Army of the Rhine 1924–7. ADC to the king 1926–30. Governor and Commander-in-Chief Malta 1927–31. Retired 1931. Died 1947.

EDMONDS, Sir James Edward (Brigadier General). Born 1861. Educated at King's College School, Woolwich. Joined Royal Engineers 1881. Instructor in fortification at Royal Military Academy 1890–6. South Africa, served as Lord Kitchener's adviser on international law. DAAG GHQ 1899–1901. In charge of MO5 (later MI5) 1907–11. Promoted Colonel 1909. GSO 1, 4 Division 1911–14. With engineer in chief, GHQ France 1914–18 (Deputy Engineer in chief, 1918). Director Military Branch, Historical Section, Committee of Imperial Defence 1919–49. Edited British *Official History*, France and Belgium. Wrote other military books. Died 1956.

ELLES, Sir Hugh Jamieson (General). Born 1880. Educated Clifton College, Woolwich. Joined Royal Engineers 1899. Served in South African War, 1901–2. Promoted Captain 1908. Staff College 1913–14. Promoted Brigade Major 1915. Commanded Tank Corps in France 1916–18. Promoted Brigadier General 1917, Temporary Major General 1918. Commanded Tank Corps training centre, at Wool, 1919–23. Promoted Major General 1928. GOC 42 Division. DMT 1930–3. MGO 1934–8. Promoted General 1938. Civil defence commissioner for south-west England 1939–45. Died 1945.

FANSHAWE, Sir Edward Arthur (Lieutenant General). Born 1859. Educated Winchester. Entered RA 1878. Promoted Captain 1886. Served in Afghan War 1878–80 and in the Sudan 1885. Major 1896. Served in First World War 1914–18, during which he was promoted Major General 1915 and Lieutenant General 1916. GOC V Corps. Retired 1923. Colonel Commandant RA 1923–34, RHA 1930–4. Died 1952.

FRANKS, Sir George McKenzie (Major General). Born 1868. Educated Marlborough. Entered RA 1887. Served Waziristan 1894–5; NW Frontier, India; and Nile Expeditions 1898 and 1899. Instructor, Staff College, India, 1909–12. Served First World War as GOC 35 Division. Promoted Major General. Inspector General of Artillery, Great Britain, 1918–20. GOC Meerut District, India 1925–8. Retired 1928. Colonel Commandant RA 1931–8. Died 1958.

FRENCH, John Denton Pinkstone (Field Marshal, first Earl of Ypres). Born 1852. Educated Eastman's Naval Academy, Portsmouth. HMS *Britannia* 1866. Midshipman 1868. Joined Suffolk artillery militia 1870. Joined the 8th Hussars 1874. Expedition to relieve General Gordon, 1884–5. CO 19th Hussars 1888. Became Colonel and AAG, War Office 1895. During South African War, dispatched to Natal, commanded mounted troops under Sir G. S. White 1899. Relieved Kimberley 1900. Promoted Lieutenant General 1902. Commander-in-Chief, Aldershot 1902–7. Promoted General 1907. Inspector General of Forces 1907. Promoted Field Marshal 1913, resigned appointment 1914 over Curragh incident. August 1914 appointed Commander-in-Chief BEF. Removed as Commander-in-Chief BEF in December 1915. Created Viscount and given command of Home forces 1916. Lord Lieutenant of Ireland, 1918–21. Created Earl 1922. Died 1925.

FULLER, John Frederick Charles (Major General). 'Boney'. Born 1878. Educated

Malvern College, Sandhurst. 1898 joined 1st Battalion, Oxfordshire Light Infantry. Served in South African War 1899–1902. Served with a regiment in India 1902–6, Captain in 1905. Staff College 1913. Transportation Officer, Southampton docks 1914. In France 1915–16, GSO 3 VIII Corps, GSO 2 of 37 Division, GSO 2 of Third Army under General Allenby, GSO 2 to Tank Corps under General Elles. Planner for battle of Cambrai, 1917. Tank branch, GS War Office, 1918. Senior instructor, Staff College 1923. Promoted Major General 1930. Retired 1933. Numerous and influential publications. Died 1966.

FURSE, Sir William Thomas (Lieutenant General). Born 1865. Educated Eton, Sandhurst. ADC to Lord Roberts, Commander in Chief, India 1890–3. Promoted Captain 1893. PSC 1897. Army HQ 1897–1902. Promoted Major 1900. DAQMG II Corps, 1902–4. Army HQ 1905–7. GSO 2 Staff College 1908–11. CO 12th Brigade RFA 1911–13. Promoted Colonel 1911. Served First World War 1914–16; GSO 1 6 Division 1913–14. BGGS II Corps 1915. GOC 9 Scottish Division 1915–16. MGO, 1916. Army Council. Retired 1920. Director of Imperial Institute 1926–34. Died 1953.

GOUGH, Sir Hubert de la Poer (General). Born 1870. Educated Eton, Sandhurst. Joined 16th Lancers 1889. Served Tirah Expedition 1897–8, South African War 1899–1902. Instructor Staff College 1903–6. CO 16th Lancers, GOC 3rd Cavalry Brigade, 1911. Promoted Major General 1914, GOC 2 Cavalry Division at first Battle of Ypres. In March 1915, GOC 7 Division, and later 1915, as Lieutenant General, appointed GOC I Corps. In 1916, GOC Fifth Army at the Somme, and in 1917, at Passchendaele. Replaced by Sir Henry Rawlinson, March 1918. Chief Allied Mission, Baltic, 1919. Retired as General in 1922. Published defence of Fifth Army in 1931. Died 1963.

GREENLY, Walter Howorth (Major General). Born 1875. Educated Eton, Sandhurst. Joined 12th Lancers in 1895. Served in South Africa 1899–1902. Lieutenant Colonel 19th Hussars 1912–16. GOC 2 Cavalry Division 1916–18. Promoted Major General. GOC 14 Division, 1918. Chief of Military Mission, Romania, 1918–20. Retired 1920. Died 1955.

HAIG, Douglas (Field Marshal, first Earl Haig). 'Lucky' Haig. Born 1861. Educated Clifton, Oxford, Sandhurst. Joined 7th Hussars 1885. Staff College 1896–7. Special service officer in Sudan campaign 1898. Staff officer under Colonel John French in South Africa 1899. 1901–2, column commander. Inspector General for Cavalry in India 1903–6. Promoted Major General 1904. DMT 1906–7. DSD at HQ 1907–9. Chief of Staff to Sir O'Moore Creagh in India in 1909–11. GOC Aldershot 1912–14. Lieutenant General 1910 and General in 1914 for distinguished service. With outbreak of war, Haig took I Corps to France. GOC First Army 1914–15. Commander-in-Chief of the BEF 1915–19. Made Field Marshal 1917. Field Marshal Commander-in-Chief of the forces in Great Britain 1919–20. Died 1928.

HAKING, Sir Richard Cyril Byrne (General). Born 1862. Educated Sandhurst. Entered army 1881. Burma Campaigns 1885–7. Promoted Captain 1889. Staff College 1892. Served in South Africa, promoted to Major 1899. Instructor, Staff College 1901–4. DAAG Staff College 1904–6. GSO 1 3 Division 1906–8. BGGS Southern Command, 1908. GOC 5th Brigade 1911–14. 1914, in France GOC 5th Brigade. GOC 1 Division December 1914. GOC XI Corps 1915–18. Went to Italy, late 1917, with XI Corps. Chief of the British Section Armistice

Commission 1918–19. Military missions Russia and Baltic, 1919. High Commissioner League of Nations, Danzig, 1921–3. Commanded British troops in Egypt 1923–7. Promoted General 1925. Died 1945.

HALDANE, Sir Aylmer L. (General). Born 1862. Educated Edinburgh Academy, Wimbledon School, Sandhurst. Joined Gordon Highlanders 1882. ADC to General Sir W. Lockhart 1896–9. Served Waziristan 1894–9 and Tirah 1897–8, DAAG HQ. South Africa in 1899–1900 with 2nd Gordon Highlanders. Military Attaché with Japanese Army, Russo-Japanese War, 1904–5. First World War, GOC 3 Division and VI Corps. Promoted Major General and Lieutenant General. Appointed GOC Mesopotamia 1920–2. Promoted General 1925. Retired 1925. Died 1950.

HAMILTON, Sir Ian Standish Monteith (General). 'Johnny'. Born 1853. Educated Wellington College, Sandhurst. Posted to Suffolk Regiment, 1872 and to 92nd Highlanders in India, 1874. Participated in the Nile expedition 1884–5 and Burma expedition 1886–7. Promoted Colonel 1891. Commander, School of Musketry at Hythe 1898. South Africa 1899–1901. Chief of Staff to Kitchener, GOC four columns. Promoted Major General and Lieutenant General. 1902, Military Secretary, War Office. QMG to forces 1903–4. Chief of Military Mission to Japanese Army 1904–5. GOC Southern Command 1905–9. AG, 1909–10. GOC Mediterranean and Inspector General overseas Forces 1910–15. March 1915, given command of Anglo-French Army to assist navy in Dardanelles (Gallipoli). Recalled October 1915. Lieutenant, Tower of London, 1918–20. Died 1947.

HARPER, Sir George Montague (Lieutenant General). 'Uncle'. Born 1865. Educated Bath College, Woolwich. Joined Royal Engineers, 1884. Served in South African War 1899–1900. Staff College 1901. DDMO War Office, 1911. First World War GOC 51 (Highland) Division, 1915–18. GOC IV Corps 1918. Promoted Lieutenant General and GOC Southern Command, 1919. Died 1922.

HEADLAM, Sir John Emerson Wharton (Major General). Born 1864. Entered Army 1883. Promoted Captain 1892. Instructor, School of Gunnery 1892–7. Served GHQ South Africa 1900–2. Became Major 1900 and Lieutenant Colonel 1902. HQ 1903–6. Promoted Colonel 1905. GHQ India 1908–13. CRA 5 Division. First World War, promoted Major General for distinguished service in the field. MGRA GHQ. Retired 1921. Colonel Commandant RA, 1928–34. Wrote a three-volume history of the RA. Died 1946.

HORNE, Baron Henry Sinclair (General). Born 1861. Educated Harrow, Woolwich. Entered RA 1880. South African War 1899–1902. CO Artillery Depot at Weedon 1902–5. Inspector of Field Artillery and then Horse Artillery Brigades in Ireland 1905–12. Inspector Horse and Field Artillery, 1912. BGRA I Corps 1914. GOC 2 Division, 1915. Dardanelles 1915. GOC XV Corps, Somme 1916. GOC First Army 1916, Vimy Ridge 1917, 1918. Promoted General 1919. Created Baron 1919, and received £30,000. GOC Eastern Command 1919–23. Retired 1926. Died 1929.

HUNTER-WESTON, Sir Aylmer Gould (Lieutenant General). Born 1864. Educated Wellington College, Woolwich. Entered Royal Engineers 1884. Promoted Captain 1892. Staff College 1898–9 (Master of Staff College Hounds). Served in South Africa 1899–1901, first in command of Mounted Engineers, then of Royal Engineers Cavalry Division. DAAG Cavalry Division. Chief of Staff to

Colonel French's Cavalry Division, and given independent command of a cavalry column. GSO Eastern Command, 1904–8. GSO Scottish Command 1908–11. Assistant DMT, War Office 1911–14. GOC 11th Infantry Brigade. GOC 29 Division in Gallipoli, GOC VIII Corps in Gallipoli and at Somme. Temporary Lieutenant General 1915, and GOC VIII Corps to end of war. Promoted Lieutenant General 1919. MP 1916–35. Died 1940.

JARDINE, James Bruce (Brigadier General). Born 1870. Educated Charterhouse, Sandhurst. Joined 5th Lancers 1890. Served in South Africa 1899–1902. Staff Officer to Colonel Callwell's column. Promoted Captain 1901. Attached to Japanese Army, 1903. Military Attaché to General Kuroki's Army during all operations in Manchuria, 1904–5. GOC 97th Brigade, First World War. Promoted Lieutenant Colonel 1917. Died 1955.

JEUDWINE, Sir Hugh Sandham (Lieutenant General). Born 1862. Educated Eton, Woolwich. Entered RA 1882. Promoted Captain 1891. Instructor School of Gunnery 1894–9. Served in South African War 1899–1902, commanded mobile column. Promoted Major 1900, Lieutenant Colonel 1908, Colonel 1912. GSO 2 Staff College 1912, and GSO 1 Staff College 1913. First World War, GSO 1 I Corps 1914, GSO 1 Division, 1914. BGGS V Corps, 1915. GOC 41st Brigade 1915 and GOC 55 Division 1916–19. CGS British Army of the Rhine 1919. GOC 5 Division on active service in Ireland 1919–22. Director General Territorial Army 1923–7. Retired 1927. Died 1942.

KENTISH, Reginald John (Brigadier General). Born 1876. Educated Malvern, Sandhurst. Entered Army 1897. Served in South Africa 1899–1902. Promoted Captain 1902. ADC to GOC 2 Division, 1910. Brigade Major, 6th London Infantry Brigade, 1912–14. 14th Brigade, 1916. Commandant Senior Officers School, Aldershot, and Brigadier General 1916–18. Retired 1922. Founded National Playing Fields Association, 1925. Died 1956.

KIGGELL, Sir Launcelot Edward (Lieutenant General). 'Kigg'. Born 1862. Educated Ireland, Sandhurst. Gazetted to Royal Warwickshire Regiment 1882. Adjutant of 2nd Battalion 1886–90. Staff College 1893–4. Instructor at Royal Military College 1895–7. DAAG South Eastern District 1897–9. Staff, South African War 1899–1904. DAAG, Staff College 1904–7. GSO Army HQ 1907–9. DSD, War Office 1909–13. Commandant, Staff College 1913–14. Director of Home Defence, War Office 1914–15. CGS to BEF (GHQ) December 1915 to January 1918. Promoted Lieutenant General 1917. GOC and Lieutenant Governor of Guernsey, 1918–20. Retired 1920. Died 1954.

LINDSAY, George Mackintosh (Major General). Born 1880. Educated Radley. Joined Royal Monmouthshire Royal Engineers (Militia). Commissioned in Rifle Brigade 1900. Served South African War 1900–2. Adjutant Customs and Docks Rifle Volunteers 1907–8 and of 17th Battalion the London Regiment 1908–11. Instructor at School of Musketry, Hythe, 1913–15. Instructor, Machine Gun Corps Training Centre, Grantham 1915–16. Brigade Major 99th Infantry Brigade 1916–17. Chief Instructor Machine Gun School 1917–18. Machine Gun Officer, First Army, 1918. CO 41st Battalion Machine Gun Corps, Germany 1919. Attended Staff College 1920. GOC No. 1 Armoured Car Group, Iraq 1921–3. Inspector Royal Tank Corps, 1925–9. BGGS Egypt Command 1929–32. GOC 7th Brigade 1932–4. Major General

1934. Commander Presidency and Assam District, India 1935–9. Colonel Commandant, Royal Tank Regiment 1938–47. Died 1956.

LUCKOCK, Russel Mortimer (Major General). Born 1877. Educated Harrow, Cambridge. Gazetted into King's Own Regiment 1900. Served South Africa 1899–1902. Assistant Instructor School of Musketry, Hythe 1908–11. Staff College 1913–14. Brigade Major 24th Brigade 1915. GSO 1 17 Division 1915. GSO 1 Fourth Army 1916–18. GSO 1 Staff College, Camberley 1919–21. Promoted Colonel 1922. Commandant, Small Arms School, India 1922–5. BGGS Southern Command, 1928–32. Promoted Major General 1932. GOC 54 Division 1934–8. Retired 1938. Died 1950.

MACDONOGH, Sir George Mark Watson (Lieutenant General). Born 1865. Entered Army 1884. Captain 1892, Major 1901, and Lieutenant Colonel 1909. GSO 1, War Office, 1912 when he was promoted Colonel. Served in France 1914–16. Promoted Major General and DMI, War Office 1916–18. AG 1918–22. Died 1942.

MALCOLM, Neill (Major General). Born 1869. Educated Eton, Sandhurst. Entered Army 1889. Served Northwest Frontier of India 1897–8, Uganda 1899, South Africa 1899–1900, and Somaliland 1903–4. First World War CGS to Gough's Fifth Army and GOC 66 Division. Promoted Major General. Undertook British Military Mission to Berlin 1919–21. Appointed GOC Malaya 1921–4. Retired 1924. High Commissioner for German Refugees, 1936–8. Died 1953.

MAXSE, Sir (Frederick) Ivor (General). Born 1862. Educated Rugby, Sandhurst. Commisioned into 7th Fusiliers in 1882. Captain Coldstream Guards 1891. Seconded to Egyptian Army 1897–9. Lord Roberts's Staff in South Africa 1899–1902. CO 2nd Battalion Coldstream Guards 1903–7, and Coldstream Regiment of Foot Guards 1907–10. GOC 1st Guards Brigade 1914–15. Promoted to Major General and GOC 18 Division 1915–17. Promoted Lieutenant General in command of XVIII Corps 1917–18. Inspector General of Training to the British Armies in France 1918–19. GOC Northern Command, 1919–23. Promoted General 1923. Retired 1926. Died 1958.

MONRO, Sir Charles Carmichael (General). Born 1860. Educated Sherborne, Sandhurst. Gazetted to 2nd Foot in 1879. Staff College 1889–90. South Africa 1899–1900. Chief Instructor, School of Musketry, Hythe, 1901–3, and Commandant 1903–7. GOC 13th Brigade, Dublin 1907–12. GOC 2 Division 1914. GOC I Corps in December 1914. Promoted Lieutenant General, 1915, and commanded force at Gallipoli, GOC Third Army, 1915. GOC First Army in France 1916. Promoted General 1917. Commander-in-Chief, India 1916–20. Governor of Gibraltar 1923–8. Died 1929.

MONTGOMERY, Sir Archibald Armar (Field Marshal). 'Archie'. (Assumed name of Montgomery-Massingberd 1926.) Born 1871. Educated Charterhouse, Woolwich. Gazetted into RA 1891. Served in South Africa 1899–1902. Staff College 1905. Entered First World War as GSO 2 4 Division. Acting GSO 1 when Lord Rawlinson became GOC Fourth Army. Became Chief of Staff IV Corps 1915, and of Fourth Army 1916–18. Promoted Major General. 1919, Chief of Staff Army of the Rhine. Deputy Chief of General Staff, India, 1920–2. GOC 1 Division 1923–6. GOC Southern Command 1928–31. AG 1931–3. Lieutenant General 1930. CIGS 1933–6. Field Marshal 1935. Died 1947.

OXLEY, Reginald Stewart (Brigadier General). Born 1863. Educated Charterhouse, Sandhurst. Entered KRRC (King's Royal Rifle Corps) 1884. Served at Manipur 1891. Brigade Major, 12th Infantry Brigade, South African War 1899–1900. Appointed DAAG Northwest District 1901–4. GSO 1 Staff College 1912–14. Brigadier General, GOC 24th Brigade 1915–16. DA and QMG 1916–19. Died 1951.

PHILIPPS, Sir Ivor (Major General). Born 1861. Educated Felsted. PSC. Served in Militia 1881–3 and in Indian Army 1882–1903. Served Burma 1887–9, Chin Lesnai 1889, Miranzai 1891, Isazai 1892, Northwest Frontier 1896, Tirah 1896–7, China 1900–1. Promoted Major 1901. Liberal MP, Southampton, 1906–22. CO Pembroke Yeomanry, 1908–12. Brigadier General, 1914. GOC 115th Brigade. Parliamentary Secretary to Ministry of Munitions, 1915. Raised and served as GOC 38 Welsh Division, 1915–16. Removed as GOC. Made honorary Major General in 1916. Governor of Pembroke Castle, 1917. Died 1940.

PILCHER, Thomas David (Major General). Born 1858. Educated Harrow. Joined 5th Fusiliers, 1879. Served Niger 1897–8. Raised 1st Battalion West African Field Force 1899, and commanded expedition to Lapai and Argeyah. CO 2nd Bedfordshire Regiment. South Africa 1899–1902, commanded mounted column. Promoted Colonel. 1901, appointed ADC to the king. Major General 1907, held various commands in India until 1914. First World War, GOC 17 Division, 1915–16. Author of several volumes on military matters. Died 1928.

PLUMER, Herbert Charles Onslow (Field Marshal, first Viscount Plumer). 'Plum'. Educated Eton. Joined 65th Foot 1876. Served in Sudan, 1884. Staff College 1885. Raised the Rhodesian Horse at Bulawayo, 1899. Served in South Africa 1899–1900 and again 1901–2. Promoted Major General 1902 and QMG 1903. Commanded 5 Division (Irish Command) 1906–9. GOC Northern Command 1911–14. GOC V Corps 1915, GOC Second Army, 1915–17. GOC Italian Expeditionary Force, November 1917–March 1918. GOC Second Army 1918, and GOC Army of the Rhine 1919. Governor and Commander-in-Chief Malta 1919–24. High Commissioner for Palestine 1925–8. Died 1932.

PULTENEY, Sir William (Lieutenant General). Born 1861. Educated Eton. Joined Scots Guards 1881 and served Egypt 1882. Employed Foreign Office in Uganda, 1885–95. Served in South Africa 1899–1902. From 1908–9 GOC 16th Infantry Brigade and then GOC 6 Division, the Irish Command, 1910–14. First World War, GOC III Corps. Undertook mission to Japan 1918. Black Rod to House of Lords from 1920. Died 1941.

RAWLINSON, Sir Henry Seymour (General and Baron). 'Rawly'. Born 1864. Educated Eton, Sandhurst. Commissioned to King's Royal Rifles, 1884. Served in India and Burma 1884–9. Transferred to Coldstream Guards, 1892. Staff College 1892–3. DAAG to Kitchener in Sudan, 1898. Served in South African War, commanded mobile column. Brigadier General and commandant of Staff College 1903–6. GOC 2nd Brigade 1907–9. Promoted Major General 1909. GOC 3 Division 1910–14. ADC to the king. GOC IV Corps 1914–15. Given temporary command of First Army 1915. Lieutenant General and GOC Fourth Army 1916–17. General 1917. Served as British military representative on Supreme War Council, 1918. GOC Fifth Army, which he reconstituted as Fourth Army, 1918. Commander-in-Chief, India 1920–5. Died 1925.

ROBERTSON, Sir William Robert (Field Marshal, first baronet). 'Wully'. Born

1860. Educated private school. Enlisted in ranks, 16th Lancers, 1877. Troop sergeant 1885. Lieutenant 3rd Dragoon Guards India, 1888. Transport officer, Niranzai and Black Mountain, 1891. Staff Captain and DAQMG Intelligence Branch, Simla 1892–6. Staff College 1896, the first 'ranker' to enter. Head of foreign section, intelligence department War Office, 1900–7. BGGS Aldershot, 1907–10. Promoted Major General 1910. Commandant Staff College 1910–13. DMT 1913–14. Quartermaster General, GHQ France until early 1915. CGS, GHQ, 1915. CIGS 1915–18. GOC Eastern Command 1918. GOC Home Forces, 1918–19. Commander-in-Chief, British Army on the Rhine, 1919–20. Promoted Field Marshal 1920. Died 1933.

RYCROFT, Sir William Henry (Major General). Born 1861. Educated Eton, Sandhurst. Joined 71st HLI (Highland Light Infantry) in 1879. Served in Nile Expedition 1884–5 and with Egyptian Army 1886–7. Transferred into 7th Dragoon Guards 1888. Attended Staff College 1891–2. DAAG York 1895–6. Joined 11th Hussars 1896, which he commanded 1904–8. In 1897–8, served Northwest Frontier of India. DAAG Cairo 1898–9. On staff, South Africa, 1899–1900. Served in Somaliland 1902–3. Staff in South Africa, 1911–12. AQMG Southern Command, 1913–14. First World War, promoted Major General, GOC 32 Division, 1916. Removed. Retired 1921. Died 1925.

SANDILANDS, Henry George (Brigadier General). Born 1864. Entered Army 1884. Promoted Captain 1893. Served Northwest Frontier India 1897–8, South African War 1899–1900. Promoted Major 1900. Member of Australian Military Forces in 1907–9. Lt Col. 1910, Colonel 1913. First World War, GOC 104th Brigade. Retired 1919. Died 1930.

SHEA, John Stuart MacKenzie (General). Born 1869. Educated Sedbergh, Sandhurst. Joined Royal Irish Regiment, 1888. Lieutenant 15th Lancers, 1891. Chitral 1895. Promoted Captain 1899. Served South Africa 1900–2. Promoted Major 1906. First World War, promoted Major General, GOC 30 Division. GOC Central Provinces District, India, 1921–3. Promoted Lieutenant General 1921. AG India 1924–8. Promoted General 1926. GOC Eastern Command, India. Retired 1932. Served in Second World War. Died 1966.

SMITH-DORRIEN, Sir Horace Lockwood (General). Born 1858. Educated Harrow, Sandhurst. PSC. Commissioned in 95th Foot 1877. Zulu War 1879. Raised and commanded Corps of Mounted Infantry, Egyptian War, 1882. Nile 1884. Sudan 1885–6. Served in India 1889–98. DAAG Bengal 1893–4, AAG Punjab 1894–6, DAAG Chitral 1895, Tirah 1897–8, Nile 1898. Served in South Africa 1899–1901, where he commanded a Brigade and a Division, and was promoted Major General. AG India, 1901–3. GOC 4 Division, India, 1903–7. GOC Aldershot 1907–12. GOC Southern Command 1912–14. Lieutenant General 1906 and General 1912. GOC II Corps in August 1914. GOC Second Army, 1915. Removed. GOC First Army, Home Defence 1915 and Governor of Gibraltar 1918–23. Retired 1923. Died 1930.

SNOW, Sir Thomas D'Oyly (Lieutenant General). Born 1858. Educated Eton, Cambridge. Commissioned in 13th Foot, 1879. Zulu War 1879, Sudan 1884–5, Sudan 1898. Promoted Major into Royal Inniskilling Fusiliers. 1903, AQMG of IV Corps (later the Eastern Command). AAG in 1905. BGGS, 1906. GOC 11th Brigade in 1909. GOC 4 Division in 1911. Took this Division to France in 1914. GOC 27 Division in 1915. Later GOC VII Corps, 1915–18.

GOC Western Command 1918–19. Promoted Lieutenant General 1917. Died 1940.

STEPHENS, Sir Reginald (General). Born 1869. Educated Winchester. Served in South Africa 1897 and in Nile Expedition 1898. In South Africa 1899–1902. First World War, promoted Major General, GOC 5 Division. Corps commander 1918–19. Commandant Royal Military College, 1919–23. GOC 4 Division 1923–6. Promoted Lieutenant General 1925. Director General of Territorial Army 1927–31. Promoted General 1930. Retired 1931. Died 1955.

STUART-WORTLEY, the Hon. Edward James Montagu (Major General). Born 1857. Educated Eton. Served Afghan War 1879–80 and South African War of 1881. Appointed Military Secretary to General Valentine Baker in Egypt 1882. ADC to General Sir Evelyn Wood in Egypt 1883–4. Served in Nile Expedition 1884–5. Military Attaché to Sir H. Drummond Wolff's special mission to Turkey in 1885. DAAG to Sir F. Grenfell. 2nd in command, gunboat flotilla, 1897–8. Brigade Major 1893–6 in Malta. PSC. Served South Africa 1900–1, commanded Battalion of Rifles at relief of Ladysmith. Military Attaché in Paris 1901–4. GOC 10th Infantry Brigade, 1908–12. GOC 46 (North Midland) Division to 1916. Removed. GOC 65 Division in Ireland. Died 1934.

SWINTON, Sir Ernest Dunlop (Major General). Born 1868. Educated Rugby, Cheltenham, Woolwich. Commissioned in Royal Engineers 1888. Served in South African War 1899–1902. Promoted Captain 1899. Promoted Major 1906. Chief instructor in fortification and geometrical drawing, Woolwich 1907–10. Assistant secretary to Committee of Imperial Defence 1913. Deputy Director Railway Transport, 1914. Official War Correspondent 1914–15. Promoted Colonel 1915. Given appointment to command training of new tank corps, 1916. Became Assistant Secretary, Committee of Imperial Defence, 1916. Accompanied Lord Reading to United States 1917 and 1918. Colonel Commandant of Royal Tank Corps 1934–8. Numerous publications. Chichele Professor of Military History, Oxford, 1925–39. Died 1951.

TURNER, Richard Ernest William (Lieutenant General). Born 1871. Educated Quebec. Served in South Africa with Royal Canadian Dragoons under Smith-Dorrien. CO, King's Royal Colonial Escort at coronation, 1902 and of 10th Queen's Own Canadian Hussars, 1905. Commanded 3rd Eastern Townships Cavalry Brigade, 1907. In 1914, GOC of 3rd Canadian Infantry Brigade. Assumed command of 1 Canadian Division in 1915. Promoted Major General 1915, GOC 2 Canadian Division 1915–16. GOC Canadian Troops in British Isles, November 1916–18. Promoted Lieutenant General 1918. Died 1961.

WATTS, Sir Herbert Edward (Lieutenant General). Born 1858. Entered Army 1880. Promoted Captain 1889. Adjutant, Militia 1894–9. Promoted Major 1899. Served South Africa 1899–1902. Promoted Lieutenant Colonel 1904 and Colonel 1908. Commanded No. 9 District, 1910–14. Retired 1914. GOC 38 Division and XIX Corps, First World War. Promoted Lieutenant General. Died 1934.

WHIGHAM, Sir Robert Dundas (General). Born 1865. Educated Fettes College, Sandhurst. Joined 1st Battalion of Royal Warwickshire Regiment, 1885. Served Nile Expedition 1898 and South African Campaign 1899–1902. First World War, Deputy CIGS 1916–18. GOC 62 (West Riding) Division, 1918.

AG 1923–7. GOC Eastern Command 1927–31. ADC to king 1930–1. Retired 1931. Died 1950.

WIGRAM, Clive (Colonel, first Baron Wigram). Born 1873. Educated Winchester. Gazetted into RA 1893. Served in India, ADC to Lord Elgin, Viceroy of India 1895, exchanged to 18th Lancers, Indian Army 1897. Northwest Frontier, 1897–8. Served in South Africa 1898–1902. Assistant to the Chief of the Staff during HRH the Prince of Wales' visit to India 1905–6. Indian Staff College 1906–8. Military Secretary to GOC Aldershot Command, 1908–10. Assistant Private Secretary and Equerry to the king 1910–31, Private Secretary and Equerry 1931–5. Married Nora, only daughter of Sir Neville Chamberlain, in 1912. Died 1960.

WILSON, Sir Henry Hughes (Field Marshal). Born 1864. Educated Marlborough. Repeatedly failed to gain entry to Woolwich and Sandhurst. Commissioned in Longford Militia 1882. Transferred to Rifle Brigade 1884. Burma campaign 1885–9, and 1887–9. Staff College 1892–4. Staff Captain Intelligence Division 1894–7. Brigade Major, 2nd Brigade, Aldershot 1897–9. Served in South Africa 1899–1901, DAAG Army HQ. AAG, military training branch of War Office 1903. AAG Army HQ 1903–6, ADSD War Office 1904–6. Commandant of Staff College and Brigadier General, 1907–10, DMO War Office 1910. DMO at Army HQ 1910–14. Promoted Major General 1913. Assistant CGS, GHQ, 1914. Chief liaison officer with French GQG, 1915. GOC IV Army Corps 1915–16. Mission to Russia 1916–17. Promoted Lieutenant General and GOC Eastern Command, 1917. British military representative, Versailles, 1917. CIGS 1918–22. Field Marshal 1919. MP 1922. Assassinated 1922 by Sinn Fein.

WOOD, Sir (Henry) Evelyn (Field Marshal). Born 1838. Educated Marlborough College, Barrister Middle Temple. Entered navy 1854, transferred to army during Crimean war. Served in 17th Lancers in India campaign, 1858. VC in Indian Mutiny, 1859. Staff College 1862–4. Ashanti 1873. Zulu War 1879. Egypt 1882–3. GOC Aldershot 1889–93. Nile Expedition 1894–5. Promoted Lieutenant General 1891. QMG at War Office 1893–7 and General 1895. AG 1897–1901. GOC II Corps District 1901–5. Promoted Field Marshal 1903. Several publications. Died 1919.

Select Bibliography

I UNPUBLISHED SOURCES

1 *British Library, London*

Lieutenant General Sir Edward Hutton Papers
Lieutenant General Sir Archibald Murray–General Sir William Robertson
   Correspondence
General Sir Horace Smith-Dorrien Papers

2 *Churchill College, Cambridge*

General Lord Rawlinson of Trent Papers

3 *Imperial War Museum, London*

Major General S. C. M. Archibald Papers
Lieutenant Colonel J. H. Boraston Papers
Lieutenant General Sir Richard Butler Papers
General Sir Stanley von Donop Papers
Lieutenant Colonel B. Fitzgerald Papers
Lieutenant General Sir Aylmer Haldane Papers
General Lord Horne Papers
Lieutenant General Sir Hugh Jeudwine Papers
Major General A. I. MacDougall Papers
General Sir Ivor Maxse Papers
General Sir Horace Smith-Dorrien Papers
General Sir Reginald Stephens Papers
Field Marshal Sir Henry Wilson Papers

4 *The Library, the Staff College, Camberley*

Reports of General Staff Conferences, 1906–1914

5 *National Army Museum, London*

Major General Milward Papers (6510–143)
General Lord Rawlinson of Trent Papers (5201–33)
Field Marshal Lord Roberts Papers (7101–23)

6 *National Library of Scotland, Edinburgh, Scotland*

Field Marshal Earl Haig Papers
Lieutenant General Sir Aylmer Haldane Papers

7 Public Record Office, Chancery Lane and Kew

1901–2	WO 13/483	Machine Guns – Committee of Major General C. W. H. Douglas
1912	WO 13/767	Machine Gun Transport Office
1915	WO 32/5453	Formation of Machine Gun Corps (1915)
1911	WO 32/7067	Machine Guns – Relative Value of Patterns
1912–14	WO 32/7069	Light Machine Guns for Aeroplanes (1912–1914)
1909–14	WO 32/7071	Committee on Automatic Rifles
1867–86	WO 32/8901	Machine Gun Reports (1867–1886)
1901	WO 32/9029	Machine Gun Committee (1901)
1912–14	WO 32/9089	Machine Guns vs Aircraft (1912–1914)
1915	WO 32/11239	Formation of Machine Gun Corps
1916	WO 32/11392	Machine Guns
1916	WO 32/11393	Tanks
1870–1	WO 32/22	Reports on Mitrailleurs (1870–1871)
1872	WO 33/24	Director of Artillery (1872)
1872	WO 33/24	Second Report on Mitrailleurs (1872)
1905	WO 33/350	Reports on Manchuria (1905)
1910	WO 33/504	Report on Automatic Rifles (1910)
1911	WO 33/571	Second Report on Automatic Rifles (1911)
1915	WO 33/721	General Staff, GHQ, Tactical Notes
1915	WO 33/725	General Staff, GHQ, Tactical Notes
1916	WO 33/756	General Staff, GHQ, Notes on Artillery
1916	WO 33/802	Emergency Scheme for Machine Gun Companies' Mobilization (1916)
1915–16	WO 33/881	Minutes of Army Council (1915–1916)
	WO 79/61	Charteris Papers
1914–15	WO 79/62	General A. J. Murray Correspondence
1914–15	WO 79/63	Secret Correspondence (Kitchener)
1915	WO 79/63	General A. J. Murray Correspondence
	WO 79/66	Cavan Papers
	WO 79/69	Cavan Papers
1918	WO 95/749	V Corps Files
1918	WO 95/953	XVIII Corps Files
1915–16	WO 106/308	General Staff, GHQ Appreciations
1915–16	WO 106/310–11	General Staff Appreciations for War Cabinet
1915	WO 106/390	Handling of Reserves at Loos
1916	WO 106/396	GHQ Papers
1915	WO 106/1510–11	Directorate of Military Operations
	WO 106/1519	Directorate of Military Operations
1904	WO 108/267	Reports on Equipment from South Africa
1916	WO 157/8–10	Intelligence Reports GHQ
1916	WO 157/171	Fourth Army Intelligence
1915	WO 158/5–6	Intelligence Reports GHQ
1915–16	WO 158/17–19	General Staff Notes on Operations
1915–16	WO 158/21–4	Secretary of State for War and CIGS
1915–16	WO 158/181–5	First Army Operations
1915–17	WO 158/193	First Army Summary of Operations
1916	WO 158/233–6	Fourth Army Somme
1915	WO 158/288	Motor Machine Gun Batteries
1917	WO 158/298	Machine Gun Lessons

1916	WO 158/344	Fifth Army Lessons of 1916
1915–16	WO 158/831	Tanks
1916–17	WO 158/897	Macdonogh–Charteris Correspondence
1914–15	WO 159/2–10	Creedy–Kitchener Papers
1914–	WO 159/15	Von Donop Papers
1914–15	WO 161/22	New Armies 1914–1915
1914–15	WO 162/1	Adjutant General's Decisions
1910	WO 163/15	Army Council Minutes
1914	WO 163/20	Army Council Minutes
1915–16	WO 163/21	Army Council Minutes
1915	WO 163/45	Military Members Committee
1915	WO 163/46	Army Council Minutes
1915–18	WO 256/4–24	Haig Diary
1915	Supply 6/170	President, Ordnance Board
1910	Supply 6/175	Ordnance Board Minutes
1911	Supply 6/534	Small Arms Committee, Report
1900–20	Supply 6/643	Reports on Army Matters
1906	Supply 6/653	Small Arms Committee, Report
1915	PRO 30/57	Kitchener Papers
	Cab 16/52	Cabinet *Official History* Committee
	Cab 44/27–8	1927 Draft of Loos Chapters, *Official History*, and comments by Haig, Brigadier General Haking and Brigadier General Charteris
	Cab 44/428	Reflections by Edmonds on *Official History*
	Cab 45/120–1	Postwar *Official History* Correspondence, Loos
	Cab 45/130	Postwar *Official History* Correspondence, St Eloi
	Cab 45/132–8	Postwar *Official History* Correspondence, Somme
	Cab 45/140	Postwar *Official History* Correspondence (includes Cab 45/33 Gough correspondence *re* Flanders 1917), Ypres
	Cab 45/141	Postwar *Official History* Correspondence, 1914–1915
	Cab 45/182	Headlam and Jeudwine Papers
	Cab 45/183	Haig–Edmonds Correspondence
	Cab 45/184–7	Postwar *Official History* Correspondence, Third Army (includes some Somme material)
	Cab 45/190	Postwar *Official History* Correspondence, Fourth Army
	Cab 45/192–3	Postwar *Official History* Correspondence, Fifth Army (includes some Somme material)
	Cab 45/196	Postwar *Official History* Correspondence *re* 1914
	Cab 45/200	Tanks (1916–1918)
	Cab 45/201	Major General G. S. Clive Diary
	Cab 103/110	Postwar *Official History* Correspondence, Passchendaele
	Cab 103/112	Postwar *Official History* Correspondence, Passchendaele
	Cab 103/113	Edmonds *Official History* Correspondence

8 *The Royal Artillery Institution Library, Woolwich*

Brigadier E. C. Anstey Papers
Lieutenant Colonel S. W. H. Rawlins Papers
Major General Sir Hugh Tudor Papers

9 *University of London, King's College, Liddell Hart Centre for Military Archives*

Major General G. S. Clive Papers
Brigadier General Sir James Edmonds Papers
Lieutenant General Sir Launcelot Kiggell Papers
Sir Basil Liddell Hart Papers
Colonel R. Macleod Papers
Major General Sir Frederick Maurice Papers
Field Marshal Sir Archibald Montgomery-Massingberd Papers
General Sir William Robertson Papers
General Sir Edward Spears Papers

10 *West Sussex Record Office, Chichester, Sussex*

General Sir Ivor Maxse Papers

II Films (1899–1918)

Imperial War Museum, London

IWM	037	Patiala (Machine Guns)
IWM	244	Infantry Training
IWM	438	Lewis Gun Training
IWM	1025	Boer War
IWM	227	Machine Gun and Lewis Gun Training
IWM	68	India
IWM	1081	Boer War
IWM	191	Somme
IWM	207	Western Front
IWM	131	Western Front
IWM	485	First World War Recruiting
IWM	243	Machine Gun Training
IWM	570	Western Front
IWM	371	Western Front
IWM	580(3–12)	First World War (Land, Sea, Air)

III Printed sources

Official Material, Books and Articles:

Altham, Major General E. A., *The Principles of War* (London, 1914).
Amery, L. S., *The Problem of the Army* (London, 1903).
Applin, Captain R. V. K., *Machine Gun Tactics* (London, 1910).
Arthur, Sir George, *Lord Haig* (London, 1928).
Articles from *The Journal of the Royal United Services Institute*, 1898–1914.

Articles from *The United Service Magazine*, 1897–1914.

Articles from *The National Review*, 1899–1901.

Articles from *The Cavalry Journal*, 1913–14.

Articles from *The Army Review*, 1913–14.

Articles from *The Contemporary Review*, 1900–12.

Articles from *Review of Reviews*, 1899–1903.

Articles from *The National Review*, 1901.

Baden-Powell, Major B. F. S., *War in Practice: Some Tactical and Other Lessons of the Campaign in South Africa* (London, 1903).

Baden-Powell, Lieutenant General R. S. S., *Scouting for Boys: a Handbook for Instruction in Good Citizenship*, revised edn (London, 1908).

Baker-Carr, Brigadier General, *From Chauffeur to Brigadier General* (London, 1930).

Banning, Lieutenant Colonel, *Tactics Made Easy* (London, 1912).

Bloch, I. S., *Is War Now Impossible?* (London, 1899).

Blunden, Edmund, *Undertones of War*, Penguin edn (Harmondsworth, 1982).

Calwell, Colonel C. E., *Tactics of To-Day*, 2nd edn (Edinburgh and London, 1909).

Charteris, Brigadier General John, *Field Marshal Earl Haig* (London, 1929, 1933).

Cooper, Duff, *Haig*, 2 vols (London, 1935, 1936).

Coppard, George, *With a Machine Gun to Cambrai* (London: HMSO, 1969).

Dallas, Captain O., *Private Smith* (London, 1913).

Davidson, Major General Sir John, *Haig: Master of the Field* (London, 1953).

Dewar, G. A. B., *Sir Douglas Haig's Command: 19 December 1915 to 11 November 1918*, 2 vols (London, 1922).

Edmonds, Brigadier General Sir James, editor and chief official historian, *History of the Great War: Military Operations, France and Belgium*, 14 volumes (London: HMSO 1922–48).

Edmonds, Charles, [Carrington], *A Subaltern's War* (London, 1929).

Field Service Regulations Part I, Operations (London: War Office, 1909).

French, Gerald, *French Replies to Haig* (London, 1936).

French, Lieutenant General Sir John, 'Introduction', in von Bernhardi, *Cavalry in Future Wars* (London, 1906).

French, Lieutenant General Sir John, 'Preface' in von Bernhardi, *Cavalry in War and Peace* (London, 1910).

Fuller, Major General J. F. C., *The Last of the Gentleman's Wars* (London, 1937).

Fuller, Major General J. F. C., *Memoirs of an Unconventional Soldier* (London, 1936).

Gilbert, Major Gerald, *The Evolution of Tactics* (London, 1907).

Goltz, von der, *The Nation in Arms* (London, 1914).

Gough, General Sir Hubert, *The Fifth Army* (London, 1931).

Graves, Robert, *Goodbye to All That*, Penguin edn (Harmondsworth, 1960).

Haig, Major General Douglas, *Cavalry Studies, Strategical and Tactical* (London, 1907).

Haking, Brigadier General R. C. B., *Company Training* (London, 1913).

Hamilton, Captain Ian, *The Fighting of the Future* (London, 1885).

Hamilton, Sir Ian, *A Staff Officer's Scrap Book During the Russo-Japanese War*, Vol. 1 (London, 1905).

Hamilton, General Sir Ian, *Compulsory Service* (London, 1910).

Hamilton, General Sir Ian, *National Life and National Training* (London, 1913).

Handbook for the .303 and .303 Converted Maxim Machine Guns (London: War Office, 1907).

Hart, Captain B. H. Liddell, *Reputations* (London, 1928).

Hart, Captain B. H. Liddell, *The British Way in Warfare* (London, 1932).

Hart, Captain B. H. Liddell, *The Ghost of Napoleon* (London, 1933).

Hart, Captain B. H. Liddell, *Through the Fog of War* (London, 1938).

Hart, Major General Sir Reginald Clarke, *Reflections on the Art of War*, 3rd edn (London, 1901).

Henderson, Lieutenant Colonel G. F. R., *The Science of War* (London, 1905, 1906).

Hutchison, Lieutenant Colonel G. S., *Machine Guns: Their History and Tactical Employment* (London, 1938).

Infantry Training Provisional (London: War Office, 1902).

Infantry Training (London: War Office, 1905).

Infantry Training (London: War Office, 1914).

James, Major W. H. (ed.), Count Yorck von Wartenburg, *Napoleon as a General*, 2 vols (London, 1902).

James, Lieutenant Colonel W. H., *Modern Strategy* (Edinburgh and London, 1903).

Knox, Major General Sir Walter, *The Flaw in our Armour* (London, 1914).

Lewis, Cecil, *Sagittarius Rising* (London, 1966).

Linesman, *The Mechanism of War* (London, 1902).

Longstaff, Major F. V., and Atteridge, A. Hilliard, *The Book of the Machine Gun* (London, 1917).

Maude, Lieutenant Colonel F. N., *Cavalry: Its Past and Future* (London, 1903).

Maude, Lieutenant Colonel F. N., *Notes on the Evolution of Infantry Tactics* (London, 1905).

Maude, Lieutenant Colonel F. N., *The Evolution of Modern Cavalry* (London, 1905).

Maude, Lieutenant Colonel F. N., *The Science of Organisation, and the Art of War* (London, 1912).

Maude, Lieutenant Colonel F. N., *War and the World's Life* (London, 1907).

Maurice, Lieutenant Colonel F. B. (ed.), *Sir Frederick Maurice* (London, 1913).

Meinertzhagen, Colonel, *Army Diary, 1899–1926* (London, 1960).

The Memoirs of Captain Liddell Hart, 2 vols (London, 1965).

Memorandum on Army Training (London: War Office, 1910).

Murray, Lieutenant Stewart, *Discipline: Its Reason and Battle Value* (London, 1894).

Murray, Major Stewart, *The Future Peace of the Anglo-Saxons* (London, 1905).

Notes on the employment of MGs and the Training of Machine Gunners (London: HMSO, 1915).

Playne, Caroline, *The Pre-War Mind in Britain* (London, 1928).

Protheroe, E., *Earl Haig* (London, 1928).

Report of the Committee Appointed to Consider the Education and Training of Officers of the Army (Command Papers 982, 983, vol. 10, 1902).

Report of the Committee ... to Enquire into the Nature of the Expenses Incurred by Officers of the Army (Command Paper 1421, vol. 10, 1903).

Report of the Committee on the Provision of Officers (Command Paper 3924, vol. 69, 1907).

Report of His Majesty's Commissioners appointed to enquire into the Military preparations and other matters connected with the War in South Africa (Command Paper 1789, vols 40–2, 1904).

Roberts, Field Marshal Earl, *A Nation in Arms* (London, 1907).

Roberts, Field Marshal Earl, *Fallacies and Facts: an Answer to Compulsory Service* (London, 1911).

Robertson, Sir William, *Soldiers and Statesmen* (London, 1926).

Roper-Caldbeck, Major, *The Nation and the Army* (London, 1910).

The Russo-Japanese War: Reports from British Officers Attached to the Japanese Forces in the Field, 3 vols (London: HMSO, 1908).

Sassoon, Siegfried, *Memoirs of an Infantry Officer* (London, 1930).

Secrett, Sergeant T., *25 Years With Earl Haig* (London, 1929).

Swinton, Sir Ernest D., *Over My Shoulder* (Oxford, 1951).

Speeches by the Right Hon. Sir Henry Campbell-Bannerman (London, 1908).

Training and Manoeuvre Regulations (London: War Office, 1909).

Training and Manoeuvre Regulations: Amendments (London: War Office, 1911).

Training and Manoeuvre Regulations 1913 (London: War Office, 1913).

'Ubique', *Modern Warfare, or How our Soldiers Fight* (London, Edinburgh and New York, 1903).

Vivian, E. Charles, *The British Army from Within* (London, New York and Toronto, 1914).

Wilkinson, Spenser, *The University and the Study of War* (Oxford, 1909).

Wilkinson, Spenser, *Government and the War* (London, 1918).

Wilson, Captain Holmes, *Offence, Not Defence, or Armies and Fleets* (London, 1907).

Wolseley, Field Marshal Viscount, *The Study of a Soldier's Life*, 2 vols (Westminster, 1903).

IV SECONDARY SOURCES

Barnett, Corelli, 'The education of military elites', in Rupert Wilkinson (ed.), *Governing Elites* (New York, 1969).

Barnett, Corelli, 'A military historian's view of the literature of the Great War', *Essays by Divers Hands*, vol. 36 (Oxford, 1970).

Beckett, Ian F. W., and Simpson, Keith (eds), *A Nation in Arms: a Social Study of the British Army in the First World War* (Manchester, 1985).

Best, G. F., 'Militarism and the Victorian public school', in Simon and Bradley (eds), *The Victorian Public School* (Dublin, 1975).

Bidwell, Shelford, and Graham, Dominick, *Fire-Power: British Army Weapons and Theories of War 1904–1945* (London, 1982).

Blake, Robert, 'Introduction', in Blake (ed.), *The Private Papers of Douglas Haig 1914–1919* (London, 1952).

Blake, Robert (ed.), *The Private Papers of Douglas Haig, 1914–1919* (London, 1952).

Bond, Brian, *British Military Policy Between the Two World Wars* (Oxford, 1980).

Bond, Brian, 'Doctrine and training in the British cavalry, 1870–1914', in Michael Howard (ed.), *The Theory and Practice of War* (London, 1965).

Bond, Brian, *The Victorian Army and the Staff College 1895–1914* (London, 1972).

Bond, Brian, *War and Society in Europe 1870–1970*, Fontana edn (Bungay, 1984).

Bond, Brian, and Roy, Ian (eds), *War and Society*, 2 vols (London, 1976–7).

Carrias, Eugène, *La Pensée Militaire Allemande* (Paris, 1948).

Carrias, Eugène, *La Pensée Militaire Française* (Paris, 1960).

Dixon, Norman F., *On the Psychology of Military Incompetence* (London, 1976).

Dupuy, Colonel T. N., *A Genius for War: the German Army and General Staff, 1807–1945* (Englewood Cliffs, 1977).

Edmonds, Brigadier General Sir James, *A Short History of World War I* (London, 1951).

Ellul, Jacques, *The Technological Society*, Vintage edn (New York, 1964).

Farrar-Hockley, A. H., *The Somme*, Pan edn (London, 1966).

Farrar-Hockley, A. H., *Goughie* (London, 1975).

French, David, *British Strategy and War Aims, 1914–1916* (London, 1986).

Fussell, Paul, *The Great War and Modern Memory* (Oxford, 1975).

Geyer, Michael, 'The German practice of war, 1914–1945', forthcoming in Gordon Craig, Felix Gilbert and Peter Paret (eds), *Makers of Modern Strategy* (Princeton, 1986).

Gardner, Brian, *Allenby* (London, 1965).

Gooch, John, *The Plans of War: the General Staff and British Military Strategy, c. 1900–1916* (London, 1974).

Goodspeed, D. J., *The Road Past Vimy* (Toronto, 1969).

de Groot, Gerard, 'Educated soldier or cavalry officer? Contradictions in the pre-1914 career of Douglas Haig', *War and Society*, vol. 4, no. 2 (1986), pp. 51–69.

Hannah, W. H., *Bobs: Kipling's General* (London, 1972).

Hart, B. H. Liddell, *History of the First World War*, Pan edn (London, 1972).

Hayes, Denis, *The Conscription Conflict* (London, 1949).

Higham, Robin, *The Military Intellectuals in Britain, 1918–1939* (New Brunswick, 1966).

Horne, Alistair, *The Price of Glory: Verdun 1916* (New York, 1963).

Howard, Michael, *Clausewitz* (Oxford, 1983).

Howard, Michael, 'Men against fire: expectations of war in 1914', *International Security*, vol. 9, no. 1 (1984), pp. 41–57.

Hynes, Samuel, *The Edwardian Turn of Mind* (Princeton, 1968).

Isorni, Jacques, *Philippe Pétain*, Vol. 1 (Paris, 1972).

Janis, Irving, *Groupthink*, 2nd edn (Boston, 1982).

Keegan, John, *The Face of Battle* (London, 1976).

Kennedy, Paul M., 'The First World War and the international power system', *International Security*, vol. 9, no. 1 (1984), pp. 7–40.

Kitchen, Martin, *The German Officer Corps, 1890–1914* (Oxford, 1968).

Kuhn, Thomas, *The Structure of Scientific Revolutions*, 2nd edn (Chicago, 1970).

Leed, Eric, *No Man's Land: Combat and Identity in World War I* (Cambridge, 1979).

Lupfer, Timothy T., *The Dynamics of Doctrine: the Changes in German*

Tactical Doctrine during the First World War (Fort Leavenworth, Kansas, 1981).

Luvaas, Jay, *The Education of an Army: British Military Thought, 1815–1940* (London, 1965).

McDermott, J., 'The revolution in British military thinking from the Boer War to the Moroccan Crisis', in Paul Kennedy (ed.), *The War Plans of the Great Powers, 1880–1914* (London and Boston, 1979).

Macdonald, Lyn, *Somme* (London, 1983).

Magnus, P., *Kitchener* (London, 1958).

Marshall-Cornwall, General Sir James, *Foch as Military Commander* (New York, 1972).

Marshall-Cornwall, General Sir James, *Haig as Military Commander* (London, 1973).

Middlebrook, Martin, *The First Day on the Somme* (London, 1971).

Middlebrook, Martin, *The Kaiser's Battle* (London, 1978).

Myatt, F., *The Soldier's Trade: British Military Developments 1660–1914* (London, 1974).

Pakenham, Thomas, *The Boer War* (London, 1979).

Phillips, Gregory, *The Diehards: Aristocratic Society and Politics in Edwardian England* (Cambridge, Mass. and London, 1979).

Porch, Douglas, *The March to the Marne: the French Army, 1871–1914* (Cambridge, 1981).

Rapoport, Anatol (ed.), *Clausewitz on War*, Penguin edn (Harmondsworth, 1968).

Reid, Donald, *Edwardian England, 1901–1915* (London, 1972).

Riesman, David, *The Lonely Crowd*, Yale paperback edn (New Haven and London, 1961).

Sixsmith, E. K. G., *British Generalship in the Twentieth Century* (London, 1970).

Snyder, Jack, 'Civil-military relations and the cult of the offensive, 1914 and 1984', *International Security*, vol. 9, no. 1 (1984), pp. 108–46.

Spears, Major General Sir Edward, *Liaison, 1914*, 2nd edn (London, 1968).

Spiers, Edward M., *The Army and Society, 1815–1914* (London, 1980).

Strachan, Hew, *European Armies and the Conduct of War* (London, 1983).

Taylor, A J. P., *The First World War*, Penguin edn (Harmondsworth, 1966).

Terraine, John, *Douglas Haig: the Educated Soldier* (London, 1963).

Terraine, John, *Mons: the Retreat to Victory*, Pan edn (London, 1972).

Terraine, John, *The Road to Passchendaele: the Flanders Offensive of 1917: a Study in Inevitability* (London, 1977).

Terraine, John, *To Win a War: 1918, the Year of Victory* (London, 1978).

Terraine, John, *White Heat: the New Warfare, 1914–1918* (London, 1982).

Thompson, Paul, *The Edwardians* (London, 1975).

Travers, T. H. E., 'The offensive and the problem of innovation in British military thought, 1870–1915', *Journal of Contemporary History*, vol. 13, no. 3 (1978), pp. 531–53.

Travers, T. H. E., 'Technology, tactics and morale: Jean de Bloch, the Boer War, and British Military Theory, 1900–1914', *Journal of Modern History*, vol. 51, no. 2 (1979), pp. 264–86.

Travers, T. H. E., 'The hidden army: structural problems in the British officer corps, 1900–1918', *Journal of Contemporary History*, vol. 17, no. 3 (1982), pp. 523–44.

Travers, T. H. E., 'Learning and decision-making on the Western Front 1915–1916: the British example', *Canadian Journal of History*, vol. 18, no. 1 (1983), pp. 87–97.

Van Creveld, Martin, *Command in War* (Cambridge, Mass., 1985).

Van Doorn, Jacques, *The Soldier and Social Change* (Beverly Hills and London, 1975).

Van Evera, Stephen, 'The cult of the offensive and the origins of the First World War', *International Security* vol. 9, no. 1 (1984), pp. 58–107.

Weller, Jac, *Weapons and Tactics, Hastings to Berlin* (London, 1966).

Williams, Jeffrey, *Byng of Vimy* (London, 1983).

Winter, Denis, *Death's Men: Soldiers of the Great War* (London, 1978).

Winter, Denis, *The First of the Few: Fighter Pilots of the First World War* (London, 1982).

Wintringham, Tom, and Blashford-Snell, J. N., *Weapons and Tactics*, Penguin edn (Harmondsworth, 1973).

Wolff, Leon, *In Flanders Fields: the 1917 Campaign*, Penguin edn (Harmondsworth, 1979).

Woodward, David, *Lloyd George and the Generals* (Delaware, 1983).

Wynne, G. C., *If Germany Attacks: the Battle in Depth in the West* (London, 1940).

Index